# AFTER LONG SILENCE

## ALSO BY THE AUTHOR

# AFTER
# LONG SILENCE

Michael Straight

W·W· NORTON & COMPANY
*New York London*

The text of this book is composed in 11/12 Garamond, with
display type set in Janson.
Manufacturing by The Haddon Craftsmen, Inc.
Book design by Nancy Dale Muldoon.


First published as a Norton paperback 1984


Library of Congress Cataloging in Publication Data

Straight, Michael Whitney.
After long silence.

Includes index.
1. Straight, Michael Whitney. 2. United
States—Officials and employees—Biography.
3. Journalists—United States—Biography.
4. Novelists, American—20th century—Biography.
I. Title.
CT275.S8779A32 1983      327.1'2'0924 [B]      82–14543

ISBN 0-393-30186-9

W. W. Norton & Company, Inc., 500 Fifth Avenue, New York, N.Y. 10110
W. W. Norton & Company Ltd., 37 Great Russell Street, London WC1B 3NU

3 4 5 6 7 8 9 0

# CONTENTS

6 After Long Silence

INTERLUDE
*The Wild Blue Yonder*

PART THREE
*The Long Road Back*

# LIST OF ILLUSTRATIONS

# Part One

The Wind and the Blown

# AFTER LONG SILENCE

AFTER *Long Silence,* Yeats called one of his poems. For me the long silence ended on March 24, 1981.

At noon on that day, I drove to my home in the suburbs of Washington. An unfamiliar car was parked in front of the house.

Two strangers were waiting for me in my living room. "Mr. Straight?" said the first man, holding out his hand. "I'm Angus Macpherson, the Washington correspondent of the London *Daily Mail.*

"I must apologize for barging in on you like this," he added, "but my editors felt that it was a matter of some urgency.

"Would you mind," he said, "if I asked you a few questions?"

"Not at all."

I knew what was coming. I had been waiting for this day—and dreading it—for thirty-five years.

"Mr. Straight, were you a student at Cambridge University in 1937?"

"Yes, I was."

"Were you acquainted at that time with Anthony Blunt?"

"Yes."

"Mr. Straight, the *Daily Mail* is running a series of articles on the Soviet spy network in Britain. They are being reprinted in the London *Times* and, indeed, throughout the world. In tomorrow's article, you are mentioned as the man who unmasked Blunt—Sir Anthony, as he was then. You are not mentioned by name, I should add, but the author of the series has informed my editors that the individual in question is in fact you."

"Go on."

"Mr. Straight, have you any comments to make for the readers of the *Mail?*"

"I don't know. I'd like to see the article first."

"Mr. Straight, this is a matter of some urgency. Did you know Sir Roger Hollis?"

"I've never heard of him."

"He was the head of British Intelligence. He came under suspicion as the result of actions that you took back in 1963. The prime minister, Mrs. Thatcher, is due to make a statement about him in the House of Commons on the day after tomorrow."

"I'd still like to see what you wrote."

Macpherson nodded. "I'll wire the London office," he said. "I'll have it here for you tomorrow morning."

The next morning, he came back to my house with his companion, who proved to be a press photographer. He handed me a teletyped copy of the relevant paragraphs taken from the article that had been published that day.

> Anthony Blunt was in fact a much more important Soviet agent than has yet been realized.
>
> His crimes against his country, dragged out of him during hundreds of hours of taped interrogation, were such an indictment of wartime security that every effort has been made to cover them from public knowledge.
>
> I can reveal precisely what it was that happened in late 1963 which led to his unmasking.
>
> A middle-aged American belonging to a rich and famous family was invited to undertake a political task by the White House. Having a guilt complex about his secret past, he went to the F.B.I. headquarters in Washington hoping to clear himself before accepting the White House post.
>
> There he confessed that he had been a communist while in England at Cambridge University, had been recruited to Soviet intelligence and had served the Russian interests for several years.
>
> He named the man who had recruited him as Sir Anthony Blunt and said that he was prepared to give evidence against Blunt in court if necessary.
>
> The F.B.I. passed this information to M.I.5 and it was only when confronted by it in April 1964 that Blunt decided to confess after being first assured that he would never face prosecution.
>
> Blunt has said publicly that he felt free to confess because something that happened in 1964 "freed him from loyalties to his friends." The sanctimonious hypocrite confessed because, for the first time in his treacherous life, he was frightened.

'. . . hoping to clear himself. . . . had served the Russian interests for several years. . . .'

"Those statements about me are all wrong. And they're very damaging," I said.

Macpherson nodded. "Mr. Straight," he said, "you have one simple recourse. Tell us the true story."

In five hundred words? If I had a hundred thousand words, where would I begin?

In March 1937?

The Spanish Civil War was raging in March 1937. The British economy was foundering, and the Soviet Union seemed to be the only nation that could stand against the armies of Nazi Germany.

All that was true, but it was not enough to account for my actions.

Nor did I want the one acid line in my life to survive as my epitaph.

If I were to tell the true story, as I saw it, I would have to go back, long before March 1937. 'A middle-aged American belonging to a rich and famous family. . . .'

The part about my family at least was true.

# MY FATHER

MY father, Willard Straight, worked his way through Cornell as an artist.

"Had I only peace of mind," he wrote, "I could make a good artist out of myself."

Lacking peace of mind, he set out for China to stamp his mark upon the world. But he took his paints and pastels with him, recording history as he helped to set its course.

An exhibition of his artwork was staged by Cornell in 1974. I walked past his familiar portraits of Japanese admirals and Chinese houseboys. Then a seascape beckoned to me; it was so serene.

I found the explanation for its serenity in my father's inscription in one corner of the painting: *Southampton, L.I.; Sept. 2, 1916.*

That was the day after I was born.

My mother had been in labor for twenty-seven hours, thanks to my Extra-Large size head. I could envision the next day: in the darkened room, my mother, asleep at last; on the beach, my father painting—sand, sea, sky.

My father sent a telegram to the band of diplomats with whom he had once shared a house in Washington: "BE IT KNOWN THAT ON THIS, THE FIRST DAY OF SEPTEMBER THIS YEAR OF OUR LORD 1916 AND OF WOODROW WILSON WE HOPE THE LAST, WAS BORN TO DOROTHY AND WILLARD STRAIGHT AN EIGHT CYLINDER FULLY EQUIPPED MAN CHILD WEIGHING NIGH ONTO TEN POUNDS. THE CHILD SHALL HENCEFORTH BE KNOWN AS MICHAEL, FRIEND OF THE PEOPLE. GOD SAVE THE KING."

My father sent a less exuberant message to the editors of *The New Republic,* the journal that he and my mother had founded. A letter came back addressed to me:

Dear Michael:

Let me welcome you to a good world! Good not because all is nice and lovely in it. Far from it. But good because there never was a better chance to help make it nicer and lovelier than it is; never when we had more justifiable faith that we could bend this hulking, reeling world a little closer to our heart's desire. We have this faith despite our humility that man can only do ever so little, and that great mystery we call God, so much.

You come into the world fortunately, most fortunately in your choice of parents.

Good luck to you!

Felix Frankfurter

The reference to my parents is, I am afraid, revealing. The letter was addressed to me, but written to them.

—⟨∞⟩—

Life is expressed through action, according to Aristotle, and its end is a way of action rather than a moral attitude. My father shared that view. Like Theodore Roosevelt, whom he knew and admired, he believed in America's future as a world power. He worked furiously to raise war loans for the Allies. He took military training at Plattsburg. In his spare moments he drew designs around the baby photographs in the album that my mother made for me. Then, seven months after I was born, he enlisted in the army.

One photograph only was taken of our family, outside our home in Old Westbury, Long Island. My father stands grave and erect in his uniform. My mother stands beside him, her face shaded by a large black hat. Biddy, my sister, aged three, is dressed up in a soldier's suit. So is Whitney, my brother, aged five, who is scratching his bare midriff. I am perched in the crook of my mother's elbow, staring with a puzzled expression at the photographer, who must have been making animal noises to attract my attention. It is late afternoon—the shadows cast by the November sun reach almost to the boxwood that surrounds our house.

There are, after this photo, no more designs in my album—my father sailed for France in December 1917. There are scores of photographs that were taken that winter and the next summer. They show Whitney and Biddy and me: seated on the back of a brown pony; nestled between the claws of a stone dragon that our father brought back from Peking; standing on the dashboard of an early limousine; posing in patriotic attitudes on the beach in Southampton. Whitney and I grip wooden rifles; Biddy waves an American flag.

There are adults in some of the photographs: nurses clad in starched white uniforms and bonnets; a groom in a checked cap, holding the pony; a uniformed chauffeur standing beside the limousine. There is no sign of mother—she had immersed herself in war work.

She wrote to my father in France, describing her war work. He replied: *"June 10, 1918:* . . . I am proud of you for all you've done and are doing. . . . It's splendid. But . . . don't let these things keep you in town from early morn 'til late at night, so that you never see the children. They need you, Best Beloved, all the more because they can't say so. They don't know how much they need you. You must give to them of yourself; not of your tired self only, but of your real, thoughtful self; not *en passant* but all the time. . . . Give them a ground work. . . ."

On the night before he sailed for France, he wrote to Whitney:

. . . You may never see this letter. I hope you never will. But should anything happen to me I want you to have a word—you as the oldest— that you may have it for yourself and your blithe young sister and your brother Michael.

My father died when I was seven years old, and I had no word save such as my mother gave me. She was taken too, before I knew what she meant.

I trust for your sake and the sake of all three of you, your mother will be there to guide you. All the best in you comes from her; all the finest in you will be brought out by her. You are blessed as no other children have been blessed in your mother. May your worship for her—for it will be with you as it is with me, reverence and real worship—guide you and lead you to treat all women with chivalry. . . .

His one desire when he enlisted was to lead his own men into battle. Instead, he was kept in staff work. His sense of frustration mounted. His letters to my mother voiced his uneasiness about the future. *"October 14, 1918:* . . . We should have made our bargain with the Allies when we first came in. . . . Now, we will be apt to get . . . a peace which will, instead of being founded upon a League of Nations, have the foundations for other wars. . . ."

Colonel Edwin House, President Wilson's principal adviser, arrived in Paris on October 25. He called in my father to help him with the preparations for the Peace Conference, adding that he wanted my mother to help them: *"November 15, 1918:* . . . The Colonel . . . said that you were one of the very few people in America who saw the whole thing clearly, and that you could be the greatest help in the world if you could come over and be here, smoothing out kinks. He was quite wonderful about you. . . ."

House hoped that my mother would establish the kind of informal salon that the British and French governments had created for after-dinner diplomacy. My father feared at first that House was planning to make use of my mother for his own purposes. Then his doubts were overcome by his longing to have her beside him: *"November 19, 1918: . . . Are you coming? That's all I'm thinking of. . . ."*

That was his last letter. He had woken on the morning of November 19 with a chill. It proved to be septic pneumonia.

Several doctors were summoned to his bedside. They said that since he had a strong constitution he would survive. But as his young friend Walter Lippmann noted, "He had been through the fire and the swamp."

He developed a high fever and became delirious. He died on December 1, the day before my mother was to have sailed with Woodrow Wilson to France.

On the first anniversary of my father's death, Walter Lippmann wrote to my mother:

Dear Dorothy:

This day is green, not having yielded to Winter, and unconquerable, like Willard's soul. There are kind, strong winds blowing through dusty places, messengers it seems today of him. He had become the wind and not the blown—that is what war and France and the conduct of affairs had meant in the last four months.

As I think back, through many days when loneliness was all too close to heartbreak, this is what I most remember. He had ceased to accept the valuations placed by the world upon its aims and institutions, had seen these values in all their dimensions, and was in an ultimate sense free of them. They were not his final values, his highest hopes, his determinants.

And yet the men who believed in them and acted on them were still more important than their theories or his, for they were human beings, friendly beings, queer beings.

He seemed to strangers the ideal man of action. I don't think of him that way. The final way in which he saw the world was the way the artist sees it, as a sight delicious and exhilarating apart from anything anyone does or says or thinks about it. He combined with perfect sophistication about the way things are done, that blessed innocence of the eye as to what they are. And the enormous fertility of his practical suggestion was, I believe, a phase merely of a playful and free fancy that touched all things eagerly.

War had broken down the compartment wall between the submerged artist and the practical administrator. They had been, I think, separate, alternative, almost antagonistic. But in France, at the Staff College, at the Marne, and finally at Bouilly during the Argonne, he saw with lurid clarity the human cost of practical decisions. In G.3. he did not move paper divisions across a map, but sons and lovers and glorious boys across mud and wire and filth against other boys. He had known but now he saw and felt and was certain. Complacency and routine, favoritism and dullness, caste and intrigue were no longer abstract evils but things intolerably costly, improvident, destructive. . . . A weaker man endowed so sensi-

tively would have recoiled totally, but the impulse in him moved trium-
phantly toward new invention and organization. . . .

'. . . the wind and not the blown. . . .' My father had become the
wind before his death, as Walter Lippmann wrote. In his absence, we
three children became the blown.

# MY MOTHER

CAN we trust our earliest memories? Why is it that some sink
beyond recall while others remain vivid after six decades? One in
particular haunts me. I am struggling in the grip of my nurse in our
home in Old Westbury. We are facing the door that leads to my
father's study—a room whose paneled walls are hung with Chinese
beheading axes and ceremonial swords. The door is opened by my
nurse; I see my mother, sitting at my father's desk. Her head rests on
her arms; she is weeping. I am thrust toward her, to comfort her, but
I am frightened. I scream and struggle, trying to escape.

As children, we were not much comfort to our mother. Nor were
her brothers, her sister, or her childhood friends. She had moved
beyond the boundaries of their world when she married my father.

In her isolation, she reached out to him.

Once, in the Cathedral at Langres, he had sensed her presence
beside him. "I stood there with you," he wrote. So now she traveled
to the cathedral, hoping to be with him once again. She journeyed to
Maryland to consult a medium, Mary K. In the course of many sessions with Mary K., she asked about our futures. She was told not to
worry. Whitney would have a life of worldly interests, like her brothers; Biddy would develop her artistic talents.

"What about Michael?" Mother asked. The answer: "He will be
more literary. . . . He will have a very deep mind, and problems of
all kinds that he will have to be taught to meet."

Still reaching out for my father, she returned to the beach where
he had painted the seascape on the day after I was born. There, she
sensed his presence beside her so powerfully that she was overwhelmed.

She never spoke of these experiences, but when my closest friend
died of cancer in 1958, I mentioned in a letter to her that he had

experienced in Indonesia one of those rare moments beyond the boundaries of poetic inspiration, when color and form are intensified and one's relationship to the universe is clarified and thus settled. She replied that she understood: "Three times in my own life it has occurred—a kind of sudden lifting of one's whole being to another level of vision where everything falls into place—where every object, every person, every detail of the pattern assumes an undreamed-of perfection that makes one want to cry. I suppose it is really a state of ecstasy —so intense that one can never doubt again that life and consciousness can be stretched beyond anything we have seen or imagined, and that death is only a transition to another plane."

My father was very much a part of his time; my mother reached beyond it. She was concerned with all earthly things but she was not, as we were, earthbound. It may be without significance, but on the night of December 13, 1968, her close friend Irene Champernowne went into her study for no apparent reason and saw my mother standing before the fireplace. She was at first irritated, thinking that my mother had entered her house without knocking. Then she was overcome, knowing that my mother had just died.

She was born in Washington in 1887. Her father, William C. Whitney, was secretary of the navy. President Cleveland, his Cabinet, the members of the Supreme Court, and the leaders of the Congress, all attended her christening.

So did her uncle, Oliver Payne. He was unmarried and immensely wealthy. He had an almost obsessive love for his sister, Flora. He had chosen Whitney, his roommate at Yale, to be her husband. When they were married, he bought large mansions for them and paid most of the bills.

Flora was forty-five when my mother was born. She became ill and, in her seclusion, accused her husband of having love affairs with a number of women, including a beautiful widow, Edith Randolph. She died in 1893; three years later, Mrs. Randolph and my grandfather were married.

Oliver Payne was outraged. He swore that he would ruin my grandfather. Summoning the elder children to his home, he told them that if they would renounce their father, he would bestow his vast fortune upon them. If they stayed with their father, they would receive nothing from him.

Harry, the eldest child, declined his uncle's offer. As the husband of Gertrude Vanderbilt, he was already very wealthy. In contrast, Payne and Pauline chose to abandon their father and ally themselves with their uncle.

My mother was ten years old. Her father told her that the family had broken apart. He gave her the choice of joining her uncle, her brother, and her sister, and being wealthy, or of staying alone with him and sharing whatever he might earn on his own.

She chose to stay with him.

My grandfather had played a leading role in the election of President Cleveland. It was widely believed that he would be the next Democratic president. Instead, when his family broke up he left public life to make his own fortune, throwing away "the usual objects of political ambition," as his friend Henry Adams wrote, "like the ashes of smoked cigarettes."

He was successful, despite the efforts of Oliver Payne to force him into bankruptcy, but his life was shattered. Two years after she married my grandfather, Edith Whitney was horseback riding with my mother when she struck a bridge and broke her back.

She lived on for fourteen months at Old Westbury. A few days before she died, she called for my mother. "She asked me to stand by her bed," my mother wrote. "She wanted to tell me herself about menstruation and the shock it might cause me. And so, from this last tragic moment in her life, I learned that she was thinking of me and how to help me face the future."

From then on, my mother and her father lived alone in his mansion on Fifth Avenue. My mother remembered always the great paintings in the mansion and the evenings when Fritz Kreisler and Joseph Hoffman came to play for them. She later wrote that she "curled up on a cushion in the far corner of our great music room, feeling that it was all a world of magic."

My grandfather died in 1904. The Paynes, so my cousin Kenyon Bolton told me, were brought up to believe that the press notice that reported my grandfather to have died of peritonitis was nothing more than a cover-up. He had, they were told, been shot and killed by a jealous husband who had come upon my grandfather in bed with his wife.

My mother was seventeen when her father died. She remained in Old Westbury with an older woman—an orphan and an heiress.

American heiresses were sought after at that time by Europe's debt-ridden, improvident aristocrats. My mother's friend, Consuelo Vanderbilt, was driven into a loveless marriage with the Duke of Marlborough. My mother's closest companion, Gladys Vanderbilt, was torn away from the man she loved and forced to marry Count Lazlo Szechenyi. My mother's sister, Pauline, had chosen to marry an adventurer who was the grandson of the Marquess of Anglesey. Pauline, in turn, pressed my mother to marry an English suitor, Lord Falconer.

My mother listened to the pleas of her sister, her brothers, and her titled suitors. Then, in Venice, she set down her own standards.

When the right person comes along, I wonder if one has doubts, even then. Many of us are immediately carried off our feet and swept away in an irresistible current of love, while to the rest of us, love comes walking slowly; and yet with sure steps he overtakes us and folds his arms around our shrinking forms.

How little we know ourselves! And yet I feel that love would come slowly and gradually into my heart, and not with a sudden onrush of emotion.

Of course, the man one marries cannot be all one dreams of having him, and I am fully expectant of disappointments. I can't help longing for certain things. He must be strong and he must be tender. He must be honest and generous and also kind and thoughtful. And—oh . . . if he will only love me tenderly, take care of me, put his arms around me. . . .

I don't think I could fall in love with a man who had no ambition and no aim in life, because I feel a great longing to be a part of his work. And then, besides, if he lacked all ambition, I couldn't admire him. . . .

She had been drawn to the charming, aimless suitors who pursued her, but she turned them all down. She reveled in the house parties in the Adirondacks and the balls that lasted until daybreak. But even as a girl, she was looking beyond the boundaries of her circle. She wrote in her diary, "I'm filled with a terribly absorbing desire to work and to help."

A series of newspaper articles asserting that her father had made his fortune at the expense of small investors deepened her sense that her inheritance was not so much a personal possession as a public trust. She worked at the Henry Street Settlement with Lillian Wald; she toured through the sweat shops of New York with Rose Schneiderman and Emma Goldman, women whom her brothers regarded as dangerous Reds.

She set out on a tour of the Far East in 1909. By then, my father had joined the diplomatic service. He had barely met her; from the American embassy in Peking, he wrote to her: "We are all awaiting you with red carpets and brass bands. . . ."

They rode one day to the Ming Tombs for a picnic luncheon and on to the Great Wall to see the sunset. She wrote to a cousin: "Mr. Straight and I used to walk along the city wall at sunset time, and watch the soft glow of the distant, purple hills and listen to the strange calls and cries of the city below. Every evening, we used to turn out the lights and sit by fire, and then Mr. Straight brought out his guitar and sang to us."

Soon, as she wrote, "The magic of China seemed to fade before the magic of a human personality."

He was, like her, an orphan. He was penniless and unknown. He met none of the requirements set forth by her brother and her sister, but he met her own standards, for he was ambitious and hard working, honest and generous, thoughtful and tender.

He courted her with a determination that she had never encountered on Long Island, bombarding her with telegrams and letters. Her brothers and her sister, her companion, Beatrice Bend, and most of her friends concluded that he was a fortune hunter and joined in denigrating him. In contrast, Theodore Roosevelt took his side and urged her to accept his proposal of marriage.

She gave in one summer evening at Old Westbury. Then, once again, she was overcome by doubts. She insisted that her engagement to my father be kept a secret; she would not set a date for their wedding. She left suddenly for Europe, and he barely managed to get a berth on her steamship.

After his death, she wrote,

> How pitifully unprepared for him I was, I now tremble to think. I came near letting the old things count the most. Willard came and lifted me bodily out of the old life, and it fell away. I never even heard it fall. Almost imperceptibly, things assumed new values and new proportions. I began to share his own vivid life of imagination and dreams, as if no other realities had ever existed for me. He tied winged sandals to my feet, and I began to soar with him to new heights of exploration. Life suddenly became an adventure, a quest on which I could risk everything. Safety did not matter any more. In teaching me to look into the heart of things, he taught me a new insight of which I had never dreamed. . . .

She was humble, as these lines suggest. Yet, at twenty-six, she possessed wisdom and perception beyond my father's. He had little interest in ideas, save as they pointed to immediate action. Her mind, in contrast, was always open to new ideas. He was concerned with winning the war. She was looking ahead to the postwar world. He gave her Herbert Croly's book, *The Promise of American Life*. It was she who suggested to Croly that he found a weekly journal of opinion. Croly accepted her offer of funds, insisting that the journal would soon pay its way. She disagreed. She added that its balance sheet was less important than its contribution to America's intellectual life.

The new journal was to be called *The Republic*. That title, a search revealed, belonged to a Boston politician whose name was John F. Fitzgerald and who was known as Honey Fitz. My father took Honey Fitz to lunch and suggested to him that he give up the name in the higher interest of a national journal. Honey Fitz replied that there was no higher interest than the distribution of his sheet to his precinct captains. His grandson, John F. Kennedy, might have agreed.

The journal was thus called *The New Republic*. Its first issue appeared in 1914. My parents had promised that they would not impose their views upon the editors. Their promise was soon put to the test. My father was an ardent supporter of Teddy Roosevelt in the 1916 presidential campaign; *The New Republic* backed Woodrow Wilson.

My father described himself as a "conservative." Had he lived, my mother might have deferred to his political views. Left on her own, she followed her own instincts and allied herself with the poor and the exploited. She defended *The New Republic* when it was denounced as unpatriotic. She became a champion of women's suffrage, and of the rights of workers to organize in trade unions. She marched in demonstrations and spoke in union halls. Nonetheless, this political orientation was a passing phase for her. After the electoral debacle of 1920, her interest in political reform, like Croly's, dimmed.

She continued, as a young widow, to play an active role in the cultural life of New York, sponsoring appearances by leading artists who were engaged in raising funds for political refugees. She rarely spoke of her own past to us, but rummaging through her papers, I came upon many engraved invitations to events held at our home at 1130 Fifth Avenue. *Mrs. Willard Straight requests your presence . . .* the invitations begin. They continue: *Mr. Paderewski will play his compositions;* or, *Mr. Joseph Conrad will read from his works.*

I wonder now what Conrad read aloud to the ladies and gentlemen who assembled in our drawing room, while upstairs in the nursery, I pushed my fire engine around the carpeted floor. Did he limit himself to *Lord Jim* and other well-known works, or did he turn to less familiar novels, such as *Under Western Eyes?*

A few sensitive men toured America after the war, describing the hardships that they and their fellow soldiers had suffered. One, the English writer Siegfried Sassoon, spoke before a gathering at the Colony Club. The American critic John Jay Chapman was in the audience that day. His only son had been killed in the war, and when Sassoon called the war a crime against humanity, Chapman stood up and denounced him for betraying his dead comrades. The meeting ended in an uproar; my mother took Sassoon back to our house, where he collapsed.

Her sympathy for men like Sassoon deepened my mother's fear of confrontation and of violence. Her early memories of family quarrels, with their disastrous consequences, and her revulsion against the war created within her a deeply felt pacifism. It was broader than opposition to war between nations; it embraced all of her being.

I never heard her utter a harsh word or raise her voice in anger. Once when we were standing on the quay at Harbour Island, in the Bahamas, a black woman began to beat her small son. My mother went up to her with tears in her eyes. "You mustn't do that; you mustn't strike him," she said. The woman stood in sullen silence while the child stared up at my mother with wide, uncomprehending eyes.

Deeper than pacifism in my mother was self-denial. She took the drumstick, the hard chair in the back of the hall. If a friend admired the overcoat that she was wearing, her impulse was to take it off and give it to her friend.

She had no sense of self-protection. She found it difficult to refuse any demands that were made upon her. Once when she was recovering from a heart attack, one of the women who preyed upon my mother insisted upon seeing her. Knowing that my mother would see her and be upset by her litany of selfish complaints, I barred the door to her bedroom.

"So!" the woman said. "You forbid me to see her!" It was as if I had defied some elemental and universally accepted convention.

My mother was not a churchgoer. She crossed swords in her militant days with the conservative bishop of New York. She was attacked as an atheist by the Reverend Martin of Dartington Village because she would not attend his church. Yet when she died, a slim volume was found by her bed in which she had written out the prayers, the psalms, the hymns, the mystical poems, and the reflections that she loved to read.

Isaiah, Campion, Shakespeare, Vaughan, Herrick, Hopkins, Emily Brontë, Francis Thompson, Walter de la Mare, Paul Tillich. . . . The entry that for me comes closest to her spirit is a passage from James Naylor, who lived from 1617 until 1660: "There is a spirit which I feel that delights to do no evil, nor to avenge any wrong, but delights to endure all things in hope to enjoy its own in the end. Its hope is to outlive all wrath and contention, and to weary out all exaltation and cruelty. . . . As it bears no evil in itself, so it conceives none in thoughts to any other. If it is betrayed it bears it, for its ground and spring is the mercies and forgiveness of God."

"I have fellowship," wrote Naylor, "with them who lived in dens and desolate places in the earth. . . ." My mother lived in great houses, but Naylor's fellowship was one that she shared.

Why do I dwell upon my mother's character? My intention is not to lay my own errors like a bouquet of withered flowers on her grave. I hold myself responsible for my own actions, but in attempting to understand them, I turn back to some characteristics that stemmed in part from her: A sense of guilt over the wealth that I inherited; a fear of hurting or even of offending others; an inability, at critical moments, to assert my own interest; a deepseated need to love and to be loved.

And a radical streak. A few days after my mother died in 1968, her second husband said of her,

When Dorothy wanted to come to the United Kingdom, just after the First World War, a message came from the U. S. authorities which said:

ADVISE DO NOT ALLOW ENTRY TO MRS. WILLARD STRAIGHT. DANGEROUS TROUBLEMAKER.

I used to try and find out what it was that made her such a dangerous troublemaker. "I did lead a march down Fifth Avenue asking for votes for women," Dorothy said. "And I used to work for recognition of the labor unions."

About thirty years later, I was at a meeting in Washington when a rather elderly gentleman came up to me. "I believe you are married to the former Mrs. Willard Straight," he said. "Will you give her a message? Just say that it isn't half as easy to get our boys out of jail as it used to be in the days when we used to count on her."

# MY BROTHER, MY SISTER, AND I

"AFTER Willard's death," my mother wrote, "I immersed myself in work of many kinds."

Why, I wonder, did she find solace in work rather than in her children?

Fashionable theorists maintained in the twenties that mothers should not be overly affectionate with their children. 'If your child cries, let him cry' was the dominant view. The saving grace of the British aristocracy, according to Bernard Shaw, was that mothers entrusted their children to nannies.

My mother accepted those doctrines. In some way, they accorded with her needs.

Whitney was entrusted to a young tutor; Biddy, to a French governess whom we were instructed to call *"Mademoiselle."* I was left with an elderly English governess, Miss Gardner.

Miss Gardner was rigid, stern, remote. By day, she armored herself in a black gown with a high, lace collar. At night, a mountain of flesh would heave itself, sighing, into the canopied bed that towered above my cot. Miss Gardner snored, and her bed creaked when she turned over. But she usually managed to be up and fully dressed by the time that I was awake. Once in a while, however, I would wake before she did. Then, my eyes would open to a horrible sight. On a table inches away from my head there would be a glass of water, and glaring at me, from within the glass, a set of ferocious teeth.

We lived in a handsome town house on the corner of Ninety-Fourth Street and Fifth Avenue. We were sent to Lincoln, a progressive school built on the edge of Harlem. Many poor children were taken into Lincoln School. Many wealthy families, including the Rockefellers, sent their children there, believing that they should be cast together with every social class—even while they maintained their upperclass lifestyle.

For the children, it was unsettling. Each morning, when we had been dressed and fed, we would step into a Packard limousine. The Packard would glide up to the steps of the school; Hutchinson, our chauffeur, would lift the Persian lamb rug off our knees and hold the door of the Packard open. We would trot up to the doors of the school; there, our underprivileged classmates would by lying in wait for us.

They resented us as they had every right to, and they were rough. I protected myself against them by forming an Alliance of the Weak. It was made up of shy boys like myself; boys who were sickly; boys like my best friend, Bernard Naumberg, who were short-sighted and fat. We banded together on our battleground, the school gymnasium. If we were threatened, I would run and get Whitney. He and his classmates—giants from the sixth grade—would charge in and chastise our enemies while I looked on, smirking.

Our school day ended with recreation. On warm days, we played cops and robbers in a nearby park. I was cast as a robber on one memorable occasion. I hid in a public latrine and when the cops found me, I resisted arrest. They dragged me through the dirt and dumped me on the school steps, where the Packard was waiting. My clothes were torn; my face was filthy; I was completely happy. Miss Gardner, who was sitting in the back seat of the Packard, failed to recognize me when I climbed in beside her. She barely recovered.

On weekends, Hutchinson would drive us out to Old Westbury. There, I tried feebly to escape from Miss Gardner's embrace. I would look on in silent wonder as a blacksmith shod my Uncle Harry's race horses and polo ponies. I would follow the Italian gardeners as they gathered up the autumn leaves. I would turn the wringers with the laundresses and sit with the handyman while he churned a bucket to make ice cream. Most of all, however, I craved the companionship of Hutchinson's son. My mother wrote of me, "He would do anything for Harry Hutchinson. He wanted to give him everything he had. He wanted to play with him all day long. His greatest desire was to satisfy all of Harry's wishes. He didn't care about the other children with whom he played. Harry claimed all of his attention."

It was a losing battle. Miss Gardner referred to me as her "Little Angel." And little angels were not supposed to play with the sons of working men.

On rare occasions, we managed to break out of our enclave. One Sunday afternoon in January 1924, for example, Whitney, Biddy, and

I went to skate on the village pond in Westbury. Hutchinson drove us there; Miss Gardner accompanied us and remained in the back seat while we ventured forth.

Whitney and Biddy rushed onto the ice. I followed them, encased in a woolen helmet and stockings.

I wobbled around on the ice until Whitney skated up to me.

"There are two boys over there who say that you look like a stewed prune," he said.

I was nonplussed. I said, "What am I supposed to do?"

"You have to fight one of them," Whitney told me. He led me to the shore where the two boys were waiting.

One of the boys was ruddy-faced and stocky; the other was pasty-faced and thin. I grabbed the pasty-faced one and hauled him onto the ice. I threw him down and sat on top of him. I was doing well until he raised his head and bit me on my knee. We both began to blubber, and, at that moment, the crowd that had encircled us parted, laughing. Miss Gardner, in her black gown and high lace collar, was slipping and sliding across the ice in a desperate attempt to rescue me. She bundled me off as if I had been mortally wounded. She put me to bed with a hot-water bottle. Never again would she permit her little angel to mingle with the common people.

Governesses feel secure within their own small sanctuaries. They would spend all their days with their charges in those sanctuaries, if they could. Biddy and I were forced to spend hours in our playground with the children of wealthy neighbors, such as the Bradley Martins, so that Miss Gardner and her fellow-governesses could sit knitting and gossiping.

The Bradley Martins were boring little boys. I remember one occasion only in all of the many days that we spent being bored with each other. On that occasion, I hopped off my end of our see-saw with no warning, leaving one of the Bradley Martins high in the air. He descended abruptly, squashing a Sealyham terrier. We were rushed from the scene lest the terrier's yelps should scar our souls.

Looking back, it seems clear that, early on, Whitney, Biddy, and I set the courses that our lives would follow.

Whitney's tutor, Albert Crystal, drove a Marmon convertible that our mother had bought for him. Whitney would make him take us to a toll road on Long Island, where he would push the Marmon up to speeds of sixty miles an hour while we hung on, gasping. On other days, we would drive to Roosevelt Field. We would stand aghast on the apron of the field as dare-devil pilots swooped around in Bellanca bi-planes, giving joy rides for one dollar. We would creep between the heavy doors of the hangars that rimmed the field. Inside the hangars, in the dim and mysterious light, stood the Jennies—the pursuit planes left over from the First World War. We would walk around them, touching lightly the wooden propellers, the steel struts, the stretched green fabric of their fuselages. Then if no one had seen us, Mr. Crystal would hoist Whitney up into the open cockpit of one of the Jennies. He would sit there for hours when he was twelve, pushing the pedals, waggling the joystick. For Mr. Crystal and for me, those hours were a diversion. For Whitney, they were a life unfolding.

Biddy and her friend Nina Fonaroff shared a passion for the theater. They would spend hours in my father's study, playing some record over and over while they choreographed a new work. When they were ready, a performance would be announced. Chairs would be set out in rows in the study; the staff, led by Grove the butler, would march in and take their seats. I would pull back the curtain—a bed sheet rigged up on a clothes line. I would turn on the gramophone, and Biddy and Nina would appear, dressed up as wood nymphs. They would pirouette around with their arms upraised. When the record had ended and they had run offstage, I would do my imitation of them while Grove hid a smile with his fingers and the cooks and maids shook with suppressed laughter.

As the youngest child, I learned to give in when I was threatened by superior strength or resolution. I was thought to be fragile, and, in fact, my breast bones failed to join together, causing a condition known as *pectus excavatum* or "funnel chest." It was caused by my inability to absorb vitamin D, and on the advice of a specialist, Miss Gardner made me swallow daily doses of cod-liver oil in the vain hope that it would make my breast bones grow. I turned my infirmity to advantage and by pretending that the cod-liver oil made me sick, persuaded tender-hearted adults to read aloud to me while supper was brought to me in bed.

The world of fiction appealed to me much more than did the world around me. I loved best the works of Thornton Burgess. They were called "Bedtime Stories," and the title was well chosen. When a story was ended, you could sink, freed from all anxiety, into sleep.

The world of Thornton Burgess was made up of one happy family: Old Mother Nature and her Little Friends. Chief among her Little Friends was Peter Rabbit. He wore starched collars in the illustrations by Harrison Cady; he had a round, humorless face. Looking back, it seems clear that Cady used Herbert Hoover as his model for Peter. Yet Peter was a happy-go-lucky rabbit whose characteristics—laziness, curiosity, and lack of respect for his elders—were, by coincidence, the characteristics of most small boys. They were bad characteristics, as Grandfather Frog kept on telling Peter. But they never landed him in serious trouble. There was no serious trouble in the world of Thornton Burgess: no old age, no death. In the Great Forest that stood beyond the borders of the Green Meadows, there were fierce beasts like Howler the Wolf. But Howler did not intrude into the happy sanctuary of the Green Meadows. As Peter explained to his friend, Danny Meadow Mouse, "He doesn't bother to hunt little people like us."

There were a few predators in the Green Meadows. There was Hooty the Owl, for example, and Billy Mink. There was Reddy Fox and his mother, who, for some reason, was called Old Granny Fox. If you thought about it, you guessed that they had to eat something in order to survive. But you did not have to worry. If they caught a mouse or a rabbit, you were not told about it. It was not a mouse or a rabbit whom you knew. Only minnows and flies were caught and eaten in your presence. The flies were "foolish," and the minnows, being cold-blooded, did not mind.

At seven, I moved on to the works of Ernest Thompson Seton. His was a world of struggle, in which each animal was born into peril and died in defeat. Wahb crawled off to breathe his last in Death Gulch; Silverspot was eaten by an owl. Krag, the Kootenay Ram, was stalked and shot in his prime; Lobo, Lord of the Currumpaw, was snared by duplicitous hunters who first trapped his wife, a white wolf. Lobo, a good husband, tried to rescue his wife. He was caught and, spurning a life spent in captivity, starved himself to death.

*Live heroically and face death bravely when it comes.* That was the message that, in dying, Seton's heroes—all of whom were male—bequeathed to the living. It was a harrowing message, and the outcries were loud. "I have been bitterly denounced," Seton wrote, "first for killing Lobo, second and chiefly for telling of it to the distress of many tender hearts."

He felt that he had no choice; he was telling the truth as he saw the truth. "For the wild animal," he wrote, "there is no such thing as a gentle decline in peaceful old age. Its life is spent at the front, in line of battle, and as soon as its powers begin to wane in the least, its enemies become too strong for it; it falls.

"There is only one way to make an animal's history un-tragic, and that is to stop before the last chapter."

Seton's stories were all tragic. I could no longer snuggle under my comforter when each one was finished, knowing that the world around me was safe as I surrendered myself to sleep. Yet I clung to his stories. In fact, I began at seven to write my own animal stories.

The titles of my stories suggest my indebtedness to the master: *Cross Fox, King of the Chewacka Range; Chink, the Story of a Chipmunk; The Story of a Moose.* Like Seton's, my stories centered in the struggle for survival, but they ended before 'the last chapter.' The moose calf's mother saved him from a pack of wolves; Chink evaded the attacks of hawks, foxes, and weasels and found a female chipmunk; Cross Fox saved his mate by leading off the pack of hounds that was pursuing

her. He led them so far afield that it took him three days to get back
to his burrow. The story ended, ". . . He travled and travled and by
the middle of the third day he saw the friendly hills and woods and
mountains of the Chewacka Range. That night if one could have been
on the edge of the woods near a stream, they would have seen in front
of a burrow two foxes licking each other, one a slim red fox, the other
a big cross fox."

That was the last glimpse my readers were given of Cross Fox, King
of the Chewacka Range. But thanks to Ernest Thompson Seton, the
tragic sense of life was imprinted on my own mind for good. I sensed,
perhaps, the reason for my mother's sadness, and so, for me, Seton's
stories had the ring of truth.

# LEONARD ELMHIRST

FROM time to time, suitors for my mother's hand appeared at Old
Westbury. One was a young Englishman named Leonard Elmhirst,
whom we were instructed to call "Jerry."

He was unknown and penniless, as my father had been. Like my
father, he was one of the "dreamers of the day."

As the son of a Yorkshire parson, Jerry had volunteered for mission-
ary work in India. In the course of a few months, he had come to
realize that India was in need not of moralistic preaching but of
practical knowledge and leadership in overcoming illness, illiteracy,
ignorance, and poverty. Turning to agricultural economics, he
worked his passage to America and enrolled in Cornell.

He lodged in the Cosmopolitan Club in Ithaca, paying his way by
working as a dishwasher. Then, in 1920, he was elected president of
the club. Later, he recalled, "The extra swelling in my chest, caused
by this magic transformation, was almost immediately deflated by the
professor/treasurer. He called me into his office as soon as the election was over. 'Mr. President,' he began, 'I think I ought to inform
you now that the Club is hopelessly in debt, and that it is likely within
a few weeks to be declared bankrupt and put up for sale by auction,
at the request of our creditors and of the bank.' "

A number of professors had signed notes on behalf of the club and
were facing financial setbacks, should their notes be called in. Together they chipped in and bought their new president a roundtrip

ticket to New York, so that he could pass his hat among the Old Cornellians. He was told to return with $80,000.

To a man, the Old Cornellians turned him down. In despair, he went to Oswald Garrison Villard, who had once spoken at the club. Villard listened to his story. He remembered that my father had worked his way through Cornell. He said, "In the whole of the United States, there is only one person I can think of who might be ready and able to do something."

Villard telephoned the one person—my mother—and arranged a meeting at the Colony Club. Jerry waited there for her; she failed to appear. He waited for her again on the following day. She failed him a second time. On their third appointment, as he was about to leave for Ithaca, she arrived. "She gave me the most abject apologies for her behaviour," he wrote later, "and in I plunged. 'Mrs. Straight,' I said, 'have you ever visited Cornell?' "

She spent a day with him at Cornell. It was the first of many visits. She helped to save the club, but her real interest was in carrying out a provision of my father's will 'for the making of Cornell a more human place.' She decided that its primary need was for a student union where all students, men and women, fraternity members and nonfraternity students, could meet.

Thirty-six years later, I took my eldest son, as a prospective student, to see Cornell. By chance, we met an elderly professor. His name, he said, was Elmer Johnson. When I introduced myself, his eyes brightened.

As an undergraduate, he told us, he had lived in Telluride House. One morning, he added, an immense Packard drew up outside his door. Inside it, he saw a chauffeur, a fashionably dressed woman, and a small boy.

The great men of the university were waiting to greet the lady— my mother. They had not supposed that she would bring me with her. One of them rushed into Telluride and grabbed Elmer. Mrs. Straight would be occupied for several hours, the man told him. He was to take care of the boy.

It was no easy task. Elmer proposed all of the conventional pastimes. I rejected each of them. As a last resort, he led me down into the ravine that crosses the campus, to the stream known as Wee Stinky.

We spent the rest of that day in Wee Stinky, turning over rocks and snatching at everything that crawled away from under them. By the time that the conferences with my mother were finished, Elmer and I had filled up a large glass bowl with crayfish, water spiders, centipedes, tadpoles, and frogs.

Elmer carried the glass bowl up to the Packard. At my insistence, he laid it on the carpeted floor of the car while Hutchinson looked on, aghast. My mother returned to the Packard and saw the bowl, lying beneath my feet. She tried to persuade me to leave my collection behind, but I howled so loudly that she had to give in. So, while the great men berated poor Elmer, we rolled away down the hill, with the bowl slopping dirty water and tadpoles all over the Packard's floor.

That was in 1924. By then, a familiar pattern of courtship had re-emerged. Jerry was entranced, as my father had been, by my mother. He pursued her with less vigor but more tact. She responded once again in her tormented manner, beckoning him to approach closer, then thrusting him away.

Herbert Croly observed it all from his office in *The New Republic.* At last, he offered my mother some advice: "If you love Elmhirst enough to marry him . . . the difficulties are relatively of small importance. . . . But I myself would be profoundly skeptical of a subsequent plan of life which called for any but an exceedingly brief residence outside this country."

Any prolonged stay in England, said Croly, would make an expatriate of my mother and it would deprive her children of their roots. If Elmhirst wanted to found a utopian community, then, Croly maintained, he should do it in North Carolina or in California.

My mother saw the advantages in that, from our point of view. She suggested to Jerry that they might find a new home in America. He shook his head. The adventure that they would undertake together had to be an English adventure. The children would adjust themselves to England, and the family would maintain its transatlantic ties.

Torn apart and tired, my mother became seriously ill. She continued to ward Jerry off and then to beckon to him, until, in exasperation, he sent off the one harsh letter that he ever wrote to her: "You have never had to live the ordinary, human life. . . . You have dealt in a fairy land that was made for you, where everything that meant struggle and effort and careful consideration for others came at the touch of the wand. . . . You never had the chance of experiencing the disciplines of poverty."

She granted the truth of his charge, adding in her defense only that "I have been able to release people from certain burdens. . . . I suppose I try to make it all an expression of love."

Her friends, fearing to lose her, united in opposition to her remarriage. Once again, as in 1910, she was forced to choose between her friends and her suitor. Jerry waited; then he made his most powerful appeal to her: the community that they would found together would extend far beyond rural rehabilitation in its aims. It would encompass education and the arts.

At that, she gave in.

They were married in the garden at Old Westbury in April 1925. My mother promised to love and to honor her second husband; she omitted—with his consent—the traditional promise to obey him.

They left for a brief honeymoon on her brother's yacht. He sailed for England, to find them a new home. She followed him and then returned to be with us at Westbury. Lying in the bed in which her stepmother had died, she took my hand and placed it on her belly, so that I might feel the new life stirring within her.

A few weeks later, we began our goodbyes. Goodbye to Bernard Naumberg and my friends at Lincoln School. Goodbye to Grove and the house staff; goodbye to the gardeners: Curly Joe, Red Joe, Little Joe, Jimmy-in-the-greenhouse; goodbye to Harry Lee, the head gardener, and to his son, Jimmy Lee.

# DARTINGTON HALL

SOUTH Devon is all curves: narrow valleys, winding lanes, rich, rolling hills. The earth, when it is turned over in the spring, is a deep, rich red. Standing on the crest of a hill you can see the barren slopes of Dartmoor on the western horizon. To the east, the land rolls away over green pastures to the sea.

Jerry chose South Devon because Rabindrinath Tagore, his teacher and guide, had praised it. He went to see the leading real estate agents in London. He never tired of recounting the interview:

"I am looking for a country estate."

"Hunting, shooting, fishing, or golf?"

"None of those."

"What then?"

"It must be beautiful. . . . It must have a reasonably productive soil. . . ."

Dartington Hall was the first place on the list that he was given. It was a Tudor manor, built in the hills that overlooked the River Dart. Richard the Second had given it to his half-brother, the Duke of Exeter, who staged jousting tournaments in its sunken garden and, for supporting Richard against Henry IV, lost his head.

The manor passed to the Champernownes in 1759; they held it until 1925 but could not keep it up. By the time that they placed it on the market, the banqueting hall was in ruins; the garden was overgrown with weeds; one wing of the courtyard, built to house the duke's knights, had been turned into farm dwellings. Pigs and chickens rooted and scratched on the lawns.

Jerry bought a car—his first—in London. He headed for Devon. He
pried open the chained gates of the estate and followed the River Dart
until the narrow road wound upward and brought him to the Hall.
He saw a skeleton of gray stone, rising in broken arches and roofless
rooms out of the Devon mud. He wrote to my mother: "I wanted to
kneel and worship the beauty of it all, and every fresh vista seemed
the more to recommend the handiwork of nature joined with the
reverend hand of generations of men. I've dreamed of it ever since
as a fit home for you and the children, and I've pictured you there—
the squire's wife."

In time the courtyard and the Hall would be restored. Beneath the
magnificent timbers of the banqueting hall, Fischer Dieskau would
sing and Benjamin Britten would play the piano. Stokowski and Stra-
vinski would lecture in the solar; Kurt Jooss and Michael Chekhov
would direct their companies in the barn that had been made into a
theater; Bernard Leach and Mark Tobey would teach carpenters and
accountants how to throw pots and draw nudes in studios that once
had stored apples and grain. Close to one thousand men and women
would work or study in the arts college, the school, the textile plant,
the sawmills, the cider press, and the two modern farms. The estate
would function like its model, the Greek city-state, in which each
member of the community knew every other member and gained
from the relationship.

In his book *The Elmhirsts of Dartington,* Michael Young maintains
that Dartington as an experimental community was based upon four
myths:

*The Educational Myth*—that mankind can be liberated through education;
*The Cultural Myth*—that a new flowering of the arts can transform a society
impoverished by industrialization and secularization;
*The Arcadian Myth*—that a community which draws the best elements from
town and country can provide in Ebenezer Howard's words, a "joyous
union" from which will spring new hope, new life, a new civilization;
*The Humanist Myth*—that the efficient operation of agriculture and industry, at least on a small scale, can be reconciled with a pervasive concern
for the individual human being.

These myths—the term is not meant to be derogatory—were
brought to South Devon by the Elmhirsts, and by the advisers whom
they recruited from Denmark, Norway, Bengal, and Cornell. They
had not been tested in a single setting since the nineteenth century,
when utopian communities had flared into life and vanished, leaving
scarcely a trace.

Could they take root in South Devon? It would have been hard to
find a more alien setting.

Eight hundred acres of farm land surrounded the Hall. Beyond
them, half-hidden in the narrow valleys of South Devon, were small
villages—primitive, impoverished, isolated from each other. They
were clusters of stone cottages with thatched roofs or slate roofs. Each
had a church, a small store that served also as a post office; a midwife;
and a hand pump from which the villagers drew their water.

Once or twice a week, buses would creep down the narrow lanes
that connected the villages to the market town of Totnes. On those
days, the villagers would go to the market, the bank, the doctor, and
the cinema. They had no electricity, no television, and only a few had
radios or gramophones. Their schools were threadbare; their cash
income was minimal. The land from which they drew their livelihood
was farmed pretty much as it had been for four hundred years.

Jerry was fond of recalling a visit that he paid to a neighboring
farmer. "Your milk cans are filthy!" he told the farmer. "They're
covered with mud and manure!" The farmer nodded, dipping his
hand into the milk and watching it drip back into the can. "No need
to keep the cans clane for the milk," he said. "Ur clanes ursel."

In listing the assets of Dartington Hall, the real estate agent in
London noted that "No fewer than two packs of foxhounds and one
pack of harriers hunt the neighborhood." The packs were patronized
by the local gentry, whose members, like the men and women who
fill the pages of Jane Austen and of Anthony Trollope, were provincial
and proud. They looked with suspicion at the residents of the neighboring counties. They were highly suspicious of Londoners. As for
Americans, I remember one grand dame opening a local fête: "I trust
there are no Americans present today," she remarked, peering over
her lorgnettes. "I can't abide Americans!"

Miss Jervoise-Smith, a leader of the local gentry, left her calling card
at the Hall and waited with increasing impatience. Her call was not
returned. The Reverend Martin sent word that the new owners of the
Hall would occupy the pew in which the Champernownes had once
been seated. The pew remained empty. The Elmhirsts did not ride to
hounds or offer the great banqueting hall, when it was restored, for
hunt balls. Their copses were well populated with foxes, but their
estate was closed to the hounds. In place of hierarchy, they brought
the practice of democracy to Devon. In place of the social conventions
of the nineteenth century, they brought the heresies of the twentieth:
coeducation, nude bathing, free love.

The carpenters and joiners of the neighborhood set off on their
bicycles each morning to work at the Hall. The gentry looked on with
increasing dismay. In the parish church, the Reverend Martin
preached a resounding sermon. Before the war, he declared, Satan
had resided in Berlin. Then he had moved to Moscow. Now, he had
taken up his residence at Dartington Hall.

# SAILING TO ENGLAND

WHITNEY was the first child to arrive at Dartington. He was thirteen, and when he saw that there were three miles of private roads within the estate, he announced that he wanted a motorcycle.

Jerry nodded. "I and your mother will put up one-half of the cost of a motorcycle," he told Whitney, "but you must earn the other half."

Earn it? How was he to earn it?

"By building a wall," Jerry said. He led Whitney to a corner of the ancient courtyard that needed a retaining wall. He handed him a pail, a trowel, and a sack of cement.

"What do I do now?" Whitney asked.

"You watch how your fellow bricklayers set their bricks. Then you do as they do."

"How do I get here?" asked Whitney, since they were living at the old parsonage, a mile away.

"You borrow my Sunbeam." Jerry said.


In mid-June, Biddy, her friend Nina, Miss Gardner, and I sailed for Plymouth on the *George Washington.* I was nine. Six years later, when I began an autobiographical novel, I described the feelings of my central character as the liner approached England:

> Suddenly there was a rush to the side of the boat. Someone, thrusting his face into the wind, had seen a light—the first fishing boat, out there in the darkness.
>
> He rushed to the side of the boat with everyone else, and squeezed in between two men. He saw the light. It was very small, but it was part of England.
>
> They passed the fishing boat. As the light bobbed past them he heard a shout from the darkness. He shouted back and listened, but Miss Gardner came for him. "Time for bed," she said, and she led him down to their stateroom.
>
> "God bless Mother and Jerry and Whitney and Beatrice and Miss Gardner. And I hope I die when she does." Hands folded and eyes shut. Lights out, but he could not sleep. A lot was going on above them: shouting, and moving baggage; a lot of fishing boats were going by. He wondered as he lay there: Would Miss Gardner's parents be waiting for her? Or were they dead? Why would she never tell him her age? Perhaps she would die soon; did he really want to die when she did?
>
> In the morning, he got up very early. The liner was cutting its way

through calm seas in the Channel; in the distance he could see the coast of England, soft and green.

In the salon, long lines of passengers were waiting; Americans here, British there. He wondered as they stood in line: Would his mother be waiting for them? Would Whitney be there? What was a "Sunbeam"?

Slowly the boat slid into Plymouth breakwater. Hundreds of gulls circled above it. Then two tugs appeared. They also circled the boat, then one came close and clenched itself to the boat's side.

They waited for hours downstairs, and on the tender. He was footsore when they landed. But his mother was waving and Whitney was beside her and Jerry was behind them.

Whitney looked older. He said that he was building a brick wall. There was a river all around the estate, he said, with trout and salmon in it. And a Sunbeam was a bicycle.

Whitney worked, building his wall. I was given a small garden to keep. A pear tree grew against a wall in my garden. In the course of the summer it produced one immense pear.

Miss Gardner left to visit her family. She returned to say goodbye. My novel comments,

As the time approached for Miss Gardner's departure, her nightly kisses became more prolonged. Half smothered by them, he began to dread the end.

It came one day when he was hoeing his garden. She came in through the gate. She told him that Biddy and Nina were going with her on the river steamer down to Dartmouth as a farewell treat. He was to go with them.

No, he said. He could not. He was too busy in his garden.

At that, her wrinkled face collapsed. Tearwet, she hugged him. Sobbing, she hurried through the gate and out of sight.

He felt weak in his knees. He worked hard, hoeing the earth. He was free for the first time. He was not sure what that meant. Soon, however, his prayers became irregular. He prayed only when he felt the need of a protector. Then he stopped praying.

# A PROGRESSIVE EDUCATION

IN September 1926, the school founded by Jerry and my mother opened its doors. The student body was made up of the three of us and fourteen waifs and strays. The teachers were an odd assortment whom Jerry had known in his Cambridge days. Manual work was stressed at his insistence. Each student had a room—another reflection of his early miseries. Permissiveness was a cardinal principle, introduced by my mother. So was self-government, and it was carried to ludicrous lengths. On one occasion the teachers and the students spent an entire morning in a meeting chaired by the head gardener, trying to decide whether the children should be driven to Totnes to have haircuts, or whether Mr. Mendham, the hairdresser, should be driven to the school.

Frankness was another antidote to the inhibitions left over from Victorian days. Students and teachers were summoned to a meeting one evening in order that the boys could be told why the girls had to be excused from games on certain days.

I and my fellow ten-year-olds were utterly perplexed. In the first place, we had no organized games. We climbed trees; we roamed through the woods; we invented our own games when the school became organized to the extent of listing Athletics on the bulletin board.

"What games did you play at your school?" my son Mike asked me in 1954. The fifth grade at his school was apparently committed to a kind of show-and-tell in which each child had to stand up before the class and boast about his father's athletic prowess. Poor Mike! "My father played third base for Hotchkiss," said the first boy. "My father played right guard for Sidwell Friends," said the next. The list of parental exploits swelled until Mike's turn came. "My father played bicycle polo for Dartington Hall," he said. The whole class burst into laughter.

The purpose of the school was set forth in an outline. "For us it is vital," it declared, "that education be conceived of as life and not merely as a preparation for life."

From that radical concept, all else flowed. Classes were voluntary and followed the interests of the teachers and the students rather than the requirements for entry into universities. Learning by doing was stressed. The students grew the vegetables that they ate and built the huts that housed their livestock. They worked with the laborers on the estate to gain from them a sense of the dignity of labor and a knowledge of how to help living things to grow.

The school was to be "A little world in itself, carrying on in a real, if elementary way, the activities of the great world around." For that reason, it had to be a self-governing democracy. Students were to participate in all the decisions that shaped their activities. Teachers were to be counselors and friends. There was to be no punishment, for punishment recalled the bitter years that Jerry had spent as a school boy at Repton. Rules and regulations were to be minimal. Self-discipline would guide the conduct of the students as it would guide them when they became adults.

One problem, which all experimental endeavors face, was how the school would relate to the rest of the world. That was rarely, if ever, considered. Whitney was fifteen when he learned that he had to master Latin if he wanted to go on to Oxford or Cambridge. Biddy, to this day, cannot spell. These pages were corrected by my daughter Dorothy, who could scarcely believe that any adult's grammar could be as bad as she found mine to be.

We could not spell when we were twelve, or read Latin, or work out equations in algebra. We were all too familiar with Freud's interpretation of dreams. There was no head of the school, since authority was regarded as regressive, but among the teachers, Wyatt Trevelyan Rawson was more equal than the others. Wyatt, as we were told to call him, had just returned from Germany, and he was well indoctrinated in the new concepts of psychoanalysis. He would seat all of us in a large circle. Then, with an ingratiating smile, he would question us about our dreams.

"You, Michael, what did you dream about last night?"

"I dreamed I was being chased by a lion."

"Aha! A lion! A well-established symbol for your repressed emotions of guilt and fear of castration! Tell us. . . ."

Wyatt also insisted on "interpreting" our writings. Thus, I wrote a story about a racing driver and was called on to read it aloud. I had cribbed the story from a film that I had seen in Totnes, but in a revised ending, I added to my hero's triumphs by producing from nowhere his long-lost father.

"Aha!" cried Wyatt. "The hidden wish is revealed!"

"I only added that part as an after-thought," I said.

"Precisely! The sub-conscious intrudes upon the conscious design!"

In some sort of premature self-analysis, I conceded that he was probably right.

Three years after the school was founded, the faculty rose in revolt against Wyatt. He accepted a post at another school, but before he departed he wrote out a final report on Whitney, Biddy, and me.

Whitney, he noted, had "great physical vigor," but "Academically he is backward in all subjects that require logical and detailed thought."

Biddy was "possessed of enormous vitality and considerable charm," but her interests were "almost exclusively directed toward dancing, painting, the movies, and lip-stick."

As for me, "Michael has been tremendously under the influence of an English governess who kept his development and his emotions arrested at an age of about five. . . ."

Wyatt concluded: "The early loss of their father, the false attitude towards them generated in others by their social and financial position, the absence of any home atmosphere, combined with the idiosyncrasies of an education at Lincoln School . . . which . . . cut them off from the conventional schooling and ideas of the average American upper-class child, their transference to England, and the arrival of a step-father have all tended to make them feel like strangers in a foreign world."

'. . . strangers in a foreign world. . . .' Shorn of the conventional ties, we continued to go our own ways.

Whitney bought himself an alto saxophone and formed his own jazz band. He bought a Riley and drove it in the hill-climbing contests at Shelsley Walsh. He learned to fly and, at sixteen, became the youngest licensed pilot in England. The school allowed him to pursue his vocation at the expense of his studies. Then, when he chose to go on to Cambridge, he was told that he would have to attend a cramming school. He managed to be accepted at Cambridge, but he was a poor student. He left at the end of his second year to devote himself to motor racing. He bought a Duesenberg, in which he broke the lap record at Brooklands. Then he bought a brace of Maseratis and formed his own racing team. He became a popular idol. Fans mobbed him at every race meeting; he was portrayed in every Sunday newspaper. He married an earl's daughter in St. Margaret's, Westminster Abbey, and when the earl brought up a busload of old retainers from his country seat, Whitney matched him by bringing up two busloads of Dartingtonians, who made the ancient walls of the Abbey reverberate when they tramped down the aisle in their hobnailed boots. He was enormously successful, yet deep within him there remained a core of alienation and hurt pride.

Whitney became more British than the British. Biddy, in contrast, put down few roots in England. She established a theater school at Dartington, under Michael Chekhov, nephew of the playwright. She took it to Connecticut in 1939 when England seemed close to war. The lack of a formal education was not as disabling for her as it was for Whitney. Yet the fracturing of her life handicapped her in many ways.

As for me, my teachers noted that I was "difficult," "withdrawn," "uncooperative," and "rude."

My mother added her own perceptive comment to these reports:

He suffers from diffidence and uncertainty about himself. He shows the
effect of having been bullied by an older brother. . . . I have often heard
Michael recount something that he has read or experienced and then
listened to Whitney pour his ridicule upon it. . . . Michael always shrivelled
inwardly under the rebuke. The effects of this vain effort to assert himself
against Whitney's domination are evident today in his outward unrespon-
siveness to people. . . . he seems to disregard people completely. On the
other hand, his fear of making any demands springs from a profound
consideration for the feelings of others. He . . . will not put forward his
own claims, for fear of inconveniencing somebody else. This has been
proven to me over and over again.

His difficulties can be traced to one source: the conflict between his
emotional and his intellectual being.

He is an intensely emotional child. He craves friendship. The interests
of his friends lie in practical things. His interests are in painting, acting,
writing. He has tried to convince himself that he enjoys gardening as much
as Oliver and horses as much as Bob, but, the conviction doesn't hold. He
feels empty; he knows only that he is wandering around without any sense
of direction. When I ask him what the trouble is, he answers simply: "I
don't know."

I gained next to nothing in classrooms. I did benefit from the
meetings on Sunday evenings to which my mother brought an exciting series of speakers: Bertrand Russell, Aldous Huxley, A. S. Neill.
. . . I enjoyed the free afternoons when we cycled into Totnes or
Paignton to see Emil Jannings tear his heart out in a Hollywood epic
while someone strummed away on an upright piano. Above all, I
loved the evenings in the school when we gathered together to darn
our socks. The teachers joined us on those evenings. So did Jerry and
my mother. We sang as we darned: *Swing Low, Sweet Chariot, Nobody
Knows the Trouble I've Seen, Cockles and Mussels,* and *Brennan on the Moor.*
Those moments provided some release for my own sadness and gave
me what I deeply longed for: a sense of belonging to some brotherhood.

-<≈>-

From time to time, my mother took a train to London. On one such
trip, she went to a production in English of *Le Tombeau sous l'Arc de
Triomphe* by Paul Raynal. She was overcome by the play, and when
it completed its brief run, she brought it to Dartington.

The central character of the play, the Soldier, returns on a twenty-
four-hour leave to his home, where the woman he loves is living with
his father. She voices doubt about her love for him; in his despair, he
reveals that he obtained his leave by volunteering for a suicidal mission, when a volunteer was called for.

A little-known actor named Maurice Browne played the part of the

Soldier. He formed a theatrical partnership with my mother and together they put on the most celebrated play of the decade, *Journey's
End*. Its influence was immense and not altogether good, for it reinforced the pacifism of the British people at a time when Hitler was
preparing to overrun Europe. But the impact of *Journey's End* is not
part of this story.

My interest lies in a comment of my mother's that has risen to the
surface of my mind after being buried in my memory for fifty three
years.

I was moved, as everyone was, by Raynal's play. But I told my
mother that the action of the Soldier made no sense to me.

"Why, if he was the best man in his company, did he have to be
the one to volunteer for the mission?" I asked her. "Why, if he loved
Aude so deeply, did he give up his whole life just to be one night with
her?"

My mother was unusually sharp in her answer. "If you don't understand that, then you understand nothing," she said. "It was because
he was the best man in his company that the Soldier had to volunteer,"
she told me. "It was because he loved Aude that he gave up his own
life."

⌁

In 1929, when I was twelve, Jerry and my mother visited the two
communities in Bengal where he had worked as an assistant to Rabin-
dranath Tagore. I was doing poorly in school and had fainted a few
times in classes, so they decided to take me along.

We went by steamship to Bombay and by train from then on. We
were not grand as travelers. To my dismay, I was given a member of
the Untouchable Caste named Quadrat whose assignment was to cater
to all of my wishes. Each morning, Quadrat brought me a chamber
pot and waited while I squatted on it. He waited in vain. When we
arrived in Santineketan, I was given special privileges by Tagore
himself. He possessed the only flush toilet in the community; one on
which he sat for hours in his majestical manner. I was given squatting
rights upon his toilet after he was done.

It was the first time that I had been cast alone with my mother and
my stepfather. Looking back, I can see that at times my stepfather was
remote, and my mother naïve. On the voyage home, for example, a
man who was a teacher in a boys school took an intense interest in me.
My mother thought that was fine; my stepfather said nothing. Some
instinct within me led me to rebuff the man's approaches to me.

We landed in Nice, in the South of France. There, a letter was
waiting for Jerry and my mother. It was from Jerry's brother, who was
acting headmaster of the school. He said, quite rightly, that the school
should be reorganized or else closed down. Jerry was ready to admit

defeat. My mother, her eyes blazing, cried no! They hurried off to England, leaving me alone in a splendid hotel in Nice.

I did not mind. A tennis tournament was under way at the hotel. Among the players was the great William T. Tilden.

I sat under a bay tree, watching the matches. Tilden won the tournament. Then, in the twilight, he came and sat down beside me.

He put his arm around my shoulder. I was thrilled. I asked him if he would teach me to play tennis. He would love to he said, but I would have to travel with him. He left Nice with his protégé—a boy of my own age. A few years later, he was arrested on a morals charge.

A new headmaster came to Dartington bringing new goals and priorities. The school ceased to be an integral part of the community, concerned with the life around it. It became a preparatory school, attempting to outdo other preparatory schools in placing its students in Oxford and Cambridge.

We began at last to study, preparing for the School Certificate examination. At the same time, I discovered new realms of literature and of love.

My home in the Hall was out of bounds in term time, I used to creep into the Hall, nonetheless, to gobble up the leftovers from tea when I was hungry or else to read by myself. My mother had placed the novels of Joyce, of Aldous Huxley, and of D. H. Lawrence on the shelves in our sitting room. For me, they were a great awakening.

As for love, it was critically important for Whitney, for Biddy, and for me. Whitney was a Don Juan, moving from woman to woman and fearing to commit himself. Biddy, in contrast, was too trusting.

I was a romantic. I believed, when I was fourteen, that *Lady Chatterly's Lover* was the greatest novel ever written. I cast myself in the role of Mellors, the gamekeeper. In searching for my Lady Chatterly, I moved out beyond my depth.

# IN LOVE WITH LOVE

WHEN she was eighty, Martha Graham told me about the day in 1920 when she came to see my mother in New York. She spoke of her ambition to create a modern dance company. My mother listened; she then excused herself, leaving Martha to play with me. We did a dance together before my mother, check in hand, returned.

She gave the check to Martha. It was substantial, and Martha said that she did not know what to do with it, since it was the first she had been given. She was told to spend it and not to worry.

My mother continued to support Martha Graham. When, in 1930, a company was formed in London by a former Graham dancer, my mother took us to its first performance.

The company consisted of four dancers and a pianist. The works that they performed were lyrical and earthy: young mothers rocking their children to sleep; Breton fisherwomen mending their nets. We agreed that the works were beautiful. So my mother brought the company to Dartington, to work in the villages and to teach in the school.

The founder of the company, and its choreographer, was an American dancer named Margaret Barr. She was dark and dramatic, like a gypsy; bold and strong, like a statue by Gaston Lachaise. She walked on the balls of her feet as dancers do, taking long strides with her head high and her glossy hair shaking behind her.

She was twenty-four.

Twice a week, she took the students of the senior school in dance classes. We did the Graham exercises: stretching, bending, leaping, rolling over, muscle by muscle, on the floor. The boys in the senior school loathed the classes; I set out to excel in them, for Margaret's sake. I proved to be a good dancer, and before long, she cast me in leading roles in the new works that she created.

She created dance/dramas and pageants, using farmhands and housewives forty years before the British Arts Council committed itself to the support of "participatory arts." Her creations culminated in an epic that at first was performed to the Second Symphony of Jean Sibelius. It reflected her political convictions, for she thought of herself as a Communist.

Jerry was cast as the Pope in Margaret's epic. A porky mill hand was the Capitalist Boss, strutting around in a top hat and gripping a long cigar. I was the Visionary; I led a large chorus of Workers out of poverty and oppression and into a new order in which, as in the world of Thornton Burgess, there was no pain.

Did my role help to shape my own developing attitudes? I do not think so. I was a dancer, stripped to the waist, with gold dust in my hair. Like most dancers, I moved without thought or reflection; I let others reflect upon the meaning of the work.

The critics came down from London for the opening night. They praised it highly. In contrast, Admiral Sir Barry Domville, who had two children in the school, took it as proof that black magic was being practiced at Dartington. He spread that word around until our solicitors silenced him with the threat of a libel suit.

I danced for Margaret, believing that I loved her. I was out of my depth. To be sure, boys and girls lived side by side in the senior school. We studied together and stood side by side in the showers. The notion that this would vaporize our adolescent desires was seen in time by our elders to be naïve. That was always apparent to us. Nonetheless, we saw ourselves as pioneers. The notion that the future of co-education in English boarding schools would turn upon our conduct was for us a powerful inhibition. We shared the same showers but not the same beds.

Margaret was on the other side of the boundary. She sensed the danger as she became drawn to me. Her sister, Betty, visited her, bringing her lover—a handsome and sophisticated writer named John Langdon-Davies. They saw what was happening and told her that it was madness.

She was twenty-five; I was fifteen. I wrote a stilted letter to her, saying that I loved her. She answered it in a guarded way. I persisted, and the day came when she handed me a letter:

Because of certain times in the past week, I expect you know that I love you. I'm saying it in my heart, to you and about you, all the time. But, to tell you has been impossible for me. We are both up against it, because neither of us really knows the other.

I've often tried to speak to you. I couldn't because I was frightened that I might frighten you. Also, I wasn't sure about your feeling. But you have been so constant in spite of certain times when I must have bewildered you that time can't go by with more misunderstanding.

You and John are the only men whom I've ever learned to love, just because you use the same tactics—of quiet persistence. I don't know if you do it consciously—John did.

You see, I've been so bound up in my work. I've seen other human beings as so much material to be used in dancing, not as people with emotions. And, as a girl and a woman, I've deliberately cut men out of my emotional life. I've had to be a good instrument. I was frightened that, in loving anyone, I should lose creativity. I know now that that is wrong; I know it consciously now that I am thinking it through. So, if this time of deliberate avoidance of you has been puzzling you—my own uncertainty has been driving me from one line of action to another; cutting you dead, trying to make you angry with me, running away from you as hard as I could. It all sounds stupid, darling, and I'm laughing at this moment. But, like as not, it will happen again.

You and Betty are so alike: idealistic, dreamy . . . you are purity itself. John and I are alike in our passionate worship of those qualities; our instinctive desire to protect them, when we find them in another. There comes the awful thought: how can you possibly care for queer creatures like us? There you have it—I shall always be in a state of wonder about you.

What on earth must you have thought when I rushed up and took you

by the arm last night and led you to my car? You were looking as black
as could be. I tried twice to explain that I was only trying to help that boy
who worked at the Hall and is tubercular, but you were about as respon-
sive as blotting paper and I knew by the feel of you that you were in your
vacuous, introspective state. Look—those people are the backbone of the
community, and I shall continue to ally myself to them.

I didn't go to the party because I knew that you wouldn't dance with
me. Why?

Well . . . it will be impossible for you to idealize me after this. And now,
do sit at another table at mealtimes. The more people there are to separate us, the more I ache, and love you. You don't eat; I get unnerved and
the result is not good for either of us.

All my trust is in you. Believe me when I say that I don't look on you
as a schoolboy. The feeling I have is that worlds are crashing, and, out
of the tumult and the confusion comes the still, quieting voice saying *you*.
It is absolutely ageless and sexless.

The danger with me is—and it may be true of you—that I can always
fall back on my imagination to support me.

How much your mother really knows, I can't judge. She doesn't know
from me what I have written here.


I carried the letter around with me all day. In the darkness, I walked
to her cottage and stood before her. "How can I make you happy?"
I asked. She said, "By loving me."

We had to meet furtively. We drove off together in her car. We
were able to steal away for weekends to the cottage in Cornwall that
my mother let us share. We read *Lady Chatterley* aloud. We were
happy, but it could only end badly. She was not Connie, and I was not
Mellors. She was even more innocent than I about contraception, and
there was no one to turn to for advice. The tension caused by with-
holding myself, added to the furtive life that we had to lead together,
left me impotent at last.

I buried myself in my studies. She stayed on at Dartington, teaching
dance. After a year or two, the arts department was placed under a
man who believed that participation in the arts should be limited to
professionals. The Jooss Ballet, when it fled from Germany, was offered a new home at Dartington by my mother. There was no room
for another dance company.

Margaret went back to London. She married a working-class man.
She wrote to me to say that he had joined the Communist party.
Before long, they emigrated to Australia.

Thirty-five years later, I went to Sydney on a speaking tour. I asked
the director of the Australia Arts Council if he had ever heard of a
dancer named Margaret Barr.

"Of course!" he said.

I waited.

"She's a thorn in our side!" he said.

She was still at work, organizing dockers, truck drivers and Aborigines in her dance/dramas. She was collecting a few pennies from the arts council, in contrast to the millions it was pouring into the productions of Classical ballet. I had sat through a lavish and sterile production of *La Fille Mal Gardée* at the Sydney Opera House. I thought to myself, *She was right.*

I was sixty; she was seventy. I called her telephone number, trembling. I heard her voice, and I said who I was. The line was silent, then we talked for twenty minutes. Once or twice, we were able to laugh.

# LONDON: THE PULL OF THE LEFT

"IN my hot youth," wrote Ford Maddox Ford, "I yearned to be both poet and soldier; having been them, I find myself to have become pacifist and prosateur."

At sixteen, I thought of myself as a poet. I had taken the School Certificate examination, but having failed mathematics, had to wait one year before going on to Cambridge.

If my interest was in writing, why did I not set out to develop my talents? One answer, I suppose, is that the world seemed to be collapsing around me. The pain that I had caused Margaret intensified my sense of obligation. I did not know what flag I should follow, but I yearned to enlist as a soldier in the political battles that were raging in Europe.

Felix Frankfurter was living in Oxford that year. Since he had written to me when I was born, I went to see him.

He sat at his desk in his study. Pacing up and down, I blurted out my intention of setting aside a university education in order to help save the world.

How did I propose to save the world, he wanted to know.

By working for the League of Nations, or some such cause, I said.

Frankfurter remarked in his dry way that if I could spare the time to attend a university, the world might survive for another three years.

What, then, should I do? Frankfurter had the answer. He sent me to see his close friend Harold Laski, professor of political science at the London School of Economics; a frequent contributor to *The New*

*Republic;* a man despised by the right wing in Britain as a Socialist, an intellectual, and a Jew.

Laski motioned to me to sit down in his small and stuffy parlor. He brought out a decanter of port. "The last of old Haldane's," he told me. He poured me a very small drink.

The telephone rang. "Is that-ah-you-ah Ibn Hamid?" said Laski. "I am delighted (a) to hear your voice, and-ah- (b) to infer that-ah- I shall be seeing you soon."

I explained my situation to Laski. He listened with a grave air, sucking in from time to time through the dark stumps of his teeth.

"In my-ah-opinion," he said, in his nasal twang "you should-ah-attend the-ah-London School of-ah-Economics-ah-for one-ah-year."

I said that I would be happy to go to the LSE, but that I doubted if I could get in.

"That-ah-will depend on-ah-the Committee on-ah-Admissions," said Laski, "and-ah-since I happen to be-ah-the-ah-Committee on Admissions-ah-I-ah-suspect that it might-ah-be arranged."

So I turned, or was turned, from literature to economics.

I moved to London. Whitney had left Cambridge by then. We rented an elegant house in Mayfair from the writer P. G. Wodehouse. As a parting gesture, he gave a dinner in our honor to which he invited his glamorous friends. He raised his glass to toast us, and when the ladies had departed, voiced his conviction that Hitler and Mussolini were strong leaders who deserved our wholehearted support.

Whitney prided himself on his aesthetic sense. No sooner had Wodehouse departed than he sent me around to the studio of Ben Nicholson, an avant-garde painter, with orders to buy five or six large canvases to hang on Wodehouse's walls. He had the dining room redone in luminescent paint, and he installed a monkey on our top floor.

The luminescent paint failed to glow as Whitney had supposed it would, when the candles were blown out and our male guests settled down with their port and cigars. The paintings were praised, but the monkey proved to be ill-smelling, bad-tempered, and an alcoholic. It was presented to Lady Astor's Siamese cat when they were both promenading in Hyde Park. It sprang upon the cat and gave it a nasty bite. Whitney brought it down one evening when he had a glamorous actress named Wendy Barrie to dinner. The monkey remained in our sitting room when we went down to dinner. Then it emptied our glasses of sherry.

We returned to the sitting room, and Wendy draped herself along a sofa. From its perch, high up on a curtain rail, the monkey glared down at her. It raced around the top of the room, shrieking insults at Wendy. Then it leaped down onto her and drenched her golden evening gown with vomit.

Whitney was scheduled to join the European racing circuit with his Maseratis, his mechanics, and his valet, Dewdeney. He hired a young footman to care for the monkey and for me.

He instructed the young man in our needs. When he had bowed and departed, Whitney turned to me.

"He is to be called John," he told me.

"But . . . his name is Albert——"

"All footmen are called John," said Whitney. With that, he departed for Milan, leaving me alone in the house.

———✦———

Each morning, after "John" had served me breakfast, I left our elegant mansion and took the tube to Aldwych. There, along with thousands of shabby students, I made my way into the grim, Victorian interior of the London School of Economics.

On my first evening at the London School a debate was staged in the student union. Three hundred students crowded into the debating hall, smoking furiously and chattering away. In time, the president of the union and two speakers appeared.

The first of the speakers was the renowned scientist J. B. S. Haldane. He was immense, with bushy eyebrows and a walrus moustache. The second speaker Gates, made no impression on anyone.

The president, Frank Meyer, was an American. He looked like an Aztec priest, with his high cheekbones, his arched, sensual lips, and his long, narrow nose.

The union was a training ground for the Inns of Court. No sooner had the secretary of the union completed his brief, innocuous report than a dozen would-be barristers were on their feet, demanding to be heard. They belabored the poor secretary with useless points of order and preposterous motions: "That this House demands more sugar for its coffee . . ." and, "That this House affirms that the school's waitresses take away the plates too soon. . . ."

Meyer sat in his high chair as an Aztec priest might have sat on his throne. A student standing beside me whispered in awe that he was "a revolutionary."

So, apparently, were many of the students. Haldane had publicly announced that he was joining the Communist party. Before and after his speech, he was loudly cheered.

I wanted very much to gain some identity in my new surroundings. I saw my opportunity when the secretary announced that the fund that had been created to aid the refugees from Nazi Germany had, in the course of seven weeks, taken in two pounds six shillings and ten pence ha'penny. I went to the president's office the next morning and introduced myself to Frank Meyer. I said that I wanted to contribute to the refugee fund.

Meyer nodded, working away on his papers. "How much?" he asked. "Twenty pounds," I said.

I volunteered to play field hockey, and since I had an old Ford convertible and could drive other players to the matches, I was placed on the LSE team.

Among the members of the team was an Oxford graduate, Peter Floud. He spoke about street fights with the local Fascists as we drove back and forth to our matches. He became my first friend at the London School.

At Floud's urging, I became a member of the Socialist Club. I went with him to its meetings. They were tense, for a caucus calling themselves Marxists had captured the key positions in the club. They were rigid and humorless; against them were ranged a number of equally humorless Socialists. One was a Hindu with an arrogant manner and cavernous eyes. His name was Krishna Menon. He was a perpetual student, in a perpetual rage. He fought on every issue, and every issue was inflamed by his venom.

I did not understand what the arguments were about. Nor when I went to a debate in the House of Commons, could I gain any sense of where the government of Great Britain and the opposition Labour party stood on the great issues of the day. Hitler had taken power in Germany. He had denounced the disarmament treaties and the League of Nations. What was England's response to be? Sir John Simon, the foreign secretary, seemed mildly dismayed by Hitler's actions. Anthony Eden, his deputy, sat, nodding at his side. The leaders of the Labour party berated the government for not pressing ahead with disarmament. Churchill, in his gloomy way, spoke of the threat to the empire. No one mentioned the League of Nations—the one cause that could have rallied my generation.

I did not know it, but in the dark recesses of the London School, a jurisdictional struggle had been developing between Frank Meyer and the director, Sir William Beveridge. In my second week at the school, it broke into an open fight. The union became a battlefield, and on every bulletin board, notices were posted, summoning all students to an emergency meeting.

The meeting began with the customary trivialities. Then a motion was introduced supporting Meyer. Liberals, Socialists, and Marxists spoke in favor of the motion. The Conservatives tried to prevent it from coming to a vote.

The hall had to be cleared at 10:30. At 10:25, the leader of the Conservatives introduced a substitute motion censuring Meyer.

Meyer leaned forward in his high chair. "Mr. Ingerson, you are required to give one day's notice before introducing any motion."

"Mr. President, I demand that my motion——"

"Mr. Ingerson, will you please sit down."

"No, sir, I will not!"

"Mr. Ingerson, I order you to sit down!"

"I won't!"

Meyer called for the vote on the first motion. I reached my hand up as high as I could. With Ingerson still standing and shouting, the tellers counted the vote. They handed the tally to Meyer, and he announced that the motion supporting him had carried. At that, most of the students in the hall stood, cheering wildly and hurling their papers into the smoke-filled air.

In the street outside I came upon Floud, talking to an earnest radical named Geoffrey Marmont. We set out for a Lyons corner house. I wanted to go over every detail of the debate, but Marmont dismissed it as "bourgeois romanticism." Floud, who had sat through many such evenings, soon changed the subject.

He had been paying twelve shillings a week for his lodgings, so he said. The night before he had brought his girl home with him, and, that morning, his landlord had thrown them both out. "I'm not keeping a brothel!" the landlord had told him. He had repeated it to Floud's father, a high-ranking civil servant.

"You must be mistaken," the civil servant had said, "my son sleeps only with ladies."

At eleven, we moved on to a café. Meyer was seated there with a group of his supporters. An orchestra was playing *Land of Hope and Glory*. It scraped its way to the end, and one of Meyer's group demanded that the musicians play the *Internationale*. The musicians said that they did not know that number. Meyer and his friends stood up and sang it unaccompanied. When they finished, they raised their clenched fists in the air.

Marmont stood up for the *Internationale* although he did not sing it. He sat down again and at once launched into an attack upon W. H. Auden—"a fence sitter," he said.

Auden had come to Dartington. I knew many of his poems by heart. "You call him a fence sitter," I said, "but the fence is a wide fence. The middle class is the majority in England and they are not revolutionary."

"They will be," said Marmont, "when the crisis comes."

At midnight, Marmont and I walked from the Strand to Piccadilly Circus. There, knowing that I had no key to my house and fearing that "John" would be waiting up for me, I said that I had to walk home.

"I'll walk with you," Marmont said.

I protested, saying that it was out of his way.

"Bourgeois manners!" said Marmont. "How false they are!"

"You are bored." He went on. "You are weary of listening to me."

"That's not true!"

"No? Perhaps your mistress is waiting up for you."

"I have no mistress."

"Who then?"

"My brother's footman," I said, filled with shame.

"If you are ashamed of your way of life," said Marmont, "then do as I did—reject it!"

We walked on toward Mayfair.

Marmont told me that his father was a high official of the Imperial Tobacco Company and that he had been sent to a fashionable preparatory school. He hated the school, and he hated his father's way of life. So he left his school and his home. He was working his way through LSE as a film critic and an editor of a radical magazine, the *Student Vanguard*.

"You should follow my example," he said.

No, I told Marmont, I would never give up my family. But I could give up the money that my mother had given to me.

I had no right to hold on to that money. Yet I was not prepared to part with it. I cherished the independence that it gave to me; I liked to surround myself with beautiful things. I had bought an early Picasso in Paris; I wanted to clasp it to myself before I handed it on to a museum.

"Michael is driven by guilt," a friend told my first cousin, Jock Whitney, when I returned to America in 1937. "He feels guilty because he's wealthy."

"Wealthy!" Jock snorted. "What makes him think he's wealthy?"

I was practically a pauper by Jock's standards. By the standards of my fellow students at the London School of Economics, I was unconscionably rich. That placed me at a perpetual disadvantage in dealing with radicals such as Geoffrey Marmont.

We did not discuss our feelings at the London School. We related to each other through a superstructure of beliefs. Night after night, in Lyons coffeehouses, I defended my beliefs. Marmont dismantled them in his methodical way. He was more articulate than I was, but the attractive power of his position was deeper than ideology. I felt alone and isolated; he was part of a purposeful brotherhood.

In stable societies, institutions exert their claims upon the individual; traditions provide a sense of continuity and brotherhood. Transplanted as I was, I lacked a sense of loyalty to British or American institutions; I was not held in place by a national tradition. I had been uprooted; I was waiting to be reclaimed.

I believed in equality; I feared violence and war. Was Marmont an advocate of violence? Of course not, he said. It was the ruling class that would inflict violence upon the people, through the army and the police.

We were on our way to the German embassy to join in a demonstration. It was a damp, gray day. There were only a few hundred demonstrators standing around and a score of policemen. We stood in the drizzle, shouting "DOWN WITH HITLER!" The police stood beside us nodding; it all seemed peaceable enough. Then, for no reason, a student sprang onto a policeman's back and tried to throttle him. Shocked and offended, the police overpowered the student. They drove him away in a paddy wagon, leaving a dark stain of blood on the pavement. A woman knelt beside it. "The blood of the workers!" she shrieked. I looked at Marmont. He shook his head.

On May Day, 1934, trade unionists and students, Socialists and Communists marched together throughout Europe. I joined in the student contingent that marched to Hyde Park.

It was drizzling when we took our places in Aldwych. The streets were dank, and the marchers were disconsolate. We shuffled through side streets to our assigned rendezvous, clutching the bedraggled banners that we had been given.

The students formed in one contingent: LSE at the head of the column; Oxford and Cambridge, Manchester and the other universities, behind us.

A student leader walked along the column, handing out sheafs of paper on which were printed the slogans for the day,

> SCHOLARSHIPS, NOT BATTLESHIPS!
> DOWN WITH THE GOVERNMENT OF STARVATION AND WAR!
> GIVE A YELL, GIVE A YELL, GIVE A GOOD SUBSTANTIAL YELL.
> AND WHEN WE YELL WE YELL LIKE HELL
> AND THIS IS WHAT WE YELL:
> DOWN WITH THE BILL!
> DOWN WITH THE BILL!
> DOWN WITH THE UNEMPLOYMENT BILL!

We stood waiting in the rain. None of us had the heart to give 'a good substantial yell.' Then the first contingent of hunger marchers passed us on their way to Hyde Park. They had marched all the way from Yorkshire and the Clydeside. They were shabby and footsore. But they held their banners high, and as they passed, we let out that yell.

The last contingent passed us. We joined in behind them. I was in the second rank, and Krishna Menon was at my side.

A student leader hurried alongside the column. "Scholarships, not battleships," he muttered. We picked up the cry in a ragged chorus, "SCHOLARSHIPS, NOT BATTLESHIPS!"

"Down with the government of starvation and war," the student muttered. We shouted again, "DOWN WITH THE GOVERNMENT OF STARVATION AND WAR!"

A young policeman walked along beside us, the rain dripping off the rim of his helmet. I could see his lips moving as he repeated the slogans.

Somewhere ahead of us, a contingent of hunger marchers began to sing the *Internationale*. The students around me joined in. I felt ashamed, not knowing the words.

As we marched up Oxford Street, the rain ceased to fall. Crowds were lined up on the sides of the street, and as we marched past, some of them cheered. We passed beneath the imposing front of Selfridge's. The street resounded as we shouted, "GIVE A YELL, GIVE A YELL, GIVE A GOOD SUBSTANTIAL YELL!"

We marched on, under Marble Arch and into Hyde Park. There the orators of the day were waiting on a number of open wagons. Thousands of supporters crowded around them. Soon the speeches began. James Maxton, the leader of the Independent Labour party, spoke first, his arms flailing the air in grand gestures, his long black hair shaking. "We must bring down the whole rotten system!" he shouted. From the crowd a woman's voice came back, "I'll do it, Jamie! I'll do it with all my heart!"

On the largest of the wagons stood a fraternal delegation from the Confédération Générale des Travaileurs, flown over from Paris for the day. Once again, my need to establish my own identity led me to ask if the French comrades had a translator.

No, I was told, they had no one.

"I'll do it," I said.

My French was dreadful; I had never spoken to an audience of more than fifty people. But I clambered up onto the wagon. I stood there with the leading radicals of England. I looked out on five thousand faces and thought, *What have I done?*

A heavy-set Frenchman moved to the microphone. I took my place at his side. He shouted, pumping his arms up and down. Then, after two minutes of florid oratory he turned to me.

I had understood only half of his words at most but had caught his drift. I shouted out, "On this historic day . . . consecrated with the blood of countless martyrs . . . the workers of France . . . dedicated as always to the cause of liberty . . . of equality . . . of fraternity . . . the workers of France, I repeat . . . stand shoulder to shoulder with the peace-loving masses of England . . . with the freedom fighters of Vienna . . . with the gallant anti-fascists, who even today defy the monster Hitler and his Gestapo. . . ."

I shouted out the familiar clichés. Then I motioned to the Frenchman. I stepped aside, and he started off again. His voice rose, his arms pumped faster as he cranked himself up. I realized to my dismay that he was advancing from generalities to specifics and leaving me stranded. I caught something about the plight of countless thousands of refugees, driven from their homelands, and about the aid given to them by the international peace movement. I struggled through that much when, once again, it was my turn to translate. Then I remembered that he had used the word *commissariat*.

"In addition," I shouted, "the Commissariat of the League of Nations has done splendid work. . . ."

"'Ere!" shouted a little man with a rat's face who had forced his way up to the wagon. "'E's not talking about the League of Nyshuns! 'E's talking about the police styshun!"

"Oh," I said. I stood there, helpless, until someone behind me muttered, "Get on with it!"

I started again. "In addition, the refugees have been held like prisoners in police stations . . ."

I stumbled through that bit. I motioned to the Frenchman to keep going. He looked at me with raised eyebrows. *"Mais . . ."* He began again, but in phrases that were utterly beyond me. I thought for one moment that I could bluff my way through one more round. Then I knew that I was hopelessly lost.

The Frenchman completed his burst of incomprehensible rhetoric. He stepped aside to make way for me. I looked out at the thousands of faces. I stood there, paralyzed.

A rumble started up in the crowd, led by the rat-faced man. "Get him down! . . . Throw him out! . . . If you cawn't speak French, let someone who can get up there!" The shouts grew louder. From the back of the wagon, someone grabbed the Frenchman and pushed him back to the microphone. *"Mais . . ."* He shrugged his shoulders and started off once more. As he shouted his sonorous phrases, I slipped off the back of the wagon and fled.

I forced my way like a fugitive through the crowd. At its rim, I paused to regain my breath. I hoped that no one would recognize me, but a small, dark man came toward me. He smiled and stretched out his hand. "My name is Leo Silberman," he said. "I am a German refugee. I cannot say that I admired your French, but I must tell you that I admire your spirit."

I wanted only to escape. I hurried away, and he trotted along beside me. He suggested that we go to his house. I was too humiliated to say no.

We sat in his parlor. The conversation dwindled. Silberman excused himself and left the room. To my astonishment, he reappeared clad in a pair of tight shorts and a sleeveless shirt. He sat down beside me and took hold of my hand.

Nothing at Dartington had prepared me for any such experience. I stood up and started for the door.

Silberman watched me. "I thought you were one of us," he said.

At the London School, the conflict between Beveridge and Meyer reached its climax. The *Student Vanguard,* Marmont's journal, published an article charging that a faculty member was in fact an intelligence agent, spying on Indian students. Beveridge banned the *Vanguard* from the school and started a libel action against it. Meyer in turn charged that Beveridge had exceeded his authority. He ordered that copies of the *Vanguard* be returned to the student common room.

At that, Beveridge expelled Meyer, Marmont, and four other students from the London School and forbade them to set foot on its premises.

I hurried down to Aldwych when I heard the news. The grim old building was in an uproar. An announcement by the director entitled TO ALL CONCERNED was pinned to the Bulletin board in the main hall. A mob of students crowded around it, arguing.

I forced my way to the bulletin board. A dozen students grasped hold of me.

"Have you seen the story in the *Daily Herald?*" shouted the secretary of the Marxist Society. "We're on the front page!"

"Would you be so good as to inform me," said an Indian. "What is your opinion?"

"Meyer was a fool," said a graduate student. "If he had waited for the union to back him, he would have landed Beveridge in the soup."

"The question is," Floud said, "what do we do now?"

We formed in ragged ranks outside the London School. We marched around Aldwych and the Strand, shouting ragged slogans: "DOWN WITH BEVERIDGE!" and "BRING BACK FRANK MEYER!" It was no use. The week of examinations was approaching; the time for agitation had passed. Beveridge stood firm, and his board supported him. Sir John Simon, the home secretary deported Frank Meyer. The academic year ended, not with a bang but a whimper.

Were we foolish in supporting Meyer? I suppose so. Were our teachers under any obligation to help us in gaining wisdom, as citizens? I still do not know. I read Beveridge's book *The London School of Economics and Its Problems* in 1982 in the hope that it would cast some light on this unresolved issue. It bore the same resemblance to those days as a brown kipper does to a bright herring in the sea.

Beveridge does mention, in passing, that the London School was ruffled by a "psychological disturbance" in 1933 and 1934. He recalls that "six or seven students, led by a very red politician from America," disobeyed his order and were expelled by him. He adds that one of them was "forgiven" by him.

Beveridge notes that it was his Emergency Committee that nudged the home secretary to deport Meyer, saying that he "was better suited to the United States." He makes no mention of Meyer's defense of his position. Instead, Beveridge quotes in full a letter from an admiring student who wrote to him when the "psychological disturbance" was over, to tell him how wonderful he was.

In his remoteness and his condescension, Beveridge offered little guidance to students like myself. Laski did share our preoccupations, but his concern masked his own political ambivalence.

Beveridge notes in his autobiography that he chastised Laski for writing articles for the *Daily Herald* on the great issues of the day. Laski, he pointed out, was earning a supplemental income through his articles, and he was being paid quite enough as it was.

The truth, I fear, was that faculty members at the LSE were supposed to be content within their own little enclaves. Neither the students nor the threat of war were to interrupt them in their own academic pursuits.

I was seventeen in 1934. Meyer and Marmont and Floud were not much older. Nor was Leo Silberman. Even Krishna Menon, the perpetual student, was a young man then.

We were all carried along in a powerful current. It cast us up on many distant shores.

Krishna Menon became the foreign minister of India.

Marmont killed himself, soon after I left the London School.

Silberman was murdered in a plot in which the intelligence services of South Africa and other nations were involved.

Floud became a leading Communist intellectual. His younger brother, Bernard, committed suicide while he was under interrogation by British intelligence officers. I may have set in motion the events that led to his death.

Frank Meyer returned to America. I heard no more of him for seven years. Then one day as I was working at *The New Republic,* there was a knock at my door.

"Come in!" I cried; and in came Frank.

He was as pale and as gaunt as ever. He sat down and sighed. He had been a leader of the Young Communist league he told me. He had gone to work for the league, after his enforced return to New York. Then he had broken with the league, and with the Communist party. He had gone to the Un-American Activities Committee of the House of Representatives, taking his files with him. He had given the committee the names of all the Communists whom he knew.

He had come to my office after leaving the committee. He said, "Now what do I do?"

He found a new home in time as the literary editor of a right-wing journal, the *National Review*. I felt at the time that he was exchanging one pseudoreligion for another, but now that seems unkind. We discovered that we shared a common enthusiasm for the works of J. R. R. Tolkien. We kept in touch until he died.

# JAMES AND JOHN

FROM the London School of Economics I went to Trinity College, Cambridge. On my first evening there, in the autumn of 1934, I wandered into a candlelight service in Kings College Chapel. I sat, staring at the stone columns that arched upward into the darkness and listening to the thin voices of the boys choir. It was a new world for me; I was alone in it and in awe of it; I was content.

I lived as a first-year student in a lodging house on Trumpington Road. My landlady, Mrs. Roff, was a kind woman. She twitted me only because I fed crumbs to the mice that crept around my sitting room, glancing up with their bright eyes at the desk where I studied.

My field was economics. Maurice Dobb, the tutor to whom I was assigned, was a leading member of the British Communist party. He was a shy man, but a persuasive one when he turned to politics; as an economist, he had little influence.

In Cambridge and throughout the free world, economic doctrine was dominated by the overpowering intellect of John Maynard Keynes. The largest lecture hall in Cambridge was crowded when Keynes, in a series of talks, set forth the principles of his General Theory. It was as if we were listening to Charles Darwin or Isaac Newton. The audience sat in hushed silence as Keynes spoke. Then, in small circles, he was passionately defended and furiously attacked. On one occasion, a noted economist, Hubert Henderson, denounced the General Theory as a hoax. Keynes himself paled at that, and for days the tremors could be felt up and down Kings Parade.

Conventional doctrine, as it was set forth by the Classical economists, relied upon the self-righting mechanisms of the market place. It was no guide to action in an age characterized by giant corporations, powerful trade unions, and widespread unemployment. Keynes, in contrast, demonstrated in his General Theory how mass unemploy-

ment could develop in a free society and how through the use of
government, it could be overcome.

Needless to say, I became an ardent follower of Keynes. I felt, as
I listened to him, that I was riding the crest of a great wave.

I left Dobb as soon as I could. As a member of Trinity College, I
was assigned to Denis Robertson. He was a Classical economist and
a sensitive, vulnerable man. We were deeply attached to each other,
and I hurt him by asking if I could leave him to study under Joan
Robinson, the most brilliant of Keynes's disciples.

Robertson released me, but the shift to Mrs. Robinson took some
time. I had first to force my way to the front rank of the two hundred
students who were enrolled in the Economics Tripos. I worked furiously, driven as I was by a desire to excel. The results of the first
examination were posted, and I saw my name at the head of the list.

I sat at my desk past midnight, six nights a week. Each morning,
while it was still dark, a gentleman's gentleman whom Whitney had
bequeathed to me stepped silently into my bedroom. He would pour
a jug of hot water into a basin so that I might wash and shave. He
would set out my socks, my shirt, my student's gown, and the tie that
he felt was appropriate. Then, standing over my bed, he would inform
me in a low and deferential voice, that it was time for me to arise.
Once a week he would ask if I wished him to "draw" a bath. The word
"draw" was scarcely adequate to describe the process of preparing the
bath that I and three other lodgers shared. The bathtub was high and
narrow. It stood on four ornate legs and had a copper boiler at one
end. After two pennies had been dropped in a slot, the boiler would
rouse itself with fearsome creaks and groans. They would be followed
by a hissing sound. At that moment, when the boiler seemed about
to burst, an irregular spout of steam and rusty water would sputter
from the faucet and would go on sputtering, scalding the unwary
student who failed to sit hunched up at the far end of the tub.

Why risk it? My attitude toward the bath was that of the master of
Trinity College. He was asked by the college architect how many
baths should be installed in Whewell's Court. "Baths?" he said. "Why
install any? The young gentlemen are only here for ten weeks at a
time."

The only student in our lodgings who made use of our bathtub was
the Honorable Philip Lever, the son and heir of Lord Leverhulme, the
soap king. He lived in the rooms above mine and on Sundays he had
his friends from the Pitt Club in for lunch. Looking out of my bay
window on Sunday mornings, I would see a solemn procession winding its way down Trumpington Road. It was made up of porters from
the Trinity College kitchen, dressed in blue-and-white-striped aprons
and bearing immense silver trays on their heads. Fish and fowl; claret
and champagne; buckets of ice, and strawberry mousse . . . they would

trudge up the stairs past my room, set down their dishes, and trudge back the long mile to the college. At 1:00 P.M. the young bloods would arrive in their checked jackets and caps. A two-hour celebration would follow during which I found it difficult to study. In the late afternoon, the procession of elderly porters would reappear and trudge off with their trays on their heads.

It was a four-mile walk for them, but they never complained. Nor did the waiters in our dining hall, but I noticed that they slipped scraps of meat from our plates into their pockets when no one was looking.

I asked one of them if he did it because he was hungry. "It's not for me, sir," he said. "It's for the young 'uns."

Should I leave more slivers of meat on my plate each evening when I dined in the hall? My concerns were not shared by my fellow students, who sat in lines along the ancient oak tables. "Damn these waiters!" they shouted; "Why can't the beggars look sharp!"

I felt ashamed of the privileges that the students took for granted. I told my gentleman's gentleman that I could not keep him any more.

"Am I charging too much?" he asked. I was paying him four dollars a week.

"I just don't believe in being waited on," I said.

"But sir, if young gentlemen like you don't employ us, what's to become of us?"

"I don't know."

-∞-

I was on my own in Cambridge, but I was not left alone for long. One evening in November, when I was hunched over my desk and the mice were nibbling at the crumbs I had set out for them, our doorbell rang. Mrs. Roff allowed as how there were two young gentlemen come to see me. Two students in black gowns stood in my doorway. One had a birdlike head and manner; his name was James Klugman. The other had black, curly hair, high cheek bones, and dark, deep-set eyes. His entire body was taut; his whole being seemed to be concentrated upon his immediate purpose. His name was John Cornford.

James and John. James is seen now as a legendary and sinister figure; John has attained the timeless stature of the hero. Yet no one knew much about them when they were alive. The brilliant students of 1912 —the last prewar generation—discussed their own feelings for days on end; James and John would not waste five minutes in talking about themselves.

It was in 1979 that I learned that James had been born into a prosperous Jewish family in London and had attended a fashionable preparatory school. It was in 1937 that I discovered that John stood at the center of the Cambridge tradition.

John's father, I discovered, was a leading authority on Classical Greece; his mother, a poet, was the granddaughter of Charles Darwin. They had named their son Rupert John, in memory of their friend Rupert Brooke, a British poet who died in the First World War. John himself was a fine poet. He had, as a student, shared a room in the town of Cambridge with a working-class girl who had borne him a son.

I learned all that when I sorted out John's papers, after he had been killed in Spain.

I had hung reproductions of paintings by Cézanne and Picasso in my sitting room on Trumpington Road, in place of Mrs. Roff's chromolithographs of *Highland Cattle at Dawn*. Mrs. Roff asked only if I had painted the pictures myself. James and John wandered around the room, looking at the paintings. Then James slumped into my easy chair. He sat there, smiling. John stood by my fireplace. When he grinned, it was as if the grin had been wrenched out of him.

James explained why they had come to see me. They were second-year students at Trinity, he said, and members of the Cambridge University Socialist Society. My name had been passed along to them by some comrades at the London School. They asked if I would join the society. I said that I would.

I went to the meetings of the society from then on and spent many hours with James and John, arguing about political principles. They were patient but persistent, as Peter Floud and Geoffrey Marmont had been. On one occasion, I balked when John insisted that the class struggle was the central reality of life in Britain. I had lived for eight years in Britain, I said, and it was not the central reality for me. For once, John was exasperated. He picked up my copy of the *News Chronicle* and searched through its pages. He found a story about a strike in a plant in Norwich.

"There! There is the class struggle for you!" he said.

I read the story. It seemed like an isolated incident to me.

"You mean that this strike is a symbol of the class struggle," I said.

"No, dammit! It *is* the class struggle!" John cried.

In the course of that winter I learned that, at Cambridge, as at the London School of Economics, the Socialist Society was dominated by a Marxist core. It was, at heart, the point of entry into the student Communist movement. That movement, which took its directives from the head office of the British Communist party in King Street, was led by James and John.

The Socialist Society had two hundred members when I went to Cambridge and six hundred when I left. About one in four of them belonged to Communist cells. There were a dozen students in the Trinity College cell when I joined it early in 1935.

Moving from the outer fringe of the Socialist Society to the inner core of a Communist cell sounds like a major step in 1981. It did not seem to be in 1935. Several large trade unions were led by Communist party members in 1935; most of the poets whom I admired belonged to the party or allied themselves with it. On all the issues that we cared about, militant Socialists and Communists held the same opinions. The main objective of the British Communist party was to create a United Front of Communists, Socialists, and Trade Unionists —the broad front that dominated the political scene in France and in most European democracies. The United Front, in turn, was part of the larger strategy pursued by the Soviet government. It had turned from an aggressive strategy of fomenting revolution to a defensive one of creating a common front of all nations in resisting Hitler's armies, which even then were multiplying. It stood for the League of Nations and for collective security.

When John and James went to Cambridge in 1933, the party line was dogmatic and sectarian. Then, in 1934, the Seventh World Congress of the Communist International transformed its stance to one of outward respect for democratic institutions and procedures. It took John a month or two to adjust to the change; from then on, he was more ardent than any Social Democrat in mobilizing students to canvass for the Labour party candidates in local elections. As for James, he was by nature tolerant, flexible, and receptive to new ideas. He came back from a conference in Paris full of praise for the French Communists for opening their party conferences to public scrutiny.

We met once a week in a student's rooms in Trinity. We discussed immediate tasks: organizing a protest against the Blackshirts in Cambridge; raising relief funds for Abyssinia; combating pacifist tendencies within the local branch of the League of Nations Union.

The student Communist movement had no name and no visible ties to the Communist party or the Young Communist League. Within its broadening circle, there were three kinds of members.

There were firstly those who, like myself, were student members of a student movement. We were interested in ideas; we wanted to believe. But most of us joined the movement because it was the best-led, most active movement in the university, advancing the short-term objectives that we felt were right. We carried no little green cards in our pockets; we took no party assignments with us when we left Cambridge at the end of each term. I loved and admired James and John. I got along very well with Harry Pollitt, the working-class leader of the British Communist party to whom, at James's urging, I gave as much money as I could without feeling the pinch. But I felt no sense of loyalty to the party as such. It never occurred to me that it could impose its discipline upon me. My actions were shaped by my own free will.

The second group of student members was less active than we were, and less visible. A few of them were known as "moles." Moles were students who were preparing to earn their livings as barristers or as civil servants. It was understood that they would have to subordinate their beliefs to their professional ambitions, but their reticence was seen as discretion, not deception.

The third group of student Communists was made up of dedicated party members. They pasted stamps in their green books, week after week. They checked in at their local party headquarters when they left Cambridge for their home towns. They went to London from time to time, to meet with party organizers. They believed not in other individuals but in the party itself. James Klugman was writing the official history of the Communist party of Great Britain when he died in 1978. From Spain, John wrote to Margot Heinemann, "I love you with all my strength and all my will and my whole body. . . . The Party was my only other love. . . ."

I could not have forced my hand to write those lines. In John's hand they rang true.

So within the student movement, the three kinds of members led intertwined but separate lives politically. Casual members like myself did not ask who James or John talked to in London. We made no effort to intrude if they met secretly upon occasion with the "moles." In turn, they did not press us further than we were prepared to go in committing ourselves to the party to which they were wholly committed.

Keynes was not alone in believing that the Communist movement was the outgrowth of respectable antecedents in England's past. According to his biographer, Sir Roy Harrod, "He attributed it to a recrudescence of the strain of Puritanism in our blood, the zest to adopt a painful solution because of its painfulness."

The primary pull of the movement, I have argued, was its energy in pursuing short-term objectives. At a deeper level, Keynes perhaps was right.

# THE USSR
# A SUMMER PILGRIMAGE

I SPENT July 1935 in the fishing village of Brixham. It was famous for its fleet of trawlers—magnificent black boats with long bowsprits and rusty-red sails. The fleet was dying out; I wrote a report for the University of the South West on the reasons for its decline. I spent my days with the fishing captains, going over their records. I concluded that the fleet could not be saved. The reason had nothing to do with the class struggle. The trawlers were sailing ships, and the days of sailing ships had passed forever.

A Communist student, John Madge, organized a group tour to the Soviet Union that summer. In August, six of us boarded a Soviet ship in London and set off for Leningrad. We were joined by a recent graduate of Cambridge, an art historian named Anthony Blunt. He was very pale, very slender, very tall. He listened in silence to the discussions that John Madge organized on shipboard. When we landed in Leningrad, he went off on trips by himself.

All of us, in time, went our separate ways. Anthony now suffers in seclusion, stripped of his knighthood and all else save for his reputation as a scholar. Charles Fletcher-Cooke is a Conservative member of Parliament; Charles Rycroft has distinguished himself as a psychiatrist; Michael Young, who gained world renown as a sociologist, is now a spokesman for Britain's new Social Democratic party; Brian Simon is a leading educator and a member of the Central Committee of the British Communist party.

Brian alone retains some lingering belief in Soviet Communism. Most of us shared that belief in 1935. We looked in awe at a husky woman who worked as a deck hand on our ship. We worried that we were squandering the resources of the Worker's State if we put two lumps of sugar in our tea. We tried not to see the poverty, the squalor, the primitiveness that surrounded us wherever we went. It was not easy. We took an aged train from Moscow to Kiev. In its lavatory was a poster made for those who could not read. It showed a stupid peasant squatting on top of the toilet bowl and spraying his excrement around the floor. In an accompanying picture, an intelligent worker sat on the bowl with his trousers down and a beatific expression on his face. Judging by the state of the lavatory, most of our fellow passengers chose the first method.

The train journey took two days and two nights. It was hard to breathe and almost impossible to sleep. The Russians who shared our

car smoked and talked and boiled their tea. We were aroused one
night by gunfire. The train lurched to a halt; the gunfire continued.
We made our way to the end of our coach. We saw, huddled against
the iron steps, a dozen half-starved children. They had boarded the
train in the darkness, and the guards were firing their rifles to drive
them away.

We huddled inside our illusions, responding as *Intourist* intended
we should to a dozen carefully staged interviews. Just once, in Moscow, I was able to leave the beaten track. I had been commissioned
by the manager of the Jooss Ballet to try to arrange an exchange visit
with the Vakhtangov Theatre Company. I made my own way to the
theater, named after the Soviet Union's most renowned director; I
introduced myself to his widow, a most distinguished lady.

We spoke in French about the terms of the exchange. When that
was completed, she asked me about my family.

"My father . . . that is to say, my stepfather . . . he runs an experimental enterprise . . . that is to say, a sort of Greek city-state. . . ."

My French failed me. "My father is a farmer," I said.

"A kulak!" said Madame Vakhtangov. I could see that an indelible
image of Jerry had formed in her mind; he was the class enemy.

"And your mother?" she said.

I pictured my mother reading Shakespeare with the music students
at Dartington; walking through the terraced gardens; providing the
spiritual leadership that held the community together. It was hopeless.

"My mother is a farmer's wife," I said.

"Ah!" Madame Vakhtangov painted a lurid picture of my mother
slaving over her pots and pans. "Such," she said, "is the sad fate to
which women are condemned in your capitalist society!"

# "A TERRIBLE BEAUTY
# IS BORN"

IN my second year at Cambridge, I moved into Trinity College. I
shared a room with Hugh Gordon, a fellow radical.

I hung huge paintings of clowns by my friend Hein Heckroth on
the walls of our sitting room. I brought in an EMG gramophone with
an enormous horn, and a collection of records: Mozart and Beetho-

ven; Benny Goodman and Red Nichols. To add to the noise, there were meetings on most evenings in our suite, K5. They ended, just before curfew, in singing and shouting.

An old recluse lived in the suite above us. I never paused to read his name, stenciled in black paint on the wall at the foot of our stairwell. He would feel his way like an old crab down our stairs and set forth for a brief outing in the winter sunshine, a long scarf covering his mouth and his nose and an old hat crammed down on his head. At night, he would tap angrily with his cane on our ceiling, when the noise in K5 became unbearable. We never paid the slightest attention to him.

In time, the tapping of his cane grew fainter. Then it ceased. A few elderly professors puffed up our stairwell; a doctor or two followed them. Then two porters came and carried the old man away.

A handyman appeared at the bottom of our stairwell with a brush and a pot of paint. I glanced up at the old man's name as he began to paint it over; it was A. E. Housman.

He had seen his last cherry tree, hung with bloom along the bough. We did not pause to mourn him. The poets of our own generation were the ones who moved us. Cambridge—the Cambridge that we knew—was no country for old men.

Living in college, I found myself at the center of the political life of the university. I was well enough ahead in my studies to be able to coast and so, for the first time, I took on a political role. I worked with Dobb on his Anti-Fascist Exhibition. I helped to plan demonstrations and parades. I canvassed for the Labour party. I made speeches demanding sanctions against Italy in response to Mussolini's invasion of Abyssinia.

I went to occasional lectures. Most of them bore little or no relation to life in England. There was only one lecturer whom I respected, apart from Keynes—John Hilton. He had the long, angular face of a prophet. He was invariably ten minutes late. He rushed into the lecture hall fumbling with piles of papers and muttering to himself. He spoke incoherently, but from his ramblings, there emerged a deep concern for the English people. We became good friends, and he helped me on a project of mine—to get students to work in unemployment centers and in factories as part of their training in economics. It was to be a sort of extension course that would come into being during vacations, and Hilton was all for it. But in Cambridge, life and learning had to be kept rigidly apart.

Keynes invited me to lunch in his rooms in Kings College one Sunday. I spent that morning selling *Daily Workers*. I had to run the two miles back to Whewell's Court to change. Even then, I was late.

Keynes forgave me in his charming way. He leaned forward in his easy chair, pressing his slender fingers together and looking at me with his limpid eyes. We talked about the ballet and about sanctions against Italy until 3:45.

That evening, I returned to Keynes's rooms for the first meeting of his Political Economy Club. It was made up of a dozen young professors and graduate students, a few third-year students, and four of us who had gained First Class honors at the end of our first year. At each meeting of the club, a paper was read aloud and then discussed. A draw was held, and those who picked slips of paper with numbers on them had to stand before the fireplace and speak.

A European economist read a paper that evening. It was entitled "The Price Level and Stabilization." The draw was held, and, to my dismay, I drew a slip with number nine on it.

The paper dealt with differential movements within the price level. "If the differential reaction of commodity A upon commodity B is taken to be inversely affected by the function of the elasticity of the substitution factor, then the demand curve for commodity A, projected as an algebraic equation, may be expressed by the formula *alpha minus A over beta plus B . . .*" and so on. I did not understand a word.

Two other second-year students had to speak. Peter Bauer, a brilliant little Hungarian, spoke so rapidly that no one could understand him. The son of Josiah Stamp told some story about a traveler and a map. I made the mistake of saying something about the paper. I compounded my error by asking its author for his comment on my comment.

He said that he was sorry, but he had been unable to grasp my point.

I turned to the circle of learned men and asked in a strangled voice if *anyone* could see the point in what I had said. They sat in silence. Then Keynes, in his noble way, came to my rescue. "I think I know what you mean," he said. He outlined a concept that, if anything, was more obscure than the paper itself. I had not a clue as to what he was talking about, but I nodded vigorously, and when he ended, I said yes, that was precisely what I had had in mind.

Keynes knew better, of course, but when he glanced at me he did not even smile, as if to lay claim to my gratitude.

I described the scene to my mother in a letter the ending of which must have dismayed her, "I cook my own breakfast every morning—tea and two fried eggs. I haven't had a bath for three weeks, and I can't see myself having one until the municipal elections are over."

Why did the municipal elections prevent me from having a bath? The answer, I suppose, was that in order to take a bath in Whewell's Court, you had to march across the cobbled stones of the courtyard in a dressing gown and slippers, carrying a towel and a bar of soap. You went down a flight of steps into some dark catacombs; you felt your way around until you slipped on the greasy floor of the showers.

Then you turned on a tap and jumped up and down under a cold stream of water. Not exactly enticing, but then the master of Trinity for whom the court was named had not been famous for pampering his students. Only on the rarest occasions did he deign to mingle with the undergraduates in what were known as "stand-ups." An observer at one stand-up described him as "radiating repulsion."

The Keynes Club met a second time in October. David Champernowne, a graduate student and a member of the family that had owned Dartington, read a paper on Karl Marx's *Theory of Value.*

Dobb was not there. Piero Sraffa, an Italian refugee and a Marxist, refused to speak. That left me. I had opened the impenetrable volumes of *Capital* for the first time on the evening before the club met, but David referred the first hard question to me. I answered it in my unintelligible way, but no one knew enough about Marxist theory to dispute what I said. I was priding myself on carrying the day for the old German when Keynes stood up to speak.

He stood like a great bear in front of his fireplace. He rocked back and forth. Marxism, he said, was even lower than social credit as an economic concept. It was complicated hocus-pocus, the only value of which was its muddleheadedness. He had read Marx, he said, as if it were a detective story, trying to find some clue to an idea in it and never succeeding.

It was the only instance that I can remember of a leading intellectual at the university challenging the new orthodoxy that had fastened itself upon the minds of the undergraduates.

David was crushed. Sraffa was silent as we walked at night along Kings Parade. I was shaken, but my political allegiance was unchanged. Intellectually, I was a follower of Keynes; emotionally, I was dependent upon James and John. Sadly, in those days, I separated my head and my heart.

I had other friends who held Marx in contempt. One was the mystic Gerald Heard. He was a close friend of my mother, and she relied upon him for guidance. Perhaps she asked him to keep track of me. In any event, he wrote to me saying that he was coming to Cambridge in November and hoped to see me. I asked John to join us for luncheon in K5.

Gerald had an astonishing mastery of unrelated facts. He moved swiftly, as he always did, from one analogy to another. John kept pace with him, and they circled each other for an hour. They came to grips at last, on the subject of dictatorship.

"Do you really believe," asked Gerald, "that any individual is wise enough or good enough to hold unchallenged authority, even for an hour?"

John paused at that. He said at last, "We have to put the fear of God into the bourgeoisie."

The University Union Society was the main political battleground in Cambridge. Its Gothic walls contained a dining room, a library, and a number of reading rooms. Its debating hall was modeled on the House of Commons, with rows of benches facing a central aisle, an overhanging balcony, and a high, timbered ceiling.

On Tuesday evenings, the hall filled up with students. The president, elected for one term, entered the hall, followed by the vice president and the secretary. Two students and two visiting speakers came next and took their places on the front benches. They wore evening dress.

The two students opened the debates, proposing and opposing a motion that the president had selected. The visitors spoke next. Then, on both sides of the aisle, students stood up, hoping to speak. Those whom the president recognized advanced to the secretary's desk. They had five minutes apiece, and they were handed cards with two-minute and one-minute warnings. Then a card marked STOP was handed to them; if they ignored it, they were silenced by the tinkle of the president's bell.

At the end of each debate, the students filed out as members of the House of Commons do, and tellers at the doors counted their votes. The motions had no force, of course, yet the debates were watched from beyond the boundaries of the university, for it was assumed that those who led the Oxford and Cambridge unions in the thirties would lead the House of Commons in the seventies.

In the summer of 1935, James and John decided to make an open assault upon the union. John undertook to lead the assault; he chose to take me with him. His action transformed my life as a student, for I would never have joined in the union debates on my own.

The first debate in each new academic year was on the Parliamentary motion: *This House has no confidence in His Majesty's government.* It was by tradition proposed by a leading member of the opposition party in the House of Commons and opposed by a Cabinet minister.

In October 1935, the motion was moved by Leonard Miall, a student member of the Labour party. The visiting speakers were D. N. Pritt, a Socialist M. P., and J. H. Thomas, a doughty old trade unionist, who in 1931 had abandoned the Labour party along with Ramsay MacDonald and had become a minister in the National government.

Pritt served up a lawyer's brief in opposing the government. Thomas never stooped to reason. He began with a coarse joke; he went on to make a personal attack on Leonard Miall. Leonard stood up, claiming a point of personal privilege. Thomas crushed him with a brutal insult. Two hundred conservatives shouted their approval; Leonard sat down, staring at the floor.

Pritt had described how he had watched the unemployed grow thinner. Thomas turned on him. "You don't know anything!" he shouted. "You're completely ignorant! What do you know about the unemployed? I'm a worker! I know how they feel! Their flesh is my flesh! Their blood is my blood!"

More cheers.

At the end of his harangue, Thomas turned to the subject of the debate. "Under the National government," he shouted, "Britain has made by far the greatest recovery of any country in the world!"

"What about Sweden?" said Pritt.

"I said 'any first-class country!' "

"On a point of order," said Pritt, "you said 'any country.' "

Thomas never paused. "I was under the impression that I was speaking to first-class people who, if they had any brains, would know what I meant!"

Loud cheers.

"In any event," said Pritt, "the rate of recovery, as a percentage of national income, is far higher in America than in Britain."

"Percentages!" cried Thomas. "What do percentages matter? I had a slacker working for me once. He claimed to have raised the local membership of our union by fifty percent. 'How many members were there?' I asked him. 'Two,' he said. There's your percentages for you!"

Prolonged laughter and cheering among the conservative students; sullen silence across the aisle.

John and I were sitting in the balcony of the debating hall. We looked at each other. We had agreed that we would take on the union together. The prospect filled me with apprehension, and John with disgust.

I could not tell which he despised more: the simpering mannerisms of some of the undergraduate debaters or the rantings of Thomas, whom he regarded as a traitor to the working class. He went off muttering to himself; one week later, he took his place among hundreds of other students and stood, waiting to be recognized. The president nodded to him; he stepped to the speaker's box and said what he had to say, emphasizing his words with cutting gestures, as if he were slicing meat with both his hands.

The president decided to test the seriousness of John's commitment to the union. Guy Fawkes Night was celebrated on November 5, and for that evening's debate, he invited John to propose the motion: *That this House regarding Parliamentary institutions as an obstacle to progress, deplores the failure of Guy Fawkes.*

John understood that he was being trapped. He realized that if he were to propose the motion, he would have to put on evening dress in place of the threadbare jacket, the flannel trousers, the ragged shirt, and the scrawny tie that he habitually wore. He rebelled at that until he remembered Lenin's rebuke to Trotsky when Trotsky balked at wearing a morning coat and striped pants to the peace conference at Brest-Litovsk.

John had no dinner jacket, but we were the same build. I telephoned my mother and asked her to send my dinner jacket and dress shirts so that John could make his appearance in the union.

An hour before the debate was due to begin, he came to K5. He had never tied a bow tie. As I faced him, fumbling with the knot, I saw that his hands were trembling.

He grinned. "The bastards have got me nervous," he said.

He spoke quietly and effectively about the failings of Parliamentary democracy. He made no effort to adjust his style of speaking to the union, but the students listened to him, and the *Cambridge Review* congratulated him for a "sensible and well-argued speech."

One month later, I was invited to propose a motion on government control of the press—*That Fleet Street is too close to Downing Street.* I was panic-stricken. John grinned, seeing my alarm, and gave me a letter of introduction to four of his pals in London: three staff members of the *Daily Worker* and Claude Cockburn of *The Week.*

The bearer of this note is Michael Straight, who wants to get some dope on the question of the ownership and control of the press. The reason is this. He has to move a motion in a fool debate in the Cambridge Student Union: *That Downing Street is too close to Fleet Street* or some such nonsense. The importance of this otherwise silly debate is that it is important to get a Communist elected to the Committee which he can do if he makes a speech that goes down well.

I did not make use of John's letter. I was not prepared to be identified as a Communist beyond the boundaries of Cambridge, and I did not think that I could learn much from John's friends, save for Cockburn, a former correspondent of the London *Times.* Instead, I went for help to three of my own friends: Harold Laski, Gerald Barry, the editor of the *News Chronicle,* and Kingsley Martin, the editor of the *New Statesman.*

We lost John's motion; we carried mine. He and I spoke each week in the debates, and at the end of the term, we ran together for the union committee. We were both elected with the support of a good many Socialists and Liberals.

John loathed the debates; I lived for them. So from December on, he went back to his own work, leaving me in command.

I discovered in the autumn of 1935 that I had the power to lead my own generation and to take my place with the leaders of England in debates. I was "someone" at last in the country to which I had been carried as a child. I was, for the first time, the Wind and not the Blown.

I lived in a state of continuous excitement and heightened awareness. The love that I felt for my fellow students was doubled and redoubled by the recognition that they awarded to me.

I accepted the responsibilities of leadership. I seemed to be certain of my convictions in the presence of those who were uncertain. Within myself, however, I was deeply uneasy. I wrote to my mother,

> My actions are based upon my personal needs rather than my convictions. I spend an hour arguing with a non-Communist. I'm left at the end not knowing if I myself am convinced by what I'm saying.
>
> Worse still, I'm bringing new people into the movement, wondering all the time if I am damaging their lives.
>
> I want to believe. Is it because I have to challenge authority? I find myself challenging it in all its forms, Communist as well as Capitalist.
>
> I don't know why I do what I do. That's why I want to go to the North of England, to see conditions there for myself. For there's no sound basis for communism in Cambridge, and there may be in the North. If I go there, I'll convert my psychological pretense into something solid or else I'll give it up entirely.

For me, the superstructure of Communist ideology was little more than a 'psychological pretense.' It was the sense of brotherhood that had opened up a new life for me. I had come to deeply distrust my own feelings after my failure with Margaret. I blamed myself for hurting her. As I wrote to my mother, in November 1935, "I'd lived in fear that I'd become incapable of loving. Now I've learned that I'm able to love the Communist students, even if I don't love Communism itself."

In that same letter, I wrote of my feelings for John, for James, for Maurice Dobb: "I'm filled with a violent, uncontrollable love for them; an extraordinary sense of comradeship. It's unreasonable and inexplicable. It burns within me and I can't express it; I can't get it out."

The paragraph that follows in that letter startled me when I came upon it in 1981. "James in particular is so delightful. I've been with him, and Whitney's friend Guy Burgess and an art historian named Anthony Blunt all evening. Now at half past eleven I sit here and try to describe the terrible significance of it all."

It was, I am sure, a memorable evening. I was, as I have noted, in a state of heightened awareness and sensitivity. I must have been enthralled by the worldly brilliance of Guy and Anthony and flattered by the interest that they took in me.

But why did I use the word *terrible?*

I was, I believe, echoing the poem that I admired above all others: Yeats's *Easter 1916.* The word *terrible* recurs like a constant chord in that poem. Each stanza ends: *A terrible beauty is born.*

The theme of the poem, after all, is the theme of my letter: the sense of communion that transforms those who are bound together by a shared experience.

The Easter Rebellion was an event more tragic and more ennobling than the day-to-day life of a student in Cambridge, but it was of the same order of experience. And Yeats's final stanza bore upon my own state of mind. He meditates in that stanza upon the state of mind of his countrymen who were condemned to death for leading the rebellion. He does not criticize them for their lack of understanding; he asks simply,

> And what if excess of love
> Bewildered them till they died?

Was it excess of love, in part, that bewildered me?

"He would do anything for Harry Hutchinson," my mother said of me, when I was eight. When I was nineteen, she might have added: "He would do anything for James and John."

It was true. I would have done anything for James Klugman and John Cornford. James, for one, knew that, and so did others. It is that, perhaps, which gives the evening I spent with James and Guy and Anthony a terrible significance—one that I was wholly unaware of at the time.

Guy Burgess left Cambridge in June 1934. He had become a part of a Soviet espionage network, and he had agreed to draw students from Cambridge into it. That was presumably one of the reasons he kept coming back to Cambridge.

Anthony Blunt returned to Cambridge from a year in Europe to become a teaching Fellow of Trinity College. It was in November 1935, so he said later, that Burgess recruited him into his network. His assignment, presumably, was to recruit others.

November 1935, is therefore a critical moment for all of us.

Had Guy selected me as the first of the undergraduates to be brought into the network? Had he instructed Anthony to become a close friend of mine in order to draw me in? Was that why I was invited to spend an evening with them?

I think so. It was from then on that Anthony took a close interest in me.

And James, whom I loved, did he know what was going on that evening? Was he a part of the snare?

In his book *Their Trade Is Treachery*, Chapman Pincher refers to James as "an even more sinister Communist agent" than Anthony. It was James, according to Pincher, who led John Cairncross, another Cambridge student, into a life spent in espionage, by introducing him to the Soviet agent who called himself "Otto." And, Pincher adds, it was James who recruited Bernard Floud, the younger brother of my friend Peter, into the same network, causing him to commit suicide when he was interrogated by British intelligence officers in 1967.

As late as 1981 I found these assertions painful to read and difficult to accept. I turned for guidance to others who were student Communists at Cambridge. We agreed, on reflection, that in his description of James's role if not of his character, Pincher was probably right.

James, we agreed, would have looked with distaste on deception in all of its forms. But in his gentle way, he would have justified it as a "historical necessity."

"Look, comrades," he would have murmured, "the historical era in which we live imposes hardships of many kinds upon those who participate in its decisive events. The roles to which we are assigned may seem questionable to us, but, in the end, our actions will be measured by the general happiness that will be shared by all mankind." Clothing his own conscience in generalities such as these, James could have sanctioned Guy's role as a secret agent of the Soviet Union. He could have rationalized his own role in delivering students younger and less knowledgeable than he was into Guy's hands.

Would John have played out the same role? I and my friends think not.

Why not? We asked ourselves that question; in answering it, we came up with the same phrase: "He was a Romantic."

John inherited a keen sense of personal honor from his father, a Classical scholar. He believed in the Communist party as a contemporary expression of that sense of honor and of obligation. He saw it as a cleansing force in his own time as well as in some future era. He treasured it as a human experience, not as the instrument of some vast historic trend.

For John, a proposition had to be right if it was to move himself and others to action. For James, it had only to be 'correct.'

John, to be sure, would have responded to some romantic image: the decisive moment, perhaps, at which Communists all over the world stand upright at their posts and advance together toward victory. But John's image would have differed from James's in this: his comrades might be holding posts in which they were unseen, but they would have taken up those posts consciously and willingly, as volunteers.

He would have conceded the necessity of underground activity. He might have turned a blind eye to the work that Guy was engaged in. But he would not, I think, have abetted Guy in that work. He would not have looked on the Trinity cell as an antechamber to a Soviet intelligence service. He would not have walked all the way to my lodgings on Trumpington Road, on the night that we met, had he known that Guy was waiting in the shadows to take advantage of his matchless ability to win others over to his own beliefs.

# MOTOR RACING
# MY BRIEF CAREER

As a racing driver, Whitney moved into the front rank, competing against the incomparable Nuvolari and the unscrupulous Chiron. I worked in the pits at Brooklands and was with him when he crashed at Monte Carlo. I had bought a sports car, built by Reid Railton around a Hudson engine. So when Whitney and his team mate Dick Seaman were invited to compete in the first South African Grand Prix, they asked me to join them.

Whitney's chief mechanic, Giulio Ramponi, stripped down my car and tuned up its engine. He sailed by boat for South Africa with our three cars. We followed, in December 1935, in a rented airplane.

Our plane was a De Havilland *Dragon*. It cruised at 110 mph—10 mph less than *Hengist* and *Horsa,* the two airliners that had opened the air route to South Africa. They flew from dawn to dusk; to reach their stopping places, we had to take off and land in darkness.

The *Dragon* was equipped with very few instruments: an altimeter, a tachometer, a compass that was none too accurate, and an airspeed indicator that failed when we first took off and never worked again. We had no radio, but that did not matter much as there were no radio aids in those days.

We took off from Heston in the darkness. Flying against a strong headwind, we managed to average 60 mph. It was dark when we landed in Marseilles.

We flew to Cairo the next morning. We fell into our beds and set out again before dawn to fly the twelve hundred miles to Khartoum.

On the next day we began to see big game. A hippopotamus clambered out of a mud hole and lumbered into the Nile as we flew over him. A herd of elephants stampeded as we passed them, flying at five hundred feet.

On the morning of December 19, we arrived at Salisbury, Rhodesia. We were planning to fly to Johannesburg, but our plans were abruptly changed. The air was thinner at Salisbury's altitude; the *Dragon* failed to lift itself off the runway. We leaped over an irrigation ditch, tore through a barbed-wire fence, scattered a herd of gnu that was grazing by the airport, and came to rest on the plain.

The fabric of the *Dragon*'s lower wing was ripped apart. Still worse, according to the De Havilland maintenance crew, one main strut was cracked. The crew chief pronounced our plane unfit to fly and refused to touch it. So we spent two days sewing the fabric back together with heavy needles and covering our patchwork with dope.

At dawn, on the morning of the next day, we climbed back into the *Dragon*. Using up all of the longest runway, we managed to stagger into the air. In the late afternoon we flew over an airport at which a large crowd had gathered, their banners saying WELCOME. It was East London, a town on the coast of South Africa and the site of the Grand Prix.

The Grand Prix was a road race; six times around a fifteen-mile course. The course wound along the cliffs that bordered on the sea for a couple of miles; it climbed steep hills and plunged into ravines. Most of it was paved, but some stretches consisted of loose gravel and dirt.

The course had been described in the London *Daily Mail* as 'hazardous.' We decided, after we drove around it, that the phrase was apt.

We had only two days in which to practice, thanks to our crash. The second day was cut short when millions of locusts settled onto the course. They added to my anxiety through a sleepless night, but at dawn on the day of the race a wind arose and blew the locusts away.

Thirty-five thousand spectators gathered on the course that morning. We made our way with some difficulty to the pits that faced the grandstand.

The Grand Prix was a handicap race. I was to start in sixteenth place. Dick Seaman, who was killed in a road race two years later, was in seventeenth place in his M. G. Magna. Whitney was in eighteenth place in his Maserati.

Ramponi, our mechanic, would not allow me to start up my engine until the last moment. It would be bad for my spark plugs, he said, and bad for my nerves—as if I had any nerves left.

The fifteenth car moved onto the starting line. With a shrill screech of its tires, it churned off when the flag fell. "Now!" Ramponi shouted. I heard him from a great distance. The Railton seemed to start up on its own.

I lost my sense of limits when the flag fell. As we rounded the first corner, I felt the inside wheels of the Railton lift off the road.

That brought me to my senses. "Easy," I said to myself. "Easy!"

I passed one car on my first lap—smashed flat into a rock face. I passed a clump of pines that had been torn out of the ground on my second lap—another car had uprooted them as it went over the cliffs and onto the rocks one hundred feet below the road. I passed four or five cars on my third lap; on my fourth lap, Dick Seaman passed me. I caught a glimpse of him on my fifth lap, sitting on the roadside, cleaning his spark plugs.

On the sixth lap I saw the Maserati coming up behind me. Whitney waved as he passed me. Then I was heading for the finish; an official was holding a checkered flag for me; thousands of people were on their feet, cheering. I drew into the pits and Ramponi ran up and kissed me.

Whitney had won the Grand Prix at an average speed of 95 mph. I had come in third at an average speed of 81. Ramponi insisted that I had a great future as a racing driver. I was too elated to tell him that the Grand Prix was my first race—and my last.

We started home the next morning. At noon, a wall of thunderstorms forced us down. We landed on an emergency strip in desolate country. It was an earth strip, and when we tried to take off, the wheels of the *Dragon* sank into the mud.

The skies had cleared; the hours were passing. It was decided that I would get out, to lighten the load and to push the *Dragon* into motion. Whitney would fly Dick and Dewdeney on to Mbaya, the next stop on the air route; then he would come back for me.

Our plan was an initial success. The *Dragon* slithered off through the mud and vanished in the sky. I stood on the mud strip, alone.

A band of Africans appeared at the edge of the strip. They advanced toward me, clapping their hands. I clapped my hands in turn, and they led me to their village. There, they gave me food and drink. The drink, I learned, was a mixture of cow's blood and cow's urine. The meat, which tasted like veal, was, I suspected, human. I chewed it slowly and managed to swallow it while my hosts squatted in a circle around me.

I wondered what would follow our luncheon. My question was answered when a lorry rumbled into the village. An Englishman, dressed in khaki shorts, stepped down from the lorry and introduced himself to me. He was, he said, the resident commissioner for the region. A runner from the village had informed him of my arrival, and he had hastened over.

It was some months, said the commissioner, since he had talked to another white man. But we spent little time in talking. In fact, our conversation was limited to one exchange.

"Do you play golf?" the commissioner asked me.

"After a fashion," I said.

"Good!" The commissioner went to his lorry and returned with a golf bag. He took one iron and one golf ball for himself; he gave one iron and one golf ball to me.

We walked in silence to a patch of sand, which, the commissioner told me, was the first tee. We followed our balls in silence from then on, for the commissioner took the game very seriously.

He teed his ball up on the sand. He whacked it off among the ant hills and the thorn trees. He nodded to me. I teed my ball up and took a practice swing. Then I asked him where the first green was.

He pointed in the precise direction in which his ball had flown.

The greens, it appeared, were where the commissioner's ball happened to land after his third or fourth shot. The holes were the ant hills nearest to the spot where his ball happened to be lying.

I whacked my ball off from each tee in the general direction in which his ball had gone. I pitched it as close to his ball as I could. It was as difficult for me as it would have been for Bobby Jones to match his accuracy.

We played nine holes in the course of the afternoon. Needless to say, the commissioner won them all.

The ninth hole brought us back to the edge of the village. The commissioner collected my iron and my ball. He climbed into his lorry and departed, well satisfied.

I waited at the air strip. As the daylight dimmed, I heard the welcome sound of the *Dragon,* returning. It landed and slithered up to me. We took off and, in the twilight, put down in Mbaya.

Eight days later, we pushed a path through rain and fog to London. My mother was waiting for us. She had not had one good night's sleep since we had set off, but she said nothing. Whitney was a fine pilot, and we were very lucky.

# CAMBRIDGE: MY COMMITMENTS

WHITNEY and Dick and I returned as celebrities to London. They flew off to race again in Italy. I took a slow train to Cambridge and became, once more, an undergraduate.

I dined at the college on my first evening back at Trinity. James Klugman came up to me, smiling.

"I was at a peace conference in Paris," he said, "and a French comrade brought me a newspaper with an article about you and your brother. He asked if I knew you, and I said, 'Yes; he is one of us.' "

I did not disagree with James, but for me, the phrase did not ring true. I called myself an anti-Fascist when I spoke at a mass rally on the Cambridge Commons; when I was called on to oppose the new Public Order Bill in the union, it was Harold Laski to whom I turned for guidance.

The bill, backed by the Conservative party, gave the British government broad powers to control and to forbid political demonstrations by extremist groups. In criticizing it, Laski drew a sharp distinction between Sir Oswald Mosley's British Union of Fascists and the British Communist party, led by Harry Pollitt. He wrote to me:

Any state has the right to protect itself from disorder; still more from a policy intended to secure, as in the issue between Fascism and democracy, say, the suppression of essential institutions. The case for special legal action against Fascists does not touch Left parties however extreme, because:

1. They do not wear uniforms;
2. They do not use violence as a method of propaganda;
3. They do not propose the overthrow of the state. Accusations against Communism to this end are inaccurate. Communism is not a philosophy of a *coup d'état*—that is *Blanquism.* Lenin pointed out in 1917 that revolution should be attempted only:
   a) When the defense forces of the state are no longer loyal;
   b) When the machinery of government is dislocated;
   c) When there is profound revolutionary class feeling;
   d) When there is an organized revolutionary party to direct that feeling; i.e., when there is the kind of chaos that existed in Paris in 1870 or in Russia after February 1917.

Apart from such conditions, communist propaganda has not been directed to any ends not legal, and has used methods that are legal. Insofar as its members have offended against the law, the record shows that the law has been amply able to deal with them. No Communist has preached racial or religious hatred in this country. The maintenance of democratic institutions is an official principle of the policy of the Communist International—note the Popular Front in France. Its purpose is to save the masses from the result Mosley is seeking.

The test of the right to suppress is surely whether the organization involved is using methods which are a clear and an imminent threat to public order. That is true of Mosley; it is not true of Pollitt. On the meaning of this definition, see Holmes, J. in *Abrams v. U. S., U.S.A. Law Reports* for 1919. So long as you stick to that test you are on safe ground. The principle of democracy does not mean a license to Mosley to leave injured people wherever he goes.

Laski's letter, on which I based my speech, was, I am sure, legally correct. Was it politically wise in its assumption that an 'official principle' proclaimed by the Communist International could be taken as a guide to the International's underlying aims?

In his political role, as chairman of the Labour party, Laski argued against collaboration with the Communist party. But his arguments were advanced behind closed doors. In offering guidance to students like myself, he maintained simply that the Labour party and the Communist party were both "Left parties."

That view accorded with the outlook that Laski associated with his role as a political scientist and an historian. He thought of himself as a Democrat and a champion of civil liberty. He also thought of himself as a Marxist. In fact, he was fond of repeating a remark he had once made to a colleague: "Both of us carry on the teaching of Karl Marx; you in your way, I in his." He knew that Marx had developed his concepts from the mainstream of European thought, and that Engels had continued to believe that democracy could survive in England through reform. He knew also that Marx's guiding principle for a Communist society—*From each according to his ability; to each according to his need*—stemmed from ancient values held by Christians and Jews. Thus, to note that Laski reached out on one side to grasp the hands of Felix Frankfurter and Justice Holmes, while on the other, he embraced Marx and Lenin, is not to assert that Holmes and Frankfurter were dupes. It is simply to affirm that, as late as 1936, men who were wise and well informed still sensed that there was a continuity based upon a long and an honorable tradition between the parties of the Left.

-─<∞>─-

Trinity College was in an uproar in May 1936. I was regarded as the cause of it all.

The Trinity cell had decided to take up the cause of the college servants. A petition was prepared, stating what the servants were paid and protesting that it was less than a living wage. I had voiced my concern for the servants; I had gained some academic distinction. I was therefore identified as the organizer of the petition—and I had signed it at the top of the page. It was also signed by my friend David Layton and by six graduate students of the college.

The petition was bound to raise some eyebrows in the college. It was made a good deal more offensive because, without informing the signatories, the student who had taken charge of it sent it not only to the council of the college but to all of the Fellows as well. That was deeply resented by the council, on which Denis Robertson and my supervisor, J. R. M. Butler, served. For it implied that the members of the council would take no action unless pressure was brought to bear upon them.

Three of the signatories happened to be applicants for fellowships. Without consulting me, they circulated a second letter to the council and to all of the Fellows, implying that I had deliberately deceived them. They were mistaken, but I sent a third letter around the college, taking the blame for all that had happened and adding that I was very sorry. I then spent three days tramping around Trinity Great Court and the courts that surrounded it, explaining to all of the Fellows why I had done what I had not done.

Some of the Fellows, including Denis Robertson, were kind to me. Some were very cold. They made it plain that while agitation against the government of Great Britain might be tolerated, interference in the administration of Trinity College was not to be borne.

To make matters worse, the steward of the college let it be known that he had been on the point of raising the wages of the servants, but that he had been forced to reconsider his action lest anyone should conclude that I had brought it about.

It seemed clear at that moment that if the servants of the college were to be punished through no fault of their own, I would have to organize a second, more serious protest, even though it might lead to my expulsion from the university.

Luckily for me, a number of friends went to work on my behalf. David Layton called on all of the Fellows. So did Anthony Blunt. Each evening, Anthony came by my rooms to assure me that the weight of opinion was shifting. The Fellows were coming around to the view that I was foolish rather than malign.

The wages of the college servants were raised. My trespasses were forgiven. The petition survived in the annals of Trinity College. A year or two after I had departed, the American ambassador was invited to dine with the Fellows at the High Table of the college. In proposing a toast to the United States, the master of Trinity spoke of two brothers who had added to that country's local renown. They were known, he said, as "The Motor Car" and "The Petition."

I had written to my mother about the 'violent love' that I felt for my friends at Cambridge. Almost all of them were men. There was no physical element in the love that I felt for them, or that they felt for me. Yet most of my friends, I came to realize, were or had once been homosexuals. Guy was an exhibitionist; Anthony, in contrast, was wholly discreet. Denis, I suspected, had been deeply and unhappily in love with other men. Keynes himself had been the lover of the painter Duncan Grant.

A close friend of mine described, one evening, how he had lain in bed beside a member of the Nazi Youth Corps, listening to the church bells of Munich striking the hours. That same evening, a fellow radical revealed his obsessive love for choir boys. I was sympathetic but incredulous, so he invited me to join him and his current lover for tea on the following afternoon.

I knocked on the outer door of my friend's rooms, in his college; he let me in. A rosy-cheeked boy of eleven was sitting on his sofa, munching a cream bun. I sat beside him for an hour, sipping tea and talking about cricket scores. My friend kept nodding to me as if to say, "Isn't he beautiful?"

I did not think so, but I could not point to a lover of my own by way of contrast. I had lived through three years of self-denial, following my failure with Margaret Barr.

A dozen young women came to Dartington as dancers with the Jooss Ballet. One was a fair-haired girl from Essen named Herta Thiele. She was as cautious in committing herself as I was. She never asked for more than I could give.

We were content at Dartington to lie for hours with our arms around each other. But we could be together for only two months a year. I was determined to be faithful to her, but I was not cut out to be celibate.

A student of unearthly beauty came to Cambridge in my second year. Her name was Teresa Mayor. She had the gaunt nobility of Yeats's beloved, Maude Gonne, and some of Maud Gonne's cold fire.

I was stricken by Tess as my friend Brian Simon and other students were. I used to invite her to tea at K5. I would push Hugh Gordon out of the lodgings that we shared. I would set the stage with care, playing a Mozart concerto over and over on my gramophone and pretending to be reading a volume of Yeats's poems as Tess came in.

It was no use. Tess needed as I did to love and to be loved. But there was a knot within her that I could not untie.

The Jooss Ballet returned to England from a long tour in the spring of 1936. My mother persuaded Kurt Jooss to release Herta for a day so that we could be together.

I drove up to London in the Railton and brought her back to Cambridge. We strolled through the colleges; we went to a meeting of the Socialist Society and on to a party in Anthony's rooms. We went to a candlelight service in Kings College Chapel.

I believed in those days that in becoming lovers we would be entering a commitment akin to marriage itself. I was ready after three years of chastity to make that commitment once again. Herta and I agreed as we parted in London that we would meet in Paris in June. We would become lovers and drive around Europe together.

I did not know it at the time, but John was also going through an upheaval in his private life. His lover, Ray Peters, had gone to London to give birth to their son James. He had brought her back to Cambridge, but he was moving away from her. He had met a student Communist named Margot Heinemann, who was his intellectual equal. He broke with Ray and wrote his "Sad Poem" to her. It is characteristic of him in its directness, its intensity, its absence of any false sentiment or embroidery.

> *I loved you with all that was in me, hard and blind*
> *Strove to possess all that my arms could bind*
> *But something is broken, something is gone,*
> *We've loved each other too long to try to be kind.*
> *This will turn to falseness if it goes on.*
>
> *Though parting's as cruel as the surgeon's knife*
> *It's better than the ingrown canker, the rotted leaf.*
> *All I know is, I have got to leave,*
> *There's new life in me, fighting to get at the air,*
> *And I can't stop its mouth with the rags of old love,*
> *Clean wounds are the easiest to bear.*
>
> *Else feel the warm response grow each night colder,*
> *The fires of our strength in each other ash and smoulder,*
> *Nothing that we do can prevent that we have grown older,*
> *No words to say, no tears to weep.*
> *Don't think any more dear, rest your dark head on my shoulder*
> *And try to sleep now, try to sleep.*

John knew that he had to be with Margot. He wrote to me: "What I want to know is this. From April 7 on, will there be any chance of you being able to put up me and my girl? For about a week. We're looking for somewhere to go for a holiday that isn't in the middle of a town and isn't in a youth hostel where you have to sleep apart."

Several notes followed, including this one:

Two things. First of all, we shall get to Totnes next Friday at 4:36. Is that o.k.? I can't get there earlier because I've got to appear in a police station on Thursday on a charge of wilful obstruction for giving out leaflets at the Lucas factory. Not very much fun, but quite interesting. Is that too late or is it o.k.?

Secondly, would it be possible for Margot's brother, Henry to park himself on you for the same time? The position is, he is suffering under a family in London and wants to get away, and if it were possible, it would be a good thing. But say if you think it's like conducting an invasion of the premises.

'The position is . . .' John wrote as he spoke, and he analyzed the problem of Henry Heinemann as he would analyze the problem of the British economy. His letter is so characteristic that, when I read it after forty years, I can see John standing beside me, slicing the air with both hands to emphasize his point.

John, Margot, and Henry arrived after two more changes of plans. We had a fine week, driving to the sea at Bantham; sailing down the Dart; playing golf at Thurlestone; walking along the narrow Devon lanes. The members of the Chekhov Studio gave a party one evening, and we joined them in Russian songs and dances. We went to our rooms late that night, and Margot must have lingered in the bathroom for I was woken by John's shout, "FOR GOD'S SAKE, WOMAN, COME TO BED!"

# ON THE EVE

WHEN the summer term ended, I set out for France in the Railton. I reached Paris at midnight. Herta was waiting for me at the Hotel Vendôme.

We drove south from Paris to Blois. We stayed in a hotel that had once been the home of the Duc de Guise. We walked in the city gardens with our arms around each other. We could hear old men and women sighing, "Ah, to be young!" and "Ah, young love!"

We drove on along Roman roads and through pine forests to St. Jean de Luz. We stayed there for a week. I went out to sea to catch tuna with the crew of a Basque fishing boat. In the evenings we sat in open-air theaters with the Basques, watching performances of *Robert the Devil* and other ancient dramas. Then we drove inland, heading for Provence.

In early July, festivals were held throughout the Basque country. The villages were bright with flags. We stopped many times on the road to watch the dancing and the games of *pelota*. Then, as we climbed, the Pyrénées reared up on the horizon, blue, with the snow still on their summits, blinding white. Beneath them, the green hills rolled in powerful rhythms beside us, and on the sides of the road, the fields of corn were tawny and golden.

Suddenly, on the road to Carcassonne, we were hailed by a young

woman with a knapsack on her shoulder. We drew in to the side of
the road, and as she ran toward us, a man rose wearily from the grass.
They told us they were Austrian students on their way to Spain. They
had walked eighteen miles that day and were very tired.

We had no room in our open car, but we squeezed the woman in
beside us and buried the man beneath our luggage in the back seat
so that all that we could see of him was his sunburnt face.

We questioned them as we drove; they were guarded and vague.
The secret police were everywhere in Austria they said; militarism was
being revived in the schools; the Social Democratic party and the
Communist party had been outlawed; the chancellor, Kùrt Schu-
schnigg, was a dictator in everything but name.

It seemed clear where their sympathies lay. I whistled the *Internationale*, watching the girl in the mirror of the car. She glanced toward
me and looked away. For a hundred miles we talked of other things.

In the evening we came to the tiny town of Foix. We had dinner
by lamplight on a hotel terrace overlooking a dark, rapid river. By
then, they could see that we meant no harm. They told us that they
were members of the underground Communist party of Austria. They
said that it was strong and growing; that it was organized in units of
four; and that it was working closely with remnants of the Social
Democrats. They were going to Spain on some mission, but they
would not say what it was.

At eleven, we began a search for lodgings. We went first to the
cafés, since they had the cheapest rooms.

At the entrance to one café in the town square, a heavy-set man sat
at a table alone. He seemed to be drunk or asleep—his body slouched
over the table, his head low. Hearing us talking in German, he jerked
his head up, straining to listen.

There were no rooms in the café. We wandered away until we
heard a cry behind us. We turned and saw the man, lurching beneath
the lamplight like a dancing bear.

He staggered up to us, muttering. He thrust his hand out to the girl,
saying in German that he had known her in Saarbrücken. She insisted
that she had never been there, but he swayed toward her.

"You look just like Kathe from Saarbrücken," he said.

"Kathe? Which Kathe?" said the male student.

"I knew a Kathe in Saarbrücken."

"So. You are from Saarbrücken," the student said.

*"Ja, ja; Ich bin Saarbrückener,"* the man cried.

"In that case," said the student, "you must know Paula." He was,
I gathered, using the code words of the underground.

"Paula . . . Paula. . . . There are lots of Paulas. . . . What's her other
name?"

"Paula has no other name. Paula is big and strong."

"No . . . I don't know Paula. . . . But if my friend were here.
. . ." The man shook his head to clear it. "It's just that I can't remember names."

There was a pause.

"So . . . you're from Saarbrücken," the student said. "Very interesting! Perhaps the political wind has blown you this way."

"*Ja. Ja,*" said the man. "I left after Hitler moved in."

"Would you go back?"

"Perhaps. If I could."

"But you can't; is that it? You're a Communist, I suppose."

The Saarlander grinned again in his drunken way. "*Ja,*" he muttered. "Ich bin Kommunistisch."

"Then why are you down here?"

"The Red Aid," said the man. "The Red Aid sent me." He drew
himself upright. "I'm a mechanic," he said, "a skilled man.

"I'd like to go back," he added, "in a way. But here . . . I have a
good job here; at good wages . . . I can do what I like here!" he cried,
his voice resounding in the silent square. "I can say what I like!" He
spread his arms wide, embracing the empty town. "*Hier,*" he shouted,
"*hier bin Ich frei!*"

He stood there listening, as if his challenge might evoke an answer.
There was no answer.

"Yes," he went on. "And here, I earn my living by honest means."

"So," said the student with bitter irony. "You are an honest
man!"

"Yes, I'm honest."

"You think you're honest! You call yourself honest because you can
say what you like!" The student turned to his girl and said, "*Wie ihnen
der schnabel gewachsen ist!*" ("How the moss has grown!")

There was a long silence. The Saarlander stood, grinning and swaying. Then he leaned toward the student. "And you," he said, "what
are you doing down here?"

"Holidays."

"From Berlin?"

"Yes," said the student after a pause. "From Berlin."

"Why did you have to think so long about it?"

"Did I think so long about it?"

"You thought for too long!"

"Did I? Why shouldn't I tell you, if I'm from Berlin?"

"Of course . . . of course . . ." Then, with sudden cunning, the
Saarlander said, "But you wouldn't be down here just for that!"

The student ignored him. "Tell me," he said, "where can we get
some cheap rooms for the night?"

For a moment the Saarlander was sullen. Then he laughed. "Oh,
there are plenty of cheap ones, but you won't get out of them alive!

The bedbugs are as bad as the Social Democrats here, for pestering you!"

At that we said good night and walked back to the hotel.

"A pity," said the student as we sauntered across the square. "He was in the underground, all right. He cracked up, and they sent him here for a rest. Now, he's been demoralized by too much freedom. He's no use to anyone."

We drove on together the next morning, under the brilliant sun and the deep-blue sky. Fifty miles from Foix, we came to a crossroad. There, we stopped and said goodbye. The two Austrians hoisted their packs up onto their shoulders and trudged off down the road that led to Spain. Herta and I drove on toward Carcassonne and Cézanne's country.

Twelve days later, the Spanish Civil War began.

# TOTAL COMMITMENT: JOHN CORNFORD

ON July 18, 1936, a group of generals, led by Francisco Franco, began their uprising against the elected government of Spain. The uprising was well organized and heavily financed. In a somewhat shamefaced manner, Whitney told me that he had sold an aeroplane to one of Franco's agents for a very high price.

The Soviet government and the Communist parties of Europe were unprepared for the rebellion. Three months passed before they began to organize the International brigades. John was no more farsighted in sensing that Spain would become a testing ground. He had planned a holiday with Margot in the South of France and, on a whim, he changed his plans. "The idea suddenly occurred to me," he wrote to his father, "to go to Spain for a few days. I expected [that] the fighting would be over very soon; so, in a tremendous hurry, I got a letter of introduction from the *News Chronicle* and set out."

John spent three days in Barcelona; then he headed for the front. He had realized, so he wrote to his father, that the military threat to the Republic was much greater than he had supposed. For that reason, he decided to join the Spanish militia. He was the first British volunteer.

He was in Catalonia. The working class, he discovered, was led not by Communists but by Anarchists. His own column was dominated by Trotskyists, and while he found their lack of discipline "deplorable" he could not fault them, or the ex-Communists who fought beside him, for their lack of either courage or revolutionary zeal.

John wrote some fine and little-known poems about the war. One begins

> We buried Ruiz in a new pine coffin
> But the shroud was too small and his washed feet stuck out.
> The stink of his corpse came through the clean pine boards.
> And some of the bearers wrapped handkerchiefs
> round their faces.
> Death was not dignified.
> We hacked a ragged grave in the unfriendly earth
> And fired a ragged volley over the grave.
>
> In the clean hospital bed, my eyes were so heavy,
> Sleep easily blotted out one ugly picture,
> A wounded militiaman moaning on a stretcher
> Now out of danger but still crying for water
> Strong against death, but unprepared for such pain.

John had been taken to a field hospital; he had a grave stomach disorder. Tom Wintringham, another British volunteer, found him there, "ill with fever and exhausted."

He was too weak to rejoin his unit when he was released from hospital. He was given three weeks leave and returned to England on what he described as "a special propaganda mission." He felt like a deserter he told me, but he knew where he was needed. He had to warn the leaders of the British Communist party that the situation in Spain was far less hopeful than they were claiming in all their pronouncements. And he wanted to recruit a band of English volunteers, one that by "shaving every morning and . . . acting as a disciplined formation, would give some kind of example to the extremely irregular levies that were . . . fighting the war."

He arrived in England on September 16. I wrote to him, suggesting that he and Margot come to Dartington for as long as they could stay.

He came alone, since Margot was working. He seemed greatly changed. He was silent for the most part; somber. He was, in his own mind, still in Spain. He worked in his bedroom, writing his *Report on Catalonia.* I typed it up for him.

"I have two things that I need," he told me. "A helmet and a revolver." We searched through the attic of the Hall and found nothing. We tried Totnes and Paignton with no luck.

We drove on to the coast, where we had played golf on those

carefree days in April. We wandered over the troubled country that borders the estuary of the Avon River at Bantham. We came upon a band of Boy Scouts engaged in some reconnoitering. For one moment, we staged a mock attack upon them, crouching behind hillocks of bracken and salt grass.

In the courtyard at Dartington I asked John to stand still while I took his photograph. I crouched beneath him with my Leica. It took me a minute or two to adjust the focus and the exposure. I thought to myself: *He wouldn't stand still for this long if he believed that he was coming back.*

I went with John to London. It was hard to read in the train, so we talked for four hours. He did not want to talk about the war in Spain, so, for the first time, we talked about ourselves. I said that I was disturbed by the intensity of my own desire to excel in everything that I did. He grinned and said that it was the same with him, only a thousand times more so.

Maurice Thorez, the leader of the French Communist party was in Moscow that week, so the historians tell us, persuading the Soviet government to support the formation of an International Brigade to fight in Spain. John did not know that at the time; neither did Harry Pollitt, the secretary of the British Communist party, whom he went to see in London. He won Pollitt's support in organizing a British contingent within the Spanish Army. He recruited seven volunteers, including a writer, John Sommerfield, and a Classics scholar from Cambridge, Bernard Knox.

"The worst thing about war," John told them, "is not discomfort nor even danger but boredom." They set out for Spain with knapsacks, revolvers, and books; John took *Capital* and a volume of Shakespeare's plays.

# CAMPAIGNING FOR
# THE LABOR PARTY

I SPENT the rest of September campaigning for the Totnes Divisional Labour party. It was barely alive, but I had become close friends with a working-class couple—the Ramsdens—and, together, we managed to revive it.

The member of Parliament for the division was a retired soldier: Major Ralph Rayner. I planned to run against him in my own time, but I was only just twenty. And I was an American. That was brought home to me when I went to the American Consul in Plymouth to get my passport renewed. The consul turned red with rage as he handed my passport back to me. He flourished a newspaper clipping about Whitney in my face. "If you choose to give up your country," the consul shouted, "don't parade your disloyalty to the press as your brother did!"

I listened in amazement. I had no sense at all that Whitney had acted disloyally in becoming a British citizen, or that I owed any loyalty to the United States.

I realized then that running for Parliament was not as simple as I had supposed. I and my friends in the local Labour party settled on an inoffensive haberdasher named Henwood as our candidate. I drove him around the division trying to stir up support for him. It was not easy. The press ignored us until I challenged Rayner to a debate on foreign policy. Then the campaign came to life. "TOTNES M. P. CHALLENGED TO DEBATE!" cried the posters in every town and village. Strangers came up to me and slapped me on the back while the discomfited Henwood looked on.

A few days later, Thomas, the butler, hunted me down. Mrs. Rayner and two of her friends were at the front door, he said. They wished to be shown around.

We walked through the great hall, the jousting court, the barn theater. We were strolling across the courtyard when Mrs. Rayner stopped and stared at me.

"Are *you* the one who's opposing my husband in the next election?" she said.

I shook my head.

"I see," she said. "It's your older brother who's being so beastly."

"No," I said. "I'm afraid that it's me. Only, Mr. Henwood is the candidate."

"That little man!" She let out a scornful laugh. We headed for the garden, talking about *Vaccinium corymbosum* and *Enkianthus perulatus.*

# "I DON'T LIKE FIGHTING"

IN the autumn of 1936, the balance of hope and of fear began to turn against us.

The bombing of the civilian population in Spain by Hitler's *Stukas* seemed like an open breach in the whole fabric of civilization. The British and the French governments looked the other way. The young generals whom we revered—Lister, Modesto, Gustavo Duran—were fighting losing battles. In the test that we had accepted as decisive, we were facing defeat.

In Moscow, the purge was beginning. Only the hardened party members were prepared to argue that the confessions of Stalin's new-found enemies were genuine. The rest of us simply refused to think about the trials. We would not peer into the dark recesses of the Kremlin while Russia was arming itself against Hitler and sending arms to Spain.

John was fighting in Spain; James was working in Paris. Without them, the Communist movement in Cambridge was leaderless. I chaired one meeting in K5, but I was given no responsibility and I wanted none. The work of the leadership—coordinating the college cells, passing on the new recruits, meeting with the party organizers in London, and briefing the "moles"—was entrusted to a few hard-core members, such as George Barnard, who, at twenty, was already a bureaucrat.

George and his superiors decided that some basic education was in order. He summoned a number of us to a seminar on Marx's *Capital.* Reading from copious notes, he told us that Marx had proved by his Theory of the Falling Rate of Profit that capitalism was doomed.

George, I felt, was intruding into my realm of economics, where I was master of my own beliefs. In addition, his seminar was being held in my sitting room. So I scoffed at his assertions. Marx, I said, had assumed that the productivity of labor was a fixed element in his equation, whereas, in fact, it was a variable. For that reason, Marx's theory, which George had described as the core of *Capital,* was nonsense.

George's face darkened. He chastised me for my heresy. It was, on the surface, insignificant, but George sensed the underlying danger. Students like myself owed no allegiance to the Communist party as such. We had enlisted *as students* in response to two extraordinary individuals, and, without them, we were adrift.

From time to time, word came back from John. His father wrote to me on November 29.

Margot Heinemann has sent me two letters from John which reached her *via* Klugman in Paris. Both I think from Albacete; the second about a week old and censored. He was training with an international column there, and was well satisfied with the prospect of winning the war. Expecting to go to the front about now. He says the organization is good, and that his district is under control of the Party which is now popular with the Anarchists who shout *Viva Russia!* Not much else in the way of news, but this is good as far as it goes.

'. . . his district is under control of the Party . . . this is good as far as it goes.' Francis Cornford was a lifelong liberal but he, like the rest of us, had to narrow his choices in politics to the forces that were in place on the battlefields of Spain.

--◦◦◦◦◦◦◦◦◦◦◦◦◦◦◦◦◦--

I was running for the presidency of the Cambridge Student Union that autumn. It was an all-out contest between the Left and the Right. My opponent, John Churchill, was a well-established Conservative.

The most important issue that was scheduled for debate was *"That this House would prefer the triumph of Fascism to the dictatorship of the proletariat."* It pitted a conservative student against me, and that did not worry me. It also brought me up against one of the most formidable orators in England, Sir Oswald Mosley. He had been one of the most promising Labour members of Parliament. He had left the Labour party in disgust and had become the founder and the leader of the Blackshirts—the British Union of Fascists.

I cast aside all my studies to work on my speech. It forced me to define my own position. I made no mention in my draft of communism as an ideology, or of Soviet Russia as a society. I cast the speech simply in terms of the contrasting attitudes of the Nazi and the Soviet governments toward war as an instrument of national policy. I did not mention Stalin. I spoke instead of Georgi Dimitrov, the Bulgarian who had defied Hitler and who, as secretary of the Communist International, had become a spokesman for all left-of-center parties in defense of collective security.

It was the best argument that I could construct, but I was anxious. I wrote to my mother,

"If Mosley comes, the nervous strain will be almost too much for me. I don't rise to the occasion. I don't like fighting."

I learned my speech off by heart and practiced it in front of a mirror. I tried to study. As the day of the debate approached, the newspapers began to carry stories about the illness of King George V. He died on the night before the debate was due to take place, and it was cancelled.

The race for the presidency of the union continued. The Conservative party urged all students to join the union so that they might vote. The Socialist Society followed suit. On election day, clergymen from all over the county arrived by car and by bicycle and headed for the union. Our friends, in turn, hurried off between classes to vote.

I walked to the union when the votes were counted. My knees were like rubber strands. Gerald Croasdell came out of the old building to greet me. "You made it—just!" he said.

So I became the secretary and, later, the vice president of the union. I was scheduled to become the president in the autumn of 1937.

# THE APOSTLES

ONE day in the Autumn of 1936, David Champernowne came to see me. He was, he said, the last of the students who had been enrolled in a secret society; one called the Cambridge Conversazione Society, whose members were known as the Apostles.

The society, David said, had been founded early in the nineteenth century. Its members had included most of the university's great men. It had declined in numbers during the thirties, since the elder members of the society had encountered few young men whom they regarded as "Apostolic." They had, in fact, come to the conclusion that if the society could not be revived, it should be allowed to die.

The same men, David added, looked on me as Apostolic. They were prepared to place the future of the society in my hands.

I asked if I might be told the names of some of the members of the society. David pledged me to secrecy, then told me that Keynes was its most influential member. Denis Robertson was a member; so were Sheppard, the provost of Kings; G. M. Trevelyan, the historian; the novelist, E. M. Forster; and the philosopher, G. E. Moore. Some of my friends were members, David added: Victor Rothschild, for example, and Guy Burgess and Anthony Blunt.

The decision seemed simple to me. I said that if Keynes and Robertson and Trevelyan were willing to spend their evenings with me, I would be only too happy to meet with them.

We met in Keynes's rooms. I held up my right hand and repeated a fearful oath, praying that my soul would writhe in unendurable pain for the rest of eternity if I so much as breathed a word about the society to anyone who was not a member. It seemed a bit harsh, but Sheppard, who carried a cushion with him wherever he went, patted me with his free hand and told me not to be alarmed.

"You see," he explained, "our oath was written at a time when it was thought to be most unlikely that a member of the society would speak to anyone who was not Apostolic."

I asked Sheppard how he would define the term *Apostolic.* He beamed at me in his childish way. "One must be *very* brilliant and *extremely* nice!" he said.

I had not thought of myself as being in either category. I asked if any member had ever been found to be unworthy of the society.

Sheppard frowned. "There was a horrid man long ago," he said, "who was thought to be Apostolic, and who was indeed elected to the society. He then said that his only interest was in being elected, and that he could not afford to waste his time by attending our meetings.

"His name is never mentioned in the society," Sheppard said.

Keynes, of course, was more precise. In his beautiful essay *My Early Beliefs,* which was written as a paper to be read to his friends and was published after his death, Keynes set forth the "habits of feeling" that he and Moore and Lytton Strachey and Leonard Woolf and Clive Bell shared when they met together as undergraduate members of the society in 1902.

> . . . We were at an age when our beliefs influenced our behaviour, a characteristic of the young which it is easy for the middle-aged to forget, and the habits of feeling formed then still persist in a recognizable degree. It is those habits of feeling, influencing the majority of us, which make this Club a collectivity and separate us from the rest. . . .
>
> We were the forerunners of a new dispensation; we were not afraid of anything. . . . Nothing mattered except states of mind . . . timeless, passionate states of contemplation and communion. . . . The appropriate subjects of passionate contemplation and communion were a beloved person, beauty and truth, and one's prime objects in life were love, the creation and enjoyment of aesthetic experience and the pursuit of knowledge. Of these, love came a long way first.

Did Keynes see beneath my preoccupation with political activity? Did he discern that his prime objects in life were mine? I think so. He understood also how fragile those prime objects were:

> We were among the last of the Utopians. . . . We repudiated all versions of original sin. . . . We were not aware that civilization was a thin and precarious crust . . . only maintained by rules and conventions skillfully put across and guilefully preserved. We had no respect for traditional wisdom and the restraints of custom. We lacked reverence. . . . And, as the years wore on towards 1914, the thinness and superficiality as well as

the falsity of our view of man's heart became more obvious. . . . I can see us as water-spiders, gracefully skimming, as light and reasonable as air, the surface of the stream without any contact at all with the eddies and currents underneath.

It was my task as the youngest member of the society to arrange our meetings. Keynes gave me all the help he could:

February 3, 1937

Dear Michael:

For the meeting of the Society we fixed I think Saturday February 20th in my rooms; and I was to let you have some suggestions as to who might be asked.

For King's I suggest Sheppard, the two Lucas's, Rylands, Richard Braithwaite and Watson; also most certainly Champernowne if you can get him to Cambridge.

For Trinity—G. M. Trevelyan, G. E. Moore and D. H. Robertson, and of course the younger people such as Blunt, Rothschild and the others.

Then there is Sykes-Davies from John's and quite likely there may be others I have forgotten for the moment.

Yours ever

J. M. K.

One of the Apostles who came back to Cambridge for our meetings was Guy Burgess. Did he share Keynes's beliefs? He derived an almost sensual pleasure out of any discussion of ideas. He craved the companionship and the physical love of other men, which seemed to be a binding tie for many members of the society. With his curly hair, his sensual mouth, his bright blue eyes, his cherubic air, he seemed at first sight to embody in himself the ideal of male beauty that the Apostles revered. Then, on a closer look, you noticed the details: the black-rimmed fingernails; the stained forefinger in which he gripped his perpetual cigarette stub; the dark, uneven teeth; the slouch; the open fly. If he was angelic, you sensed that he was a fallen angel. That sense was heightened when he spoke to you. He smiled before he said anything, but most of his comments had a cutting edge.

As an undergraduate, Guy had been a member of the Communist cell in Trinity. I did not know that. He had broken with his Communist associates in 1934 in a manner that some of his friends found bizarre. That also was unknown to me. I knew only that he lived in London, and that he was working for Captain Jack Macnamara, a Right-Wing member of Parliament who had close ties to the Nazis. In a sidelong phrase, Guy would joke about the homosexual encounters he had taken part in with Macnamara and his Nazi friends. In a moment of elated intoxication, he would hint that he had learned something of importance through the indiscretion of a Nazi diplomat.

There was a suggestion that Guy was up to something; but what? He was close to the Rothschilds; were they supporting him? Jews were deeply concerned about the developing ties between Hitler's agents and the Conservative party. So were others. For those ties were of immense potential significance. If the Conservatives were resolute in resisting German expansion peace might be prolonged. But if a Conservative government established secret ties to Hitler. . . .

The Anglo-German Link, established by our old antagonist, Admiral Sir Barry Domville, was too disreputable to sponsor an alliance that was in the making. The Anglo-German Fellowship, in contrast, was led by powerful men. The Prince of Wales was known to favor closer ties with Germany. The Cliveden set shared his views, and it included the hard core of the Conservative party. Its aims were never discussed in public, but the opposition of students like myself to rearmament stemmed in part from an intuitive sense that the government was rearming not to resist Hitler's armies but to divert them to the East.

What was Guy really up to? No one asked him. Most of us were interested in politics; he had to wedge his way to the center of the political stage. Some of us were ambitious; he had to obtain power to satisfy his fantasies. He dreamed of using power for his own, capricious ends.

In his guise as Captain Macnamara's secretary, Guy pointed to fascism as the wave of the future. He voiced no such opinions in the meetings of the Apostles. In any discussion of ideas he was always ready with an apt quotation, an amusing anecdote, a suggestive analogy, a mocking riposte. If the question before the society was political, he spoke in metaphors that were distant and obscure. If he was challenged to state his own convictions, his bright blue eyes would widen. He would look at the challenger with a beguiling smile, and then speak of other things.

-⟨∞⟩-

"Tell me," said Sheppard, "do you have any friends who are not members of the society?"

"A few," I said.

I went to a party one evening where I met a lovely young American whose name was Catherine Crompton. She had married a young English scientist, and her family had moved to Cambridge for a year, bringing their youngest daughter, Belinda, with them. We spent many afternoons together.

I spent another afternoon with Arthur Waley, the translator of *The Tale of Genji,* and his lover, Beryl de Zoete. We walked up the Cam to Grantchester, past the pool where Rupert Brooke had spent so many hours. All the trees were in flame along the river that afternoon. Jackdaws rose, protesting from their branches, and in the distance, we could see the spires of Cambridge thrusting into the sky. An autumn wind was blowing, and Arthur was swept like a wisp along the tow path.

Arthur came with us when we went to Klosters to ski. And when Jerry and my mother organized an exhibition of pottery by the Japanese master, Hamada, they invited Arthur to open it. He was in the South of France at that moment. It was a long and expensive journey by rail and Channel steamer to Dartington. But Arthur alone, they felt, could do justice to the occasion, so they paid his return fare.

A large crowd assembled in the solar for the opening of the exhibition. Jerry stood up and delivered a fulsome introduction of the great scholar and student of Zen who had journeyed so far to make his speech. No Westerner, he said, was better able to express the inner essence of Hamada's art than was Arthur Waley.

Arthur nodded. He stood like an amber statue until the applause had died away. Then, in his high and quavering voice he delivered his speech. He said,

> *I hope—that you will enjoy this exhibition—*
> *as you would—if you were eating—a peach.*

At that, he sat down again. He remained sitting with a contemplative smile upon his face.

# "WHAT I AM AND I SHALL BE"

ONE morning in mid-January 1937, I returned from a class to K5 and found a note that had been left for me: "Come to my rooms as soon as you receive this—George Barnard."

I set out for St. John's College. George met me in its courtyard. He said, "John's been killed."

"Where?"

"At Cordoba."

"When?"

"On December twenty-eighth."

"Who told you?"

"They called me from King Street."

"Are they certain?"

"They checked it twice in Madrid."

"Who else has been told?"

"You're the first."

I knew that I would have to be the one to break the news to John's father and to Margot. I started off, then I ran after George.

"Did they tell you how it happened?"

"There was a story. He'd been on a night patrol, and as he came in, he was shot by his own sentries."

I told George to never mention that story again. It proved to be untrue. John was killed in a vain effort to hold the bare ridge above Cordoba that became known as the "English Crest."

I bicycled out to the Cornfords' house at Conduit Head. I had never been there and I had to stop to ask the way.

I rang the front doorbell. I stood there, waiting.

Professor Cornford, a tall man, opened the door. "You've brought some news of John," he said, as I passed him. He followed me into his sitting room saying, "Is he coming back?"

"He's never coming back," I said. I started to cry.

He sat down heavily in his armchair. After a long time, he looked up at me. "Are you certain?" he asked. "Are you absolutely certain?"

I nodded.

"Then I must tell his mother," he said.

I bicycled back to Trinity. I hunted down Margot's brother Henry, and we set out for Birmingham in the Railton. We arrived there at dusk. We went to the Victorian house where Margot was living. It was dark, and the door was locked. We waited in the narrow alcove of the doorway. Margot returned from work and blundered into us.

John had told her that he would come back to her one day without warning her. She reached out for me, thinking that I was John. Then she recognized us and at once she understood.

We drove to London the next morning. We talked mostly about the memorial meeting that we would hold in Cambridge and the article that I would write about John for the *Left Review*. I remembered the old pledge of the Chartists when I said goodbye to Margot: We are at one, and we will keep to each other.

I spent three days in John's bedroom at Conduit Head, copying out lines from his letters and his poems.

His letter to his mother when he was sixteen explaining why he had to leave his boarding school: "My trouble here is that I can get through a whole day without having to make a single new response to a new situation of any kind."

His poem on the assassination of Kirov:

*Nothing is ever certain, nothing is ever safe,*
*Today is overturning yesterday's settled good,*
*Everything dying keeps a hungry grip on life.*
*Nothing is ever born without screaming and blood. . . .*

His last poem to Margot:

> *Heart of the heartless world,*
> *Dear heart, the thought of you*
> *Is the pain in my side,*
> *The shadow that chills my view.*
>
> *The wind rises in the evening,*
> *Reminds that Autumn is near.*
> *I am afraid to lose you,*
> *I am afraid of my fear.*
>
> *On the last mile to Huesca*
> *The last fence for our pride,*
> *Think so kindly dear, that I*
> *Sense you at my side.*
>
> *And if bad luck should lay my strength*
> *Into the shallow grave,*
> *Remember all the good you can*
> *Don't forget my love.*

His letter to Margot from Aragon:

. . . I love you with all my strength and all my will and my whole body.
Loving you has been the most perfect experience, and in a way, the biggest
achievement of my life.

The party was my only other love. Until I see you again, bless you my
love, my strength. Be happy. I worked for the party with all my strength,
and loved you as much as I was capable of. If I am killed, my life won't
be wasted. But, I'll be back.

We held a memorial meeting for John in the union, and another in
the town of Cambridge. Some Communist party hack came down
from London and spoke at the town meeting. He referred to John as
"the finest type of a middle-class comrade," as if he had been a "type"
and not a unique individual. He drew the correct party lessons from
John's death.

John's friend, Pat Sloan, was another speaker at the meeting. I
drove him to the railway station on his way back to London. I remembered, as we drove, a line from the second verse of John's poem on
Kirov: "Only in constant action was his constant certainty found." I
said that the line was true for John as well as for Kirov. I added that

he had seemed less certain to me when he had returned from Spain.

Sloan glanced at me for a moment. He said nothing.

"You seem to have the same sense of certainty that John had when he was in Cambridge," I said. "I don't have it. I don't know what I believe in anymore."

Sloan nodded. "There are only two things that you must believe in," he said. "The certainty of the ultimate victory and the necessity for continuous, organized, disciplined struggle."

There was no one in Cambridge at that moment whom I wanted to be with save for Bernard Knox, who had gone to Spain with John. He had fought in several battles and at University City had been left for dead on the battlefield, with a bullet through the base of his neck. He had returned to Cambridge, unemployed, low in spirits, and broke.

Two other people were broke and homeless: Ray Peters and her small son, James. I talked to John's sister about them; her husband wrote to me, ". . . I do not want to raise the question of Ray with Professor C. He never liked her. . . ."

I found a job for Ray at Dartington and a home for James with my working-class friends, the Ramsdens. They were childless and they revered John's memory. They lavished affection on James, and he responded. He was bright and sensitive and, although the school at Dartington was filled, Jerry persuaded its principal to take James in.

Professor Cornford accepted my plans for Ray and James. He was infirm, and his wife was ill. John's sister wrote to me:

"We had a very generous letter from Ray this this morning, offering to bring James here before she goes down to Devonshire. My father had to ask her not to because I don't think my mother could stand it. He is so exactly like John at that age."

One more letter from Margot, ". . . I am off to Paris tonight. I wanted to thank you for everything you have done. I'm afraid that this has been damnably rubbed in for you, but I feel good about it now and I hope you will. I am absolutely all right and very proud."

And a poem enclosed with the letter:

> For my pain and my distress
> I forgive his father's house
> And the poplars at the side
> And the old man's handsome head.
>
> I forgive the lettered page,
> And the singers on the march,
> And the Commune's dying shout,
> And the only worker's state.
>
> I forgive him strength and sense,
> I forgive him love and loss,

*Fine desire and furry head*
*His own hand and his own blood.*

*I forgive with open eyes*
*All that took him where he is.*
*What I am and I shall be*
*He and time have made of me. . . .*

# "HORRIBLY STARTLED"

*UNDER Western Eyes* was published in 1911. It is perhaps the most perceptive of Joseph Conrad's novels.

Kyrilo Sidorovitch Razumov, the central character, is a third-year student at St. Petersburg University in Russia. He is regarded by his fellow students as being an "altogether trustworthy man." But, Conrad adds, he had no family: "No home influences shaped his opinions or his feelings. He was as lonely in the world as a man swimming in the deep sea."

Razumov returns to his lodgings one winter evening. His mind is on the essay that he is writing, which he hopes will advance his career. "I shall put in four hours of good work," he says to himself as he opens the door to his room.

But, no sooner had he closed the door than he was horribly startled. All black against the usual tall stove of white tiles gleaming in the dusk, stood a strange figure, wearing a skirted, close-fitting, brown cloth coat strapped around the waist, in long boots, and with a little Astrakhan cap on its head. It loomed lithe and martial. Razumov was utterly confounded. It was only when the figure advancing two paces asked in a grave untroubled voice if the outer door was closed that he regained his power of speech.

Razumov sees that the figure is Victor Haldin, an older and highly respected student. He is mildly irritated, thinking that Haldin has dropped by for a chat.

He is mistaken. Haldin has just assassinated an odious tyrant, the minister-president of Russia. He has come to seek Razumov's help.

"All I want you to do," Haldin tells Razumov, "is to help me vanish. No great matter, that."

Razumov is stunned: "He saw his youth pass away from him . . .
his strength give way; his mind become an abject thing. . . ."

Razumov promises Haldin that he will help him. Instead, he betrays
him to the police. Haldin is captured and hanged. Razumov appears
at first to be unscathed. But he has lost his independence. He can
never again call his life his own.

It is an unpleasant story. As if to reassure his readers, the narrator
of the story states at the outset: "This is not a story of the West of
Europe. It is unthinkable that any young Englishman could find himself in Razumov's situation."

Is it?

Two weeks or so after the news of John's death had reached England, Anthony asked me to meet him in his rooms.

They were elegant rooms, in the loveliest court in Trinity. I made
myself comfortable on a gray sofa. Anthony settled down in an easy
chair. We spoke about a few familiar matters. I assumed that he
wanted to talk to me about the Apostles, or about Victor Rothschild's
unhappy wife.

Instead, he asked me what I planned to do when I graduated from
Cambridge.

I had given no thought to my own future. I was under no compulsion to think about it, since I did not have to earn my own living.
I had taken it for granted that I would become British, as Whitney
had done. I had been asked to run for Parliament by the Plymouth
Labour party. I had assumed that before long, I would be offered a more promising constituency. In the interim, I guessed that I
might stay in Cambridge, writing a book about Malthus or David
Ricardo.

I mentioned all of those possibilities. Anthony listened. Then,
"Some of your friends," he said, "have other ideas for you."

"Other ideas?"

It was not as easy as I might suppose, Anthony said, to gain British
citizenship. Sir John Simon had infuriated Keynes by warning him that
I would have to curtail my political activities if I wished to become
British.

Furthermore, Anthony went on, was it really the best course for
me? Britain was a declining nation, governed by heartless Conservatives and weak-kneed Socialists. It was on the eve of a catastrophic
war. America, on the other hand, was an immense country, one that
was bound to play a larger role in world affairs.

"America?" I barely knew the country. I had shunned the few

Americans who were students in Cambridge, feeling that I had little or nothing in common with them. My home, my family, my friends, my interests were all in Britain. Why, then, would I go back to America?

"Your father worked on Wall Street," said Anthony. "He was a partner in J. P. Morgan. With those connections, and with your training as an economist, you could make a brilliant future for yourself in international banking."

"I don't want a brilliant future in international banking," I said. "I have no interest whatever in becoming a banker."

"Our friends have given a great deal of thought to it," said Anthony. "They have instructed me to tell you that that is what you must do."

"What *I* must do? . . . What friends have instructed you to tell me——"

"Our friends in the International. The Communist International."

"*They* instructed *you?* . . . You are a part of it?"

Anthony nodded. "My instructions are to inform you of your assignment, and to assist you in every way that I can."

"My assignment? What assignment?"

"To work on Wall Street. To provide appraisals, economic appraisals, of Wall Street's plans to dominate the world economy."

"Why on earth would anyone suppose that I'd take on an assignment like that?"

"For the same reason that John went to Spain."

I had no answer to that. After a moment, I said, "Why do they tell me this now?"

"Because of John's death."

"I don't understand."

"It will be necessary for you to cut all your political ties. It had been assumed that you would do that after you left Cambridge, but . . . this way seems . . . more convincing."

"More convincing? I still don't——"

"Since John was so close to you, and since you have obviously been so affected by his death . . . this seems to be the logical time to make the break."

"Seems to whom? Who would——"

"To our friends. Our friend," said Anthony, correcting himself. "He has given a great deal of thought to it."

"How would he know what I——"

"He knows you and respects you."

"Then why doesn't he——"

"He would like to talk to you himself. He regrets very much that he is not permitted to identify himself to you."

We sat in silence. I fumbled with Anthony's sentences, trying to make some sense out of them.

"You want me to stage some kind of nervous breakdown," I said, "some crisis of belief."

"It will be seen that way.

"Everyone knows," Anthony continued, "that your loyalty was to John rather than to the party. It will come as a blow to them, but in time they will accept it."

"I stage a break with all my friends," I said. "I leave my home and my family. I go back to a country that I barely remember. I live a life of deceit——"

"John gave up his life, remember that.

"Well," said Anthony, "why don't we get some sleep. We'll meet again tomorrow evening, when you've had a chance to think about it."

He laid a hand on my shoulder as I left his rooms.

"I hope you get some sleep," he said.

---

Razumov lies down on a hard, horse-hair sofa after he sends Victor Haldin to his death. He is exhausted; he tries to sleep: "Several times that night, he woke up shivering from a dream of walking through drifts of snow. . . ."

In the morning he awakes: "The light coming in through the window seemed strangely cheerless, containing no new promise as the light of each new day should for a young man. It was the awakening of a man mortally ill, or of a man ninety years old. . . . An incredible dulness, a ditch-water stagnation was sensible to his perceptions, as though life had withdrawn itself from all things."

I think to myself now: *How could Conrad have known?* It is as if the man who read aloud his fiction in my home in New York while I played in my nursery, had me in mind when he wrote those lines.

I too felt as if life had withdrawn itself from all things when I awoke in my small cell in K5. The omelette that I made for myself tasted like sawdust; Hugh seemed like a total stranger to me. I went through the motions of the day as if I were repeating phrases and gestures that I had learned in some prior existence.

In the evening, I returned to Anthony's rooms. I told him that I would not return to America to live out my days as an international banker. I said that the prospect of a life of deceit was repugnant to me. I pleaded to be released from the commitment that had been imposed upon me in the name of my dead friend.

Anthony nodded. He praised me for not collapsing the night before. He promised to carry my plea back to his friend. He assured me that it would be considered very carefully. He said that he would let me know their decision within a week.

*Their* decision about *my* life.

At the week's end, I went to Anthony's rooms once again. He was waiting for me.

Careful consideration had been given, he said, to the arguments that I had made. It was conceded that my staged break with the Communist movement in Cambridge would cause a good deal of consternation among my fellow students. It was granted that I was more British than American. If I refused to become a banker that would be accepted. But my appeal was nonetheless rejected. I was to go back to America, and I was to go underground.

I had regained some strength by then. I protested against the decision that had been made.

Anthony listened to my protest. He never raised his voice. He would carry back my appeal once more, he said. This time, it would be considered in the highest circles in the Kremlin. It might take weeks to resolve the issue; the time would be granted to me, on one condition: I would have to start my staged breakdown at once. For if my apparent break with the Communist movement were to be based upon my reaction to John's death, it could not be delayed.

That was the bargain that was offered to me. I accepted it. My part of the bargain would, I knew, be painful. Yet in a way it accorded with my own state of mind. I had never supposed that my ties to the Communist movement would outlast my student days. And, in a sense, they were already broken. In the course of a week, I had moved out of the noisy, crowded world of Cambridge into a world of shadows and echoes.

On the day after Haldin comes to his rooms, Razumov reflects upon the position in which he finds himself: "Fatality enters your rooms while the landlady's back is turned; you come home and find it in possession, bearing a man's name. . . . you don't know enough to take it by the throat and fling it downstairs. . . . 'Sit down,' you say. And it is all over. It will cling to you forever. Neither halter nor bullet can give you back the freedom of your life and the sanity of your thought."

Why didn't I take Anthony's scheme by the throat and fling it away? These pages, I hope, have suggested the answer.

If I had been English by birth or American by upbringing, I would have been held in place by the traditional loyalties. But these loyalties were no buttresses for me.

If I had been self-centered, as most sensible people are, I would have asserted my own self-interest against Anthony's claim upon me. I lacked the will to do that; I lacked the sense of self.

If Anthony had approached me later on, as he had intended to, I would, I think, have balked at his demands. But in the weeks that followed John's death, my defenses were down. I wanted to be a martyr. I needed to sacrifice myself, as John had done.

In the absence of other allegiances, my response was shaped substantially by Anthony's own personality.

If he had been a stranger, he would have exerted no claim on me. But in the months that preceded our meeting, he had become a wise and a valued counselor for me.

If he had been overbearing, he would have antagonized me. He was, on the contrary, compassionate; he seemed as unnerved as I was by the sadness of the situation in which we found ourselves.

If he had been didactic or doctrinaire, that in itself would have aroused forces of resistance within me. But he was as untouched as I was by the dull core of Communist ideology. In all the hours that we spent together, we never spoke of Communist principles or of Soviet practices. On one occasion only, we wondered together what a Marxist theory of aesthetics might be. He was writing an article on art for a journal of opinion. In an effort to be helpful, I developed the preposterous notion that works of art might be considered in terms of their historic impact rather than their intrinsic worth. It was an indication of Anthony's own lack of political indoctrination that he incorporated my notion in his article. He was scolded for it by his fellow art historians—as he should have been.

Do psychiatrists point out the innate submissiveness of the youngest child in each family? I expect so. In any case, for the reasons that I have mentioned, and no doubt for others that I cannot discern, I failed to reject Anthony's scheme out of hand. If my reasons seem unconvincing in 1983, so be it. It is hard for a man, said Cato, to live in one age and to be judged by another.

Razumov went at once to the police; I did not. His life was brief and tormented; mine has been long and richly rewarding.

Does it follow that our two stories have little in common?

Conrad maintained that his novel "could be reduced to the formula of senseless desperation provoked by senseless tyranny." But why reduce the novel to a political formula?

Earlier, in his Author's Note, Conrad asserts that his sole purpose in writing *Under Western Eyes* was to "express imaginatively the general truth which underlies its action." He does not tell us what the 'general truth' is, but surely it relates to a larger theme. It concerns the fate of the individual who is caught up in the current of history and carried out of his depth, as I was in February 1937.

# BREAKING THE TIES

IN the weeks that followed my third meeting with Anthony, I made it plain that I was in an emotional crisis. In part it was staged, under Anthony's tutelage; in part it was real. The two were interwoven, so much so that, in my weariness and my confusion, I did not know whether the anger, the bitterness, the disillusionment, the grief that I expressed were façades forced upon me, or if they came from the deepest part of me.

I quarreled with my fellow members of the Socialist Club and failed to turn up for meetings of the Trinity cell. I upset the Communist caucus in the union by instructing them to vote for a Conservative, John Simonds. I said that I might not return to Cambridge in the autumn to serve out my term as president of the union. I voiced my disgust at the adolescent nature of its debates.

I saw the worried glances of my fellow radicals. I heard their whispers: "He's obviously in a deep depression." "I think he's a bit better today. . . ."

Day after day, the student Communists who were closest to me came around to K5. They lingered in our sitting room and tried to talk to me. They asked me if I needed companionship, and if they could be of help. They said that they understood, but only one of my friends guessed what was happening. He too was approached by Anthony in the spring of 1937; he balked at being recruited, saying that he was not strong enough to survive years spent underground. He came to my rooms when I was alone one evening. He stood in the doorway and said, with a sad smile, that he knew what was happening to me.

I was on the other side of the mirror by then. I said that I did not know what he was talking about.

I set out deliberately in those weeks to drive myself toward a nervous breakdown. I sensed that it might be a way of escaping from Anthony and his superiors even while I was obeying their orders. I kept myself awake long after midnight, reading Tolstoy and Thorstein Veblen. I hoped that my body might give way under the strain of sleeplessness, but it proved to be resilient with a will of its own to survive and to be strong.

I learned that there were resources within myself that I had not sensed before. I took some pride in my capacity to withstand punishment. I even wrote a satirical song: *Let's Liquidate Love*. It was performed by a chorus of students at the Annual Dance of the Socialist Club.

I formed new friendships. Bernard Knox was one companion; the American girl, Belinda Crompton, was another. John Simonds was drawn to her, as I was, and the three of us spent many afternoons together.

I went to no lectures save for those given by Keynes. I did no work. I stayed on for a time as president of the Socialist Club and raised money for the Spanish Loyalists. By then, the *Luftwaffe* was in control of the skies over Madrid, and the armies of the Republic were in retreat.

In a desperate gesture, I invited the leaders of the Labour party to come to Cambridge to discuss with us their reasons for supporting the Conservative government of Britain in its policy of nonintervention in Spain. To my surprise, Clement Attlee, the leader of the Labour party, accepted my invitation. He came to Cambridge with his deputy, Hugh Dalton, looking over his shoulder.

We argued for two hours about the necessity of standing up to the Fascists. Attlee had been an army officer in the First World War, and the memory of it seemed to paralyze him. Yet we were the ones who would have to fight.

The room grew darker as the winter afternoon wore on. The old platitudes broke across it like a succession of waves. I thought of John and I grew very sad. His death seemed such a crying waste.

Dalton remembered me from his visits to Dartington. When our meeting was over he came and stood over me, fixing me with his pale eyes, like a hunter about to finish off his prey.

I did not have the heart to speak to him.

I said nothing to my mother about the catastrophe that had overtaken me, but she sensed from my letters that something was wrong. She wrote to Keynes and begged him to watch over me.

He did all that he could. He invited me to his rooms to talk over the future of the Apostles.

He invited me to the opening performance of the Royal Ballet at the theatre that he had built in Cambridge. I turned down his invitation, but I did go to the dinner that he gave for the stars of the Ballet. I found myself sitting beside a young ballerina with dark, appealing eyes and raven hair. I tried in my arrogant way to engage her in conversation. Since I knew nothing about the ballet, I concentrated on the visual arts. The National Gallery, The Louvre, The Hospice in Beaune with its Triptych by Rogier van der Weyden. . . . I tried them all; she listened and made no response. At last she looked at me with those appealing eyes. She said, "I don't think you realize that I'm only fourteen."

"No," I said, "I had not realized that."

I tried to remember the subjects that had interested me when I was fourteen. It was no use. We sat and ate in silence.

Her name, I remembered later, was Margot Fonteyn.

※

There was another evening in the spring of 1937 that is still vivid for me. Julian Bell, the son of Clive and Vanessa Bell and the nephew of Virginia Woolf, had returned to England from China. He was determined to join the International Brigade in Spain. He wrote to his mother, "It's too late for democracy and reason and persuasion and writing to the *New Statesman* saying it's all a pity. The only real choices are to submit or to fight."

Julian was an Apostle. He came to Cambridge clad in a black bearskin coat and an Astrakhan hat. He read a paper to the society. He praised the military virtues in his paper and identified the soldier as his new-found ideal.

The paper marked his break with the pacifism of his Bloomsbury forebears. His letters made it plain, in time to come, that he meant precisely what he said, but those who listened to him did not know that. I for one assumed that he was speaking metaphorically. He was, I thought, saying that in a world in which no cause was flawless, he would carry out his obligations with the soldier's detachment, placing his own life at risk and obeying without much reflection the orders that his superiors would hand down to him.

I was shaken by what he said, for it bore upon my own willingness to accept the orders that Anthony had given to me. When my turn came to speak, I attacked Julian's paper, saying that the war in Spain called not for the soldier's detachment, but for the intellectual and emotional commitment of the partisan.

Julian nodded. He said that perhaps he had not made his sense of partisanship plain enough. He left for Spain a few weeks later; he was killed in the battle for Brunete.

※

Week by week, life in Cambridge became harder for me. Hugh treated me with open contempt after a time. My former friends barely spoke to me.

My final examinations loomed like monsters on my horizons. I could not gain First Class honors for a third time after cutting my classes all year long. I could not face the prospect of getting a lesser degree.

I sat alone in my rooms. One evening, Brian Simon, Tess Mayor, and another girl came to find me. They had bought four tickets to a concert in the Corn Exchange, and they dragged me along.

The performance was by a chamber group. The first pieces that they performed were enchanting. Then, after the intermission, they played Mozart's G Minor Quintet. His biographer, Alfred Einstein, refers to the Quintet as Mozart's "Agony in the Garden." I did not know that in 1937; I had never heard the work. Yet somehow, in the isolation and heightened sensitivity in which I was living, the barriers of time and of place seemed to fall away between the composer and myself. I was unraveled, and the mood of despair that flowed from me to my companions was so oppressive that they rushed out of the hall when the music ended and waited for me in the fresh night air.

The pressures built up. I told Anthony that I could not face my final term at Cambridge.

He was very sympathetic. He agreed that it would be best for me not to return. So when the spring term ended, I drove to Dartington, knowing that I would have to tell my mother that I was not going to take my degree at Cambridge, and that I would be going back to America to live.

I assumed that she would accept my first decision, and that the second would come as a heavy blow for her. I was wrong. She nodded when I spoke of America, as if she had known all along that the day would come when, like Biddy, I would return to the country where I had been born. But when I said that I was not going to return to Cambridge, she lashed out at me.

"My brother Harry was a brilliant student at Yale," she said. "William Sumner used to say that Harry was the most promising student he'd ever taught. But he ran away. He ran away from every hard challenge; he couldn't face the possibility that he might fail. He squandered his great gifts, and that is something that you cannot do!"

I was taken aback by the vehemence of her response. I could not explain to her why I had to leave Cambridge, so I gave in. I agreed to go back, and to face what seemed to be certain humiliation and defeat.

Anthony and Guy and Brian Simon drove down to Dartington in early April. I took them to a rehearsal of the Jooss Ballet, and Guy praised the dancers—the male dancers—for the beauty of their bodies. Anthony and Guy drank a great deal of whiskey; they talked a great deal about art. My mother drew Anthony aside on one occasion. She voiced her deep concern about me and asked him to watch over me. He promised her that he would.

My stepfather made a brief visit to New York that April. I went with him. It seemed wise to see America once more before I returned there for good.

From the ship, I wrote one more plea to Anthony. I cited every argument I could think of for resisting his claim upon me. I even offered to turn over all the wealth that I had if I were released.

On the docks in New York, my mother's old retainers were waiting for us. George Owens, Jesse's cousin, handed out twenty-dollar bills to speed us through the customs inspection; Matty, the chauffeur, drove us out to Old Westbury. Harry Lee and his younger son, Jimmy, waved to us as we rolled up the gravel driveway. Curly Joe and Red Joe and Little Joe were lined up with the household staff at the front door. I slept in the narrow bed where once I had curled up, listening to the stories of Thornton Burgess and Ernest Thompson Seton. I sat on the see-saws and the swings in our playground, trying to make sense out of my own life. The tulips were yellow and scarlet in the Chinese Garden, and along the path to the playhouse, the lilacs were coming into bloom.

My stepfather, Jerry, and I went on to Washington. We had tea with President and Mrs. Roosevelt in the White House. I began my search for a job.

Jonathan Mitchell, the Washington correspondent for *The New Republic*, took me on a tour of New Deal agencies. I had no civil service rating, but "Keynes" was a name that opened every door. Roosevelt said that the National Resources Planning Board was the best place for me. Its director, Charles Merriam, was eager to take me on.

I kept clear of the sensitive departments of the government. I pushed all thoughts of Anthony out of my consciousness. I was ready to return to America. I was beginning to identify myself with the New Deal.

❦

I wrote to Anthony, saying that I would be returning to Cambridge. He did all that he could to be helpful. On his plea, the bursar of Trinity College gave me rooms of my own in New Court. I shut myself up in my rooms, and for the rest of my days in Cambridge, saw almost no one, save for Anthony and John Simonds and my American girl.

I knew that there was no way in which I could make up a year's work in five weeks. I compiled a list of all of the questions that had been given in the final examinations of the Economics Tripos over the prior ten years. I plotted them on a graph, and I made up a probability curve from the graph. Then I went to work on the 10 percent of the questions that I guessed might recur.

I was lucky. When, once again, I was given First Class Honors the economics faculty met and revised the examinations system. My name became an epithet among economics students for years to come.

# THE LION OF JUDAH

FROM the torment and the misery of my last days at Cambridge, one splendid occasion stands out.

It sums up for me all that was brave and right in the instincts of my generation.

In October 1935, Mussolini's armies invaded Ethiopia. It was a case of unprovoked aggression and for the League of Nations, it was a decisive test. The league began by imposing sanctions on Italy. Then at the instigation of the British government, it abandoned sanctions and, with them, the last hope that peace could be preserved through collective security.

Haile Selassie, the emperor of Ethiopia, went to Geneva to plead with the assembly of the league. The assembly ignored him. By then the Italian armies had captured Addis Ababa. The emperor refused to become a puppet ruler. He moved to England and took up residence in Bath.

The presence of the emperor and his entourage was in itself an embarrassment to the British government. It could not drive the emperor out of England in its efforts to appease Mussolini, but early in 1937, a number of inspired stories appeared in the Conservative newspapers. They suggested that the emperor and his entourage would be happier in another country.

Ronald Gibson, a member of the Liberal party, had been elected to serve as president of the Cambridge Union in the summer term of 1937. He read the newspaper stories inviting the emperor to get out of England. He decided that he would make the emperor an honorary member of the union.

Only two individuals had been so honored in the twentieth century: Admiral of the Fleet Lord Beatty and Admiral Sims. Ron decided that the emperor should be the third; I, as vice president, was all for it. We inquired if the emperor would be receptive to our invitation. We were informed that he would be. We sent off our invitation, and he sent his equerry to Cambridge to arrange the details.

The great day was set; Ron announced it to the press. *The Daily Herald,* the *News Chronicle,* and the *Manchester Guardian* chortled with delight. Conservative newspapers frowned upon the irresponsibility of the young who meddled in affairs of state.

The governors of the university were nonplussed. They began by disassociating themselves from our childish prank; we ignored them. They insisted that our invitation be withdrawn; Ron declined to withdraw it. They attempted to take over the occasion; Ron reminded them that he was the elected president of the union. They gave in. They informed us that the master of Trinity and Lady Thomson would be honored to receive the emperor and his entourage as their guests. They suggested only that they be allowed to invite a few colleagues to meet His Majesty at tea time. Ron graciously acceded to their request.

The day came when Ron and I stood on the platform of the Cambridge station, waiting for the emperor's train. It arrived, and the equerry appeared, followed by His Excellency Blaten Gueta Horony. Then a small but regal figure descended the steps of the carriage: Haile Selassie, the Lion of Judah, the Elect of God, the King of Kings.

He stood there, bareheaded in his black, embroidered cloak. We advanced and bowed before him. The equerry presented us. We shook hands. We led the emperor and his party to the line of ancient taxis that we had hired. We rattled through the streets of Cambridge and drew up under the massive gate of Trinity, which Henry the Eighth had commissioned and which bore his Royal Coat of Arms.

A crowd had gathered in front of the college. They cheered the emperor as he stepped down from our taxi; he bowed to them. Two college porters, dressed in top hats and morning coats, escorted us through the archway and across Trinity Great Court. We walked slowly, knowing that from every window in the Court we were being watched.

We came to the Master's Lodge. The head porter rang the bell. The door opened, and we saw Lady Thomson standing there. She was tightly corseted and very tense. She sank a few inches in a shallow curtsey; she raised herself again. She stammered something in a language that none of us recognized. The emperor turned to his equerry; the equerry turned to me. I could not help them.

Lady Thomson grew desperate. *"Chambre. Chambre,"* she cried. I explained to the emperor in my mediocre French that she was asking him if he would like to go up to his room. He bowed and followed her upstairs.

Ron and I looked at each other, grinning. Then we ran off to a ready-made tailor's shop to rent our white ties and tails.

That evening, every seat in the union was filled an hour before we made our way into the hall. Students were crouched on the stairs; in the balcony, rows of journalists from London looked down on us.

Ron rapped his gavel. I delivered the speech of welcome that Anthony had translated into French.

Conservatives, Socialists, journalists, everyone stood up and cheered when the emperor in his dainty way stepped forward to the speaker's stand. He signed our register. He spoke in his light, thin voice. He ended with a bow to all of us.

At that moment, an explosion of fireworks lit up the night sky. It was the beginning of a party put on by Barbara Rothschild for me and for my friends.

Entering the Rothschild's house that night was like entering the Athenian Wood in *A Midsummer Night's Dream.* "I am to discourse wonders," said Bottom when he emerged from the Wood, "but ask me not what."

Few of us could remember what had happened when we assembled for breakfast the next morning. John Simonds had the worst headache, and he was seated at the emperor's side. His French was none too good at the best of times, and he soon ran out of conversational phrases. After one awkward silence, he said to the emperor, *"Est-ce-que il-y-a-de* beer *en Abyssine?"*

We waited in silence. The emperor nodded. Among his many wives, he said, he had three whose special assignment was to brew the imperial beer.

*"Il est bon?"* asked John.

The emperor smiled. *"Excellent!"* he said.

When breakfast was over, we assembled in three rows beneath the stone front of St. John's College. Stiff and solemn, we posed for a photograph.

The emperor sits, hands folded, in the center, with Ron on his left side and me on his right. John Simonds is at the far right of the photograph; Maurice Dobb stands at the left side, with Abba Eban beside him; he was Aubrey Eban then.

Many of the students in the photograph were fellow radicals: Gerald Croasdell, Hugh Gordon, Leslie Humphrey, Peter Astbury, Jakes Ewer, Pieter Keuneman, who became the leader of the Opposition Communist party of Ceylon, Kumaramangalam, who went to prison as a Communist in India.

Some, including John, were killed a few years later in a war that might have been prevented had the world heeded the emperor's plea.

British troops cleared a path for his return to Ethiopia. He entered Addis Ababa in triumph on May 5, 1941, and resumed his throne.

Twenty years after the photograph was taken, Whitney called on the emperor in his capacity as chief executive of the British Overseas Airways Corporation. The emperor greeted him warmly. "You are Michael's brother," he said.

*Part Two*

*A Stranger in America*

# "WHEN THOU SEEST AN EAGLE"

IN July 1937, John Simonds and I sailed for America. We bought a car in New York City and drove north to the Adirondack Mountains. We spent a week tramping through forests of white pine, sleeping on balsam boughs, fishing for brook trout and lake trout, and cooking our fish over camp fires.

On the days that it rained, we both wrote letters to Belinda Crompton, who was staying for another year in Cambridge. I wrote also to Herta. She and I had driven through Europe for the last time in June. We had watched Hitler's storm troopers marching through Munich; we had stood in awe before the Isenheim Altarpiece of Mathias Grunewald in Colmar. Now I had to tell her that our days as lovers were over.

Roger Baldwin, the founder and the head of the American Civil Liberties Union, learned that John and I had arrived in America. He invited us to join him in a tour of the Middle West. It would be a grim trip for the most part he said, for the summer of 1937 was marked by violence as the newly formed Congress of Industrial Organizations struggled to unionize the great manufacturing plants of the United States. But, Roger added, he was heading for St. Louis, "where I plan to take a day or two off for a canoe trip if the weather is right. . . . There will be room for you," he added, "so bring along a bathing suit and sneakers and an old pair of pants."

John and I started out at daybreak from our camp on Little Tupper Lake. We drove into Pittsburgh that night and met Roger and his young friend, Trueman Peebles.

The next morning, we called on Philip Murray, the president of the United Steel Workers and, next to John L. Lewis, the leading figure in the C.I.O.

Murray had brought his union through a hard battle. Ten steel workers had been killed and sixty wounded in one fight with company police. It was known as The Chicago Massacre.

Roger was a pacifist; he loathed violence in all its forms. He was also a radical, and he held the companies to blame for the massacre. He feared that it had set back the union, but Murray insisted that it was a victory. He had gained a foothold in the largest mills. He was moving to gain political power over the sheriffs, the police, and the municipal judges so that there would be no more massacres in the steel towns.

We drove on and came to Terre Haute. There, martial law had been in force for three months as the result of a labor dispute. We talked to the chief of police, who told us that the mayor was an agent of the employers. We spent an hour with the secretary of a vigilantes committee, who said that his committee had bribed the police to beat up the strikers. He added that he had obtained a list of the strike leaders and that he had given it to the aging and inert parent of the C.I.O.—the American Federation of Labor. The A.F. of L. had seen to it that the men were fired from their jobs.

We went to the local prison. One hundred and fifty strikers were being held there. We found them packed in with bank robbers and other criminals, in a few cells that were dark and as hot as furnaces.

The cells were in the basement of the prison. Upstairs, we came upon another cell, whose iron door was open. Inside, on a bare cot, we saw a leg, a man's leg. It was pink and shiny, with a leather strap attached to its thigh and a brown sock in a black shoe over its foot.

The owner of the leg hobbled into the cell as we stood there. He apologized for leaving his leg in full view. It got wet he said, when he sweated in the summer heat. He had taken it off to dry it out.

He was hitchhiking to California he told us. He hoped to find work there. He had been felled by the heat in Terre Haute, and the Warden had given him permission to rest in the jail until the weather cooled off a bit.

A good place for a rest, Roger said. He had spent the war in jail as a conscientious objector he told the man. He had been allowed out on Sundays and only once had he caused any trouble. Coming back one Sunday evening, he had found the jail locked. The guard on duty did not like his looks, and he had had one hell of a time talking his way back inside the jail.

The hitchhiker nodded. He asked Roger for the loan of a cigarette; Roger gave him an entire pack. At that, the hitchhiker began to cry.

We drove next to St. Louis and arrived there on the night of the championship fight between Joe Louis and Max Schmeling. Louis won, and all night long, Negro kids roamed the streets, banging on tin cans and yelling, "WE WON!"

A C.I.O. organizer in St. Louis mentioned a series of bombings carried out by an A.F. of L. union to intimidate nonunion companies. I did not believe him, so Roger took me around to the offices of the *Post-Despatch*. The city editor opened his files for me, and after reading them, I knew that the story was true.

We went for lunch that day to a nearby cafeteria. I parked my car and walked back along the street. Next door to the cafeteria was a store that sold firecrackers, conjuror's sets, and Halloween costumes. I saw in the window of the store a trick bomb, made to be attached to cars. So half way through lunch I nudged John. Excusing myself, I said that I had to buy some toothpaste in a nearby drugstore. I bought the bomb and wired it to two spark plugs in Trueman's car. When I sat down again at our table, I wondered aloud if the labor bosses who had been bombing the nonunion plants might try to knock off a visiting head of the Civil Liberties Union for being too inquisitive.

Roger laughed and said pooh pooh. I nudged John again. I conceded that maybe I had been reading too many scary newspaper stories; nonetheless, I said, I thought that Roger should be careful.

We paid our bill and walked outside. Trueman and Roger climbed into their Ford and started it up. There was a piercing whistle, then a tremendous BANG! Clouds of black smoke billowed out from under the cowling of their car.

Roger and Trueman sprang out of the Ford and fled down the street to the corner where John and I were standing, doubled up with laughter. They saw us and the four of us stood there laughing like madmen in the center of a small crowd.

Trueman and John left us in St. Louis. Roger and I set off on a two-day trip in a rented canoe. He had been a passionate libertarian throughout the few days that I had known him. As we stepped into our canoe, he became a passionate naturalist. Water snakes, snapping turtles, parula warblers, wood ducks, they all lived in our new surroundings, and Roger was at home with all of them. Sitting in the front of our canoe, in his shabby clothes, he was wholly content.

It was the first of many canoe trips that Roger and I took together. We went on our last one in the summer of 1978, when Roger was ninety-four years old. He put down his paddle only to pick up his field glasses; the sight of an otter filled him with joy.

"Have you made your peace with your creator?" asked the minister who was brought to Thoreau's bedside when he was near death. Thoreau said, "I did not know that we had quarreled."

Roger shared Thoreau's spirit. He never ceased to fight against intolerance; he never quarreled with life itself.

"I have no objection to dying," he told me when he was ninety-six. "I just don't like being uncomfortable." He was having difficulty breathing by that time, so he could not move beyond the reach of an oxygen tank.

"You can see," he said, "that I'm anchored fast."

My daughter Dinah sent him a Valentine that year. A letter came back:

When the old and the young strike up an understanding like ours, both get the rewards. So I gain as much as you. It's a lovely gift to share and I cherish it.

Your oldest, devoted Valentine

Now, when it is too late, I bitterly regret my inability when I was twenty to share with Roger the story of my own entrapment. But that bitter regret is overcome by a sense of gratitude for the good times that we had together.

I think now of Blake's lines when I remember Roger:

> *When thou seest an eagle lift thy head;*
> *for thou seest a portion of eternity.*

# MORAL SOLITUDE

ROGER and I celebrated my twenty-first birthday in a German beer garden. We headed toward New York, stopping in several cities where he spoke at meetings organized by chapters of the American Civil Liberties Union. He was militant in attacking the corporations for violating the civil rights of their employees. But he never wavered in his assumption that industrial strife in America would be resolved through reliance on the Bill of Rights.

His speeches were wholly persuasive for me. The tension that we had encountered was far greater than anything that John Cornford could point to in his efforts to convince me that the class struggle was the central and enduring characteristic of English society. But the strikes that we had witnessed were part of an industrial struggle, not a class struggle.

The radical tradition that Roger stood for had been embalmed in England by the trade unions. In America it had been refreshed by the New Deal. It was all that I needed, in the way of political leadership. *But at my back I always hear. . . .* The coil that held me was too distant to be visible, too dim to be identified, and, at the same time, too shameful to be revealed to Roger or to anyone else. Like a threatened animal, I could only act as if the threat were not there.

Was it there all the time? My plea to be released had been reviewed by Stalin, so Anthony told me when I had returned to Cambridge. It had been rejected, and I was trapped in a way that neither Anthony nor I could assess.

He had carried out his assignment; we spoke no more about it. But when the time came for me to leave Cambridge, he asked me to meet him in London.

I picked him up on Oxford Street. He directed me to a roadhouse on the Great West Road. There, a stocky, dark-haired Russian met us. He barely smiled, and very little was said. It was a sweltering day, and the Russian spent most of his time in a large and crowded swimming pool. When he heaved himself out and dressed, he ordered a beer. He said a few trivial things about telephoning from public booths to avoid detection. Then he departed. He was more like the agent of a small-time smuggling operation than the representitive of a new international order.

I drove back to London with Anthony. There was little to say. He said only that I would be on my own for some time in America. He asked me as we parted for some highly personal document. I searched in my pockets and found a drawing that had been given to me. He tore it into two ragged pieces. He handed one piece to me and kept the other, saying that it would be handed back to me by the man who some day in the future would approach me in New York.

---- ∽ ----

Razumov leaves Victor Haldin lying on his bed the evening Haldin comes to his rooms. He goes out into the winter night and stands in the snow, wondering what to do. If he aids Haldin, he becomes an accomplice in a criminal act. If he goes to the police, then, as he comes in time to realize, he betrays not only Haldin but also himself.

"He longed desperately for a word of advice," Conrad tells us. In one of his own, reflective asides he continues, "Who knows what true loneliness is—not the conventional word, but the naked terror? To the lonely themselves it wears a mask. The most miserable outcast hugs some memory or illusion. Now and then a fatal conjunction of events may lift the veil for an instant. For an instant only. No human being could bear a steady view of moral solitude without going mad."

Roger and I parted company when we arrived back in New York. John Simonds was there but within a few days he sailed for England.

I was altogether alone. I had no roots in America; no old friends; no accepted tradition to lean against; no rational hope to look forward to. I could not go to Roger or to the police. I could not reconcile myself to the position that I was in. Yet if it continued, I would spend the only life that I had in deception. I would in time become ingrown, suspicious, unloving. I would never be able to share my mind and my heart with another human being.

I had some sense of moral solitude, yet, as Conrad knew, no man can bear it for long. If strangers approached me and wanted to talk to me, I watched them warily and waited. Beyond that, I shut all

thoughts of Anthony out of my consciousness. I pretended to myself
that the trap that I was in was an illusion. I told myself that the ragged
piece of a drawing that had been taken from me would never be thrust
back into my hand.

# HUNTING FOR A JOB

I NEEDED to find a job in America. I began my search by calling
my father's old friends—businessmen and bankers, diplomats and
retired generals. All of them spoke of my father with reverence. Most
of them spoke with such venom about President Roosevelt and his
wife that I wondered if they would support an armed uprising against
the government of the United States.

America was in a recession in the autumn of 1937. As it deepened,
the hopes that I had of finding a job dimmed. I had been promised
jobs with the National Resources Planning Board and the National
Labor Relations Board. Those promises were broken—as they had to
be when the New Deal agencies were cut back. Secretary of Labor
Frances Perkins kept a clerical position open for me, but Jonathan
Mitchell told me not to take it. I wrote to my mother, "Jonathan says
that she commands little respect in Washington. She is like someone
with a jewel he says, who instead of enjoying it, is obsessed by the fear
that it will be stolen from her."

I went to see Roosevelt in his White House study. He tried to think
of agencies that might take me on; he gave up. "Why not get some
outside experience and *then* join the government," he said.

For lack of anything better to do, I went to Fiorello LaGuardia's
headquarters in New York. I signed on as a volunteer in his campaign
to be re-elected as the mayor of New York. I asked if I could work
on the East Side, for LaGuardia. I was given a stretch of Park Avenue
and told to get out the vote for LaGuardia's runningmate, Thomas E.
Dewey.

Dewey was elected in November. I set out once again in search of
a job. I listened, during many interviews, to sad stories about the state
of the American economy. I nodded politely, in response to a good
many apologies.

My Godfather, Henry Fletcher, was the one who told me to face
reality. There was only one place in America, he said, where my

qualifications would enable me to find a position—the Department of State.

How, I asked, was I to gain an entrance to the department? My Godfather, who had sworn in 1932 and again in 1936 that he would renounce his American citizenship if "that man" were elected president, looked at me with a grim expression.

"You must ask Mrs. Roosevelt," he said.

A radical Quaker named Don Stephens appeared at Old Westbury with his wife, Inky. I mentioned my need to hunt down Mrs. Roosevelt. Don said that he was in hot pursuit of her.

I put on my best blue suit, my best white shirt, my shiniest shoes. Inky drove us to the nearest railroad station, and Don and I set out for the coal mines of West Virginia.

We stayed overnight in a Quaker home near Arthurdale and arose with our host while it was still dark. We wanted to be helpful, but neither Don nor I could milk a cow.

We borrowed a car and drove to the planned community built by the Roosevelt administration to resettle the families of miners who were unemployed. At ten, Mrs. Roosevelt arrived with Doris Duke, a young heiress whom she hoped to interest in social work. They went into the miners' homes, and we followed them. In each house, Mrs. Roosevelt settled down as if she had lived among the miners all her life.

Doris Duke departed at noon. Mrs. Roosevelt drove to a section of the community that was still under construction. There, her Packard limousine sank up to its axles in two feet of mud.

Mrs. Roosevelt sat serenely in the back of the limousine. A group of miners waded into the mud to rescue her. I looked on for a moment—then joined them. We pushed and heaved; the wheels of the Packard spun around. By the time that it rolled up onto solid ground, I and the miners looked as though we had been sculpted in mud.

I groped my way to the window of the Packard and introduced myself. I was mortified by my appearance, but Mrs. Roosevelt found it reassuring. She invited me to sit beside her and kept me beside her when she made a speech to the residents of the community. "Years ago," she began, "I and this young man's mother. . . ." It made me proud and happy to be standing at her side.

She had to drive fifty miles to catch a train to New York. She asked me to drive with her, so we were alone for an hour and a half.

She said that in every town she had visited, men and women had been told that they would lose their jobs unless the Democrats were defeated in the 1938 campaign. The recession, she believed, was in part a deliberate maneuver by the great corporations to force the president to repeal his reforms.

"I would be a Communist," she said, "if I thought that Russia was comparable to America."

I made no response to that. Instead, I mentioned my own desire to work for the administration. The State Department seemed to be my best chance, I added. She promised to write a letter on my behalf to Sumner Welles, the under secretary of state.

She kept her word. One week later, I went to Washington to keep an appointment with Welles. I arrived in time to learn all that I could about him from Jonathan Mitchell. Jonathan's stories were disconcerting to say the least; they barely prepared me for the man.

He was tall and forbidding, with a thin moustache and cold, green eyes.

"Ignore his forbidding exterior," Jonathan had told me. "It's his wife's fault. Underneath, he's as shy and as vulnerable as they come."

Welles did not seem vulnerable to me. He stretched out a hand that felt like a frozen mackerel. He stood in silence, waiting for me to speak.

I told him what I hoped to do in Washington. His expression never altered.

"You have a long, hard road in front of you," he said.

I walked from the department to 1718 H Street, the house that my father and his friends had shared when they were young bachelors, working for the State Department. George Summerlin, the chief of protocol for the department, met me at the door. He was a little old man with white hair and a wicked smile. "Call me Summy," he said.

Summy made two old-fashioneds. He proposed a toast to the Good Old Days. He kept on "freshening up" our drinks until it was time for him to dress for dinner.

Summy dined out, as he did every night. I studied the rows of solemn faces in the photographs that lined the room; the starched collars; the righteous looks. I settled down with a book. At midnight the front door opened an inch at a time. Summy crept in on tiptoe. He turned twice in a pirouette; he saw me and froze, swaying slightly. To cover his embarassment, he poured us both a whiskey-and-soda. He talked for half an hour, mostly about the spare ribs that his hostess had fed him. He placed his fingers on his lips and blew an imaginary kiss to their memory.

A second meeting kept me on in Washington. The two hundred soldiers who had sailed to France under my father's command in 1917 had formed an association named for him. They were to meet in the Willard Hotel to celebrate the twentieth anniversary of their departure for France, and I had agreed to address them.

They were insurance salesmen and store managers; solid citizens from the small towns of America. Most of them had been drinking for an hour or more by the time that I arrived at the banquet. They tried to appear sober as Mel Ryder, the secretary of the association led me around the room. "Mike," they kept saying, "Mike . . . it's an honor . . . an honor. Your father was a prince—a prince among men."

We sat down to dinner. When it was over, Mel stood up. He held a sheaf of telegrams and letters from members of the association who had been unable to make it to Washington. "Here's one from old Jim," said Mel swaying back and forth with the tears rolling down his cheeks. "Terribly sorry . . . just can't make it. My doctor tells me . . . give my regards. . . .

"Good old Jim," said Mel as he laid the letter down. He picked up the next letter. "Here's another—terrible, terrible sorry. . . ."

"Who's it from?" everybody shouted.

"How should I know," Mel murmured. He wandered off to be sick.

I looked on, dismayed. I wanted very much to establish some bond with these men who had followed my father to France. In my best Cambridge Union manner, I had written out and memorized an address that I had assumed would move them all to tears. It included lines from my father's letters to my mother in which he had prophesied that there would be no lasting peace. I had added the words spoken by the soldier in *Le Tombeau sous l'Arc de Triomphe.*

Those texts were almost sacred for me. I did not want to dishonor them. But if I set them aside, what could I say?

I stood up when Mel introduced me. I rushed through my quotations; my father's words of warning; the Soldier's bitter cry: "Remember us. Only remember us. That is what men say at the front. . . . Let him stand forth whose voice is strong enough to speak for us. . . . He will only have to remember. . . . His cry will echo down the ages. When history is dust, his voice will still be ringing. Who knows, it may even reach to us! And then, in what peace we shall sleep!"

There was a long silence when I finished. Then Mel heaved himself up and called on everyone to rise. He held up his glass with the last of his whiskey in it. "To the Major!" he cried, and they all echoed: "To the Major!"

As if that was a signal, the doors opened. A man in a well-worn dinner jacket came in, carrying a sheaf of musical scores. A woman in purple satin shorts and a white satin shirt followed and perched herself on top of a piano.

The healthiest of the veterans formed a circle around her. They wanted her to join them in the old songs: *Mademoiselle from Armentieres* and *Tipperary,* but she had never heard of those songs. She sang the ones that she knew.

Most of the veterans were ready for bed by then. As they left, they came up to me to shake hands once more and to say one more word about "the Major."

One little man named Tommy Shiels came back four times to shake my hand. My father, Mel explained, had bailed him out of several jails in France, and Tommy hadn't forgotten.

"Mike," he said, each time that he gripped my hand, "Mike, I'm Tommy."

"Yes, Tommy; I know."

"Mike, your father was a great man . . . He was the kindest sweetest, ablest, greatest man I ever knew. *And that's no bullshit!*"

Mel was offended for my sake. "Tommy," he said. "You've been drinking."

As if Tommy didn't know.

# THE DEPARTMENT OF STATE

THERE were no openings in the Foreign Service or in the specialized staff that worked in Washington for the Department of State. I was accepted as an unpaid volunteer, working on temporary assignment in the Office of the Economic Adviser.

The economic adviser was a diminutive historian named Herbert Feis. Other men would comb their hair as they hurried down the corridors of the Old State Department in response to a summons from Secretary Hull. Feis, who looked like Harpo Marx, would ruffle up his sheepshead of white curls.

He lived in Georgetown. He haunted the watering places of the Establishment, such as the Metropolitan Club. His wife, who was a Protestant, made a point of drawing his young assistants aside and confiding to them that she had suffered greatly in the social circles of Washington because she was married to a Jew.

Feis did not know what to make of me. He was uneasy about my ties to the White House. He sensed that I was too headstrong to survive for long. He took me out to lunch after I had been on his staff for a few days. He warned me of all the obstacles that I would face if I tried to make a career for myself in the department. The distrust of originality; the insistence on conformity; the abhorrence of independence; the fear of reform. . . . Feis ticked them off on his fingers. There were only four or five original minds in the department, he said; all the other men avoided responsibility, expressed no personal opinions, and probably had none.

He looked at me sharply. "What is it that you wish to accomplish in the department?" he asked.

"I want to write a long report."

"On what?"

"On Hitler's capacity to wage a major war."

Feis nodded and told me to go ahead.

I went to work with a good deal of pent-up energy. For five months I had been arguing about Europe with my American friends. They were isolationists for the most part. They believed that Europe's quarrels were none of their concern; they assumed that America's protection lay not in the free nations of the world but in the inhibitions imposed upon our own government by the Neutrality Act.

I had encountered these attitudes in the editors of *The New Republic* and in political leaders whom I admired, such as Senator La Follette. I did not know, as Feis knew, that the same attitudes were prevalent within the Department of State.

Feis's principal adversary within the department was Secretary Hull's own economic adviser, an owlish little man named Leo Pasvolsky. He believed in the laws of classical economics and, accordingly, was convinced that Hitler would drive Germany into bankruptcy if he embarked on a major rearmament effort or a prolonged war.

I had no access to classified documents; I did not need them. Working from published sources, I set out to demonstrate that, given centralized control and management, Europe had enough raw materials, enough industrial capacity, enough food and manpower to enable Hitler to rearm Germany and to go to war.

I worked for three months on my report. It was absorbing work for me, but in my letters to my mother, I noted that I was meeting a number of interesting men. One was "a really intelligent man named Dean Acheson"; another was a liberal congressman named Maury Maverick.

Maury invited me to supper in his apartment in Washington. Charles Beard, the historian, and his wife were there.

Beard chuckled about the description of himself in *Time:* "Old Man Beard, now deaf and senile. . . ." He told a nice story about Nicholas Murray Butler, the president of Columbia University. "Have you read Beard's last book?" someone asked Butler. He said, "I certainly hope so!"

When supper was over, Maury read aloud the draft of a speech that he was preparing to deliver on foreign policy. It was not very good. I asked if I might work on it, and Maury handed it to me. I rewrote it, and the *New York Times* gave it a full column.

I lived at 1718 H Street with Summy, Joseph Alsop, the columnist, and a banker, Major Heath. We were cared for by an elderly couple,

James and Julia, who had been there in my father's time. James would serve us breakfast each morning, laying a copy of the *Washington Post* beside our napkins. We would read the *Post* over coffee, pausing to nod when Major Heath groaned aloud in rage and despair, on learning of Roosevelt's latest assault upon the banks. At nine, Summy and I would walk together to the Old State Department—the ornate mass of gray stone, with its high ceilings, its circular staircases, and its long, resounding corridors. I would scribble away at my desk through the mornings and a part of the afternoons. But the department was still a place of employment for gentlemen, and gentlemen were not supposed to overexert themselves at work. We lingered over luncheon, and by six, we were supposed to have cleaned off our desks and departed. Jay Pierrepont Moffat, the chief of the European division, would pass my open door on his way home from the department. If he saw me still at work, he would pause. Glancing at his watch, he would remind me that I had only an hour in which to bathe and dress if, as he assumed, I was dining out.

I was an "eligible bachelor" in those days and therefore in some demand. My antecedents, my income, and my financial prospects were matters on which the hostesses of Washington prided themselves on being well informed.

At Mrs. Robert Low Bacon's and at Mrs. Truxtun Beale's, the hostess and her contemporaries moved from the dinner table to the bridge table after coffee had been served. The Young Set—Joe Alsop and I and the unmarried ladies who had been seated beside us—were sent off to another room with instructions to amuse ourselves by playing "The Game." Obedient as we were, we divided into teams, and, one by one, acted out some word that the opposing team gave to us, which our team had to guess. We spent many evenings writhing around on well-polished floors while our teammates shouted "Train!" and "Snake!" and the seconds ticked by.

It was a well-ordered life while it lasted; it could not last for long.

# "MICHAEL GREEN"

"HE had the blind passionate innocence of a boy," says Graham Greene of one of his characters; "like a boy, he was driven relentlessly toward inevitable suffering, loss and despair, and called it happiness."

In the spring of 1938, the Crompton family returned from Cambridge to their home in Rye. It was my hope that their youngest daughter and I could share a happy life together.

She knew nothing of my underground life in Cambridge; I persuaded myself that it would never catch up with me. Then, as I was sitting alone in 1718 H Street, one evening in late April, the telephone rang.

I picked up the receiver and said hello. I heard the thick voice of a stranger, speaking in a European accent.

"Mr. Straight? . . . I bring you greetings . . . from your friends in Cambridge University. . . ."

He was in a nearby restaurant, so he said. I agreed to meet him there.

Sitting alone at a table for two, a dark-haired man in a tight-fitting business suit was watching the entrance to the restaurant. As I walked in, he nodded to me.

He stood up, smiling a warm, friendly smile, as I approached his table. He stretched out his hand and held mine in a firm, friendly grip.

"My name is Michael; the same as yours," he said.

I waited.

"Michael Green," he said, still smiling.

So . . . my fantasy that my past would never cross the Atlantic Ocean was a fantasy, nothing more. I sat down, feeling as if I had been clubbed.

Green, in contrast, was perfectly at ease.

A waitress hovered above us. I shook my head. Green waited until she had wandered away. Then he bent toward me.

"I must first of all apologize," he began. It had taken him some time to find me, he said, since he did not know where I was living. He could not produce his half of the drawing; it had been "mislaid."

He had ordered a substantial dinner. He ate it with relish; I watched him as he ate. He was dark and stocky, with broad lips and a ready smile. His English was good; his manner was affable and easy. He seemed to be enjoying his life in America.

He asked in a routine way about the work that I was doing. He seemed to be only mildly interested in my reply. He was not disconcerted when I said that I was only an unpaid volunteer on temporary assignment in the Department of State. He suggested simply that when interesting documents crossed my desk, I should take them home "to study."

I told him that no documents were routed through my desk. He nodded. Not for the present, he seemed to be saying, but in time. . . .

He ended up his dinner with coffee. As he sipped it, he delivered a monologue on the developing perspectives of the peace movement. It was apparently part of his assignment, for I was given a set lecture every time that we met. He asked if I had any questions when he completed his remarks. I had none. He called for his bill, saying that he had to catch a train.

I drove him to the Union Station. We drew in under its tall columns, and, for a minute, he sat in the darkness of my car. He would be back in a month or so, he said. He would telephone me. Meanwhile, he wanted me to memorize the name and the telephone number of a friend in Brooklyn, whom I might call in case of an emergency. I repeated the name and the number and at once forgot them. I knew that they would never be used by me.

He seemed well pleased as he thrust out his hand. For me, his appearance was a disaster, yet we parted as friends.

Was it my Apostolic attitude that led me to see him as an individual rather than as a cog in a Soviet machine? Why did I see him at all?

It would have been hard for me at that moment to have defined my political beliefs. I was not a Communist yet I had underlined the words of Pietro Spina in Silone's novel *Bread and Wine:* "The only Christian life today is a revolutionary one." I was not able to repudiate John Cornford and my own past in Cambridge. Nor was I willing to be a Soviet agent in the Department of State.

I was too stunned to think clearly as I drove back down Pennsylvania Avenue. I knew only that I could not stay on at the State Department for long.

Who then would help me to escape? He did not know it, but my ally was to be Maury Maverick, the congressman from San Antonio.

# MAURY MAVERICK

MAURY was never a handsome man. He had a thick neck and an immense head. He looked a bit like a bullfrog.

He had enlisted as a private in the First World War and was badly wounded. His back was broken; his body, twisted. It was painful for him to stand, but he never mentioned his pain.

Maury was elected mayor of San Antonio during the Depression. By aligning himself with Roosevelt and Lyndon Johnson, who was running the Texas office of the National Youth Administration, he was able to accomplish a great deal for his city. Among the projects that he carried through was the preservation and restoration of an original Mexican village. It winds along the San Antonio River and is known today as *La Villita.*

Maury was elected to Congress in 1934. He soon became a leader of the Southern liberals. In the counteroffensive of the Conservatives, in 1938, he was challenged by a radio commentator who had the strong backing of the businessmen and the bankers of San Antonio.

Maury sensed that he was in trouble. He needed funds. He would not come to me himself, but he asked Roosevelt's aide, Tom Corcoran, to approach me. Tom went in turn to Joe Alsop, and, with a good deal of hemming and hawing, Joe took Tom and me to lunch.

The New Deal was in retreat in 1938, but Tom was still at the height of his power. He was forceful and eloquent—a field commander in action and an Irish poet at heart.

Tom's imagery was startling. Joe complained at lunch about the way in which the White House was using the Works Progress Administration as a political tool. Tom sighed.

"Joe," he said. "Joe! You are the Pegasus of politics!"

Tom took me aside when our luncheon was over. The bankers and the businessmen, he said, were in the field, well armed, after four years of acquiescence in the New Deal. They were setting out to defeat the best of the New Dealers in the Democratic primaries, and if they succeeded, the gains made by Roosevelt would be undermined.

"You are a friend of the president's," Tom said. "You come from a great American family, with a long tradition of supporting the best elements in our national life."

I still did not know what was coming.

"Maury is the best of the Southerners," Tom said. "His defeat would be a bitter blow for the president. Nonetheless, he's facing defeat unless we can get some money to him."

"Go on."

"Maury wouldn't ask you himself," Tom said, "but he asked me to ask you. Can you help him?"

"I can give him ten thousand dollars," I said.

"Great!" said Tom. "I want you to go down to San Antonio," he added. "I want you to watch the campaign. It will be an introductory course in American politics for you. If you take to it, as I think you will, I want you to come back and work for me."

A kindly old messenger named Clarence laid the *Economist* and other journals on my desk in the State Department as he moved slowly on his rounds. Late in June, he brought me a letter with a postmark *San Antonio.* It was from Maury.

132 AFTER LONG SILENCE

Dear Mike:

The campaign here has broken out like the smallpox, only it is on such a low plane as to make certain other diseases more appropriate for identification.

The Sun shines bright and hot. There is a great thundering about the C.I.O. and Communism is bandied back and forth across the ether.

I have an idea that this will be interesting to you because it is new to most Americans. As I've told you, we have 100,000 Mexican-Americans in San Antonio. The lives and the habits of the people are entirely different from other parts of the United States.

We can show you slums *par*—I started to say *par excellence,* but I should say *par degredado.*

Mainly, I want you to know that you will be welcome here. You will be treated like a bum. At the end of a week, I predict you will be a bum, actual and perfect. But, if your young lady comes, we will treat her like a young lady, so everyone will be happy.


My young lady's parents thought it unwise for her to go to San Antonio with me. I went alone and stayed for ten days with Maury and his wife, Terrill.

Each morning, Maury and I drove downtown to his office in the city. A hundred or more Mexicans would be waiting outside his door, holding their babies in their arms. He spent his mornings trying to help them. In the afternoons, he toured the city, speaking in schools, in churches, in market places, and in union halls.

At one rally in the Mexican quarter, three men wearing *sombreros* plucked their guitars and sang. They sang a mournful ballad that they had written, and Wanda Ford, who had studied at Dartington, translated it for me: "In San Antonio/before Mister Maverick was our Mayor the V.D. rate/ was seventy nine percent. . . ."

I took my Leica camera with me when I went to San Antonio. Maury insisted that I carry it with me wherever I went. After a day or two, I noticed that I was being treated with undue deference. People nodded and tipped their hats to me; they stepped off the pavements to let me pass.

I mentioned it to Maury; he shrugged his shoulders. Then, one morning, the reporter who was covering the campaign for the San Antonio *Light* drew me aside.

"Tell me," he said, "how are things at the bureau?"

"The bureau?"

"Sure; what's J. Edgar up to?"

"J. Edgar?"

"Hoover. We all know you work for the F.B.I.!"

"The F.B.I.!" I was naïve in those days, but I knew that to J. Edgar Hoover, impersonating an F.B.I. agent was the most dastardly crime that anyone could commit.

I asked Maury where on earth that rumor had started up. He grinned. He admitted that he had spread the story around that I was an F.B.I. agent, sent down by Roosevelt to make sure that his opponent did not steal the election. I was, supposedly, taking pictures with my Leica that could be used as evidence later on.

I protested mightily. Maury laughed. If I should be arrested, he said, he would put in a good word for me with Hoover.

The reporter from the *Light* asked me another question:

"Where is Maury getting all his money from?"

"Is he getting a lot of money?"

"Enough to give me twenty bucks for every story that I write about him."

Maury nodded when I mentioned this exchange to him. "It's a bad practice," he said. "It began during the Depression, when the reporters were hungry, and it never stopped."

Negroes were banned from all public facilities in San Antonio in 1938. They were banned as guests in almost all white households.

The household where Maury lived with his mother was no exception, but Maury paid no attention to the ban. He invited his black friends into his mother's home.

"Maury," said his mother when his guests were departing after a barbecue, "it seems to me that some of your guests were mighty dark-skinned."

"I was going to keep up the pretense," said Maury; "then I thought, oh, what the hell. The old lady might as well face the truth. So I said to her, 'Momma, you know something, you been entertaining some goddamn niggers in your house!'

"She looked at me long and hard," said Maury, "but she never said a word."

We laughed a good many times in the course of my ten days in San Antonio, but the laughter could not go on for long.

Maury's opponent had a major radio station at his command. He broadcast his commentary night after night, and he used it to discredit and to weaken Maury. As voting day approached he began to describe the dresses that his wife was buying in preparation for their move to Washington. I thought he was being gauche, but his confidence proved to be well founded. When half of the returns were in, Maury knew that he was beaten. Even the Mexican wards had turned against him. He guessed that they had been bought, but he never mentioned it. He conceded defeat at his headquarters; we drove home to his house. His political life was over.

# MY LIES

MY time was not bound by office routine, since I was a volunteer rather than an employee for the State Department. So when my mother rented a house in Woods Hole in the summer of 1938, I joined her there.

In September I returned to my desk in the State Department. Neville Chamberlain was on his way to Munich by then. War was close at hand. But in the department, life continued at its leisurely pace.

My report on Europe went the rounds of the department and came back to my desk with a number of comments attached to it. Secretary Hull wrote "Splendid!" across its cover. Acheson praised it. Alger Hiss called me down to his office to discuss the points that I had raised. Charles Yost noted quite rightly that it amounted to a plea for American participation in a common effort to resist Hitler. The Neutrality Act, he argued, was a better safeguard for peace.

Feis said nothing, and he gave me no new assignments. Left to myself, I wrote a second report for Secretary Hull on the political situation in England. I argued that the Labour party was incapable of winning an election or of forming a government. Where the alternative leadership to Chamberlain would come from, I did not know.

A position opened up in September in the Office of the Economic Adviser. Rather reluctantly, Feis offered it to me. I was waiting to hear from Tom Corcoran and, to Feis's surprise, turned his offer down.

Green came to Washington in June and again in September. I gave him copies of my report, and of the trade summaries that I had prepared. He disappeared with them and, reappearing after an hour or so, handed them back to me. They were of little or no value to him —we both knew that. He did his best nonetheless to be patient, hoping no doubt that in time the State Department would offer me a job in which I would have access to something of interest to Moscow.

I said nothing to him about the job that I had turned down. But when he came to Washington in October, I told him that I was leaving the State Department.

"Leaving the State Department! And where will you go?"

"To the Department of Interior."

"The Department of the Interior!"

I nodded. Ben Cohen worked there as general counsel of the National Power Policy Committee. Tom Corcoran used the committee as a field command post for his political activities. He had offered me a job, writing speeches for the president, the cabinet, and the liberal leaders of the Congress. I had accepted his offer. For me, it was a great opportunity as well as a welcome escape.

It was an escape from the trap that had held me captive. I could not present it in that light to Michael Green.

For his sake, as well as for my own, I had to invent some reason for my action that he could pass on to his superiors.

I was a poor liar, but, lying awake through many hours of darkness, I had built up a casual remark of Tom's into a convincing lie.

"I will be working for Secretary Ickes," I told Green. "He is to be appointed secretary of war. When he moves over to the War Department, I'll move with him."

"Ickes is to be secretary of war?" Green's dark eyes widened.

I nodded. "No one knows it yet," I said.

"Very good!" said Green. Then he looked closely at me. How, he wanted to know, had I learned of this interesting development?

"From Tom Corcoran," I said, and that much at least was true.

Tom knew that the New Deal was over. He believed that Roosevelt would spend his remaining days in the White House in building up our defenses or else in waging war. He sensed that Roosevelt would have to place civilian leaders in the War Department whom he could work with and whom the nation would respect. He had little knowledge of international affairs and not much feeling for military matters, beyond his loathing for the Corps of Army Engineers. He saw the War Department as a citadel to be captured, and, in one of his wilder moments, he had wondered aloud if Harold Ickes might take over the department from Harry Woodring, the political hack whom Roosevelt had allowed to serve as secretary of war.

Documents published for the first time in 1982 reveal that Tom Corcoran was not the only man who had his eye upon the War Department. From his seat high up on the Supreme Court, Felix Frankfurter was hard at work in 1938 in an effort to replace Woodring with a strong supporter of the Allies.

Roosevelt, so the documents indicate, told Frankfurter that Ickes was one of three men whom he was considering for the War Department. Frankfurter dismissed all three as unworthy of serious consideration. He sensed, as I did, that Roosevelt was playing a political game, and that he would never turn Ickes loose among the generals.

Pretense was a part of Roosevelt's game, but Michael Green could not know that. So the pretended candidacy of Harold Ickes served another, unseen, purpose for me. Short of physical violence or of blackmail, Green could not have prevented me from leaving the State Department, but his assent to my move made it easier for me.

I had not freed myself from my own past, but in moving from a sensitive department of the government to a job that was purely political, I had gained my first, small foothold on the possibility of leading an honest and an honorable life.

# CORCORAN AND COHEN

CORCORAN and Cohen were a famous team in the great days of the New Deal. They were men of contrasting but marvellously matched talents.

Tom was the Bold Man, resolute in action. Ben was the Wise Man, meticulous in thought. Tom would embark on a course that led to confrontation with a powerful antagonist. Ben would insist on a settlement in his mild-mannered way. Tom would listen, shaking his head, as Ben reasoned with him in his quavering voice. He would sigh deeply. "Brother Ben," he would say. "Brother Ben, you are too good for this world."

Ben was born in Muncie, Indiana—the place, as he was fond of pointing out, that Robert and Helen Lynd had portrayed in their study: *Middletown.* For them, Muncie was a model of provincial America, but there was nothing provincial about Ben. He had been an active Zionist as a law student and had worked in New York until Tom brought him to Washington. He was the equal of Felix Frankfurter in critical intelligence and in legal draftsmanship but lacked Frankfurter's compulsion to secure for himself all that the legal profession could offer in statute and renown.

He owned one, navy blue suit, which was mottled with old cigarette ashes. His diet, as far as I could tell, consisted of coffee and cigarettes. He worked through many nights and never seemed to tire.

Once, in the course of an all-night session, a fourth member of our speech-writing team, Jim Rowe, looked at his watch.

"It's three in the morning," he announced, "and I'm going home to bed."

Ben did not even glance up from his papers. "The trouble with you, Jim," he said, "is that you need too much sleep."

Tom was the grandson of an Irish immigrant. His mother used to point to the immigrants who were still pouring into America from Ireland when he was a boy. "The cowards never started," she would tell her son. "The weak died on the way."

He fought his own way upward in America. He made a fortune on Wall Street, in the boom and lost it in the crash. He went to Washington during the Depression to work for the Reconstruction Finance Corporation. Roosevelt spotted him there and sent him up to Capitol Hill to push through legislation regulating the stock exchange. He soon became the president's political commander in the field.

Tom was a romantic, passionate in his convictions, emotional in his judgments, tender and generous with those whom he loved. He revered his heroes and rarely forgave his enemies. The man whose mind and style he most admired was Oliver Wendell Holmes, the great jurist whose law clerk he had been after his graduation from Harvard Law School. He had an armory of appropriate quotations from Holmes, and he turned them to his own uses. Some pedants questioned whether all of the quotations were authentic; Tom ignored them. His attitude, as Jim Rowe noted, was: "Well, . . . Holmes would have said it if he'd thought of it."

Like Ben, Tom cared little for the trappings of power. He had no car, no wardrobe, no place to lay his head, save for the pokey apartment that he and Ben shared. He had no imposing office of his own and no staff, except for Peggy Dowd, who did his typing, took his messages, sent for his coffee and sandwiches, and straightened his tie.

He was always on the move. When he arrived at any resting place, his first question was Can I use your phone? He talked on the telephone from dawn until midnight. On the rare occasions when Peggy dragged him off to parties, he would take his accordion with him. He did not drink, but when those around him were well primed, his host would call for silence. Then Tom would bring out his accordion and sing. The songs that he sang were sea shanties, ballads, Irish airs. The one that he loved best was about a Confederate veteran in the days of Reconstruction that followed the Civil War. Its last line was "I won't be reconstructed, and I don't give a damn!" Tom would sing that line with tremendous gusto; he would draw one last chord from his accordion, then he would burst into laughter.

Speeches were important in the days before television transformed the political scene. Writing speeches was a small but necessary chore for Tom and Ben, and I was able to help them in a minor way. If a Roosevelt supporter in the Senate needed a speech, I would write it, emphasizing always the dual necessity of resisting Hitler and protecting the social gains made by the New Deal. If the members of the Cabinet asked for help, Tom would talk through with me the themes that he wanted to stress, and I would write a first draft for him. If Roosevelt was to make a speech, he would talk it over with Tom and Ben. They would prepare a draft for Roosevelt, and I would help them polish it.

The major political speech that had to be drafted each year was one that Roosevelt delivered at the Jackson Day dinner of the Democratic party. The dinner was the principal ingathering of the faithful in noncampaign years; Roosevelt, in his role as party leader, used the occasion each year to set forth the basic line that he wanted the party to follow.

Jackson Day 1939 was a difficult moment for the president. He was approaching the end of his second term in office. He had used up his political reserves in a futile effort to pack the Supreme Court. He had failed in his effort to defeat six of his conservative opponents in the primary elections of 1938. That effort, known as The Purge had been initiated by Harry Hopkins, who was determined to punish a senator from his native state of Iowa. It resulted in one minor victory—the replacement of Representative John O'Connor in New York—and in five costly defeats.

Roosevelt had been fond of saying that a man should be known by his enemies. He had criticized his protégé, Lyndon Johnson, because Johnson in his hunger for affection was willing to be all things to all men. Then, as war approached in Europe and the 1940 campaign loomed larger, Roosevelt sensed that he had to gain the support of his former enemies.

What banner could he raise for the faithful to rally around on Jackson Day? Support for the British and the French was the most divisive and dangerous of issues. The New Deal was in decline. His own future within the Democratic party was a matter that he could discuss with no one.

The speech that Tom and Ben prepared was a masterpiece. It began with an imaginary conversation with the ghost of Andrew Jackson. It ended with one of Tom's stories about the Orangemen and the Fenians in the Irish Civil War. In between was an impassioned appeal that was directed as much to the president himself as to his party—to move to the right, *but not too far.*

It was a line of battle that could not be held for long. I wrote to my mother in February, "Everyone is gloomy. Joe Alsop says that he has lost interest in the 1940 campaign. He hopes only that Roosevelt will establish a sound foreign policy before he departs from the White House, or is driven from it."

Tom drove himself to exhaustion. He ended up in a hospital. He left the hospital against the advice of his doctor and collapsed.

He was taken back to the hospital. I visited him there. He had a high fever; his hands were restless, and his eyes were unnaturally bright.

"This is going to be a quiet time for us," he told me. "There's nothing that we can do just now. It's like watching a forest fire advancing across your land and burning everything you own. Sometimes you've got to sit and watch it, waiting until it burns itself out."

Roosevelt was scheduled to make another speech in May. I wrote a first draft, based on Tom's ideas. It was scrapped. Ben prepared a second draft and I rewrote it. It too was scrapped.

Tom and Ben prepared a third draft and took it over to the White House. I climbed into my car and drove to Maryland. The dogwoods were in flower that day; the trees were filled with warblers, moving through the region on their way north. I spent the day searching them out in the foliage, as they paused to utter their feeble songs.

I lost the ache in my eye sockets. I went back to our office in the evening and found Tom and Ben hard at work on a fourth draft. Tom smiled at me. "You see how interesting it is," he said, "to watch the transmogrification of a speech."

We worked steadily, cutting, strengthening, sharpening the text. Ben lay down on his couch for an hour at 3:00 A.M. Tom worked on. I crawled through a window and sat on the roof of the Interior Department. The night was bright and still. I could see the Washington Monument in the distance. It became darker in silhouette as the morning light filled the sky.

We left the office at 6:45 A.M. We walked back to the apartment that Tom and Ben shared. The city was silent; the streets were bare, save for the milkmen and garbage collectors.

We worked through the next day in the White House and finished up at 5:30 P.M. At 7:00, we took our places in the banqueting hall of the hotel where the president was to speak.

He made his way on crutches to the dais. He stood there, smiling, as everyone rose and cheered. By then, it seemed to me, we had hammered his speech into an inert and shapeless mass; I was mistaken. When he spoke, the words that we had labored over for so long flamed into life.

# A SMALL HOUSE
# ON PRINCE STREET

"I'D like to take a few days off," I told Tom Corcoran. It was two in the morning, and we had just finished the draft of a speech.

"What for?" Tom asked.

"To get married."

"Why now?"

"Because there's going to be a war."

Tom nodded. He said, "Is she healthy?"

"Oh, sure."

"Did she have a happy childhood?"

"As happy as most kids."

He nodded again. "Get married on a Saturday," he said. "Then you can have the weekend for your honeymoon."

"That's what we plan to do," I said.

He was impressed by my devotion to duty. "Take three days off," he said. Then, perhaps, he thought of Peggy, who was typing our draft in the outer office.

"For those three days," he added, "make her think that she's the only thing in the world that matters to you."

―⚭―

We were married under an oak willow in New Hampshire and set off to spend our three days on Nantucket. The trees were beginning to turn in early September; the nights were already chill.

In Washington, we went house-hunting. We settled on a little brick house in Alexandria—the old town that lies just below Washington, on the Potomac River. The house was on Prince Street, a cobbled lane that slopes down to the river. It was one of a row of houses built by sea captains in the days when Alexandria was a great port. In later days, Prince Street had become a red-light district. There were still some faint numbers on our bedroom doors.

We lived in a light-blue bedroom. The sunlight woke us up in the mornings as we lay in bed. It was an idyllic life, save for a few alarms.

One night, for example, we were woken by the sound of scraping on the window beneath us. It was being forced open by an intruder.

The newspapers had been filled with stories about a Soviet defector, General Walter Krivitsky, who had been found dead in his room in a Washington hotel. He had, it was thought, been murdered by the Soviet secret police. For one moment, I thought: *They've come for me.*

I crept downstairs. The intruder was nowhere to be seen. The only object that was missing was the small mongrel that we had rescued from the local dog pound to be our guardian.

I hunted for her in vain until I heard her faint whines. She had crawled under our refrigerator in her panic and was unable to crawl out again.

―⚭―

War brought a number of Europeans to Washington. Six who visited us in Alexandria are vivid in my memory.

Wystan Auden came to stay with us in February 1940. He seemed to me a queer, cold creature. He drank fifteen cups of coffee a day; he sat in silence. We had a great deal in common and very little to say to each other.

He had fled from England, from Spain, from his own past as a Leftist. "Why did you come to America?" I asked him. "It's the future," he said, "and I can best come to terms with the future by meeting it here."

Julian Huxley was the opposite of Auden—warm, companionable, fun-loving. We gave a party for him, and eighty people wedged themselves into our little house. We played a game of strip poker and bid him down to his long woolen underwear. He was laughing so uncontrollably by then that he could barely move.

In March 1940, Esmond and Decca Romilly moved in with us. Esmond had fought in Spain and had written a fine book, *Boadilla,* about the battle that he survived. He was Winston Churchill's nephew; Decca was one of the Mitford sisters—famous for their beauty and their political eccentricities.

Esmond was brilliant, colorful, often hilariously funny; sometimes unspeakably cruel. Decca had a fine satirical mind. Together, they captured Washington by defying all of its conventions.

We took them to a party given by a left-wing group, the American Youth Congress. The room was filled with liberated Negroes and Jewish students from New York, talking, smoking, sipping drinks, and dancing rather self-consciously with each other.

Esmond took one look around the room, and the Churchill blood surged up in him. He whispered, "Five dollars for the first one who says out loud: 'Thank God for the British Empire!' "

It was no contest. I had barely started up an argument with two leaders of the congress when I heard an uproar at the far end of the room. Esmond had shouted out his phrase to the amazement and disgust of those around him. He hurried toward me to collect his five dollars. My companions, two earnest Marxists, looked at me in disbelief.

Esmond and Decca wrote a series of irreverent articles for the *Washington Post.* The owner of the *Post,* Eugene Meyer, was enchanted by them and invited the four of us to dinner. He stood in front of his fireplace when dinner was over and delivered a solemn little speech about the war. "There is one thing you can say for the British," he declared. "They never steal other people's property."

I glanced at Esmond. He was filling up his pockets with Mr. Meyer's most expensive cigars.

Esmond drank too much good brandy. It was midnight before we could drag him away. As we drove back to Alexandria, an argument erupted. We said that Esmond was insensitive; he called us bourgeois philistines and various other names.

The Romillys went to their room for the night. We could not come to terms with Esmond, so he left the next morning, dragging Decca behind him and taking along an ample supply of my shirts, socks, and ties.

Stafford Cripps was another Englishman who came through Washington. He arrived in April on his way back to England from Delhi, where he had been as a special representative of the war Cabinet.

Cripps had stopped off in China. He was anxious to share his views with leaders in Washington, but no one was able to organize his meetings for him. So I volunteered.

He was a sparse, austere man. He put forward a brave line in public. In private, he was deeply pessimistic. He sensed that China was about to break apart, and that India was heading for repression.

I organized a fine dinner for Cripps at the home of Mrs. Gifford Pinchot. He made a speech about the Chinese industrial cooperatives. We allowed half an hour for questions; then, in an extemporaneous comment that had been carefully rehearsed, I stood up. I had been deeply impressed, I said, by all that the speaker had said. I wondered if there was any way in which I could help the movement that the speaker had praised so highly. Yes indeed there was, said the speaker. We took a thousand dollars from a highly conservative audience.

I took Cripps to see John L. Lewis the next day. They spent an hour together. Lewis could have learned a good deal by listening. Instead, he talked continuously, pausing only to draw in his breath. In orotund phrases, he informed Cripps that Roosevelt was finished, and that the C.I.O. was getting out from under him before he collapsed.

I traveled to New York with Cripps, repeating our act. I lengthened my extemporaneous question until, at Carnegie Hall, I was howled down by an impatient audience. Our take for the evening was meager; Reinhold Niebuhr, the chairman of our meeting held me to blame.

I saw Cripps off in New York and sent a telegram to his liner: COME BACK SOON AND BRING PEACE WITH YOU. The message was slightly garbled by the ship's radio operator. "Thank you for inviting me to come back and to bring Peach with me," Cripps wrote from London, "but my wife insists on knowing, who is Peach?"

A sixth visitor came to our house in the summer of 1940—Guy Burgess. He had set out for Moscow, taking Isaiah Berlin with him. They hoped to join the staff of the British embassy, but Cripps, who had been named ambassador, refused to accept them. They had flown as far as Washington when they were ordered to return to London.

Guy called me from Washington and invited himself to dinner. Reveling in the scatological, as always, he described his life in Paris in words that Proust might well have put into the mouth of M. de Charlus. He was, said Guy, a good friend of M. Edouard Pfeiffer, *Chef du Cabinet* to Premier of France M. Daladier. He and Pfeiffer and two members of the French Cabinet, he said, had spent an evening together at a male brothel in Paris. Singing and laughing, they had danced around a table, lashing a naked boy, who was strapped to it, with leather whips.

When supper was over, Guy slumped into an easy chair, gripping his fourth glass of whiskey. We spoke for a time about the Apostles. I was anxious to hear about the friends whom I had sponsored for the

Apostles. Guy in turn mentioned a scholarship student named Leo
Long whom Anthony had brought into the society. Anthony had been
enraged, so Guy said, when another Apostle had tried, unsuccessfully,
to seduce Leo during a drunken party that had followed the annual
dinner of the society in 1938.

I remembered Leo as a quiet and resolute member of the Trinity
College cell. I thought to myself, *If Anthony has taken Leo under his
wing, that can only mean one thing.*

Guy glanced up at me in his sly way. "By the way," he said, "I have
a request to make of you."

I waited.

"I've been out of touch with our friends for several months," he
said. "Can you put me back in touch with them?"

So it was Guy who had been the invisible man behind Anthony. It
was Guy who had drawn me out of my own world in Cambridge, and
into this nether world. I had always suspected it; now I knew.

Was he testing me, to find out where I stood? It did not matter.

"I can't put you in touch with your friends," I said, "and I would
not if I could."

Guy smiled and talked of other things. After an hour or so, I drove
him back to Washington.

Here I should add that my wife knew nothing of Guy's role or of
Anthony's. That night, when I told her, she was, of course, very
disturbed. She asked me to promise to break off contact with Michael
Green by early the next year. She had nothing to do with my underground political activities, then or at any time.

# RESPONSES IN WARTIME

ON August 23, 1939, the German and Russian governments signed
the Nazi-Soviet Pact. On September 1, Hitler's armies invaded Poland. On September 3, Britain and France declared war on Germany.

Michael Green came to Washington in late October. The Red
armies were advancing into Finland when we met.

Green's dark eyes were bright as we sat in a restaurant below the
Union Station. The Soviet soldiers would be hailed as liberators—so
he said. Revolution, starting in the East, would spread like wildfire
across Germany and France. "Great days are approaching!" he said.

I listened to all that Green had to say. Then I handed him a memorandum setting fourth my views on the Nazi-Soviet Pact.

I conceded that the pact had been a military necessity, given the refusal of the British and French governments to join in a common front against Hitler. I went on to plead that the pact not be extended from a military alliance to a political partnership. A political partnership, I argued, would become more than a momentary understanding between the German and the Soviet governments. It would embrace the Communist parties in all nations and it would mobilize them in a worldwide effort to weaken the Allies.

I had done a good deal of reading in the course of preparing my memorandum, and I had cited several examples to demonstrate my point. Already, as I was able to show, the Communist parties in Britain, France, and the United States were doing all that they could to undermine the Allied war effort. They were opposing the efforts of Chamberlain and Daladier to honor the commitments that they had entered into, and they were mouthing the empty slogans of isolationism and anti-imperialism in America in order to weaken Roosevelt in his tentative efforts to lean to the Allied side.

It was, I argued, a course that could only end in disaster. It would destroy the Communist parties and their followers in the free nations; it would isolate the Soviet Union. And it would not make a partner out of Hitler for long.

Green folded my memorandum and thrust it into his pocket. I asked him to read it while we were sitting in our restaurant. He read it in silence. Then he folded it and thrust it into his pocket again.

I had given him four or five commentaries of my own in the months that I had been working at the Department of the Interior. None of them had contained any restricted material; and none of them had been as critical of Soviet policy as my memorandum on the Nazi-Soviet Pact. I asked him if he would forward it to the Kremlin. He looked at me in silence; then he said that he would.

Green vanished sometime in 1942, so I was told in 1963 by the F.B.I. They assumed that he had been summoned back to Moscow. Many, if not most, of the Soviet agents who were abroad in 1939 were recalled in the same manner. Then they were summarily tried and executed, on Stalin's orders.

Was Green among them? Did he suspect, as he thrust my memorandum into his pocket, that if he forwarded it to Moscow, it might be used against him? It seems more than possible to me that, in writing the memorandum and in urging him to send it on, I was pushing him down the road to his death.

The sense of optimism bordering on euphoria that Green felt on the outbreak of the war was apparently shared by my old friends at Cambridge. Stalin had foiled an anti-Soviet conspiracy by signing the pact with Hitler; the capitalist nations had blundered into a war against each other; the war would soon lead to mutinies and uprisings that in turn would culminate in world revolution.

A letter to me from my old Cambridge roommate, Hugh Gordon, expressed that view.

January 11, 1940

Dear Michael:

Jolly glad to get a Christmas card from you. I was wondering what you were thinking and doing and you summed it up in a few words.

What you fear, I hope for and attempt to hurry on, partly because I have not got a nice little bank balance. Yet I doubt if this would make much difference. Over here it all seems so much just around the corner that one feels one must spend more and more time on what I might describe as work of a non-academic kind.

Watch events in France. Someone just back from Paris tells me that troops on the march there cannot be stopped from singing that old song which used to make the walls of K5 echo at the end of our drinking parties.

Just a straw in the wind, but significant.

yours, Hugh.

"That old song" was, of course, the *Internationale,* and Hugh was right. We had ended many drinking parties in K5 by standing in a circle and singing *"Arise ye Prisoners of Starvation,"* while poor old Housman gnashed his teeth in impotent rage in his room overhead.

◦—◦

A profoundly different attitude was expressed in letters to me from my brother Whitney. As a pilot in the Air Force Reserve, he was called to active duty in 1939. His letters voice the low-key, casual attitude of those of whom Winston Churchill said, "Never in the course of human history was so much owed by so many to so few."

29 September, 1939

. . . I am serving with a night-flying Fighter Squadron. It is very exciting, and it leaves the days more or less free. We have the sort of aeroplanes I used to dream about, and the Air Force life is really grand. . . . We have a good band, composed mostly of people from Jack Payne's orchestra, in which I play the double bass. . . .

A protective mechanism develops which enables one to concentrate on unimportant events. For example, the high spot of our day at Camp is the arrival of cake for tea. It comes every day from Lyons, and the question is whether it will be a nauseous pink, a dirty white or a camouflage brown. This having been ascertained, we sink back in to a comatose condition to await what the next day will bring.

Three months later, he wrote again.

January 7, 1940
... I am sitting in my room in Tangmere Aerodrome, Sussex. It is as cold as charity, and I am more or less sitting in the fire.

This is the most delightful part of England and there is an abundance of things that make life and war bearable such as flying, fishing and food.

We fly a hell of a lot—mostly at night. And bloody cold it is at 20,000 feet. We do get some glorious sensations—spiritual as well as intestinal. I think you would like the life, and certainly, I have never been happier. One's horizon is limited. One's objective is simply shooting down Germans. Other things are unimportant.

Soon after he wrote, Whitney and the squadron that he was commanding were sent to Norway. He was ordered to make his base on a frozen lake. He protested, saying that it would lead to a disaster; his protest was overruled. Within a few days of his arrival, the *Luftwaffe* bombed the lake, sinking all of his planes and killing many of his men.

He made his way to the American embassy in Bergen where his godmother, Daisy Harriman, was ambassador. He was so badly wounded that she failed to recognize him. Yet by the time that he was able to write to me, the Norwegian expedition had become "my little party." "I have practically recovered from my little party in Norway," he wrote. He went on to say that he had been to Dartington. It was, he said, "infested with évacué children, chocolate dripping from their mouths." He added, "The Devon hills rattle with the screams of the little ones who find the peace and quiet of the country terrifying after the noise and stink of London."

As for our mother, "Mother is becoming as bloodthirsty as anyone. Recently, I took her down a rifle with which she was practising furiously in the hope of nabbing a parachutist on the wing."

He flew a Hawker Hurricane through the Battle of Britain. It began in August 1940; in March 1941 he wrote to me,

... We have beaten the Germans in the air by day, and we shall shortly do the same by night. The Army has defossilized itself and will make mincemeat of any tourists who come without a visa.

The bombing has been bad, but it will be fun re-building. London will be the finest, most efficient, most beautiful city in the world—mark my words.

You will also see a pretty good social system. War is a great equalizer, and people want peace to stay that way. We shall have a truly socialist state.

A socialist state? It seems strange today to recall that my brother, who prided himself on his pragmatism, was dreaming in 1941 of a new social order. His dream was the inward aspect of the spirit of the pilots of the Royal Air Force whose outward stance was marked by emotional detachment. Only by a purging and a purification of the society that had blundered into war, could the willing sacrifice that the R.A.F. exemplified be redeemed.

# CONFRONTATION IN WASHINGTON

As war approached, the doors of the White House began to close to Tom Corcoran and Ben Cohen. The president was moving to the center of the political spectrum. He wanted advisers who were less opinionated, less controversial, more easily bent to his will.

Ben continued to pore over his legal briefs. Tom rarely appeared in our offices in the Department of the Interior. There was little for me to do.

Left on my own, I turned to another assignment—helping Mrs. Roosevelt as she struggled to maintain the ties between the administration and the radicals in America.

The radical movement was made up of the industrial unions, the American Labor party, the American Youth Congress, and elements of many other organizations. Within its loose structure, the Communist party held key positions of power. It followed Soviet directives, and, as I had feared, its entire thrust after the Nazi-Soviet Pact was signed in 1939 was to undermine the Roosevelt administration and the Allies.

I was a New Dealer by then and a supporter of the Allies. In working with Mrs. Roosevelt, I came into confrontation for the first time with the movement to which I had belonged in my student days.

The American Youth Congress was the organization with which Mrs. Roosevelt was allied. It was a coalition, and many non-Communist organizations were affiliated to it. Nonetheless, a Communist caucus, working under cover and in many guises, was able to manipulate the congress in ways that Mrs. Roosevelt could never comprehend.

The American Youth Congress organized a national rally in Washington in February 1940. By then, Hitler had conquered Poland, and his armies were preparing to conquer France. The rally was called an "Institute on Government," but in the minds of its organizers, it was destined to become a nationwide demonstration in opposition to American involvement in the war.

Mrs. Roosevelt sensed the danger. Nonetheless, she did all that she could to make the Institute a national event. She secured the auditorium of the Department of Labor for its plenary sessions. She saw to it that the networks carried the sessions on the radio. She persuaded the army and the Washington hotels to provide free accommodations for the delegates. She obtained a fleet of buses to drive the delegates to the meetings.

I worked with Mrs. Roosevelt on the preparations for the Institute. I wrote the speeches for the Cabinet members whom she had asked to speak. I met with some of the planners of the Institute—Betty Shields-Collins and Abbott Simon are the two whom I remember. It was a mark of my own ambivalence that we got along well together.

A few days before the Institute was convened, Mrs. Roosevelt invited my wife and me to supper at the White House. My wife sat at Roosevelt's left. She and the president talked about Cambridge and about Poughkeepise. Then, leaning on the dining table, he called out to me.

"Well, Michael, have we any liberal thoughts left?"

"I think so," I said.

He nodded. "This year," he said, "will be the testing time."

The Institute held its opening session on a Friday evening. Three thousand delegates gathered in the Department of Labor auditorium. Four members of the Cabinet were seated on the stage.

One of them was the attorney general of the United States, Robert Jackson. He was a noble man, and he was Tom's choice to succeed Roosevelt as president, if Roosevelt decided not to run.

It was the beginning of the election year. The speech that I had written for Jackson was a defense of the Allies and a reaffirmation of the liberal spirit of America. It was, I believed, a position that could make him president.

He delivered the speech with quiet resolution. A young black stood up in the audience and denounced it. Jackson, he said, was supporting the British and the French empires, which were oppressing the colored peoples of the world.

It was a line of attack that we were to encounter many times before the Institute was over. Jackson listened to the young man; he was courteous but unyielding in his response. The exchange was carried on our national radio and when the session was over, Jackson felt, as I did, that he had carried the day for Roosevelt and the Allies.

The next day was a disaster.

An immense crowd gathered on the lawn in the rear of the White

House. A fine rain was falling. Jack MacMichael, a Southern clergyman who was chairman of the Youth Congress, made a moving appeal to the president to keep up his fight against poverty and prejudice. We waited, and from the dark recesses of the White House, the familiar figure appeared. He worked his way onto the balcony. He stood there, waving in response to our cheers.

It was Mrs. Roosevelt who had insisted that the president speak to the delegates. His own instinct was all against it. The Institute had come at a critical moment for him. The nation was divided; the congress was defiant; the Democratic party was rebelling against him; his political career was very much in doubt. He was facing the greatest test of his presidency; he looked down on the crowd that stood beneath him in the rain and, no doubt, sensed that they were making his task harder.

Jonathan Mitchell was standing in the crowd beside me. He said, "He doesn't like the smell of the Albatross that his wife has hung around his neck."

Roosevelt discarded the hopeful and constructive speech that had been written for him by one of my friends. He scolded the delegates in a rebuke that extended beyond the Left to the liberals and to his own wife, who stood beside him, leaning against a tall white pillar.

He had no words of hope for the uncommitted; no encouragement for those in the audience who shared his objectives. He ended abruptly, raised his hand in a curt gesture, turned, and worked his way back into the darkness with General Watson guiding him and Mrs. Roosevelt moving in silence a pace behind them.

The audience stood there, too disheartened to applaud, too wet to boo. Woody Guthrie, who was there, wrote a song about that moment. It was addressed to the audience of young Americans, and it began, *"Why are you standing in the rain?"*

Many well-intentioned people asked themselves the same question as they trooped disconsolately out of the White House grounds.

That afternoon the delegates filled the auditorium. They were ready to cheer any speaker who would trample upon the president, and the organizers of the congress made the most of their opportunity. They brought in John L. Lewis, the president of the C.I.O., and they gave him a thorough briefing. He was one of the great orators of the age, and he hated Roosevelt with a vengeful passion that was ground into his Welsh bones.

Lewis praised the young people that he saw before him for their courage and their concern. He spoke with heavy scorn of Roosevelt's attitude of condescension toward them. He clubbed Roosevelt's image into a shapeless mass, and the audience cheered at each new blow.

Mrs. Roosevelt was in the auditorium. She had refused to take a seat from one of the delegates. She sat on the floor. She applauded with everyone else when Lewis ended. He passed her on his slow, triumphal procession to the exit. She shook his hand.

The Communist party members and their supporters were in high spirits as they left the auditorium. In their midst I saw a man who had been a student with me at Dartington. I made a bitter remark about Hitler's allies on the Left; he turned on me. "Don't criticize your betters!" he cried.

Monday's session in the auditorium was devoted to foreign policy. Mrs. Roosevelt was on the panel of speakers. So were two spokesmen for the Left.

A Cuban opened the attack upon the administration. Rajni Patel, whom I had known as a Communist in Cambridge, spoke next. He was introduced as a spokesman for the millions of Asians who were oppressed by British imperialism. "America," he shouted, "will not follow Roosevelt into an imperialist war!"

At that, most of the delegates stamped and cheered. Their cheers redoubled when a leader of the National Maritime Union flogged the fallen image of the president. He was brutal, so brutal that once when he paused for applause, the audience was silent. But soon he had everyone cheering again, as if they were in a bull ring, thirsting for blood.

Mrs. Roosevelt was the last of the panelists to speak. She moved to the microphone. An arc light, focused upon her by the newsreel cameramen, seemed to intensify her isolation as she stood there, a dark silhouette against the white background of the stage. The crowd that had been uproarious was silent; the only sound in the darkened auditorium was the whirr of the cameras; holding up one hand, she silenced them.

She spoke in a whisper. She was very pale. A few of us tried to give her some support by applauding her. Once again, she held up her hand to silence us.

She could have said that the president of the United States needed no defenders. She chose instead to defend everything that he had said and done. Her endorsement of him came as a heavier blow than his own speech, for none could question her courage or her concern.

It was a fearful ordeal, and both she and the audience were exhausted at its end.

# A LONG LETTER FROM JOHN

JOHN Simonds returned to Cambridge in September 1937. He spent many days with Belinda, who was known as Bin, but he made no effort to win her love. He broke with the Conservatives in the course of a debate in the Union. He joined the Socialist Society, then he moved further to the left. That much seemed plain from a long letter that he wrote to me soon after he joined the British Army. It was in two parts.

June 1, 1940

There's no need to tell you, Mike, that 'though it's many months since I last wrote to you, you have been deep in my thoughts. Forgive me, old friend, for having left it so very long. . . .

Today I've a few hours free—almost the first since the invasion of Holland. I'm writing this on my back, sun-bathing in the field opposite my barracks. It's a lovely day and I'm sleepy. This will be a drowsy letter.

It's strange to look back on the two months that we spent in America, and at our friendship since its beginning.

It's difficult to think of 1937 without thinking of you. You loomed very large in my life that year.

I remember the first time I heard you speak. It was your first Union speech. You'd learned it off by heart and you gabbled through it with impressive incoherence.

You were very intense in those days. I was drunken and irresponsible. We were a darned funny combination!

I liked you from the start. For all your magnificence, you were very childish, and I've always liked to see the child in people.

Also, I was curious about you. You represented a point of view that I'd never attempted to understand. There seemed to be something big and important about it all.

John too seemed to contain within himself a great movement, a great struggle, a large part of the future.

John's death, the next term, affected me in a way that I couldn't altogether understand. I remember very vividly the night when we spoke about him in the Union. Partly it was that your grief and your friends' grief communicated itself to me. Partly, I felt that something young and precious had come and gone and I had had none of it.

That was the term when I started to work. I wanted to succeed. I wanted to show the world. I wanted to spatter that. . . John Churchill—and all the complacency he stood for—on the Union walls.

I don't quite know why we grew so much closer that term. Partly it was the change in me. But there was more, and I've tried to piece it together in my mind.

Then, and still more after you'd decided to go to America, you seemed
to avoid your old friends, and your old work too. Maybe because I wasn't
associated with those things, you saw more of me, and of Anthony.

I remember being surprised by your reaction to John's death. I'd expected that his death would plunge you into feverish activity in his tradition. Instead, it seemed to break something in you.

I used to say in those days that you'd become more human. Certainly
it became easier for us to get along together. Some kind of prop which
had held up a large part of your life had gone.

Maybe it had been John's cause, John's ideas that you had worked for,
and without him, the cause and the ideas meant less to you. Probably,
your whole approach had been too personal, too emotional, right from
the start. I don't know. But, certainly, you changed deeply, and, in a sense,
the change "let me in."

I remember a crowd of incidents: the last day of the Spring Term when
we raced our cars to London; the first day of the summer Term. You told
me about your plan to return to America that day. I thought about it very
largely in terms of my moving up in your absence to be Vice President
of the Union.

I remember the visit of the Emperor, and that lecherous party at the
Rothschild's where Anthony performed considerable feats of sexual
acrobatics, displaying an enviable versatility.

And all through that Term, a growing love in both of us for Bin; something that might have divided us, but actually drew us closer.

I shall fall asleep in a minute. I warned you that this would be a drowsy
letter. I seem to have drowsed through a good many years. . . .

June 17

I'm in a different mood today. The sun is shining but there's a cold East
wind blowing. It's too cold to lie in the sun, and I'm not sleepy enough
to reminisce any more. . . .

You wrote in one of your letters, Mike, that one day you would write
a book about John Cornford and yourself and me.

I'm proud if anything has come through you to me. But, I want to know:
*how much of John has stayed with you?* Very little that I can see from
here, as far as your job and your activities are concerned.

You may identify yourself with us, and with the future that we are
working for and will secure. I think that you have no right to do this. The
issue today is such that if you aren't with us then you are against us;
against our future; against the work that we shall do. There is one way
and one only in which you can work with us. Without it, the rest is
mouth-honor, breath.

This isn't intolerance, nor a sectarian narrowness. It's an objective fact.
You may be right or you may be wrong. But if you take a different road
on this immense issue, then there is no holding of hands. You cannot help
us, we cannot help you. We shall move further and further apart, and not
all the best intentions, the most beautifully liberal thoughts, the most
sentimental memories, the most nostalgic associations can bring us together again.

Over the last few months, Gerald and I have often thought of you and wondered about you. Many other friends—Betty Shields-Collins, Margot and others who have seen you in America—have wondered about you. We have wondered just how far you have gone to the other side; how much of 1936 is left in you.

If you are convinced intellectually that you were wrong in the old days; that John was wrong and Gerald was wrong, then one day you must tell me fully what has convinced you. I want very badly to understand you. It is not as if the developments of the last nine months have essentially altered your approach. That, for many people, would be easy to understand. But it had changed already by the time I left you in America.

It's a great regret to me that when we went to America together, I hadn't changed as I did later. You helped me enormously, but I wasn't able to help you in the way that you really needed help. I helped you in the wrong way. . . . These are critical times for our people. Very soon, there may be a sudden turn in events and, once again, you and your people will be asked to play the role assigned to you. I ask you to consider deeply how you can best use your influence to help our struggle for liberty and for justice. . . .

We shall win without you. But your people will be wounded unless they join with us; unless they refuse to take the shameful, disastrous course which will be set before them.

I don't know, Mike, just what you are thinking these days. Are you still a pal of Senator Pepper's for instance? Are you writing his very fine appeals for intervention?

At a time like this, old friend, I feel that I have to write all that is in my heart and in my mind, if I am ever to write it. If I have made any mistakes, forgive me.

You and Bin and me. The three best friends in the world. A fine friendship, with so much humor and love and wisdom in it. It has been a huge part of my life and it always will be.

You have made Bin happy, my friend, and you know how important that is to me.

One day soon, I'll be over in the flesh—as much as I've got left. I'm looking forward to that.

Meanwhile, dear friend, be happy. Think deeply about what I've written, for I feel it deeply.

A long handshake to you, with all my friendship in it; for both of you. My love

John.


I read John's letter many times over. It made me very sad. I wanted to share the truth with him; I could not.

'If I have made any mistakes, forgive me. . . .' John's letter, of course, was based upon a mistaken notion about me; one which, as he noted, many others shared. 'We have wondered just how far you have gone to the other side . . .' My apparent defection had hurt them, as I had told Anthony that it would. They had come to suspect me of ignoble motives, in part to protect their own beliefs. It was painful for me to be told that, but it did not matter. In a way, I welcomed the pain.

In his earlier letters, John had said nothing to me about joining the Communist party. Yet the evidence was laid out in the second part of his letter, in many code words. 'My friends and I. . . . the future that we are working for and will secure. . . . sectarian narrowness. . . . an objective fact. . . ." I recognized the familiar phrases. I recognized also the guarded references to the period of Nazi-Soviet collaboration and to the revolution that he felt was imminent. 'The sudden turn of events,' he called it. Judging from his reference to 'the shameful disastrous course' that would be set before the American people, he feared that the rulers of Europe would look to America to help them suppress the revolution that would put an end to the war.

'. . . if you aren't with us . . . then you are against us. . . .' That thought had pitted man against man for five thousand years.

Poor John; he blamed himself for not resisting my staged break with the party. I blamed myself in turn for leading him into a life of illusion and deceit. He could not know what I knew: that the Soviet Union would turn the dedication of our generation to its own narrow ends.

If one of us stood in need of forgiveness, it was not John but me.

I went to see John's father after the war. Gavin Simonds was the lord chancellor of England, a staunch Conservative, and a melancholy figure. He and John had quarreled when John moved to the Left; they were barely on speaking terms when John left with his company for Arnhem.

He took me to lunch in the dining room of the House of Lords. He was very kind to me. He seemed to feel only gratitude, knowing that I had loved John.

I felt that I was responsible for some part of his anguish. I wanted to tell him that and to ask his forgiveness. I could only say how sorry I was that John had been killed.

# LEAVING THE GOVERNMENT

ROOSEVELT continued to move to the Right in 1940. During one particular phone call he berated Tom Corcoran for continuing to talk about the New Deal. Tom guessed that he was putting on an act to impress some Conservative who was sitting beside him in the White House. But in Roosevelt's many pretenses there was often a hard core of truth.

Tom was incapable of being sycophantic. He had always refused to join Roosevelt on his yacht, the *Sequoia,* or at his retreat in Warm Springs, because he did not want to become Roosevelt's slave. He could not change his ways to accommodate the president. He came less and less frequently to our office in the Interior Department. One morning in April, he slipped away and married Peggy Dowd.

Harry Hopkins, who had been divorced, moved into the White House to live. He feared Tom as a rival and gloated over the advantage that he had gained. "You're married," he told Tom, "and that makes a difference. You'll see the president by day, but I'll see him in the evenings, when he's tired and lonely and when he needs a friend."

Tom needed to gain stature in his own right—not simply as an instrument of the White House. Roosevelt promised to make him solicitor general. Tom's appointment was delayed when, as part of a political trade, Frank Murphy, the governor of Michigan, was made attorney general. It was blocked for good by Felix Frankfurter. Felix had been appointed to the Supreme Court, with Tom's assistance. He feared that as an Irish-American, Tom would fail to press for the legislation that would be brought to the Supreme Court by the solicitor general to aid the Allies.

Tom never mentioned these setbacks to his career. Nor did he discuss the general strategy that we were pursuing in 1940; yet Roosevelt's hidden design seemed clear.

The Republican party was divided in 1940 between the interventionists of the Eastern seaboard, and the isolationists of the Middle West. In the Democratic party, a number of able and ambitious leaders were working openly or covertly to gain the nomination for the presidency.

Day after day, the newspapers were filled with speculations as to who the Democratic candidate would be. Roosevelt encouraged the speculation. He smiled upon Paul McNutt; he praised Robert Jackson. He told Harry Hopkins in the greatest confidence that Hopkins was to be the nominee.

Tom knew and I guessed that Roosevelt was playing a waiting game. He could not give up the White House in wartime. He could not appear to be seeking a third term. He had to keep everything in suspense until the time had passed when another candidate could replace him. Then the Democratic party and the nation would have to turn to him.

It was a dangerous game. The third-term issue was a serious handicap for Roosevelt. If the conservatives, the isolationists, and the traditionalists could unite behind one challenger, the Democratic Convention might be overwhelmed.

John Garner, the vice president, was seen as the obvious challenger, and we did all that we could to discredit him. But Tom did not take Garner too seriously. He looked on him as a front-runner whose role was to keep Roosevelt at bay until the time came at the convention for the real challenger to make his move.

The real challenger in Tom's view was a fellow-Catholic—the postmaster general and manager of the Democratic party, James Farley. Tom believed that Roosevelt shared his view.

The game was played out through the spring and summer of 1940. Senator Wheeler campaigned for an isolationist plank in the Democratic platform; Farley worked to gain control of the delegates to the convention. Tom raised funds for a third term from Roosevelt's admirers.

My days with Corcoran and Cohen petered out. Tom left the government in the autumn; Ben turned to diplomacy. I looked around for another job. It did not take long for me to discover that there was no demand in Washington for ghost writers, late in 1940. I was weary and discouraged when James Dunn called me from the State Department. A desk had become vacant in the European division, he said. He offered it to me, and I accepted his offer.

My job, as it turned out, was to sit and listen to the sad stories of the American expatriates who had returned from France when it was overrun by Hitler's armies. They feared, with some reason, that the Nazis would occupy their town houses in Paris and their castles in the country. I gave them all our solemn assurance that we would place posters saying AMERICAN PROPERTY on their front doors. For all the effect that our gesture had, I might as well have given each one of them an aspirin and a glass of water.

Only one incident interrupted the monotony of my days during my brief stay in the department. Joseph P. Kennedy, our ambassador to the Court of St. James's, returned from London to meet with the president. In typical fashion, he told a vast audience, in a nationwide address that he had handed the president a highly confidential report on Britain's chances of survival.

The State Department, needless to say, was swamped with demands for the report. On the advice of my superiors, I sent out ten copies stamped STRICTLY CONFIDENTIAL—one to the Treasury, one to the Department of Commerce, and eight others to federal agencies. Two days later, Kennedy's report was spread across the front pages of the *Washington Post* and the *New York Times*.

The report held, with some qualifications, that the British were beaten.

Roosevelt, I am sure, read those newspapers with mixed feelings. He suspected that Kennedy was preparing to desert him and endorse his Republican opponent, Wendell Willkie. But publication of the report showed Kennedy up for the defeatist that he was and made his endorsement worthless.

Kennedy left the government in disgrace. When the furor over his report had died down, Roosevelt named John G. Winant to be our ambassador to Great Britain.

Winant, a former Republican governor of New Hampshire, was massive and granitic. He seemed to me, in the words of Gerard Manley Hopkins, "Majestic as a stallion, very violet-sweet. . . ."

Winant came to my office in the course of a guided tour of the Department of State. I told him that, in my view, Kennedy was mistaken, and that the British would defeat Hitler in the end.

We talked about Britain for an hour; then Winant's escort led him down the marble corridors. I picked up my telephone as soon as he was out of hearing and called Felix Frankfurter at the Supreme Court. I told him that I wanted to go to London as a member of Winant's staff.

Frankfurter did what he could for me. So did Winant. He drove out to an R.A.F. base when he arrived in England. It happened to be the base where Whitney was stationed. They met, and Winant told Whitney that he had put in a request for me.

It was Roosevelt who vetoed the request, so Tom told me. He suspected that once I arrived in London, I would resign from the embassy staff and join the R.A.F.

I had no intention of lingering in the State Department. I told Tom that I was going to leave the government, as he had done. I wanted to play some part in pushing America into the war.

My determination to get out of government service was strengthened by a telephone call from Michael Green. He had called me only rarely during the months when I worked for Corcoran and Cohen, but when he learned that I had returned to the Department of State his interest in me was renewed. That, in itself, was sufficient reason for me to leave the government for good.

Luckily, I had a place to go—*The New Republic.*

# THE NEW REPUBLIC

THE *New Republic* was founded by my mother and father in 1914.
It was a weekly journal of opinion, and its opinions were taken very
seriously during Woodrow Wilson's presidency. The editor of *The
New Republic,* Herbert Croly, was a leading political philosopher; his
young assistant, Walter Lippmann, was close to the president. "God
knows," Oliver Wendell Holmes wrote to Harold Laski in 1916, "I
have as deep a respect as anyone for the abilities of Croly and Lippmann." But he thanked Laski for not believing that "universal bliss
would ensue if the world would only get a move on and obey when
*The New Republic* says Hocus-Pocus-Presto-Change-o."

The vision of a new world order that Woodrow Wilson and the
editors of *The New Republic* shared was shattered within two years of
the Armistice. Croly turned from politics to religion in his search for
a new impulse that could regenerate America. Lippmann went to
work for the *World.* Felix Frankfurter, John Dewey, and Lewis Mumford continued to write for *The New Republic,* but through the twenties, its most distinguished contributors were British: H. G. Wells,
John Maynard Keynes, Bertrand Russell, Rebecca West, and Virginia
Woolf.

The editors of *The New Republic* were divided against themselves in
the years that followed Croly's death in 1927. Edmund Wilson and
Malcolm Cowley aligned themselves with the Communist party dur-
ing the depression. George Soule favored 'a planned society.' Bruce
Bliven had no political allegiance. Lacking cohesion and insight, *The
New Republic* failed to make headway during the great days of the New
Deal.

The outbreak of war in Europe was a greater test for *The New
Republic,* and one that it failed to meet.

George Soule, the most scholarly of the editors, had no interest in
action. He should have been a professor, teaching introductory economics in some small college in the Middle West. John T. Flynn, *The
New Republic*'s most widely read columnist, was the slave of his Irish
heritage—he could not wait to see Britain go down in defeat. Bruce
Bliven was a working journalist rather than an editor of an intellectual
journal. His attitudes had been shaped by the First World War, and
when war broke out once again in Europe, he wrote a celebrated
article entitled "This Is Where I Came in."

Bruce's feeling—that he had sat through the movie once before—
was shared by most of the readers of *The New Republic.* When they
were polled in June 1939, they divided equally between an isolationist

position and one that favored limited and conditional support for France and Britain. The comment of Allen Tate, a poet and critic, was typical: "The question is: shall we stay out of war and try to make some sort of capitalism work, or go into war and come out with a dictatorship?"

Needless to say, he opted for the first of his choices.

By the spring of 1940, France was close to collapse. George Soule's response was to write an article for the April 22 issue of *The New Republic* entitled "If Germany Wins." He began by conceding that Hitler was on his way to winning the war. He asked, What can we do? His answer was simple enough: "We can fortify ourselves only by fulfilling and invigorating our democracy. We need to re-house the nation and make its people healthy; we need to democratise our industry. . . ."

*Etcetera, etcetera.* . . . It was this attitude of smug detachment that drove Lewis Mumford to write his polemic *The Corruption of Liberalism.* He declared, "The record of liberalism during the past decade has been one of shameful evasion and inept retreat. Liberals no longer act as if justice mattered . . . as if humanity as a whole were any concern of theirs. The truth is they no longer dare to act."

The editors, to their credit, published Mumford's article in *The New Republic.* But they did not alter their own course. George Soule went on writing articles about the virtues of planning; John T. Flynn continued to spew out his hatred for the British. "I find George as cold as ice," my mother wrote to me, "and Flynn like a hurtling flare of bitterness and resentment."

My mother and father had made a pact with Croly not to interfere in the management of *The New Republic.* My stepfather nonetheless told Bruce that its approach to the war was both callous and timid. George Soule was shocked by his intervention, and for the rest of his life, Edmund Wilson insisted that *The New Republic* had been betrayed by its founder.

When Winant failed in his effort to take me with him to London, I knew what I had to do. I would become the Washington editor of *The New Republic,* writing about the necessity for all-out mobilization and driving the magazine into a position of all-out support for Britain.

I telephoned Bruce Bliven and told him what I wanted to do. He knew that I would be a loose cannon, rolling around on the decks of *The New Republic,* but he welcomed me aboard. He asked when he might expect a short article from me. I said that I had already started to work on a thirty-thousand-word report on our defense program. Bruce swallowed hard and promised to publish it as a special supplement.

Helen Fuller of the National Youth Administration volunteered to help me on the supplement. So did Bill Salant and Alfred Sherrard,

160 AFTER LONG SILENCE

two young economists who were working for the Federal Reserve Board. We collected our information each day; we worked late at night to put it together. Our report, entitled "Democratic Defense," was published by *The New Republic* as part of the issue of February 17, 1941. It was written by the editors, so the cover said, but its opening lines were directed as much to them as to their readers:

> For eight years, fascism has warred upon the world. Men have been driven in thousands before its advance. Many free nations have passed beneath its sword. Today, against the last great nation of Europe, fascism is waging war.
> A few people in this country still refuse to understand the nature of fascism—that it wants no friends, seeks no compromise, thrives on warfare and strives for world dominion. . . .

The supplement reviewed the errors made by the British in their mobilization effort. It added that we were repeating all of Britain's mistakes. It excoriated the defense agency of the Roosevelt administration—the Office of Production Management—for its irresolution. It said of the businessmen to whom Roosevelt had entrusted the O.P.M., "We have placed our defenses in the hands of men to whom the defense of democracy means the preservation of profits."

It was a rough charge, but there was truth in it. Roosevelt had decided that the defense program could not be entrusted to the permanent departments of the federal government. He had summoned a number of businessmen to Washington to lead the new wartime agencies. They meant well, but most of them were unable to act. They had been hostile to the Roosevelt administration. They knew next to nothing about the procedures that the government employed. They were unwilling to force the conversion of existing plant facilities to war production. They were reluctant to build new defense plants. Executives, such as William Knudsen of General Motors, who were bold and resolute in Detroit became timid and cautious in Washington, where they were called on to lead the nation. In condemning their weaknesses in the supplement, we were taking on an unwelcome but necessary assignment that neither the press nor Congress was willing to carry out.

Many subscribers to *The New Republic* were taken aback by the supplement, but Sidney Hillman and Walter Reuther bought hundreds of copies of it to distribute to the district directors and the shop stewards of their unions. Felix Frankfurter telephoned me to say that I had been too harsh in judging the businessmen who had come to Washington, but Mrs. Roosevelt invited me to the White House for lunch. She was thrilled by the supplement, she said, and had marked it up for the president to read.

That was all I needed. I told my superiors in the State Department that I was leaving. I persuaded Helen Fuller to join me in setting up a Washington office for *The New Republic*. We found two rooms that we rented for fifty dollars a month. They had been maids' rooms on the top floor of an old brownstone near Connecticut Avenue. My mother visited us there when she came to America. She paused as we climbed the steep, mahogany staircase. There was something about it that was familiar to her. The house proved to be the home where her parents had lived and in which she had been born.

I wrote a great many articles for *The New Republic* in 1941 and 1942. They were, I think, the best commentary that was published on the defense program. I do not mean to sound immodest in saying that. The rhetoric of the articles was my own, and it was often overblown; the information that I set forth and the interpretation that I added to it were given to me by a small circle of brilliant men whom I was able to speak for, since they could not speak for themselves.

It had been my good fortune, in the days when I was working for Corcoran and Cohen, to be associated with a group of young economists in Washington. They were troubled, as I was, by the abandonment of the New Deal; in an effort to hold our lines, we organized a weekly discussion group known as the Economic Policy Club. The club could not arrest the drift to the Right in America, but it served a historic purpose. It brought together in one cohesive group the best of the younger New Dealers, and when the center of action shifted from the New Deal to the defense program, they were able to move together to positions of commanding power. Many of them were one-time associates of Richard Gilbert, a Harvard professor, but the best of them all, I felt, was Robert Nathan. He worked for Donald Nelson, the brightest of the businessmen whom Roosevelt brought to Washington, and when his working day was over, he and I would block out the articles that I wrote for *The New Republic*.

The stakes were high in 1941, and the articles that I wrote caused a good deal of excitement. I wrote one about the conspiracy that General Electric had entered into with I. G. Farben to obstruct the production of an element urgently needed in the manufacture of armaments. General Electric responded by canceling all of their advertisements in *The New Republic*. I attacked the War Department for opposing the creation of new defense plants, and Robert Patterson, the mild-mannered secretary of the army, telephoned me in a rage to say that he had been under actual fire and would survive any verbal assaults from me. I wrote a piece entitled "The Mirage of Production." It listed our failures, industry by industry. It said of the businessmen in the O.P.M., "Their sights were set too low; they never looked ahead. They had sufficient power to act on production but they have made no dent in the production picture. The officials of the O.P.M.

in each industry division are the representatives of each industry in question. They are in Washington primarily to protect the interests of their own industries. They aren't deliberately selfish. They are simply incapable of thinking in terms of the public interest."

The article was published at the end of July 1941. By then the failures that we had railed against were generally known. One month later, Donald Nelson took over the O.P.M., and the battle for defense production was won.

# PUSHING AMERICA
# TOWARD WAR

TANKERS were sinking in flames in sight of Miami in 1941. Hitler was preparing to invade Britain. In Eastern Europe, Stalin was seizing as much territory as Hitler would permit him to take.

Within the Cabinet, Harold Ickes and Henry Stimson were prodding Roosevelt to lead the nation. In the Senate the isolationists were in control of the Foreign Affairs Committee.

Roosevelt, as Stimson noted in his diary, was like "Laocoön in the coils of the boa constrictor." He wanted to save Britain. He knew only too well the tragic lessons of the Wilson years. He called in his close friend Henry Morgenthau in May 1941 and said, "I am waiting to be pushed."

In Emporia, Kansas, William Allen White formed The Committee to Defend America by Aiding the Allies. Its purpose was less to prod Roosevelt than to offer him moral support as he inched forward. The committee supported Roosevelt's initiative in proposing the Lend Lease Program as a means of maintaining the British merchant marine. At the same time, it insisted that its purpose and Roosevelt's was to keep America out of war.

A more militant organization was formed in New York in the spring of 1941. It was called Fight for Freedom, and it presented a mass rally in Madison Square Garden that combined entertainment with speeches demanding that America enter the war.

Helen Fuller and I tried, early in 1941, to form an interventionist movement around *The New Republic.* It was a hopeless task. In a rash moment, we founded the Washington Chapter of Fight for Freedom.

We undertook to present the rally in the largest auditorium that we could hire in Washington—the Uline Arena.

We recruited a board of directors under the chairmanship of a prosperous attorney, Donald Richberg. We set out to raise money by selling tickets to our rally. We had no experience in running a mass rally and had little time to give to it, since *The New Republic* took most of our working hours. We were saved by the dedication of a few bizarre individuals, and by good luck.

Prominent among our saviors was an elderly and eccentric lady who was the wife of a federal judge. The judge, we discovered, wore a hearing aid. We came to admire him, noting that he turned the volume of the device all the way down whenever his wife began to speak. No matter; she sold all of the boxes in the Arena by bullying her friends. Her motivation, it turned out, was to be seen in the spotlights in her new evening dress, which featured a bare midriff. The spotlights failed to alight upon her, and she was enraged. "Why hold a rally?" she shouted at her husband. He nodded happily, his hearing aid turned down to zero.

Another matron who rescued us in our search for funds was Mrs. Cyrus McCormick. She was diminutive and soft-spoken. She proved to be ten times as eccentric as the judge's wife.

Mrs. McCormick invited us to dinner after writing her check. Her guest of honor was the distinguished California architect, Richard Neutra.

Helen and I went together to Mrs. McCormick's apartment. We sat in her sitting room sipping cocktails. That would have been easy enough had it not been for Mr. McCormick's Great Dane. There was nothing fierce about the beast; he was all too friendly. He came up to each of us in turn and laid his drooling muzzle in our laps. He also wagged his tail. It was a long tail, reinforced by a wad of Band-Aids that were wrapped around its tip. Suddenly, WHACK!—a glass would go flying across the room, and we would be drenched in whiskey or gin.

Mrs. McCormick became engrossed in an intimate conversation with Neutra during dinner. Her husband drank a bottle of wine. When we returned to the sitting room, he stretched out on the carpet and closed his eyes. It was hard to ignore his portly figure as he lay there, and he made it harder by letting out a series of resounding belches. After each belch, Mrs. McCormick smiled sweetly and said, "Simmer Cyrus, simmer."

She was not so sweet when she drew me to one side. She had discovered, she whispered, that Neutra was a Nazi spy. She begged me to telephone J. Edgar Hoover and warn him. I politely declined to do that.

A third prospect whom we pursued in our search for funds was Mrs.

Gwendolyn Cafritz, the Hungarian wife of Washington's most successful contractor. She invited me to the enormous mansion that her husband had built on Foxhall Road. I sat in her living room, staring at the murals of Nubian maidens bearing baskets of fruit on their heads; and I pleaded the cause of anti-fascism.

Mrs. Cafritz listened attentively. When I had finished she said, "Who is on your board?"

Her principal interest, it appeared, was in the social standing of our board members. I mentioned Mr. Richberg and her eyes brightened. She said, "Bring him here for tea."

It might have been an enjoyable occasion. Unfortunately, Mrs. Cafritz produced, along with the tea, some cookies made from her favorite Hungarian recipe. They looked innocent enough, but between their burnt-almond layers there was some substance that was very like glue. Mr. Richberg bit into a cookie. He spent the next hour trying to separate his two rows of false teeth, which the cookie had cemented together. He nodded when Mrs. Cafritz asked if he would come to dinner bringing with him the army's chief of staff. Well pleased, Mrs. Cafritz wrote her check for $100 and we departed.

That was the only service rendered by a member of our board. Helen and I struggled along, but by mid-summer it was plain that we would do well if we managed to sell half of the tickets by the time that the rally was due to be held—November 4.

Then, on June 22, the massed tanks of the *Wehrmacht* rolled across the Soviet frontier.

It took a month or so for the Communist party and its fellow travelers to recover. From then on, we were besieged by new-found friends. I was summoned to speak at lunchtime rallies in a score of federal agencies. At each rally a crowd had been assembled by the United Federal Workers Union, and tickets for the Uline Arena were sold. Posters that I had never seen were pinned up on government billboards damning Senator Wheeler and his fellow isolationists and praising us. They were, of course, in violation of civil service regulations, as Senator Wheeler was the first to point out. We did not pause to apologize; success was in sight.

The rest was easy. Bin and I waited at the airport to greet our celebrities as they flew in: Burgess Meredith, Martha Scott, Ray Bolger, Betty Field among them. Seated in rented Cadillacs and escorted by ranks of policemen on motorcycles—red lights flashing, sirens screaming—we took our stars to the Arena.

The rally itself was a triumph. The oratory was fervent; the crowd was enthusiastic; the entertainment was highly professional. A torch singer rattled the girders of the Arena with her rendition of *They Say That Falling in Love Is Wonderful*. A cast of two hundred volunteers gave a spirited performance of a patriotic pageant, written by Ben

Hecht and Charles MacArthur. At its climax, eight thousand balloons soared into the roof of the Arena, where they remained.

One month later, we convened our board. I gave them the good news—the rally had been a smashing success—and the bad news—we had been left with a $2,000 deficit.

Mr. Richberg listened to my report. He passed over the little matter of the deficit, saying that "the staff" could handle it. He and his fellow board members, he said, were gravely disturbed by the offensive posters that we had distributed. He had assured his good friend Senator Burton K. Wheeler, and he was about to inform the press, that "the staff" alone was responsible for them. Thereupon he and his fellow board members resigned.

"The staff" sat in silence, too angry to speak. The press was soon occupied with more important matters. Three days after our board meeting, the Japanese bombed Pearl Harbor.

# AT THE WHITE HOUSE

WHEN Esmond and Decca Romilly left us in 1940, they moved in with our neighbors, Clifford and Virginia Durr. Decca gave birth to a baby girl; Esmond left to join the Royal Canadian Air Force.

He was in uniform when he returned, on leave to Washington. We became good friends again. He flew to England and, in December 1941, was shot down over the North Sea.

I drove to the Durr's house with a bottle of brandy for Decca. I took her up to Old Westbury so that we could be with her on New Year's Eve.

On New Year's Day, a telephone call came from the White House. Winston Churchill was staying there and he wanted to see Decca. We hurried back to Washington.

Decca and her baby and Bin and I drove up to the White House in my venerable Ford sedan. It rumbled up the elegant driveway; under the great columns of the front entrance, it disgorged half of its insides. I and three Marine guards in full dress uniform pushed it off the roadway and onto the front lawn of the White House. Then I hurried up the front steps in pursuit of Decca and Bin.

Mrs. Roosevelt was waiting for us. She was gracious as she always was.

"I've been reading all of your articles with such interest!" she said to me. "I must say that last one about Jesse Jones rather surprised me! Are you sure of everything you said?"

"Yes, absolutely sure," I said. It was Tom Corcoran, Jones's one-time assistant at the Reconstruction Finance Corporation, who had given me the information that was so damning about him.

"Because, if you aren't sure," Mrs. Roosevelt went on, "I should think you would be very frightened at what Mr. Jones might say in reply!"

"He hasn't said anything so far."

"Then I suppose you must be right. Do you know," she went on, "I was so curious about the charges that you made that I took the article to Franklin and I told him about it. Do you know what he said?"

I shook my head.

"He said to me, 'You must always remember that the record of his past is not necessarily an earnest of his present.' So I said, 'Well, I think you'd better read Michael's article before you say anything more!'

"I took it down to him, and, after dinner, he looked up at me. He said, 'Do I have to read the article?' And I said, 'No.' And so, you see, I don't know whether he's read it or not!"

I said that I had better creep out of the White House while I could. Mrs. Roosevelt laughed, and, sure enough, who should be ushered in to join us for tea but Jesse Jones.

Churchill was in his bedroom, taking his afternoon nap. When he awoke, he sent for Decca. She was taken to his bedroom; he embraced her there. He had nothing on, save for a loose dressing gown.

He told her that Esmond and his crew had gone down without a trace in the North Sea. He said that his heart bled for her. He strode around the room, rolling off sonorous phrases about the enemy striking with brutal fiendishness at the British home and hearth. Then he remembered that Decca's elder sister was married to Sir Oswald Mosley, the Fascist leader. He explained to Decca that he had put her brother-in-law into prison and he apologized for his action. It was the best way to protect him, he said.

If he expected Decca to thank him for protecting her brother-in-law, he was mistaken.

"Protect him!" she snorted. "He should be hung!"

# THE BEST OF DAYS

WHEN America declared war on Germany and Japan I knew that within a few months I would go off to fight. From then on, a new sense of urgency dominated our lives.

Most importantly, we decided to have a child.

We decided also to buy our own home in Virginia. We found a run-down farm eight miles from Washington. It had a brick house, built in 1750, two open fields, and a steeply banked wood. A stream flowed through the wood; a small white building stood beside it.

The farm had been bought in 1878 by Captain Fountain Beatty, one of the two company commanders of the Confederate raider, John Singleton Mosby. Beatty had been named revenue officer for Northern Virginia after the Civil War. He was able, in that capacity, to close down all of the stills in Fairfax County and to manufacture his own brand of brandy and applejack. The building by the stream had been the Captain's still.

We turned the still into a cottage and recruited a Colonial Williamsburg architect to restore the house. We persuaded Beatrix Farrand, who had designed the gardens at Dartington and at Dumbarton Oaks, to help us on our small garden.

In July, we were able to move into our cottage. I wrote to my mother: "It's whitewashed on the outside. French windows bring light into our living room, where Captain Beatty once made his Apple Jack. The windows overlook the brook. A Willow tree stands by our door. A Cardinal sings in the Willow. A Mockingbird sings on our roof. A pair of Yellow Throats live in the Blackberry bushes by our bedroom. At night, I wake up, alerted by a strange sound. I realize that it is the brook flowing under our window. I go back to sleep again."

It was the happiest of times for us. In addition to all the reasons that we had for feeling happy, I had said goodbye to Michael Green for the last time.

He had appeared and disappeared in the months after I left the State Department. He had understood that I left the government for good but he kept in touch with me. He wanted to take me to dinner with Earl Browder, the secretary of the American Communist party. When I turned down his invitation, he insisted on taking me to dinner in New York with his wife. She was an American, judging by her speech. She said very little, but Green was proud of her.

He understood that I could not and would not provide him with any information. He asked me to help him in finding a place to live in Philadelphia, and in obtaining some small business that he could run. I told him that I could not help him in any way.

He came to Washington early in 1942. I told him then that I was planning to volunteer for one or other of our armed forces. He nodded as if he had expected that for a long time.

I handed one last memorandum to Green. It was a plea to the Soviet government to give up its revolutionary ideology in the interests of world peace.

The Soviet Union, I argued, could follow one of two courses. It could continue in its self-imposed isolation, holding the governments of Britain and the United States at arms length and financing the communist parties within their borders. Or, it could join in a unified effort to win the war and to rebuild the postwar world.

The first course, I maintained, and would lead to the breakup of the wartime alliance and in all probability to a third world war. The second course could lead America to provide economic aid to the Soviet Union; in time it could result in lasting peace.

Green took my memorandum and stuffed it into his pocket. We shook hands for the last time and said goodbye.

⤳∞⤳

On January 1, 1942, the governments of twenty-six states signed the Declaration of the United Nations. It was little more than a statement of good intentions, but it was enough for me. I put aside my work for *The New Republic* and set out to write a book about the future of the United Nations in the few months that I had left as a civilian.

The book was a plea to the United Nations to accept the changes that had been brought about by the war: the collapse of colonialism in Asia; the unification of Europe; the mobilization of the Western economies; the emergence of a managerial structure that could be employed when the war was won to direct a worldwide program of relief and reconstruction.

That argument, in its essence, was bold and original. It was overlaid by populist rhetoric; it ended with some mushy thoughts about the distant future. In my effort to portray a world without war, I argued that Soviet communism and Western democracy would evolve in time into a synthesis, based upon representative institutions and egalitarian values. I was trying still to reconcile my developing consciousness with my own past as a student at Cambridge. With that in mind, I dedicated the book to John Cornford and sent a copy to Margot. She chided me gently for invoking his memory in a book that did not reflect his views.

The book, which I called *Make This the Last War,* was finished in September and published in January 1943. I was in uniform by then, but I had it mailed to my friends. Frankfurter wrote me a friendly letter about it; Keynes went to the heart of the matter as he always did. He praised the book in a letter to my mother. "But," he said, "I wish that Michael could regard politics more than he does as the art of the possible."

The book was well received, save for one review in the *New York Times*. It was by John Chamberlain, a former editor of *The New Republic*. Since I was in a highly sensitized state, I found it devastating.

My overwrought style was repulsive, said Chamberlain. As a thinker, he added, I was "even more of a perfectionist than Lenin or Robespierre."

Three weeks later, a curious footnote appeared in Chamberlain's column in the *Times*. He noted that the celebrated Alexander Woolcott had just died. He added: "Woolcott's death left me with an unanswered letter accusing me from my desk. On the basis of a review which appeared in this space, Woolcott wanted to talk over Michael Straight's *Make This the Last War*. If I had only been quicker at calling Woolcott at the Hotel Gotham, I might have learned something interesting and important that now will never be said."

Our child was due to be born in late October. I told myself that I would stay on for another six weeks with my family then go off to fight.

In what uniform? I thought that the army offered the quickest route to the battle lines, but Tom Corcoran came up with one more quotation from Justice Holmes. Army life, said Holmes, who had been a captain in the Civil War, was "organized boredom."

"If you have to go," Tom said, "then go to the farthest North that men have been—the sky.

"Forget all that nonsense about wind, sand, and stars," he added. "It's still better than sticking your face in blackberry bushes and sleeping in the mud."

I followed Tom's advice and took an examination to become an aviation cadet. I filed my application on the day after Bin gave birth to our son, David. In November, I was sworn in as a private in the Air Corps Reserve.

I knew that I had to go, yet it seemed heartless to leave my family. Bin stood outside our house in Virginia with David tucked into the crook of her elbow. I stood beside her, and that aging photograph of my father, my mother, and we three children, taken in November 1917, came back to me.

I wrote to John Simonds, saying that I was about to leave for pilot training. I told him to take care of himself, for the sake of Bin and David.

John wrote back from a troop ship on its way to the action that ended in disaster in Crete. His letter was written to be read by Bin and me, and it was lighthearted. He added a postscript for me alone.

You wrote to me telling me to take care of myself.

I shall be in action before you, but you are in the army now. Therefore I tell you this Mike, for what it's worth to you before you fight.

In the last five years, I've known many women, lived for short periods with two, been fond of several. But I haven't met one who meant a fraction as much to me as Bin used to mean and could mean again.

This does not hurt. If it did, I wouldn't write to you about it. But it is a fact as things stand with me. So I want you to know, before you fight, that if by chance I survive and you do not, I shall love Bin as much as ever. I'll take care of her—if she will let me—and of your son.

# HIP, HIP HOORAY

WE had a warm spell in Washington during January 1943. I worked in our fields on weekends, cutting brambles until my arms ached. There was nothing nicer then than to lie in the grass, look at the passing clouds, and listen to the wind in the grass, the cedars stirring, a mockingbird singing; David making noises in his pram.

I was scheduled to leave on a speaking tour in February. I telephoned the Air Corps Induction Center to tell them where I would be. The sergeant who took the message asked me to wait a minute while he checked on my status. He told me that I would be on a troop train, heading for Miami Beach, in four days time.

That was on a Thursday. I did not want to tell Bin at once. We spent Friday and Saturday together in the most innocent way. But it was necessary for Milton Rose, our attorney, to be with me. So on Sunday, I had to tell her.

It snowed Saturday night. The storm passed, and Sunday was a fine day. The snow and the sunlight made the fields and the brick house look more beautiful than ever.

I dreaded goodbyes. I left David sleeping peacefully upstairs. Bin and I drove together to Union Station.

It was cold and dismal in the station. We waited in a crowd of strangers, stamping our feet on the concrete floor to keep warm, for we had been told to leave our overcoats at home.

At last a lieutenant arrived. He was not at all the dynamic type pictured on recruiting posters. His posture was bad; he wore thick glasses; his voice was thin; he was nursing a cold.

The lieutenant told us to line up. We faced him in three wavering rows. He called off our names, peering at a long sheet of paper. We answered him. There were 170 of us, standing there and shivering. The role call took twenty minutes to complete.

"Zabriskie . . . Zimmerman. . . ." The lieutenant came to the end of his list. He blew his nose into a dirty handkerchief and called for three cheers for the departing soldiers.

"Hip, hip," the lieutenant cried in his thin voice. The crowd of mothers, sisters, wives, and sweethearts responded with a feeble "Hooray."

The lieutenant had planned, I think, to march us off in a military manner. He thought better of it.

"Follow me," he muttered. We shuffled off after him, through the iron gates of the station, to the bare and grimy cars of the troop train.

*Interlude*

———————————❦———————————

*The Wild Blue Yonder*

# THE WILD BLUE YONDER

THE troop train took us to Miami Beach. We spent our days there singing the air corps anthem: *Off we go, into the Wild Blue Yonder.* The only place we went, however, was to the parade ground. There, we marched through clouds of brown dust until the blisters broke inside our army boots.

A second troop train took us north, to Marietta College. On our first day there, we were summoned to the gymnasium. Our commanding officer called the roll and demanded to know our religious affiliations.

"Catholic!" . . . "Catholic!" . . . "Lutheran!" . . . The roll call went along without a hitch until the commanding officer came to Jones.

"Jones!" he shouted, and Jones said, "No religious affiliation."

There was an ominous pause. Then, "I'm sorry for you, Jones," said our commanding officer. "And you'll be sorry, too, before you're through!" He delivered a brief but meaty version of the prevailing doctrine: in the foxholes of Europe and the Pacific there were no atheists.

I listened in alarm. I had found lodgings in Marietta for Bin and for David. I was planning to spend my Sundays with them. I made some quick calculations as the roll call continued. Then I affiliated myself with the church least likely to be found in a small town in Ohio.

"Straight!" our commanding officer shouted.

"Unitarian!" I shouted back.

He paused for a moment. Then, in a grudging voice, he said, "All right."

I was lying on my bunk the following morning when the student orderly aroused me. "There's someone to see you downstairs," he said.

I followed him down, wondering who on earth would know me in Marietta. There, waiting for me, was a little man with bright eyes.

"I'm your minister," he said. "My name is Mort."

An eloquent preacher had built up a large congregation in Marietta, so Mort told me. He had moved to Seattle, and Mort had taken his place.

"Tell me," he said, "to which of our many congregations do you belong?"

I thought it best to reveal to Mort the circumstances of my conversion. He was unmoved. We were the first detachment of soldiers to be posted in Marietta. It was a matter of pride for each church to have its quota of cadets; since I was the only Unitarian in the detachment, I was in great demand. Mort insisted that I attend his Sunday morning

175

services. He motioned to me to stand up, and when the service was over, I had to join him at the door of the church and greet my fellow Unitarians. Each family embraced me in turn and said that if I would join them for Sunday lunch, they would provide me with some real home cooking.

Bin and David arrived the next week. We had little time alone. We knew that there was no way to escape the Sunday services and the home cooking. But on Sunday afternoons, Mort insisted on taking us to the spacious house where he lived alone. There, through the few weekends that we had together, we sat in silence while Mort practiced on his tenor saxophone.

<hr />

A third troop train took us from Marietta to Maxwell Field, near Montgomery, Alabama.

At Maxwell, the air corps prided itself on being able to separate the men from the boys. The separation process was known as hazing. It was a simple system in which the cadets who had been at Maxwell for one month inflicted minor tortures upon the newcomers to see how much punishment they could take.

I and my fellow cadets were branded as zombies when we arrived at Maxwell. We walked in "rat lines." We ate "square meals." We "sounded off," repeating idiotic phrases while standing in a rigid brace, with an upper classman's nose one inch from ours.

"Why are you famous, mister?"

"Sir! New Cadet Straight, Michael W. requests permission to speak!"

"Shoot, mister!"

"Sir, I am famous for painting concentric circles on my ass with lipstick while jumping off the Empire State Building, crying, 'Look out, look out! I'm a demolition bomb!'"

It was a change of pace for me, after working for the White House and writing for *The New Republic*. But I relished my new status of equality with my fellow cadets. Curiously enough, I was the only zombie in my squadron who could rattle off my reasons for being famous without faltering. So our cadet commander, a boy just out of high school, singled me out for special treatment.

"Mister, do you know what I am going to do for you?"

"No Sir!"

"Mister, I am going to allow you to light my cigarette."

"Yes Sir! Thank you Sir!"

Later, he did me the even greater honor of allowing me to buy him a Coke.

It was all harmless enough, but at times it turned nasty.

We were blasted out of our sleep at 2:00 A.M. one morning. The lights were on in our barracks; a sergeant was blowing a bugle, close to my ear. A cadet officer shouted to us as we blinked; we were to be standing, fully dressed, outside our barracks in three minutes.

We scrambled into our uniforms. We rushed outside and formed our ranks in the darkness. In time, we saw flares approaching; a weird procession passed by.

All of us had cheated at one time or another. One cadet had been caught and court-martialed. Now he was being drummed out of the corps of cadets. A cadet commander pushed him past us, hunched up in a wheelbarrow. He was pushed out of the iron gates of Maxwell Field and dumped onto the highway. Then while we stood at attention, and the flares added to the lurid nature of the scene, an officer shouted a warning to us. Ex-Cadet Thompson, Ernest W., had been found guilty of violating the honor code and expelled from the corps of cadets by order of the commanding officer. Never again would the name of Ex-Cadet Thompson be mentioned in the corps of cadets.

When the lights in our barracks were turned out once more, most of the cadets sank into sleep. I lay there, tense with rage. The next morning, I went to see the one good friend that I had made at Maxwell, the Protestant chaplain. I told him what had happened and he was as angry as I was about it. He picked up his telephone and asked for a number in Washington.

Three days later, hazing was abolished at Maxwell on orders from the chief of air staff.

The upper classmen were stunned; the officers were incoherent. "After today's formation," one instructor told us, "there will be a tea party for the lower class. The upper class will pour."

"I understand you zombies are extra tough!" our Physical Training Instructor shouted at us. "Well, you'd better be! Today we're going on a little trot, the Maxwell Mile! You fall out for just two reasons: appendicitis and heart failure. And don't pretend that you've got appendicitis when all you've got is a little gas on your gut!"

I kept mum about my little talk with the chaplain. I ran the Maxwell Mile and, although a dozen cadets fell by the wayside, I completed the course. At twenty-six, I was the oldest of the cadets. I had spent most of my days at a desk, but I was becoming lean and strong.

From Maxwell, we went to a selection center. There, and from then on, I shouted out "pilot!" and "combat!" whenever we were offered a choice. I was determined to get to England as a bomber pilot. But two bizarre incidents barred my way.

In Nashville, we were preparing to ship out when I was summoned to the base hospital. There I faced a medical board, consisting of a major and two captains.

The major held an X ray of my chest in his hand. "I hate to tell you this," he said, "but we are taking you out of the corps of cadets."

"You mean I can't fly?" I said.

"Fly!" said the major. "You may not have long to live."

It took me a day to recover. Then I went back to the board. I stood before the three officers and bared my funnel chest.

*"Pectus excavatum,"* said the Major. He conceded that it was responsible for the distortion in the X ray that had led the board to conclude that my heart was dangerously enlarged. He explained to the two captains that *pectus excavatum* was caused by malnutrition and was found among the children of the poor.

I put on a good imitation of a slum boy, pushing to the back of my consciousness the persistent image of Miss Gardner feeding me spoonfulls of cod-liver oil. The major was very sympathetic. He reinstated me in the corps of cadets, noting that it was one way in which the underprivileged could escape from the bonds of poverty. I thanked him for giving me that opportunity, but I had missed my troop train.

I shipped out with another detachment to Mississippi. There, when I was about to graduate, I was summoned once again to base headquarters.

On one of the hundreds of forms that I had filled out, I had, like a fool, made a check against the word *French.* My check had caught the eye of a captain who was searching for pilots to train a detachment of French cadets.

My French had, if anything, deteriorated since the day when I had stood on the wagon in Hyde Park. But the examination that the captain gave me was not all that difficult.

*"Ouvrez la fenêtre,"* he said. I took one step toward the nearest window, and he cried, "You're in!"

By chance encounters such as these, our lives are shaped. My companions in Miami Beach and Marietta went on to bomb Schweinfurt and Ploesti, and many of them were killed. I was sent to Montgomery, Alabama, to fly in the rear cockpit of a trainer, behind a series of French cadets.

Our cadets were the remnants of the once proud *L'Armee de l'Air.* They were a motley crew. As for the instructors; we were, I am sure, the strangest collection of misfits ever assembled under the banners of the air corps. When we sorted ourselves out in civilian life, a few went into Democratic party politics; a few were taken into the Central Intelligence Agency. A good many became alcoholics, and one, Charlie Engelhard, won the English Derby.

We flew five hours a day with our cadets; five hours of snap rolls,

*Willard Straight, 1914*

*Dorothy Whitney Straight, pastel by Willard Straight, 1912.*

*The Straight family, Old Westbury, Long Island, November 1917.*

*Applegreen, Old Westbury.*

*Michael and Beatrice
Straight, 1922.*

*Dartington Hall.*

*Leonard and Dorothy Elmhirst, 1938.*

*Michael Straight and Herta Thiele, Dartington, 1935.*

*Anthony Blunt on a Soviet Steamship, 1935.*

*John Cornford, Dartington, 1936*

*Michael Straight, Cambridge, 1936.*
RAMSEY & MUSPRATT, CAMBRIDGE

*Cambridge Union Society, breakfast guests, May 1937. The author, fourth from left, front row, sits next to Haile Selassie, emperor-in-exile of Ethiopia, who had been awarded an honorary membership in the society. See Appendix A for other identifications.*
STEARNS & SONS, CAMBRIDGE.

*Gustavo Duran, Spain, 1936.*

*John Simonds, Adirondack, Mts. 1937.*

*Michael Straight on a Vultee*
*Valiant, 1944.*

*Michael Straight testifying*
*before the Senate Select*
*Committee on Foundations,*
*1952.*
WIDE WORLD PHOTO

*Dinah Straight, October 1956.*

slow rolls, stalls, and spins. The plane that we flew was named the *Valiant* by its manufacturer; we called it the *Vibrator*. When it stalled, it would shake its pilot as a terrier shakes a rat. Then it would plunge downward in a spin. The spin would tighten as the plane gained speed; it was like entering the vortex of a whirlpool, and, from time to time, the French cadets would heighten its effect by freezing on the controls.

We took our students as novices and made pilots out of them. When each class graduated, we held a wild party at a local café. We shouted the *Banc des Aviateurs,* a kind of fight-team-fight cheer. We sang *Peestol Packin' Mahmah* and the *Chevaliers:*

> *Chevaliers de la Table Ronde*
> *Goutons voir si le vin est bon*

The *vin* was never *bon* in wartime Alabama, but we drank it nonetheless.

I trained three classes of French cadets. Then I telephoned Tom Corcoran and asked him to get me out of the training command and into combat.

Tom called Lister Hill, the senior senator from Alabama. Lister called the general in command of the air corps. The general called Gunter Field and was told that I could not be spared.

Lister called Tom. "I asked the general to let Mike go——" he began.

Tom interrupted him. "Lister," he said, "Lister, you are chairman of the Senate Armed Services Committee! You don't *ask* the general, you *tell* him!"

Lister told the general. Two days later, special orders arrived from Washington transferring me to Lincoln, Nebraska, to be assigned to B17s.

At last I was on my way to combat. I arrived in Lincoln breathing fire. I was kept there for three weeks, listening to lectures about warm fronts and cold fronts, hard chancres and soft chancres, combustion engines, and Why we Fight.

The lecturers had one objective: to prevent their audiences from snoring too loudly. They strove to do that by a mixture of information and smut.

The lecture to aircraft commanders on first aid was a fair example. It began with shock. "How do you know if your crew member is in shock?" asked the lecturer. "Well, his pulse will be rapid and weak; his complexion will be pale; his skin will be moist; his fingernails will be blue. Now, how many of you have seen a woman unconscious from fainting or shock? About twenty of you, eh? How many of you took advantage of her? Okay! Tell me about it afterward. Now! You may have to inject morphine into a man who's in shock. Where do you inject it? Into any part of the body. You can inject it into his pecker if you want to; it's full of blood cells. When it's erect the blood is held there. That's why men with long peckers faint when they get a hard on. . . ."

On another day, we tied tourniquets onto rubber arms and legs that were disfigured by rubber wounds. I went to mail call at the end of that day. My name was shouted out in our squadron office. A letter had come to me from England, *via* Old Westbury. It was from Gerald Croasdell, saying that John Simonds had died of the wounds he received at Arnhem.

The B17s were known as Flying Fortresses and with good reason; they were solidly built and heavily armed. Flying through anti-aircraft fire and beating off the fighters that rose to meet them, they forced their way in daylight into the heart of Germany. They made their bombing runs against munitions plants and marshaling yards. Then and only then, they returned to their bases in England with wounded gunners, feathered engines, and fuselages mutilated by shell fire.

No Allied plane took more punishment, or saved more lives, through its own, indomitable strength.

I flew no missions over enemy territory in my Fortress. I saw no plane in my formations go down in flames. But on two occasions, the lives of my crew and my own life were spared because the Fortress that I was flying was so strong.

I learned to fly the Fortress in Ohio. It was a grim place to be in midwinter; I did not mind. Night after night, when my fellow pilots were out with girls in Columbus, I would lie in the darkness, too tired to study, too elated to sleep. The hours of darkness would pass; at dawn, I would hear the engines of the Fortresses growling on the flight line as the mechanics warmed them up. I would know that in two hours I would be out there, flying the great plane with no sleep to steady me. I needed none; I was confident and content.

When we finished our training in February 1945, I headed for Old Westbury, where my family and Biddy's were living. I sat with David, reading the story of the Three Bears. I watched his eyes brim over with tears as the Little Bear found someone else in his bed. Even when he was playing, his eyes would brim over at the onset of some sadness that he could not share with us.

Mike, our second child, had white hair and blue eyes. He would raise himself on his hands and his toes at eighteen months and pirouette around. Then he would flop over and lie on the carpet, laughing.

I picked up my crew in Lincoln, Nebraska, and we flew to Rapid City, South Dakota, for our final training before we were to leave for England.

We flew in formations of up to thirty-six planes; we made strafing runs a few hundred feet over the Nebraska plains; we dropped wooden bombs from ten thousand and twenty thousand feet. My crew kept warm in electrically heated flying suits. I dared not wear one, in case our electrical system should fail. Instead, I wore eight layers of clothing and ate enormous quantities of Jewish sweetmeats, sent to my Navigator, Moe Jacobs by his mother.

Moe had a sweetheart named Florence back in Brooklyn. He could not make up his mind about marrying her and it interfered with his navigation. So I became a marriage broker and talked him into a Rapid City wedding. The trouble was, there was no Rabbi in South Dakota to perform the ceremony. We hunted around and came upon a Jewish bombardier who in his civilian days had hoped to be a Rabbi. Then we persuaded Moe's mother to set aside her prejudices and accept me as Moe's best man.

The wedding party assembled in Rapid City. The bombardier put on a white skull cap and a cape. We rounded up ten Jewish enlisted men who served as witnesses. They took their places along the aisle of the church on our base.

The bombardier's wife and I marched up the aisle while an organ played. Florence failed to make her appearance. We waited while Moe hunted her down and brought her to the altar.

The bombardier held out a goblet of wine and intoned a blessing. Moe and Florence sipped the wine. The bombardier read a scroll; then he turned to me. I produced the ring, and Moe pressed it onto Florence's finger. He promised, in Hebrew and in English, to be a faithful husband. She never opened her mouth.

The bombardier sang *I Love You Truly,* very slowly and a bit off key. Reading from right to left, he invoked a blessing on the wine. Moe and Florence drank from the goblet once more. Then Moe laid it carefully on the floor of the church and stamped upon it.

The bombardier played the Rabbi's part pretty well. Moe's mother watched him closely and motioned to him whenever he hesitated. She made no sound. The ten enlisted men, in contrast, argued loudly throughout the ceremony. They drank a good deal when it was over and told several off-color wedding stories that, no doubt, had been told in Jerusalem two thousand years ago. Then they formed a circle around the bombardier and danced the *Hora.*

Moe and Florence went off to a motel in Rapid City. I hired two taxis and took the bombardier, his wife, and Moe's mother to dinner. The bombardier, well pleased with himself, became tipsy. Moe's mother sat encased in her own world. From time to time, she smiled at me. "It's a pleasure," she said, or "So nice. . . ."

My crew told me the news when we landed after a bombing run. My friend Junius Eddy was flying the plane next to mine. Junes tried and failed to get his radio operator on Intercom. When he reached him, he demanded to know just what in the hell the radio operator had been doing.

"Listening to the news, Sir," the radio operator said.

Junes bawled the man out for listening to the news on a bombing run. The radio operator waited until he had finished.

"Sir," he said, "I don't think you know what's happened."

"Well," Junes demanded; "tell us what's happened!"

"Sir," the radio operator said, "President Roosevelt is dead."

All the officers on the base were ordered to assemble outside the tactical office at eleven the next morning. I stood in the crowd. I had never mentioned my friendship with the President in the air corps; I kept my feelings to myself.

A major came out of the tactical office. He formed us in ranks and marched us to the post theater. The dogs that wandered over the base loved formations of any kind. One of them, a mongrel, trotted beside me all the way.

A prior service, attended by the enlisted men, was under way in the theater. We waited for half an hour outside its front doors. A few of the officers squatted in circles, matching nickels. The rest stood around in the sunlight, boasting about their feats with women the night before. The mongrel slouched down beside me and licked its genitals. "Don't you wish you could do that," one pilot said to another. "I'd rather you did it," said his friend.

The doors of the theater opened. The enlisted men trooped out, and we trooped in. A choir from Rapid City sang *Holy, Holy, Holy* in a dispirited way. A tactical officer read out an Expression of Sorrow, handed down from a superior command. A chaplain asked God, our Father, to bestow His mercy on His servant, Franklin. The band from the base played *Hail to the Chief*.

That was it. We moved out into the sunlight. The major lined us up and marched us back to the tactical office. "FORMATION DISMISSED!" he shouted, and we wandered away.

Roosevelt died on April 12, 1945. Two weeks later, Hitler shot himself. The war in Europe was over.

Would the Flying Fortresses be used against Japan? The answer proved to be *no*. So we were transferred to Texas, to fly B 29s.

The B 29s were known as Super Fortresses. They were the largest planes that we had built. They had been built in a hurry and were difficult to fly.

We flew in rotating shifts at our base near San Antonio. Three days of flying between midnight and 8:00 A.M.; three days from 8:00 until 4:00 P.M.; three days from 4:00 until midnight. We did not know if the food that we were eating was breakfast or dinner; nor did we care.

When we were not in the air, or asleep, we lay on our cots, listening to the radio. We learned in August 1945 that a B 29 had unloaded an atom bomb on Hiroshima and another on Nagasaki, killing or mutilating all of their inhabitants.

I roused myself from my torpor and wrote to my wife.

August 13, 1945

. . . It looks as if the war is just about over.

I should be filled with the deepest gladness for the cause that is won; the deepest gratitude for the lives that have been spared, including my own. A part of me is truly glad and grateful. Another part is empty and adrift.

Most of each day, and a part of each night, I keep thinking: if only I had joined the Marines! If only I had never said that I could speak French. If only. . . .

Useless regrets!

I left you for only one reason: to fight. From that point of view, I've wasted three years of my life. . . .

We lay in our barracks, waiting, waiting. We waited through the heat of each day for the news to come.

We grew sick of waiting. I and two other pilots, John King and Frank Pierson, climbed into my Ford sedan and headed for the hills.

We bunked down the first night in a Spanish ranch in Medina County. We rode out with the ranch hands the next morning to check the Hereford cattle and the Rambouillet sheep. The ranch hounds started up a mountain lion in the Mesquite. It was too hot to chase them and their baying died out in the distance.

We drove on that afternoon to Bandera; it was a rough little town. A rodeo was being held there; after it was over, everyone began to drink.

We found one room in the only hotel in Bandera. We lay there, the three of us, trying to sleep in the hot night while drunken men argued on the veranda beneath our window.

Distinctions of rank were dimming as the war approached its end; or so the conversation beneath us suggested.

"I say that all officers are chicken shit."

"I say that all enlisted men are chicken shit."

"I say that all officers are bastards."

"I say that all enlisted men are louses."

And on and on.

It was Saturday night. On Sunday morning, no one was up and about save for the state game warden. He was stalking around with one hand gripping his revolver. He was followed by two sorry-looking hounds.

John King had been a biology student. He engaged the game warden in a professional exchange about an endangered species of wild cats.

"Are there any Procynidae around here?"

"Come again?"

"Procynidae."

"Caint you talk English?"

"I said, 'Are there any Ring Tailed Cats around here?' "

"Hell's fire man! Why didn't you say so! Me and my dogs killed six of them critters last month!"

We drove back to San Antonio. We lay on our cots through the next day, listening to the radio.

We fell asleep toward midnight. At 1:30 A.M. we were awoken by a yell.

"The war is over," a pilot nearby us yelled. "The fucking war is over!"

# Part Three

# *The Long Road Back*

# A WORRIED MAN

LIKE many veterans, I was highly elated when I was handed my discharge papers. I barely said goodbye to John King and Frank Pierson as I set out on the eighteen-hundred-mile drive from San Antonio to Old Westbury. I drove through half the night in my impatience to be home.

Once I was there, anxiety made itself at home in my spirit. I was desperately anxious to make up for the years that I had lost; I had no idea where to start again in the postwar world. I felt that I could no longer afford to make any mistakes; my impatience in itself led me into many errors.

I sensed that the world that I had come back to had been transformed by the atom bombs that we had dropped upon Hiroshima and Nagasaki. I had to find out if the ideas that I had lived by were valid any longer. By chance, while I was still on terminal leave, I was brought into the company of some wise and worried men.

Two international lawyers, Grenville Clark and Louis Sohn, convened a conference in Dublin, New Hampshire, in October 1945. It was the first conference to consider the impact of nuclear weapons upon the United Nations, and it was my introduction to the postwar world.

Eight veterans were invited to the conference. Charles Bolte was the only one whom I knew. He was the chairman of a new organization, the American Veterans Committee, and I had been elected to its national board.

Charles and I drove from New York City to Dublin on a fine autumn day. We talked about the A.V.C. and about its founder, a sergeant named Gil Harrison, who was still in the South Pacific.

"I'm worried about Gil," said Charles. "I'm afraid that he's becoming too anti-Communist."

At the Dublin Inn, I was assigned to a double room with a former navy pilot named Kingman Brewster. We were both in uniform, and we made the most of the occasion when the day came to put on our old civilian clothes.

"How does this shirt go with my jacket?" Kingman asked me. "Can I wear a red tie with a tan shirt?" I asked.

The devastation that the United States had wrought upon Hiroshima and Nagasaki hung like an evil presence in the conference room. The nuclear scientist who attended our conference warned us that if atomic weapons were allowed to multiply, they would destroy mankind. How, we asked, were we to control those weapons? The scientist did not know.

We felt that we were at a decisive moment in the history of the world; it was for us to propose some answer to the problem that we had met to consider.

The charter of the United Nations had not yet been reviewed by the United States Senate. We lost little time in concluding that a world organization in which Costa Rica and the United States each had one vote was incapable of reaching, let alone enforcing, a meaningful agreement on the control of atomic weapons. The United Nations, therefore, was stillborn. But what could take its place?

On that critically important question, the Dublin conference split three ways.

One group at the conference was led by an oily messiah named Emery Reves. Its central tenet, which it pressed upon us as if it were a revelation of Divine wisdom, was that a world government alone could wield the power that was needed to control atomic weapons. How it was to be brought about was a detail that did not greatly concern Reves and his followers. They preferred to speak in metaphors, pointing to an invisible clock and saying that its hands were ticking off the minutes that mankind had to live.

A second group at the conference was led by Clarence Streit. In the days when Britain was threatened, Streit had published his plan for the unification of the English-speaking nations. He pressed his plan at Dublin and the powerful figure of Owen Roberts, who had recently resigned from the Supreme Court, stood at his side.

A third position barely made itself heard at Dublin. Winfield Reifler, a historian from Princeton, said in a shamefaced way that we would have to learn to live with the bomb. No one listened to him.

It was easier at Dublin to say: "a nuclear arms race *must* lead to war" than to say: "a nuclear arms race *may* lead to war." It was more dramatic—and more gratifying.

On one point, everyone at Dublin was in agreement: only a world authority could prevent a nuclear arms race.

And if the Soviet Union refused to recognize that authority?

That question was ruled out of order at the conference sessions, but it was raised when we adjourned to the bar of the Dublin Inn. "If the plan that we have been considering is presented to the Russians," I said to Justice Roberts, "and if the Russians reject it, won't that bring us closer to a third world war?"

We had to shout to make ourselves heard in the bar, and Roberts shouted at me,

"WHY ARE YOU WORRIED ABOUT A THIRD WORLD WAR? THE THIRD WORLD WAR HAS ALREADY BEGUN!"

Emery Reves was standing beside us. "If there is to be a third world war," he said, "then let it be a civil war."

We met behind closed doors at Dublin, but on the fourth day of the conference, the world intruded on us. The press had been told to expect some important announcement, and by noon, a dozen newspapermen were waiting for it at the Inn.

A drafting committee went to work. It prepared a statement that thirty of the forty-seven conferees signed. It was called the *Declaration of the Dublin Conference* and it was carried on the front page of the *New York Times*. "Recognizing a transcendent urgency to insure against an atomic war 'which would destroy civilization and possibly mankind itself,' " the *Times* reported, "a group of prominent Americans proposed today the scrapping of the United Nations Organization and the creation of a World Federal Organization."

The *Declaration* proposed that a representative legislature and a strong executive be established in place of the assembly and the staff of the United Nations. It called on the United States to take the first step in creating the new organization.

It was a bold and a well-intentioned statement. Justice Roberts refused to sign it on the grounds that it went too far toward world government; Emery Reves refused to sign it because it did not go far enough.

I signed the *Declaration*—with deep misgivings. It brushed aside the United Nations, but, I wondered, if the United Nations were discredited, would any other organization take its place? The *Declaration* was replete with words like "must," and that disturbed me. Keynes had taught me that politics was the fine art of the possible; Tom Corcoran had chided me for placing the word "must" in the draft of a speech we were preparing. He had recalled the last exchange between Elizabeth the First and her great courtier, Lord Cecil. "Your Majesty must not die" Cecil had cried as the Queen lay on her death bed. "Little man," she had whispered, "little man, the word *must* is not used to princes."

I was sure of only one thing as I drove back from Dublin to New York: it would not be possible to talk the Soviet government into surrendering its sovereignty over its own armed forces to a body that it could not control.

What, then, were we to do? And where did I stand?

I had long since shed what belief I had once held in communism, but I could not permit my own life to be shaped by bitterness over the ways in which I had been used. I no longer believed that time would bring about a synthesis between communist and democratic societies, but I was convinced that there was no issue at stake between the United States and the Soviet Union that could justify a nuclear war. My belief in the United Nations as an instrument for resolving conflicts had been shaken by the Dublin Conference. I still pinned my hopes to the conviction that Roosevelt expressed on his return from the Yalta Conference: "I have never lost my faith that some common ground will be found."

I wondered as I drove back to New York how long we had to find that common ground. I could hear Justice Roberts's cry echoing and re-echoing through the hills of New England: *"The third world war has already begun!"*

---

We rented out our farm in Virginia during the war. My wife had embarked upon her own career in psychiatry; we had to live in New York City. The tensions of the place deepened my anxiety.

I felt that it was too late to retrace my steps and rejoin the staff of *The New Republic.* I hurried from one place to another in a frantic effort to find a role for myself in the postwar world.

I became the secretary of the Emergency Committee of Atomic Scientists, a group headed by Albert Einstein, in an effort to do something about nuclear arms control.

I went to Washington to see Tom Corcoran. He said of the Truman administration: "A gang of crooks has hijacked the funeral train of a great man."

I thought of working on the staff of the United Nations. The official who talked me out of it, saying that it had no power, was Alger Hiss.

I decided to run for Congress in the district in which we were living in New York. The incumbent was a Republican, Joseph Clark Baldwin III, who was known to his Italian constituents as Joe Baldwin de Turd. I went to the headquarters of the Democratic machine, Tammany Hall. Its reigning bosses, Bert Stand and Clarence Laughlin, welcomed me with open arms as their prospective candidate. We were moving right along when Oscar Ewing, the vice chairman of the Democratic National Committee, telephoned Laughlin.

He had been informed, said Ewing, that I had been a Communist in my youth in England.

I went to see Ewing. His source, he said, was my friend the financial columnist Eliot Janeway.

That surprised me. I telephoned Eliot and asked him if it was true that he had spread the story about me.

"The question," said Eliot, "is not who spread the story but how you respond to it."

"How should I respond to it?" I asked.

"That," he said, "is for you to decide."

It did not take long to come to a decision. I had buried my Communist past; I had no desire to disinter it in meetings with Oscar Ewing,

Clarence Laughlin, the voters of the Seventeenth District, or the reporters from the *Daily News.* I called Laughlin and told him that he would have to find another Democrat to run against Joe Baldwin. Then I called Bruce Bliven and said that I was coming home to *The New Republic.*

*The New Republic* had settled back into its old ways in my absence. I wanted to liven it up. I worked up a special issue on Roosevelt that we published on the first anniversary of his death.

Churchill was one of many distinguished contributors to the issue; he was, Mrs. Roosevelt told me, coming to America to lay a wreath on Roosevelt's grave in Hyde Park. I knew that his visit would be a trying one for both of them. I feared that she would offer him drugstore liquor or none at all. I asked her if I could send up a half dozen bottles of *Château d'Yquem,* which we had kept since my father's time in our cellar at Westbury. Mrs. Roosevelt accepted them gladly: She telephoned me a week later to say that they had been well received.

"I told Mr. Churchill that one of his admirers had sent up some bottles of *Château d'Yquem* for him," she said. "I asked him if he would like to drink them at luncheon. Do you know what he said? He said, 'On one condition: that you serve them after the whiskey and before the brandy.' " Laughing, she added, "So I did!"

-—⁓⁓—-

In the spring of 1946, I sailed to England to see my mother. It was the first time that I had been back, and it was an emotional experience for me.

I went with Milton Rose, our family's legal adviser. We landed at Southampton and drove through the New Forest to Dartington. My mother and Jerry were waiting there for us; we gathered at tea time, as they always did, in Jerry's study in the Hall. Tea was brought in, and, as always, the robins and the chaffinches, the blue tits and the great tits gathered on the window sill of the study and waited, glancing at us with their bright eyes. My mother took two slices of brown toast, as she always did. She chewed on them until they were soft and mushy; then she took them out of her mouth and laid them on the sill. The birds gobbled them up.

England had changed greatly, as Whitney had predicted it would. My working-class friend, Lil Ramsden, to whom I had entrusted James Cornford, was now the Lady Mayoress of Totnes. In the valleys that surrounded Dartington, farm laborers had taken their places on the village councils, and health clinics were being built.

I met with a group of Labour members of Parliament in London. I urged them to support the plan proposed by David Lilienthal, Dean

Acheson, and J. Robert Oppenheimer for the international control
and development of atomic energy. Speaking for the group, Michael
Foot said, "We're all for it, but we're powerless. It's the Russians
whom you've got to talk to, not us."

I had no intention of talking to any Russians. The last people that
I wanted to encounter in London were Guy Burgess and Anthony
Blunt. I did go to see Margot Heinemann. I told her that the American plan for the control and development of atomic energy was our
best hope for peace. I said that it was a constructive and a generous
offer, and that if the Russians rejected it, an arms race would follow
that could end in a third world war.

Margot was well up in the hierarchy of the British Communist party
by then. She said, "Would you tell that to Harry Pollitt?"

Harry was still secretary general of the party. We sat down together
on a bench in Covent Garden. I explained the basic principles of the
American plan to him.

He listened patiently to all that I had to say. He was wholly immune
to my plea.

I quoted his comment in an article that I wrote on my return for
*The New Republic.* "This atom bomb of yours has altered the balance
of forces, and revived the old dream of destroying the Soviet Union.
But the Soviet Union will have the bomb before long, so it's a short-
term war or none at all. I take the long view."

In other words, politics as usual.

The British Communist party had no mind of its own; no will. It
would bring no pressure to bear upon the Kremlin. It would continue,
under Soviet control, to demand the breakup of the Anglo-American
alliance. It would insist that the United States share its knowledge of
atomic technology with the Russians, not as a step toward the world
control of nuclear weapons but in order that the Russians could produce a bomb of their own. Then, in Harry's opinion, "the balance of
forces" would be restored. The imperialists would forsake their "old
dream of destroying the Soviet Union," and, accordingly, the world
would be safe once again.

'. . . it's a short-term war or none at all. I take the long view.' I
quoted Harry's parting words to me in *The New Republic.* I added my
own comment on them.

I take the short view.

Peace is a short-term problem. It rests on the faith of nations in the
possibilities of compromise. That faith is dying. Once it dies, war is inevitable.

To demand the break-up of the Anglo-American coalition is to guarantee its consolidation. To demand the sharing by the Russians of the secret

of manufacturing atomic bombs is to guarantee that the secret will be kept by us.

This is no time to assert: *world control, but not for my nation.* The only objective that can be realized now is that no nation shall be able to wage atomic war.

# HENRY

HENRY Wallace of Iowa was secretary of agriculture during the first two terms of President Roosevelt and vice president during his third term. He was secretary of commerce in the Cabinet of President Truman until, at Truman's insistence, he resigned on September 12, 1946.

I had never met Wallace, but he knew my mother and my stepfather. He had stayed at Dartington and had written many articles for *The New Republic.*

In company with most liberals, I looked up to Wallace as Roosevelt's heir apparent. I cheered when he shouted to the Democratic Convention of 1944, "The poll tax must go!" I felt cheated when the convention cast him aside and nominated Harry Truman in his place. I shared his concerns when, in 1946, the wartime alliance gave way to the Cold War. As for his speech to the Stop Dewey Rally in Madison Square Garden—the cause of his dismissal—I knew that Truman had approved of the speech when Wallace showed it to him. The Communists in the Garden had tried to howl Wallace down as he delivered the speech. *The New Republic* had commented, "In attempting to expel Wallace from the progressive movement, the Communist party will succeed only in expelling itself."

I was convinced, late in 1946, that *The New Republic* could not survive in the postwar world with twenty thousand readers. I believed that with one hundred thousand readers, we could, once again, be an important force in American life. I believed that with Wallace as our editor we could gain one hundred thousand readers, and I persuaded Bruce Bliven and Dan Mebane, the senior members of our staff, that I was right.

So one week after Wallace resigned, I stood at the door of his apartment in the Wardman Park Hotel in Washington, rehearsing the short speech I had come to deliver.

The door opened. A gray poodle sniffed my trousers. Its owner, Mrs. Wallace, led me through the apartment to the terrace that overlooked Rock Creek Park. There in the autumn sunlight sat the familiar, unkempt figure, sorting out telegrams with his principal adviser, a meaty Texan named Harold Young.

I hurried through my little speech. Wallace listened, staring at his shoes. Harold fingered the telegrams, many of which were offers of lucrative contracts from publishers and lecture agencies.

To Harold Young, *The New Republic* was a prospect about as inviting as exile to Siberia. Wallace, in contrast, recalled that at moments of personal crisis, his father and his grandfather had turned to publishing. He weighed all his offers and chose *The New Republic*. One week later, we wrote out on a grubby piece of paper the terms of our association. Wallace would be the editor of *The New Republic;* I would be its publisher. He would devote himself to the magazine; I would push its circulation up fivefold, to one hundred thousand subscribers.

With the paper in my pocket, I hurried back to New York. We cleaned out a corner room in our offices for our new editor. We bought, borrowed, or stole every mailing list we could lay our hands on. We raided the fortified empire of Henry Luce and made off with some of his ablest men.

The Wallaces moved to a farm in South Salem, New York. One Sunday, Bruce and I drove up to have lunch with them. They laid out a splendid meal, made up of produce they had grown. They were especially proud of their tomatoes. "My, these tomatoes are delicious!" said Bruce to Mrs. Wallace. "What did Henry do to make them so tasty?" "He fed them with radioactive fertilizer," said Mrs. Wallace. Bruce turned pale.

As editor, Henry advocated many innovative programs. He called for an international authority to provide power and irrigation for the Jordan Valley. He proposed massive economic aid for Europe eight months before Secretary Marshall delivered the Harvard address that gave birth to the Marshall Plan. At times, however, he seemed to be insensitive to the impact of his words. He would seem to be evasive when he thought that he was being outspoken; he would give offense when he intended to give praise.

I brought in an urbane intellectual, James Newman, to work with Henry. The three of us would meet early in each week to talk over his next editorial, then Jim would prepare a first draft. We would take our places on the sofa in Wallace's office; he would sit between us, jingling the keys that he carried in a pants pocket. Jim would read aloud a paragraph or two; Henry's eyelids would lower, his head sinking inch by inch until it came to rest on his chest. The jingling would stop; Jim and I would look at each other. Then Jim would read the editorial through to its end. We would wait, and, after a moment or two of silence, the jingling would start up again. Henry's head would jerk up; his eyelids would flutter and part. "Fine," he would murmur; "that's fine."

As for the rest of the magazine, Wallace rarely read it through. We held many conferences in our efforts to improve *The New Republic;* Henry did not attend them. We recruited a staff of brilliant editors; Henry failed to recognize some of them when he passed them in our offices. He walked forty blocks from his apartment to our building on Forty-Ninth Street. Once there, he enclosed himself in a world of his own.

The organizers of the Stop Dewey Rally complained with some justification that we had stolen Wallace from them. We managed to keep them out of our offices, but we could not keep Henry in. One day, a shapeless figure arrived and closeted himself with our editor in his corner room. After an hour, they walked out arm in arm. They went out together a good many times in the weeks that followed. We tried to find out who Henry's mysterious companion was. All that we could learn from Henry's secretary was that he came from Brooklyn and his name was Max. Months later, we were told how they spent their days. Max, who was a retired grocer, would lead Henry down the streets of the East Side, stopping at one delicatessen after another. "Mister Iushewitz," Max would say, "meet my good friend Henry Wallace. Mister Wallace, meet my dear friend Eli Iushewitz." Henry would return from these excursions with his overcoat pockets bulging with tins of gefilte fish and bottles of borscht. In the immense and alien city, he found the human warmth that he needed in these men who venerated him.

It was not critical to the success of our venture that Wallace should be a working editor. We might have succeeded had he joined *The New Republic* at a time when differences of opinion could be kept within the bounds of reason.

Unhappily for us, 1947 was not such a time.

The Iron Curtain had descended, dividing Europe. The wartime alliance had given way to the Cold War. Stalin had made a satellite state out of Poland; he was threatening to take over Czechoslovakia and was inciting turmoil in Greece. In turn, powerful men in the Pentagon were saying, Better a world war now than later on, when the Russians have the bomb.

Within the United States, the political situation was highly unstable. There was general agreement that Truman was too small a man to be president. The unions were furious with him; the intellectuals despised him; the majority of voters had no confidence in him; the leaders of the Democratic party were searching for some way to replace him as their nominee in 1948.

The liberals were only one segment of the electorate, but they were a highly articulate segment. They were bound together, not by race or region, but by the convictions that they shared. Southerners and Republicans resolved their disputes in 1947; the liberals were broken apart.

Two organizations claimed the allegiance of the liberals in 1947: the Progressive Citizens of America and Americans for Democratic Action. They moved into opposing trenches, and the ground between them became a no-man's land.

The A.D.A. condemned Stalin's efforts to crush the independence of Central and Eastern Europe; the P.C.A. insisted that the unity of the great powers was our one assurance of peace. The A.D.A. held that the P.C.A. was dominated by the Communist party; the P.C.A. retorted that the A.D.A. was the tool of Henry Luce and of the Democratic party bosses: Bob Hannigan, Ed Flynn, and Mayor Hague.

Which side could bring forth a leader? The A.D.A. fell silent when that crucial question was asked; the P.C.A. pointed to Henry Wallace.

Wallace leaned from the start toward the P.C.A. Its chairman was the renowned sculptor, Jo Davidson, who was adept at flattery. Its director was Beanie Baldwin, who had been the director of the Farm Security Administration when Henry was secretary of agriculture. Its undercover organizer was the formidable Hannah Dorner. Its platform was Peace.

My own association was with the A.D.A. It had little appeal to Wallace. Its leaders, save for Mrs. Roosevelt, were intellectuals with whom he felt ill at ease. It seemed to be seeking an accommodation with Truman, and Wallace's hatred of Truman was a virus that raged within his frame.

One morning in March 1947, the telephone rang in my office in *The New Republic.* Jo Davidson was calling me. "Mike," he said, although we had never met, "my wife and I are giving a little dinner tonight. It's in honor of Henry Wallace. We'd like you to come."

So, once again, I rang a doorbell and waited.

The door to Jo's studio opened. His wife, a heavy-set woman, let me in.

The dimly lit studio was filled with disembodied heads of bronze and plaster. At its far end, four people were standing around Wallace with drinks in their hands.

Jo left the group and gripped me in a bear-hug, his beard pressing against my chest. Beanie Baldwin and Harold Young held out their hands, ill at ease. A resolute woman grasped my hand saying, "I'm Hannah Dorner." I said to myself: *Ouch!*

We ate a number of Mexican dishes that Jo and his wife had prepared. We drank several bottles of Burgundy. Jo called me *amigo* and
spoke of his close friendship with Gertrude Whitney, my Uncle
Harry's wife. Then, at some signal, they all fell silent.

Harold Young cleared his throat. "Mike," he said, "you've been
keeping Henry to yourself for long enough. We've decided that it's
time that he got out and met the people again."

*We've decided.* . . .

Hannah Dorner and Beanie Baldwin had the accumulated deficits
of their two organizations to pay off. To them, "meeting the people"
meant having Henry stump the nation under the sponsorship of the
P.C.A.

Harold Young saw himself as a king-maker if Henry could be
elected president. To him, "meeting the people" meant having Henry
work the Democratic party precincts in an effort to wrest the party
nomination from the hands of Harry Truman.

I had gambled hundreds of thousands of dollars of our family funds
in an effort to drive up the circulation of *The New Republic.* I knew that
if Henry left us to become embroiled in political battles we could lose
the magazine.

I looked at Henry to see what his response might be to Harold's
comment.

Once again, he had fallen asleep.

I left Jo's studio wondering how I could keep my hold on Henry.
I called together the senior staff of *The New Republic.* We prepared our
little plans; then, without warning, the world began to crumble
around us.

In Europe, the dictatorial government of Greece began to fall apart;
a Communist-led minority seemed ready for a civil war.

President Truman might have taken precise and limited action to
save the Greek government; instead, he proclaimed the Truman Doctrine, an open-ended commitment to intervene in any nation where
communism seemed to pose a threat.

Our government gave up all sense of strategic priorities when it
proclaimed the Truman Doctrine. It extended our obligations without
regard for our resources. It permitted corrupt and dictatorial regimes
to lay claims upon our treasury in the name of anti-communism. It
paved the way for our catastrophic participation in the Vietnam War.

Many political leaders foresaw the dangers inherent in the Truman
Doctrine. Wallace alone set out to prevent it from being embedded
in the foreign policy of the United States. Six days after Truman
proclaimed his Doctrine, Wallace denounced it in a national broadcast
that I prepared for him. Five thousand Americans wrote to him,
thanking him for speaking out and begging him to lead them. So the
issue was joined.

Wallace was ready to stump the country in opposition to the Truman Doctrine. He could not set out at once, for he had accepted an invitation to visit England under the auspices of the *New Statesman*.

His visit had been planned in the dead of winter; in March, it became a highly volatile event.

The president called on the Congress to implement the Truman Doctrine as Wallace prepared to fly to England. The Senate was by no means ready to accede to the president's request. In England, the Labour party was in power. It, too, was deeply divided by the Truman Doctrine. Many members of the British Cabinet sided with Wallace, and more than fifty members of Parliament signed a telegram welcoming him to England.

Ernest Bevin, Britain's foreign secretary, was not among the fifty leaders who welcomed Wallace. He could not sanction any break with Truman, and he knew it.

I sensed the danger when I landed in England, a few days before Wallace was due to arrive. I sent him a telegram warning him not to criticize President Truman or his Doctrine while he was on foreign soil.

That proved to be impossible. Wallace was taken from the airport where he landed to a press conference in the Savoy Hotel. Fifty reporters were waiting for him at the press conference. They demanded to know where he stood. He chose to answer the questions as he would have answered them in Washington. But he was not in Washington, and his charge—that the United States was adopting a course of "ruthless imperialism"—caused a furor on Capitol Hill.

On the floors of the House and Senate, politicians of both parties lined up to take their turns in denouncing Wallace. They set aside their measured criticisms of the Truman Doctrine and wrapped the American flag around themselves. One senator demanded that Wallace's passport be revoked and that he be forced to return.

Many Englishmen were startled, as I was, by the intensity of the American reaction. As Frederick Kuh reported in the *Chicago Sun,* "When U.S. Senators, Congressmen and the press began to storm against Wallace, this was the signal for British conservative papers to start criticising him too."

Speaking to a Conservative party rally in the Albert Hall, Winston Churchill condemned Wallace as a "crypto-Communist" who was seeking to "separate Great Britain from the United States and to weave her into a vast system of Communist intrigue." That was profoundly unjust, and Churchill soon thought better of it. With no prompting from Wallace, he disowned his own statement, claiming that he had been misquoted by the British press.

Wallace, to his credit, was not deterred by the abuse that was heaped upon him. He spoke to one-third of the British nation over the B.B.C., advocating his own Doctrine—international collaboration to raise the living standards of all peoples. He waved a copy of *LIFE* magazine—with its map of America's new empire, stretched around the world. In place of Henry Luce's vision of the American century, he offered his own vision: the century of the Common Man.

We stayed for three days at the Savoy. A number of uninvited guests came to pay their respects to Wallace. One who looked like a Shakespearian actor said that he was the counselor of the Soviet embassy. I thought for a moment that someone was playing a practical joke on Wallace; then I whisked the counselor off to an elevator before the reporters who were sitting and drinking in our suite could catch a glimpse of him.

A second uninvited guest was Guy Burgess. He had no messages to deliver; no questions to ask. He was, he said, working for Hector McNeil, Britain's minister of state. He added that he was about to leave the government for good.

I rushed him down to the Savoy Bar and bought him a double whiskey. We talked about the danger of war. I mentioned how obdurate Harry Pollitt had been when I had tried to make him face the necessity of nuclear arms control.

"Well," said Guy, "our intelligence services must at least have taken an interest in your views."

"I don't follow you," I said.

Guy laughed. Pollitt, he said, had a mistress to whom he told everything. She, in turn, reported week by week to Scotland Yard.

The *New Statesman* had arranged a speaking tour for Wallace. We boarded a night train and were met in Preston the next morning by the local M.P. We drove through the morning fog to Blackpool for the first of many receptions given by mayors bedecked in gold braid. We drove on from Blackpool to North Staffordshire and the Black Country.

The lord mayor of Stoke-on-Trent gave us a splendid dinner. His city was engaged in trying to gobble up its little neighbor, Newcastle-under-Tyne, and between the little lord mayor of Newcastle-under-Tyne and the large lord mayor of Stoke-on-Trent, there was a good deal of sword play. The large lord mayor neglected to say grace before we began our dinner, a blooper that the little lord mayor was quick to note. Much embarassed, the large lord mayor rose when the feast was over and drew his splendid robes around his middle. "For all that we have received," he intoned, "may we be truly thankful."

"About time, too," said the little lord mayor.

"Aye," said the large lord mayor, "but I couldn't say it before, because I didn't know what a splendid feast we were going to have."

He turned to Wallace, "We may not always agree," he said, "but it takes a man to speak his mind, and we love you for it."

"Aye," said the little lord mayor, "and in North Staffordshire, when we love a man, we call him by his first name."

So for the rest of the evening, we were "Henry" and "Mike." I learned when the party was over, that both lord mayors had lost their sons in the war.

It was hard to believe, in those hours, that anything mattered, save the struggle in which we were engaged. But other battles seemed to be in progress. A British contender was challenging the American holder of the Heavyweight Boxing Crown, and he, apparently, was first in the hearts and minds of his countrymen in April 1947. We stopped at a red light in Manchester and, seeing the American flag flying on the bonnet of our rented limousine, a workman came running up to us. He poked his head into our car. "Yanks are you?" he shouted to the startled Wallace. "Who's going to win the fight then?"

On balance, Kuh wrote in the *Chicago Sun,* Wallace's journey through England was a success. "Millions of Britons," he reported, "were pleased to learn that there are still prominent Americans who see Britain's destiny as something other than that of an atom absorber in a future U.S.–Soviet war."

Wallace and I flew to Norway and Sweden, where he had been invited to speak. His speeches, as the *New York Times* noted, were sponsored by broad coalitions "of all political parties." Wallace, the article continued, "drew applause with just about every second remark."

Next we flew to Paris. A large crowd was waiting for Wallace at the airport. I looked in vain for Maurice Schuman, Jean Monnet, and other moderates who, we had been told, were sponsors of his visit. I recognized two leaders of the French Communist party: the aged Marcel Cachin and the squat and ugly Jacques Duclos.

Pierre Cot had asked Wallace's permission to organize his visit to Paris, promising that it would be broadly sponsored. Had he delivered Wallace into the hands of the Communist party? I held myself to blame and was heartsick. It was not until 1979, when I read through the Wallace archives that I learned that Henry himself had chosen to walk into the trap.

Two letters from Alfred and Martha Stern pointed to that sad conclusion. One was to Cot, telling him to wire Wallace in the name of a broad welcoming committee; the other was to Wallace, urging him to accept Cot's invitation. He had not shown the letter to me.

Who were the Sterns? I asked a congressman that question in 1981; he looked at me in surprise. "He was a Connecticut businessman," he told me. "She was the daughter of Roosevelt's ambassador to Germany. They were accused of espionage on behalf of the Soviet Union, and they were indicted by a Grand Jury. They fled to Czechoslovakia." The indictment was dismissed in 1979.

Once again, through my association with Henry Wallace, I was being drawn toward the Soviet orbit. I sensed the danger in 1947, but I could not share with Wallace the knowledge that gave rise to my feeling of dread.

Wallace's main address in Paris was delivered in the Sorbonne. The immense hall was crowded. Leon Jouhaux, the elephantine president of the Confédération Générale des Travaileurs slumbered in the chair. Wallace read aloud a tactful speech that made no mention of Harry Truman. Duclos, who was sitting beside me on the platform, nodded as the speech was translated paragraph by paragraph into French.

"Very nice; very moderate," he said.

One other event on our European tour remains vivid in my memory.

In Copenhagen, the American ambassador, an old friend of Wallace's, refused to receive him. We were welcomed instead by Ole Cavling, the owner of the daily newspaper *EXTRABLADET.*

Cavling, so he said, was the founder and president of the International Society of the Long Golden Beards. It had only one regulation: whenever anyone said something pretentious, the members of the society were required to stroke their imaginary whiskers.

Wallace and I were inducted into the society in the course of a very long luncheon that Cavling gave for Henry. The initiation ceremony consisted of swallowing one strong drink after another.

The ceremony began in the sitting room of Cavling's apartment. It went on for an hour. When Cavling summoned us, we headed in the general direction of his dining room.

The dining table was set for thirty places. At each place there were four plates, stacked on top of one another. On the top plate lay one small anchovy.

Food apparently was still scarce in Denmark in 1947. Liquor, which had been hidden from the Germans, was plentiful. Around the stacks of plates were grouped six glasses: acquavit, slivovits, schnapps, and three other colorless but fiery liquids. The glasses ascended in height to a centerpiece: a silver tankard, filled to the brim with Danish beer.

To drink down the contents of each glass was a fearful prospect; there was no escaping it. Each time I looked up from the table, a Dane would be staring at me, glass in hand. I had to fumble for the appropriate glass and raise it in return.

I sat there, stiff as a board. The dining room whirled around me. Somewhere, at the far end of the table, Henry was sitting. He was, as far as I knew, a teetotaler and, I suspected, in need of protection.

But there was no way in which I could go to his aid. In the Society of the Long Golden Beards, I decided, it was every man for himself.

Our plates were taken away one by one as each course was served. We arrived at last at the bottom plate. Cavling stood up at that moment and proposed a toast: "To the President of the United States!"

I managed to stand up when the other guests stood and to mutter: "The President!"

We sat down again. The Danes waited in silence; it was Henry's turn.

I heard no sound at the other end of the table. I realized that it was up to me. I heaved myself upright and shouted: "To the King!" Everyone rose at that and echoed: "The King!" We knocked down one more glassful of some nameless liquor. I sat down again, wondering if I was going to be sick.

A few minutes passed in which no toasts were offered. Then, at the far end of the table, I heard the sound of a chair scraping along the floor.

Henry was standing and swaying, his silver tankard in his hand.

"Gentlemen," he cried. "Gentlemen! . . . Let us rise for one more toast."

We all stood up. I had no idea what was coming, and I was beyond caring.

"Let us drink," said Henry. "Let us drink . . . to the great state of Texas!"

I stared into my tankard, wondering if I could manage one sip without throwing up. I heard Cavling's sonorous command:

"Fellow members of the International Society, I remind you! When we drink to the great state of Texas, we must drain our tankards dry!"

We landed back in New York at four in the morning. Two days later, Wallace set off on a speaking tour of the United States. I went with him, but I was no longer at his side.

Beanie Baldwin and Harold Young had insisted that Wallace should make the tour. *The New Republic* staff had done all that it could to keep it under broad sponsorship, but it was no use. We had no organizers in the cities of America. The A.D.A. was turning against Wallace, and only one of its chapters was prepared to sponsor him. The P.C.A. was fully committed to Wallace, and it was strongly supported by several large unions within the C.I.O.

I spent two days with my family at Old Westbury. I took a last look at the cherry trees and the dogwoods—they were in bloom in April. I left for the airport with a heavy heart.

I had recruited a large staff at *The New Republic*. We had driven the circulation up fivefold, as we had promised to do. We had failed to bring in any advertisers, and our losses were appalling.

I had bound *The New Republic* to Henry Wallace. He, in turn, had allowed himself to be bound to the P.C.A. To whom was the P.C.A. bound? I asked myself that question and I feared the answer.

On the tour that he made of America, Wallace moved in the center of a political bodyguard of three men: Beanie Baldwin, Harold Young, and Clark Foreman, a fiery Southerner who had worked with me in the Interior Department. A fourth man joined us who dwarfed us all in size and in stature—Paul Robeson.

We moved from city to city; the rallies were always the same. Local orators would work up the crowd with verbal assaults on Truman and the militarists who were preparing to lead us into another war. Then the hall would be darkened, and we would wait in a hushed silence. A single shaft of light would turn to an entrance, and onto the stage would stride the immense and purposeful figure of Robeson. He would sing *Ol' Man River*—in his own version, which ended *Keep on Fightin' until I'm Dyin'*. . . . He would stand there, trembling as the audience stood and cheered. The cheering would be formless at first, then, prompted by unseen voices, it would harden into a chant: *"Wallace for President, Wallace for President. . . ."* Robeson would listen, his right hand cupped behind his ear, as the chant mounted in volume. When it reached its peak his magnificent voice would boom out: *"Yes! The people want Wallace for President! And if they can't have him as a Democrat, they'll know where to go!"*

A money-raising pitch by Clark Foreman would follow hard on that theatrical climax. At last, at 11:00 or 11:30, the hall would darken once more; Wallace would appear on the stage and stand, grinning in the floodlights.

By then, many farmers and working men who had come from miles away to hear Wallace would have gone home.

City by city, Wallace and his party moved West. Beanie Baldwin devoted his days to meeting with Democratic politicians in an effort to line up delegates who would vote for Wallace at the 1948 Democratic Convention. He was, I believe, sincere in his desire to work within the Democratic party, but he lacked the power to separate the party from its president. He picked up ten delegates in Cleveland; a dozen more in Detroit. Meanwhile, driven by its own dynamism and egged on by the Communist party, the P.C.A. was moving out, on its own.

I saw the change take place; I became more and more disturbed. My hostility was apparent to the men who had surrounded Wallace, and one morning a succession of visitors came to my hotel room in Chicago. Harold Young gripped my shoulder with his sweaty hand

and assured me that I was doing a great job "for the people." Clark Foreman spoke about the political heritage that we shared as New Dealers. Paul Robeson lay on my bed and talked about the production of *Othello*—his first triumph in London, which my mother had financed.

The last of my visitors was Beanie Baldwin, the soft-spoken Virginian. He was, he insisted, a loyal Democrat.

I reminded Beanie of the refrain that we were hearing at every meeting: *If the people can't have Wallace as a Democrat, they'll know where to go.* "Do you know what you're doing?" I asked him.

Beanie nodded. "It's the only way that we can make the Democratic bosses listen to us," he said. "Without the threat of a third party, we haven't a chance."

"What if it doesn't work?" I said.

Beanie looked at me and smiled.

When the trip was over, and we were back in the offices of *The New Republic,* I was able for the first time to sit down with Wallace and talk about his tour.

I went over his meetings, one by one.

"What did you think of Cleveland?" I asked him.

"It was fair."

"That was a broadly sponsored meeting, supported by the A.D.A. What about Chicago?"

"Much better."

"It was organized by a number of Communist-led unions. What about Los Angeles?"

"It was a great rally," said Wallace, and he was right. Twenty-eight thousand people gathered in Gilmore Stadium that night. The platform was packed with film stars, and Katharine Hepburn among others had made a militant speech.

"Once again," I said, "it was Communist-led."

"Can you prove that?" Wallace asked.

"No," I said. "I can't."

"Then you shouldn't say it."

We glanced at each other. We were like passengers on passing ships, Henry heading for the land of illusions from which I had come. I knew from my own experience that collaboration with the Communist party would destroy Wallace, but I could not share my experience with him. He looked on collaboration with the Communists, in or out of Russia, as an *idea.* He had traveled on a broad highway from Iowa to Washington, and by daylight. He knew nothing of the back alleys of the political world.

We were silent for a moment. Then I read on down the notes that I had made in the course of our travels.

"What did you think of Seattle?"

"Fair."

"And San Francisco?"

"About the same."

"Those were meetings that started with broad sponsorship and ended up under left-wing control. What about Portland?"

"Very good, considering Portland."

"It was organized by a Communist-led union. And Olympia?"

I moved on down my list of cities. When I came to the end of the list, I said, "What do you think of what I've told you about the Communists?"

Wallace shrugged his shoulders. "They get out the crowds," he said.

Should I have forced Wallace at that moment to choose between his new allies and me? It was not easy.

In binding *The New Republic* to Wallace-the-Editor, I had bound myself to Wallace-the-Man. I had written most of his speeches, shared most of his views, been impressed by the crowds that had gathered to hear him. I had been moved by the men who praised him.

I wanted to rescue him from the embrace of misguided men like Beanie Baldwin and of foolish men like Harold Young. My voice was stilled by a censor within myself.

I stood, irresolute, between the opposing forces of the Left. I sensed, once again, that I was trapped. This time, the trap was of my own making.

We returned in late May from our tour of the United States. In the months that followed, the Wallace movement seemed to be becalmed, "a painted ship upon a painted ocean." Henry spent the summer on his farm in South Salem; Harold Young ran his political office in Washington; Beanie Baldwin soldiered on in a futile effort to line up delegates for Wallace at the Democratic Convention. I shut myself up in my office at *The New Republic,* trying to cope with its mounting deficits.

There was no way in which I could cope with *The New Republic* and Wallace. In a moment of exhaustion, I asked Lew Frank, the son of a Detroit businessman, to join us. Lew and I had worked together in the American Veterans Committee—or rather, we had worked against each other, since Lew was on the left wing and I was on the right wing of that embattled organization. I liked Lew nonetheless and I was sure that he would dedicate himself to his task.

On that, I was right. Lew became an invaluable aide to Wallace— and an impassable barrier, isolating Wallace from liberals like myself.

In the summer of 1947, the conflict between the Communist party and the non-Communist Left was masked. The Truman administration had taken one great step forward in proposing the Marshall Plan—a program to reconstruct Europe with the help of American economic aid. The Communist line, in turn, was in flux at three separate levels of authority.

In New York, the primary concern of the Communist leaders was the Labor party—a powerful organization in which they worked in harness with the Amalgamated Clothing Workers Union. The heirs of Sidney Hillman in the union were opposed to a third party, and Robert Thompson, the leader of the Communists, promised them that there would be no third party unless they chose to support it.

At the national level, as I learned later, the Communist party was divided. The old-time officials opposed a third party, fearing that they could not control it. The young, undercover leaders were confident of their ability to manipulate mass movements; they were ready to risk their forces in an aggressive political strategy.

In Moscow, the Politburo itself was divided. Should it support the Marshall Plan in the hope of obtaining the capital and equipment that the Soviet Union urgently needed, or should it try to drive America out of Europe? The first course pointed toward collaboration with the Truman administration; the second, toward an effort to defeat it by every means at hand. Only when that choice was made, it seemed to me, could we tell what pressures would be brought to bear upon Henry Wallace.

In October 1947, the leaders of the Communist International met in Warsaw. The manifesto that they issued denounced the United States for seeking "to subjugate the world."

"The greatest danger to the international working class," said the Soviet spokesman, Andrei Zhdanov, as he released the manifesto, "is the underestimation of its own power."

I read through Zhdanov's statement in the *New York Times*. Then I telephoned Harold Young in Washington. I said, "There's going to be a third party."

"You're crazy!" Harold said.

Henry was away that week, driving through New England to see the autumn foliage. When he returned to New York, a meeting was held to plan his schedule.

We met in my house in New York City. Beanie Baldwin opened the discussion by proposing a January rally in Madison Square Garden.

I suspected that the rally would herald the founding of the third party. "Who will be the Chairman?" I asked.

"A trade union leader."

"Which one?"

"Philip Murray, Jake Potofsky. . . ." Beanie rattled off an impressive list of leaders. "We'll invite them all," he said.

"Will they accept your invitation?"

"I can only promise one at this moment."

"Who is that?"

"Albert FitzGerald," said Beanie, naming the pliant man who, with Communist party support, was struggling to maintain his hold upon the United Electrical Workers Union.

"FitzGerald as chairman of the rally? Then better no rally," I said.

I turned to Wallace for support. Once again, he had fallen asleep.

I lay awake that night, wondering what to do. It occurred to me that the best course would be to get Wallace out of the country.

*Palestine,* I said to myself; *they cannot stop him from going to Palestine.* For once I was right, and our trip was arranged.

It was up to me to talk to Wallace and to make him aware of all that was being plotted in his name. I knew that, but I kept on putting the moment off. The plane, I said to myself. I'll talk to him on the plane as we're heading for Palestine.

I left Henry alone, but I went to see Beanie. "I think that there's going to be a third party," I told him.

Beanie said: "I agree."

"I want to say this to you," I told him. "You won't get the liberals. Some of them will abandon you out of fear, some out of conviction. I'd like to be counted now as belonging to that second group. So don't count on *The New Republic* or on me."

Beanie nodded. He said, "I wish you would tell that to John Abt."

John Abt was the general counsel of the Amalgamated Clothing Workers Union. I had never met him. I went to the union headquarters in downtown New York and introduced myself.

Abt was a quiet man. He listened to what I had to say. Then: "Thank you for telling me," he said.

"What are you going to do?" I asked him.

"We'll go through with our plan," he said. "The world must be told that not all Americans have given up hope for peace."

On the following day, Wallace and I set out for Palestine. Lew Frank went with us, since Beanie and his friends did not trust me. A publicist named Gerold Frank also joined us, since the Zionists did not trust any of us.

Our flight was announced. Lew clung to Wallace's side. *Oh well,* I thought, *I'll make Lew change places with me, once we are airborne.*

The plane took off. I started to climb over Gerry Frank's knees, but he held up his hand.

"Look," he said. "I've brought along a chess set."

He held out two fists. I tapped one and drew white. By the time that the *Constellation* was over Nantucket, our pieces were well deployed.

Had I forfeited my last chance of blocking the third party? I thought so, and for years I blamed myself for all that followed. I think now that even had I forced Henry to look ahead, it would have made no difference. His course was set.

We had many memorable days in Palestine. Henry described them in his weekly column in *The New Republic,* but there was one incident that did not find its way into print.

The Stern Gang was an armed force in Palestine, bombing British army installations; burning the homes of Arabs and Jews who collaborated with the British rulers; waylaying British soldiers and executing them in cold blood. The gang was illegal, of course, but it was in touch with a few foreign journalists. One morning, the correspondent for the *New York Herald Tribune* slipped Wallace a handwritten message. The head of the Stern Gang wanted to meet with him.

Lew and I said no to that. We added that we would meet with the man and pass along to Wallace all that he had to say. So late one night, we walked up and down a back alley in Haifa. At the appointed hour, in the best Hollywood manner, an ancient cab lurched around the corner of the alley. It swerved toward us and stopped. We were hauled inside the cab and blindfolded. Still blindfolded, we were led into a building, up in an elevator, through a guarded door. We were thrust down onto two chairs. Then our blindfolds were untied.

We sat for a moment in darkness. Then the lights came on. We were seated at a dining table, covered with salami and sausages—as if we wanted to eat! Armed men were standing behind us with their pistols drawn. Across the table, staring at us was a man whose hair was dyed jet black, and whose dead-white skin was drawn tightly across a smooth, remodeled face.

He spoke in a deadly monotone. He wanted Mr. Wallace and his supporters to know that he shared their social objectives. As for violence, he and his followers took no pleasure in executing British Tommies. In another land, in another time, he too would be a liberal.

He spoke for an hour or more. We uttered a few weak disclaimers and promised to pass along all that he had said. He nodded, and his armed men stepped forward. We were blindfolded again and dumped out into the alley where we had been picked up. We wandered through deserted streets to our hotel.

We headed home, stopping off in Rome to see the pope. In New York, it became as difficult to see Wallace as it had been to interview the head of the Stern Gang. Walter Reuther and Philip Murray denounced the third party. Within a day or two, delegates from the union locals that the Communist party controlled would be closeted with Wallace, assuring him that Reuther and Murray had lost touch with the rank and file. Jan Masaryk the leader of the Czechoslovakian liberals, fell to his death from a window in a high building in Prague. On the following morning, a Czech was brought to Wallace's office.

The rumor that Masaryk had been pushed from the window was a monstrous lie he said. The man was a manic-depressive who had threatened many times to commit suicide.

Once a week, Wallace emerged from his office to have lunch with the editors of *The New Republic.* I invited Max Lerner, the liberal columnist, to join us. Max denounced the preparations that we knew were under way to create the third party. Wallace listened in silence, his head sinking onto his chest and his eyelids closing; Lew Frank suggested that Max had fallen prey to the red-baiters.

I took Wallace out to Old Westbury for the night. I asked Charles Bolte to join us, and, after dinner, Charles told Wallace the full story of our struggle against the Communist caucus within the American Veterans Committee.

Wallace sat, staring at the carpet in our living room and jingling his keys. "You can't build a movement on the basis of opposition to communism," he said.

"Nor on the basis of subordination to Soviet policy," said Charles. He tried to continue, but Wallace cut him off.

"The issue," he said, "is peace."

Helen Fuller, the Washington editor of *The New Republic,* came to New York to see Wallace. "Would you lead a third party if the liberals were against you?" she asked him.

"Most of them are for me," he said.

"Are you sure," asked Helen. "Do you mind if I urge them to get in touch with you?"

"Go ahead if you want to," said Wallace in his gloomy way.

Helen enlisted Mrs. Roosevelt and many more old friends of Wallace's in a telephone campaign. He would stand in the doorway of my office, never coming in. "Tell Helen," he would say, "that another of her friends called me today."

Wallace made no decisions. He was carried along in a current, and the current was strong. The executive committee of the P.C.A. met in December. Howard Fast, the novelist, moved a resolution calling on Wallace to lead a people's party. A bitter argument followed. At its height, Helen, who was a member of the executive committee, moved that the resolution be referred to the national committee of the P.C.A.

That would have disrupted the entire schedule, and John Abt knew it. In his quiet voice, he invoked an obscure by-law and ruled Helen's motion out of order.

So the Progressive party was born.

It was understood that Henry could not be both the editor of *The New Republic* and a candidate for the presidency. He wrote his final editorial for our January 5 issue. It was an eloquent statement of principles. Embedded within it was a revealing comment on who would control the party that he was to lead: "Many of the friends who have supported my decision argued in advance that it was dangerous because the Communists want it. But I have never believed in turning from a principled position because it happened to win the support of others."

I read the statement when it was handed to me to print. It saddened me, because I knew that it was a lie. The Progressive party did not 'happen to win the support' of the Communist party; it was created by the Communist party. The question was not, who will support the Progressive party? It was, who will control it?

Henry had chosen to blind himself to that all-important distinction. Harold Young had fallen off somewhere down the line. Beanie saw himself as the Jim Farley of the Progressive party; he believed that, like John L. Lewis, he could use the Communist organizers as shock troops and then send them to the kitchen to peel potatoes.

*The New Republic* did not denounce the Progressive party at the moment of its creation. We were too close to Wallace to do that. We gave him a page each week for a signed column, and for a few months that seemed to work. But we were moving apart, and in the nation, tensions were rising. I realized that as I sat in the hall in Boston where the United Steelworkers Union was holding its Annual Convention.

Phil Murray was the president of the union. He had allowed himself to be guided by Lee Pressman, an undercover Communist. He had denounced Walter Reuther, the Socialist who had become president of the Automobile Workers, as a red-baiter. Then, in 1947, he turned on his former allies. In a towering passion he denounced the Communist wreckers within his union. He returned to the speaker's stand again and again to repeat his charges, and each new outburst brought the delegates to a new pitch of excitement and anger. At last, with more courage than wisdom, a Communist delegate from South Chicago stood up and called Murray a tool of the bosses. At Murray's signal, a band of muscular guards rushed down the aisle of the hall and seized the man. They punched him and kicked him as they dragged him from the hall. He was unconscious by the time that they dumped him onto the street. He would have died there if a passing motorist had not picked him up and rushed him to a nearby hospital.

In its first test, the Progressive party showed surprising strength. Its candidate swamped the man put up for a seat in Congress by Ed Flynn, the Democratic boss of the Bronx.

The lesson was not lost on Clark Clifford, President Truman's sophisticated counsel. He moved the president to the left of center and thus forced Wallace to move further to the left.

I saw very little of Wallace after January. I wrote three letters to him.

The first letter informed Wallace that we were going to oppose his stand against the Marshall Plan.

The second letter stated that we could no longer run his weekly column.

The third letter was the hardest for me to write.

The fifty thousand subscribers that we had picked up in 1947 were predominantly Wallace supporters. Our competitor, the *Nation* was straddling the issue of which candidate it would support in 1948. Nonetheless, it seemed to me, we owed it to our readers—and to ourselves—to take a stand. We urged William O. Douglas, a Supreme Court Justice, to seek the Democratic nomination. He wavered and, after weeks of indecision, refused to run. The Democratic Convention handed its nomination to the president, who accepted it in a peppery speech.

I sat through the final sessions of the convention in Philadelphia. I knew what I had to do. I went back to my office in *The New Republic* and wrote to Wallace, saying that we were about to endorse Truman. My letter must have come as a bitter blow to him, but his reply was a model of courtesy and grace.

The November election was a triumph for Truman and a disaster for the Progressive party. If the leaders of the Communist party, in the United States and in Moscow, held an inquest on the campaign, they must have concluded that they had blundered. They had forced hundreds of their organizers in the trade unions to walk the plank. They had cut themselves off from the sources of their power.

They struggled on, unwilling to admit defeat. In the spring of 1949, I was scheduled to speak at Rutgers University in New Jersey. Four people turned up at the meeting; the chairman explained that the Progressive party was holding a mammoth rally in a movie house in Jersey City.

We adjourned our meeting and went to the mammoth rally. It was a dispirited affair. A thousand people were seated in the movie house, but it was filled with the stench of death.

A British member of Parliament delivered a dreary address. A fund-raiser flogged the crowd. "Ingrid Bergman and her husband have met," he shouted, referring to the marital problems of the Swedish film star, "why can't Truman and Stalin?"

As always, Wallace was held until the very end of the rally. He sat slumped in his chair on the stage, his head resting on his chest. I hoped for his sake that he was asleep.

Who among us will reveal the dreams that he nurtures within himself? Wallace, I am sure, dreamed of himself as president of the United States and as peacemaker for the world. I also dreamed of myself as a political leader in the years during which Wallace and I were yoked together.

Our dreams were reduced to vain regrets in the course of our partnership. Wallace retired to his farm in South Salem. I struggled to salvage what I could from the ruins of our publishing venture. I heard no more from him until one Sunday morning in 1953.

I was reading in my home in Virginia that morning when the telephone rang. I heard Wallace's husky voice. He was in Washington, he said. He wondered if I would join him and his family for dinner.

Wallace had left the Progressive party by then. He had acknowledged his errors. He had made his peace with Harry Truman and with the liberals. He had endorsed the policies of President Eisenhower. Nonetheless, he was being hounded by his enemies on the far Right.

A Senate subcommittee had been looking into Communist infiltration of the federal government. It had centered its investigation upon the cell established within the Department of Agriculture in the thirties whose members, according to sworn testimony, included Lee Pressman, John Abt, and Alger Hiss.

The subcommittee had summoned Wallace to testify on what he knew about the cell. His answer—*I knew nothing*—was the truth. It was not an answer that satisfied the subcommittee or its supporters.

Day after day, conservative commentators, led by Fulton Lewis, Jr., charged that Wallace was the knowing accomplice of traitors. The charge had infuriated me. Digging into some captured German documents, I had discovered that Lewis himself had sent a series of secret messages to the Nazis, advising them on how to undermine the power and prestige of President Roosevelt.

Wallace had apparently learned of my discovery. He was anxious to read the documents.

We met in the home of the Swiss minister who was married to Wallace's sister. Wallace read through my files on Fulton Lewis; then we turned to a subject that we had discussed once before in 1947.

This time, Wallace asked the questions.

"Was John Abt a Communist?"

"I think so."

"And Paul Robeson?"

"I'm afraid so."

"What about Lew Frank?"

"I've asked myself that question many times," I said. "I just don't know."

"And Beanie Baldwin?"

"Beanie wasn't a Communist—in my opinion. He thought he could use them."

Henry nodded. He said, "I blame Beanie for a lot."

The minister and his wife were waiting for us in their living room. So were Henry's daughter and her husband. We joined them and went in to dinner.

Wallace sat in silence in the candlelight. The gloom that exuded from him spread like a black cloth, smothering all conversation.

No one had any light comments to make. I did my best. I had just returned from Europe, and I described the places that I had visited. We were beginning to feel comfortable once again when Wallace interrupted me.

"Where would you live," he wanted to know, "if you couldn't live in America?"

I tried to treat his question casually. "There's a village on the Lake of Lucerne where Mark Twain used to stay," I said. "There's Tuscany. There are some lovely places in the Cotswolds, and in South Devon. There's Dittisham and Duncannon and. . . ." I wandered on down the lanes of Devon dreading the moment when Wallace would break in once again.

He broke in. He burst out in a bitter denunciation of the charges that were being pressed against him.

"Do you think," he demanded, "that the American people believe all of those lies?"

"No, no; of course not," we all mumbled.

"That's why I asked you the question!" he cried. "Because, if they believe them, I don't want to live in America any more!"

It was a sad ending to the saddest chapter in a distinguished career. But the chapter was not all sad.

There was the sunlit day when we sailed in a tiny steamboat around the Sea of Galilee. There was another day in the North of England when we drove to the village of Freckleton.

An American bomber, badly damaged and struggling to return to its base, had crashed onto the playground of the village school at Freckleton, killing all of its crew and all but two of the children who were playing there. The men at its base had rebuilt the shattered playground, fashioning seesaws and slides and a merry-go-round from the twisted metal of the wreck. They had placed a plaque on a wall:

*This playground presented to the children of*
*Freckleton by their American neighbors . . . in*
*recognition and remembrance of their common loss.*

The villagers were waiting for Wallace in the playground. The mayor made a little speech of welcome. The two children who had survived the disaster were brought up to Wallace to curtsey and to shake his hand. They were horribly scarred and were shivering in the chill wind.

Wallace stood there with his arms around the two children. He spoke about the issue that mattered most to him: peace. The fathers and mothers of Freckleton nodded as he spoke, and, all the time, a new batch of kids too young for speeches were playing on the slides and the seesaws, breaking across his measured phrases with their shrill, discordant cries.

# THE 1948 CAMPAIGN

THE *New Republic* supported Harry Truman and his running mate, Alben Barkley, in 1948. We had differed on many issues but we had this much in common: our prospects were poor; our resources were dwindling; we were going for broke.

There was only one way in which Harry Truman and the liberal Democrats could survive in 1948; that was to cut into the Wallace vote. For that reason, *The New Republic* became a significant force in the campaign. Week after week our editorials were teletyped to the whistlestops where Truman paused on his campaign tours. His ghost-writer, John Carter, copied our comments onto the pages that Truman read aloud to the crowds that gathered to cheer him on.

As a former associate of Wallace's, I was also of some use to the Democratic party. It was not a pleasant role. In every audience some spokesman for the Progressive party would stand up and denounce me as a turncoat. I accepted their comments as a form of penance. It was as if I were working my passage home.

The League of Women Voters, the Ethical Culture Society, and many other organizations sponsored forums at which representatives of the contesting parties spoke. The forums that were held in the Northeast became a traveling road show in October with an established cast. Oren Root spoke for the Republicans; Norman Thomas, who was himself a presidential candidate, spoke for the Socialists; Emanuel Bloch or O. John Rogge represented the Progressive party; and I spoke for the Democrats.

Oren was mild and courteous; Bloch was arrogant and sour. Thomas was cunning and wickedly irresponsible, but what a show he put on! He quaked; he declaimed in righteous indignation; he poured a concoction labeled Hypocrisy over the rest of us; then he set fire to us with the malicious delight of a small boy.

How swiftly he struck, and with what deadly aim! In Schenectady, for example, we spoke before a thousand voters in a school auditorium. Thomas and I dwelt upon the Communist party's control of the Progressive party. Bloch, in his turn, swore that we were lying. He had spoken to thousands of Progressive party members, he said, and not one of them was a Communist.

When our prepared speeches were completed, the meeting was opened to questions from the floor. A man stood up in the back of the auditorium. "My question is addressed to Mr. Bloch," he cried.

Bloch advanced to the microphone that stood at the center of the stage. He waited, listening.

"Mr. Bloch!" cried the man, "are you a Communist?"

Bloch seized the microphone, clenching his fists around it. "I would be betraying every one of you if I answered that question!" he shouted. "I and every member of the Progressive party are fighting for your rights when we refuse to state our political affiliations!"

Bloch stood there, heaving as his supporters in the audience cheered. Thomas stepped up to the microphone. "Just a minute . . . just a minute!" he cried. "If, as you say, no member of the Progressive party will state his political affiliations, then how do you know that there were no Communists among the thousands of Progressive party members whom you say you met?"

We debated again in New York City. Rogge, a huge attorney, spoke for the Progressives. "Are you prepared to support the Marshall Plan in October and to denounce it May?" I asked him. "Are you willing to praise Mrs. Roosevelt as a peace lover one day and to vilify her as a warmonger the next day?" The crowd waited; Rogge was silent.

A man stood up when the chairman of the meeting called for questions. "My question is for Mr. Thomas," he cried.

Thomas stood by the microphone, cupping one hand behind his ear.

"Mr. Thomas, isn't it true that in the Soviet Union they don't discriminate against anyone on grounds of race or color?"

The Progressives in the audience cheered at that. Thomas waited until the cheering had died away.

"It's true," he said, "that in Russia they don't discriminate against you on grounds of race or color. They shoot you for your opinions, whether you're black or white!"

I made scores of speeches for the Democrats in September and October. It never occurred to me that they might win. I remember one rally where I and Maurice Tobin, the secretary of labor, were the speakers. In an impassioned peroration, Tobin shouted out that Truman was on his way to victory. He waited for the cheers but no one had the heart to break the silence. I remember another evening in Chicago when I spoke for Paul Douglas and Adlai Stevenson. We put on a brave show, but when it was over, Douglas drew me aside. He told me that although he and Stevenson would run far ahead of Truman they would be beaten by one hundred thousand votes.

I was certain in October that we would be living for four years or more under President Thomas E. Dewey. Nonetheless, I took my wife, our two boys, and our baby, Susan, back to our farm in Virginia. It seemed to me that if we could live there as a family we could regain a sense of peace.

We had been separated by work in New York. In Virginia, we were together again, in a house of our own. The walnuts fell with soft thuds onto our lawn in the darkness. A mockingbird woke me at the first light with his song. David, aged five, chopped up honeysuckle vines with his hatchet. Mike, aged four, cut firewood with his saw. Susie, aged two months, growled in her perambulator. We were content.

Ed Harris, a reporter on the St. Louis *Post Despatch,* asked the staff of *The New Republic* to his house on election night. He knew that we would all become despondent if we listened to the election returns, so he cut his own record and played it at intervals on his radio/gramophone. Mimicking the voices of the network commentators, Ed announced in his first newsbreak that, contrary to all expectations, Truman was doing well in the early returns. Everyone in his living room sat up, amazed. He turned on his record an hour later and announced that Truman was sweeping the country. At that, everyone stood up and cheered. In his third broadcast, Ed revealed that Dewey had conceded defeat. At that, his guests wept and hugged each other. They insisted that Ed leave the broadcast on. It ended with two remarkable announcements. Dewey declared that he was giving up politics for good and returning to his early career as a singer in light operas. Wallace stated that he was leaving the United States to join the army of Israel.

The hoax was over. Everyone rushed at Ed and almost lynched him.

The time had come to face the realities of 1948. Ed turned his radio on; his guests heard a replay of his fantasy. All but the ending was true.

# DIES IRAE

AMERICA was victorious in war, but peace did not follow the surrender of Germany and Japan. Victory without peace can be more disillusioning than defeat, and disillusionment can lead to wrath.

As Eric Hoffer noted in *The True Believer*, "When hopes and dreams are loose in the streets it is well for the timid to lock doors, shutter windows and lie low until the wrath has passed. For there is often a monstrous incongruity between the hopes, however noble and tender, and the actions which follow them. It is as if ivied maidens and garlanded youths were to herald the four horsemen of the apocalypse."

Dreams that had been oversold were shattered in the three years that followed the war. Sacrifices that had been accepted because they seemed to be final came to be viewed as tests of will for greater sacrifices to come.

The Soviet government returned to its prewar policy of promoting world revolution. The United States became its leading antagonist. We lacked experience in the role in which history cast us. Our task was made more difficult when the cause of opposition to Soviet expansion became intertwined with other, unworthy causes.

The House Committee on Un-American Activities played a major role in shaping political attitudes in the years after the war. Its chairmen included Martin Dies, who was known for his casual cruelties; John Rankin, a fanatical racist; and J. Parnell Thomas, a small-time crook.

A lack of serious intent marked the committee's hearings. They were hampered further by the ignorance of the members of the committee and of its staff. Thus, the role of my old teacher Harold Laski was raised by one witness and led to the following exchange between Chairman Rankin and his counsel, Ernie Adamson:

MR. RANKIN: Who is Mr. Laski?

MR. ADAMSON: Mr. Laski is, I believe, one of the leaders in England of the Communist movement.

Representitive Rankin was more interested in discrediting Mrs. Roosevelt than in learning the facts about the Communist party. He was alarmed, not by the growth of Soviet power but by the spread of democracy in his state of Mississippi. The Fair Employment Practices Commission promised to provide greater opportunities for black Americans. It was identified by Chairman Rankin as "the beginning of a Communistic dictatorship the like of which America has never dreamed."

Even when it moved to the grave issue of Soviet espionage, the committee was motivated by political considerations. Its hearings were timed, as Chairman Thomas affirmed, "to keep the heat on Harry Truman" during the 1948 campaign.

---

The committee was not the first group to stumble onto the reality of Soviet espionage. In 1945, government agents had raided the offices of the magazine *Amerasia* and recovered a thousand documents stolen from the State, War, and Navy departments. In 1946, the Canadian government had arrested twenty-two officials as Soviet agents on the basis of information provided by the Soviet defector Igor Gouzenko. The impact of these events, however, was lost upon the American public. The *Amerasia* thefts were never traced to the Soviet Union; the Canadian arrests were in another country.

Unknown to the public, an American Communist, Elizabeth Bentley, went to the F.B.I. in 1945. She stated that she had taken over the management of a Soviet spy ring following the death of her lover, a Soviet agent named Jacob Golos. She named a number of United States government officials as members of her ring. She added that two high-ranking New Dealers, Harry Dexter White and Lauchlin Currie, had knowingly cooperated in her work.

Miss Bentley was brought before a grand jury in New York. She testified in secret before it, over a period of thirteen months. Eleven officials of the State Department were dismissed or allowed to resign as a result of her revelations. But no corroborative evidence was obtained from those whom Miss Bentley named and no indictments followed the grand jury's investigation.

When legal action proved to be impracticable, publicity generated by congressional hearings seemed to be the next best thing. In eight appearances before congressional committees, Miss Bentley repeated her story for the third time. She said of her spy ring, ". . . we had a steady flow of political reports from the Treasury which included material from the Office of Strategic Services, the State Department, the Navy, the Army and even . . . the Department of Justice. We knew what was going on in the inner chambers of the United States Government up to and including the White House."

The officials whom Miss Bentley named as members of her spy ring refused to discuss her allegations when they were brought before the House Committee on Un-American Activities. The committee turned in 1948 to a second witness: Whittaker Chambers.

Chambers made no mention of espionage in his initial testimony before the committee. In subsequent hearings, he swore that he had been a Soviet agent in the 1930s, and that seventy-five officials of the United States government had, in his opinion, been engaged to some

degree in espionage on behalf of the Soviet Union. One man whom
he identified as a close friend and an ardent Communist agent was a
former high official of the State Department: Alger Hiss.

For six years, I had thrust all thoughts of Guy Burgess, Anthony
Blunt, and Michael Green from my consciousness. From 1948 on,
those memories returned like the furies to pursue me.

Foremost in my mind was a sense of fear. I had made my break in
1941. I had never heard of Elizabeth Bentley or Whittaker Chambers
and had no reason to believe that they had known Green. Yet it
seemed probable that my name would crop up in some context. For
two years, whenever a telephone call came for me, I braced myself,
wondering what I would say if a reporter who had come upon some
trace of my past were on the line.

In addition to fear, I was haunted by a sense of guilt. I saw the faces
of the men who had been named in the newspapers. I read the broken
sentences of Julian Wadleigh who chose to confess. I shared some of
his pain.

I had, as a student in Cambridge, known Herbert Norman, who
killed himself after he was arrested in Canada. I knew several of the
officials whom Elizabeth Bentley and Whittaker Chambers named.
Frank Coe had been an inoffensive figure in the Economic Policy
Club; Lauchlin Currie had given me many stories in my *New Republic*
days. Donald Hiss had been a good friend of mine in the State Department. His life was shattered.

Neither in America nor in England could I escape my own past.
Milton Rose and I returned to England in 1949 on family matters. We
were walking down Whitehall when we passed Guy Burgess in the
street.

Guy told me that the Apostles were about to hold their annual
dinner. He was the chairman for the dinner and had chosen to hold
it in a private room in his club, the Royal Automobile Club. He urged
me to attend the dinner, and I said that I would.

Guy sat at the head table with the speaker for the evening, the
drama critic Desmond MacCarthy. Thirty members of the society took
their places at two long tables; I sat by a rising historian named Eric
Hobsbawm.

I remembered Hobsbawm as a member of the student Communist
movement at Cambridge. He made it plain that he, at least, had not
given up his beliefs.

I made some bitter comment about the Soviet occupation of Czechoslovakia. Hobsbawn countered with a comment about the Americans
who had been imprisoned under the Smith Act. He said with a knowing smile, "There are more political prisoners in the United States
today than there are in Czechoslovakia."

"That's a damned lie!" I cried. I continued to shout at Hobsbawm. I was aware that others were staring at me. I was not acting in a manner becoming to a member of the society.

Anthony was sitting at the far end of the room. I had managed to avoid him, but when the speeches were over and the dinner was breaking up, he came over to me.

"Guy and I would like to talk to you," he said. "We'll meet you here tomorrow morning."

We sat in deep leather chairs in a dimly lit corner of the club. We talked about what we had been doing. I learned to my dismay that Anthony had been engaged in intelligence work throughout the war. He added that he had left the government in 1945 to devote himself to his true profession of art history. He would never return to the government, he said.

Guy, in contrast, conceded that he had moved to the Far Eastern department of the Foreign Office.

It seemed to me probable that Guy was still engaged in espionage. I reminded him that when we had last met, in 1947, he had assured me that he was about to leave the government for good.

"I was about to leave," Guy said, "but then this offer came along."

He sensed my hostility. He added that he was about to go off on an extended leave and that he did not intend to return to the Foreign Office.

Where, then, did the three of us stand? We turned to the central issue of the day: the danger of a third world war. I spoke with some bitterness about the blindness of the Soviet leaders who had rejected the American proposals for the control of nuclear weapons and were attempting to disrupt the Marshall Plan. Guy's response was not to defend the Soviet government. Instead, he questioned the motivation of the United States.

Anthony listened in moody silence. I sensed that he still deferred to Guy on political issues, although his interest in politics had diminished.

The tensions between us mounted. At last, Anthony broke in.

"The question is," he said "are we capable of intellectual growth?" I said, "Exactly!"

We stood up to say goodbye. Guy looked at me intently.

"Are you still with us?" he asked.

"You know that I'm not," I said.

"You're not totally unfriendly?"

"If I were," I said, "why would I be here?"

It was a weak, evasive answer; the sort of answer I habitually gave when I faced a confrontation of any kind. It reflected my continuing inability to force an issue, to resolve a conflict, to make an enemy of another individual, and, in this instance, to break completely with my own past.

I walked away, down Pall Mall, trying to sort out my feelings. I had made my own position clear and was glad of that. But I had stopped short of any clear threat to act against Anthony and Guy.

And that, of course, was what Guy wanted to hear. He had arranged the meeting in the club in order to learn if I had already turned him in to the authorities. He had satisfied himself that I had taken no action. He had sought a commitment from me that I would not act at once, although I disapproved of all that he seemed to be doing. I had failed to stand against him.

I had accepted Guy's assurance that he would soon leave the Foreign Office, setting aside the suspicion that, once again, he would break his word to me. I had determined that Anthony had moved from the world of espionage to a world in which he and I shared the same values and ends. I had not foreseen that he would continue to act as Guy's accomplice in moments of crisis.

My fear and my sense of guilt were secret, shared by no one. At the same time, as editor of *The New Republic,* I had to share my thoughts and my feelings week by week on the allegations of espionage that were surfacing and on the larger issues that they raised.

The editors of *The Nation* were perfectly clear as to where they stood on the charges made by Elizabeth Bentley and Whittaker Chambers. "Any neurotic exhibitionist who can claim to have been a Communist," said *The Nation,* "is now assured of absolution, soul-satisfying publicity and, probably, more material rewards."

My signed editorial in *The New Republic* was less palatable to most liberals. "In general," I wrote, "we believe that the outline of Elizabeth Bentley's story is largely accurate."

I was baffled at first by Chambers's allegations about Alger Hiss; for Hiss seemed so cautious, so proper, so self-seeking to me.

Hiss had left the State Department by the time that Chambers testified before the House Committee. He had, with the blessing of John Foster Dulles, become the president of the Carnegie Endowment for International Peace. I telephoned him on the morning that the allegations made by Chambers were published in the press. I asked him what the story was all about.

"I'm as baffled as you are," he said. "I suppose it's all part of some scheme to hinder the Endowment in its search for peace."

If he had been distraught, I might have believed him. But he was calm and assured, as if he had prepared himself for years for the moment when the story would break. I sensed then that Chambers was telling the truth, and that remote as America had been from the anguish of Europe, there had indeed been Soviet agents in high positions in our government.

Hiss had been an associate and a protégé of Felix Frankfurter's. It was Frankfurter, so I was told, who had induced the secretary of state, Dean Acheson, to defend Hiss. "I will not turn my back on Alger Hiss," Acheson told the newspapers in January 1950. I chided him in an editorial for indulging in a personal luxury that could only damage the State Department and the Foreign Service.

Frankfurter was infuriated by my editorial. He summoned me to his chambers in the Supreme Court building and gave me a tongue lashing for my lack of courage. "We must never be afraid to be identified with our friends!" he cried.

The door to his office opened at that moment. His secretary looked in and told him that some important visitor had arrived to see him. Frankfurter sprang up from his desk and bundled me out of his office by a back door.

I laughed to myself as I walked through the marble halls of the Supreme Court building. But there was not much to laugh about in those days.

As early as 1946, the chairman of the Republican National Committee held that the issue in the coming election was "Communism or Republicanism." Richard Nixon was one Republican candidate who worked his way into the Congress by accusing his opponent of following the Communist party line.

The Democrats lost fifty-four seats in the House in the elections of 1946. The lesson was not lost on Harry Truman. He and his attorney general, Tom Clark, responded with their own exploitation of the anti-Communist feeling that was taking hold of America. The British historian David Caute notes in his book *The Great Fear* that "It was Truman and Clark who produced the loyalty program, who codified the association of dissent with disloyalty and legitimized guilt by association." It was Truman who set the stage for McCarthy and for our disastrous intervention in Vietnam.

Truman's Cabinet member Lewis Schwellenbach was the first to demand, in 1947, that the Communist party be outlawed. His proposal was given legislative form in the bill named for two leaders of the House Un-American Activities Committee, Karl Mundt and Richard Nixon. Their measure, the Mundt-Nixon Bill, made the legislative finding that the committee had failed to demonstrate that the Communist party was a clear and present danger to the United States. It directed the government to act against "Communist political organizations," not on the basis of their actions but in the light of the beliefs held by their members.

The Mundt-Nixon Bill passed the House with many liberal and Democratic votes. The *New York Times* called the measure fundamentally anti-democratic and added, "It could be used to impose restraints on freedom such as the American people have not known in 150 years." Yet the measure became law and was widely supported. Walter Lippmann wrote a book justifying the suppression of the Communist party. Hubert Humphrey, the leader of the Senate liberals, introduced a bill in the Senate in 1954 that made it a crime to belong to the Communist party. It passed with one dissenting vote.

David Caute's conclusion in *The Great Fear* is a sad comment upon America: ". . . during the crucial years of the great fear, the most influential faction of the American intelligentsia (largely but not wholly) abandoned the critical function that all intellectuals in all countries ought to sustain toward government . . . all available evidence confirms that . . . this willingness to defend democracy by means of antidemocratic methods spread rapidly and widely through the middle-class professions and the labor movement."

'. . . largely but not wholly. . . .' *The New Republic* devoted a special section to a reasoned attack upon the Mundt-Nixon Bill. I testified against the bill on behalf of the American Veterans Committee. I criticized Hubert Humphrey for betraying his own principles in seeking to suppress the Communist party.

Humphrey, who was a good friend of mine, called me to his office on Capitol Hill. He berated me, not for my opinions but for my apparent indifference to his career: "Don't you understand! I would have had no future in this city if I hadn't put my name to that bill!"

I was not acting in my own self-interest in opposing the Mundt-Nixon Bill. On the contrary, in attacking the bill I was placing myself at some risk. Senator Mundt, in fact, proposed to his colleagues that they should investigate and interrogate me as an obdurate opponent of the measures that he felt were essential to the safety of the United States. His colleagues voted his proposal down.

In an article in *The New Republic* of May 1, 1950, I tried to summarize all that I had learned about the Communist party: "Ultimate aims and short-term aims can never be separated and in the case of Communists and liberals are in basic conflict. The Communist Party is a recruiting ground for subversion and espionage. Whoever joins it, either through guilty conscience or idealism, ends by losing all conscience and all ideals. Yet, for the liberal, suppression is no answer. . . ."

Why not? I had been reading *A Communist Party in Action,* by a former executive-committee member of the Communist International who wrote under the name of A. Rossi. I quoted his words as a summation of my own beliefs: "The search for truth cannot go forward in the absence of heresy and opposition. . . . When the unity of a democratic society is maintained through arbitrary imposition even over a very small area, it ceases to be the kind of unity that is appropriate to a truth-seeking society. . . . Every attempt to fight error as if it were born beyond the frontiers of truth . . . not only fails as a matter of course but prevents the application of the only effective remedy. We can liquidate error only as we absorb and transcend it."

"The citizens," Rossi concluded, "must confront the Communists in the factories, in the streets, in the villages. . . . The state should step in only when Communist action takes a form that private citizens simply cannot cope with."

If I was opposed to the suppression by the United States government of the Communist party, was I willing to confront the Communists "in the factories, in the streets, in the villages"?

The answer was a qualified yes. I was willing to confront the Communists where they attempted to take over an organization in which I was a participant. I was not willing, as some anti-Communists were, to hunt them down and rout them out from their homes and their hiding places. I did not look on communism as "an absolute evil," as Whittaker Chambers held it to be. I did not want to allow my own life to be warped by bitterness and regret.

Richard Crossman once said to me, "Our political attitudes are determined by our point of entry into politics." His own point of entry, he added, was Germany in 1932. He might have joined the extreme left or the extreme right, he said, had he not seen them both in action in Berlin.

Today, Crossman's comment enables me to see some pattern in my responses when the Communist party attempted to take over an organization that I helped to lead, the American Veterans Committee.

The A.V.C. was never a large organization, but it was an important one. It, too, was a point of entry into politics for a number of returning veterans who went on to become congressmen, senators, governors, judges, and Cabinet members. It shaped their attitudes; it taught them political procedures; it gave them special insights in the course of four embattled years.

*Citizens First, Veterans Second* was the founding principle of the A.V.C. It opposed the Veterans Bonus; it fought against segregation. It worked for arms control, and for a strong world organization.

Westbrook Pegler, the columnist for the Hearst papers, branded the A.V.C. subversive. He nicknamed Charles Bolte, who had lost a leg in action, "Long John Silver." He denounced the National Planning Committee, on which I served, as a "Bunch of Reds."

That was a little hard to take, since the Communist party had also denounced us as a "Handful of Ivy Leaguers." It instructed its members to follow the masses into the American Legion; when that course proved to be futile, the Communist party reversed itself. It sent five thousand veterans into the A.V.C. We only had ten thousand members at that time.

Yuba City . . . Yokosaka . . . Tuscaloosa. . . . The chapter applications filled up sacks of mail, early in 1946. We approved the applications with barely a thought as to who our new members might be. Then, two months before our first National Convention, our two largest area councils, in Los Angeles and New York, passed under Communist party control.

From then on the National Planning Committee was divided on every issue that came before it. The Right Wing, to which I belonged, began to hold up the applications of chapters that, we suspected, had been organized by members of the Communist party. Our stand led to a memorable encounter.

Franklin D. Roosevelt, Jr., was the son and namesake of the man whose memory we revered above all others. He was a dynamic figure in his own right and, it was widely assumed, would be president of the United States one day.

Frank was a member of our committee—but an absent one. Then, as we were struggling with chapter applications one night, he made a dramatic appearance. In a speech charged with emotion, he denounced us for daring to investigate the political affiliations of veterans who had fought for their country.

I saw a good deal of Frank from then on. I reminded him of our first encounter when, two years later, he criticized me for being soft on communism.

He nodded. He had, he said, spent an instructive day with Ed Flynn, the Democratic Boss of the Bronx. It was Flynn who had persuaded him to reverse his stand.

"He told me," Frank said, "that anti-communism would be the most important issue in American politics for the next thirty years."

The A.V.C. held its first National Convention in Des Moines in June 1946. There, the divisions that had emerged within our planning committee were clearly drawn.

The Progressives, as the Left Wing called themselves, proposed that a cash bonus be paid to all veterans. The Moderates, as we were called, beat the proposal down.

The Moderates divided three ways on foreign policy. The Progressives stood for one idea: Big Three Unity.

Gil Harrison, who had founded the A.V.C., was plainly entitled to be its vice chairman. He was opposed by a Progressive candidate, Fred Borden. Delegates who had come to Des Moines from Europe, the Pacific, and the Deep South voiced their dismay on learning that their organization was divided. As if by magic, a movement sprung up to replace Borden *and* Harrison with a "unity" candidate. The "unity" candidate was found, and he announced his willingness to run. Needless to say, he proved to be an undercover Progressive.

By the third day of the convention, the foyer of the Hotel Fort Des

Moines looked more like a battlefield than a meeting place of friends. An old man staggered out of the bar in the foyer. Sensing the tension and unhappiness that surrounded him, he came up to me.

"Dump me," he said.

I did not understand him. "Where?" I asked.

"Here," he said, pointing to the carpeted floor. "Dump me right here! Watch the ketchup run!"

He thrust out his chin. "Go ahead; dump me!" he said. "It'll make you feel better."

"I feel fine," I told him. "I don't want to dump anyone." "You don't?" He shook his head. "Christ Almighty," he muttered as he staggered away.

Charles Bolte was elected our national chairman. Gil Harrison was elected vice chairman with a slate of Moderates, including me. Our margin was narrow, however, and as we headed back to New York, we knew that we were in trouble.

We were up against a highly sophisticated, tightly organized minority in the Progressive caucus. Where could we turn for guidance and help?

The classical battlefield on which Socialists and Communists had fought for power was the International Ladies Garment Workers Union. Its president was a battle-scarred adversary of the Communist party named David Dubinsky.

Oren Root, a Republican attorney and a member of our planning committee, went to call on Dubinsky. He told Dubinsky how we had fought against a Communist caucus in the A.V.C.

Oren was elegant and a bit fastidious. Dubinsky listened to what he had to say; then he laughed aloud in Oren's face.

"You?" he cried; "You?"

When he had stopped laughing, Dubinsky called in his assistant, Murray Gross. "Murray," he said, "we got a job to do."

Gross, in turn, called in his assistant, Gus Tyler. His parents were emigrants from Russia. He had grown up among the street gangs of Brooklyn. As members of the Young Peoples Socialist League, Gus and his friends had fought in every school auditorium and on every street corner with their counterparts in the Young Communist League.

"Gus," said Murray, "we got a job to do." Gus and his friends rushed into the A.V.C. to join once more in battle with their old enemies.

Our Second National Convention was held in Milwaukee in the summer of 1947. By then, Gus had transformed the loose association of Moderates into a highly disciplined force known as the Independent Progressive Caucus. Its members were organized in teams of ten, each with a team captain. One team guarded the entrances to the convention hall; another monitored the elevators; a third was in charge of greeting and briefing new delegates; a fourth ran messages back and fourth to a command post.

I had been preoccupied with Henry Wallace and *The New Republic* in 1947. I arrived in Milwaukee the day after the convention opened. I took it for granted that Gil Harrison was to be our candidate for chairman and was all for him. I was startled when a spokesman for the Independent Progressives came to see me.

"It's all been settled," he said.

"What's been settled?"

"The Caucus has decided that Gil is too controversial to be elected this time around. But he's going to hang in there as the front man, drawing the Commie fire until our real candidate makes his move."

"Who is your real candidate?"

The I.P. man pledged me to secrecy. Then he said, "Dick Bolling."

"Who is Dick Bolling?" I asked. He was, I learned, a staff organizer for the A.D.A.

That troubled me. I had been caught for months in a cross-fire between the A.D.A. and the P.C.A. My own commitment to Henry Wallace put me in a difficult position and, beyond that, I did not want to see the A.V.C. become a battlefield between external groups.

"I don't like your plan," I told the I.P. spokesman. "I don't believe in having fake candidates and real candidates; I don't believe in deceit."

In the course of the day, a dozen veterans gathered in my hotel room. Lew Frank wanted me to work out a coalition slate with the Progressives. Instead, we formed our own, center group.

Dick Bolling came to call on us when his campaign surfaced. He was handsome and self-assured. We asked him a number of questions. His answers were all acceptable until we came to foreign policy.

"What do you think about the Truman Doctrine?" we asked him.

"I think that it's a mixture of Wilsonian idealism and Kansas City pragmatism," Dick said.

"Are you for it or against it?"

"I see its good points and its bad points."

"And on balance?"

"On balance I'd have to say that I'm for it." Our interview ended there. We ran our own candidate, an ambitious black named Franklin Williams. He proved in time to be a highly successful and a most unappealing man.

Dick and his running mate were elected in Milwaukee. The struggle against the Progressive caucus continued.

In order to join the A.V.C. a veteran had to sign a pledge stating that he or she believed in the Bill of Rights. The pledge was signed by all of the members of the Progressive Caucus, including John

Gates, a veteran who was the editor of the *Daily Worker* and a member of the National Committee of the Communist party.

In June 1948, an action was brought to expel Gates from the A.V.C. on the grounds that he could not have signed our pledge in good faith.

The chairman appointed a board of three A.V.C. members to rule on the Gates case. The three whom he selected were Robert Nathan, Franklin Roosevelt, Jr., and me. So in one more twist of history, I found myself sitting in judgment on a high-ranking member of the Communist party.

We met one evening in the New York offices of the A.V.C. Gates, a resolute leader, appeared with his counsel, a cadaverous attorney named Morris Pottish.

"I don't mind saying that I do regard myself as an expert on the Communist party," said Gates in his opening statement. He went on to quote at length from several editorials that I had written in *The New Republic* on the unconditional nature of our Constitutional guarantees of freedom of speech. At three the next morning, we thanked him for coming and adjourned.

Five months later, the Third National Convention of the A.V.C. was held in Cleveland. There, the struggle against the Progressive Caucus was finally and somewhat brutally resolved.

The board on which I had served made its report to the convention: John Gates was indeed a leader of the Communist party, and in his view his loyalty to his party did not conflict with his pledge of support for our principles.

The issue was opened for debate. A motion to expel Gates from the A.V.C. was proposed by spokesmen for the Independent Progressive Caucus. It was supported by Dick Bolling and Gil Harrison, but they and their followers were placed on the defensive. Speaker after speaker invoked the spirit of civil liberty and denounced those who presumed to tell the veterans of America what they might and might not think.

I was seated in the back row of the movie theater where we met. A messenger from the Independent Progressive Caucus found me there. He brought me an urgent message from his leaders: I had to speak.

It was a difficult moment for me. As I walked down the aisle of the theater and up onto its stage, I remembered an incident in the life of Abraham Lincoln.

Clement Vallandigham, a leading opponent of the Civil War, was arrested in 1863 for encouraging desertion from the Union armies. His arrest was challenged as a denial of civil liberty and the president was denounced for sanctioning it.

In reply, Lincoln pointed to the death penalty that was imposed upon every deserter. He said, "Must I shoot a simple-minded soldier boy who deserts, while I must not touch a hair of a wily agitator who induces him to desert? . . . To silence the agitator and save the boy is not only constitutional but withal a great mercy."

I quoted Lincoln's words from memory. I compared the dozens of chapters whose charters we had disallowed to the misled soldier and Gates to the wily agitator.

It was a rough moment for me and for a thousand others in the theater. There was some applause when I finished and a massive chorus of boos. A number of veterans spat on me as I walked back up the aisle. I could feel the warm spittle trickling down the sides of my nose to my chin.

Gates was expelled from the A.V.C. The convention turned to the election of a new slate of leaders. The center caucus that I had helped to form seemed to hold the balance of power and that, I felt, placed us in an impossible position. I resigned from the caucus and did my best to dissolve it. Gil Harrison was elected to be our new chairman.

"The heart must pause to breathe," said Byron. I refused to run again for the National Planning Committee. I felt very much alone. Gus Tyler in his compassionate way invited me to become a member of the inner core of the Independent Progressive Caucus. I went to one meeting, but it made me very uneasy. I can see now that it reminded me of our cell meetings in Cambridge.

I felt for many years that breaking away from my friends and forming the center caucus in the A.V.C. was one of my many blunders. Now that I can look at it from a distance, I can see more clearly why I acted as I did.

I was, as I have noted, bound up with Henry Wallace, and, consciously or unconsciously, I tried to rationalize his beliefs.

I reacted—too strongly—against the conspiratorial methods that my friends adopted in their struggle against the Progressive Caucus.

At a deeper level, I know now, I could not share the basic attitude of the old street fighters who, on David Dubinsky's orders, saved the A.V.C.

For them, the young veterans who belonged to the Communist party were Stalinists. They were the enemy, and the enemy had to be crushed.

For me, they were individuals, like myself. They were committed to a movement to which I had been committed. If I was capable of growth and change, then so were they. If I sought redemption, I could not deny it to them. Most of them, I sensed, would leave the Communist party within a few years if they could see some friendly faces beyond its borders.

*Love Thine Enemy, but not until he surrenders.* Was that what Jesus meant? I did not think so.

Was I wrong in believing that the members of the Progressive

Caucus were not a breed apart? I do not think so. John Gates left the
Communist Party; he lives somewhere in obscurity. Dick Bolling is
the chairman of the powerful Rules Committee of the House of Representatives; he was an ardent supporter of our participation in the
Vietnam War.

Which of the three of us, I wonder, can call his soul his own?

━━◦◦◦◦━━

One other encounter in those days of judgment and wrath convinced me that I could never join the ranks of those who tell us that
we must fight fire with fire, violence with violence, evil with evil.

I went to the Annual Convention of the C.I.O. in Cleveland in
November 1949. I spent an evening in a hotel suite with two friends:
a radical priest who was close to Philip Murray and one of the leaders
of the United Steelworkers Union.

We talked for an hour or so about Truman and Murray. We had
several drinks. Then the priest turned to more pressing concerns.

"Tell me, Joe, what happened to that Commie cell at Republic
steel?"

"No need to worry about them Father; they're all in jail."

"And what about that cell in Jones and Laughlin?"

"Same thing, Father; they were last seen heading for Chicago."

"And the one in your old plant?"

"Ah!"

The Communist party had apparently entrenched itself in Joe's old
plant. Their slate was well ahead of his slate one week before the plant
elections. Then, the most popular man on Joe's slate was waylaid and
beaten late at night by a gang of thugs.

Witnesses came forward who had seen the beating and recognized
the thugs. On the basis of their sworn evidence, the Communist
leaders in the plant were arrested by Joe's friend, the chief of police,
and run out of town by his protégé, the mayor. The election was won
by Joe's slate.

The victim remained in hospital for four months and was crippled
for life. He was grateful for the pension given to him by his union.

"You know," said Joe with a grin, "to this day, he doesn't suspect
who it was who beat him up."

# A SUNDAY PILOT

I CONTINUED to think of myself as a pilot for ten years after the war ended. It was part of the romantic image that I had of myself.

I bought a Vultee for seven hundred dollars. Its tires were threadbare and it had a hole in one wing. I kept it on a cabbage patch and flew it up to Martha's Vineyard on summer weekends so that I could be with my family.

The manager of the Vineyard airport offered to keep my Vultee in his hangar through the winter for fifteen dollars a month. That seemed like a bargain until a telegram came for me: HANGAR DESTROYED BY FIRE. ALL PLANES DEMOLISHED. THINK I CAN SAVE YOUR CLOCK.

I was secretly relieved, since the Vultee was plainly unsafe. In its place, I bought a five-seat monoplane called a Navion.

I logged three hundred hours in the Navion in 1949 and 1950, flying to cities where I spoke at rallies and banquets in an effort to rebuild the circulation of *The New Republic*. I made a flying tour of the Midwest for the A.D.A.

A staff director of the A.D.A. flew with me on that tour. His office called as we were leaving to ask if a lad who was working as a student organizer could hitch a ride with us as far as Chicago. I said of course, and we packed him into the back seat.

We dropped the lad off in Chicago. I did not bother to catch his name. But twenty-five years later, I went to a dinner in honor of Senator Walter Mondale, the Democratic candidate for the vice presidency. I had seen him once or twice in casual meetings. As we shook hands I said, "You don't remember me."

"Like hell I don't!" cried Mondale. "That flight to Chicago was the longest flight I ever took in my whole life!"

I flew the Navion to Cleveland for the A.V.C. Convention in 1949. The flight back to Washington was very nearly my last flight.

It was a Sunday afternoon in late November. I had three passengers with me: a delegate named Ann Ewing; a staff organizer; and a black lad named Cyril from Jamaica who ran our mimeograph machine.

I had had no more than ten hours of sleep during the three days of the convention. I was very tired, but the flight promised to be easy. The weather charts showed that the winds aloft were tail winds; there were a few clouds over the Appalachian Mountains, but the skies over Washington were fair and the forecast was *clear.*

We flew over Youngstown at five thousand feet. The clouds above us were thickening and lowering by then. There were many steel mills in the Monongahela Valley. I could see the smoke pouring from their chimneys. The smoke over Cleveland had drifted lazily upward; now, as we flew over the valley, it was flowing swiftly across our flight path.

I knew then that there had been a sudden and unexpected wind shift. For the first time, I felt uneasy.

Clouds were forming at our flight level as we approached the mountains. I twisted down through them, searching for the airport at Cumberland. The mountains rose to meet the clouds and barred our way.

I climbed back into the clouds and kept on climbing. I hoped to break out into sunlight but the clouds rose with us. At last, at eight thousand feet, we emerged into an unearthly realm of gray mist and billowing banks of whiteness. Then all of the sky around us became white and indefinable.

I had filed a contact flight plan in Cleveland. I had violated it when I lost contact with the earth. The wise course was to head back to Cleveland; I knew that. But no pilot likes to turn back once he has set out for a destination.

I had eight instruments, a map, a gas gauge, and a clock to follow. And I had a plane to fly. At times like those a pilot must make certain assumptions and formulate a plan based upon them.

My assumptions were that the storm we had encountered was centered in the mountains, and that the skies over Washington were clear. So, I reasoned, as we flew toward Washington, conditions were bound to improve.

I did not know that the clouds in which we were flying were the front edge of a heavy snowstorm that had formed with no warning and was moving up swiftly from the South.

We flew on at eight thousand feet until we had crossed the mountains. Ice crackled on the Navion's antenna, but the carburetor heat was on and I felt snug and safe. I let down slowly, expecting at every moment to break through the clouds. Instead, the sky darkened below us. It was laced with lines of sleet.

I had one sophisticated instrument in the Navion—an automatic direction finder. I tuned it in to the Columbia Broadcasting System station in Washington; the needle picked up the station without a tremor. I turned the Navion until the needle was pointed to *zero*. I knew beyond any doubt that we were heading for Washington, and that meant safety to me.

How foolish! For Washington was more than the crossroads airport where I kept the Navion. It was a maze of radio towers and high-tension wires.

I held the needle on *zero*. A rough equation formed in my mind between the formless chances of the weather clearing and the sharp form of the needle edging toward Empty on the gasoline gauge. The moments of elation, uncertainty, fear, and finally panic that many dead pilots had experienced before they crashed became vivid to me.

I let down to nine hundred feet—one hundred feet higher than the radio towers that surrounded Washington. I could see snow-covered fields beneath us; then the dim lines of a single railroad track wavered into sight.

I checked the railroad on my map. It was a little line that ran into Washington. I flew along it, and as I flew, I gave myself a deadline. At two hours and fifty minutes, when I had ten minutes worth of gasoline left, I would put the Navion down in the first open space, no matter where we were.

At two hours and fourty eight minutes, I lowered the Navion's wheels and its flaps. We flew along the railroad track at three hundred feet above the ground.

The land on both sides of the track was rough and inhospitable. Then, a tiny pasture passed beneath us, dim beneath the lines of sleet and snow.

I pushed the propellor lever to the full high position. I pulled the Navion over in a tight turn. The pasture vanished in the snowstorm; the blurred skeleton of a water tower appeared close beside us and disappeared.

I missed the pasture on our first circle. I circled again and it came into sight beneath us. I cut the engine and pushed the nose of the Navion down. A slushy meadow rose to meet us as we made a soggy landing. All four of us burst into laughter.

We slid over a mound in the meadow and came to rest by a farm gate. I opened the cowling and we sat there in the wet, white snow. The black water tower loomed above us, its top encased in the falling snowflakes. The world around us was serene: everlasting and still.

We climbed out of the Navion and trudged through the slush, down a muddy road. In the first shack that we came to we saw four small black faces pressed in silent wonder against a window pane.

We trudged on until we came to a frame house. I knocked at its front door. We waited.

The door opened at last. A woman stood in the doorway, staring at us.

Ann and I were standing on the top step. The two men were half-hidden behind us. I asked the woman where we were.

"Herndon, of course!" she said.

I told her that we had just made a forced landing in a nearby meadow. I asked if we could come into her house. She nodded. She turned to lead us in.

I remembered then that we were in Virginia. I thought to myself: *She'll never let Cyril stay in her parlor, being a Virginian. She'll turn him out.*

I had been calm from the beginning to the end of our flight. As we moved into the parlor, I was overcome by anxiety; I began to shiver and sweat.

We flopped into the easy chairs that were grouped around the fireplace. Cyril lay spreadeagled on the most expensive of the chairs. The woman stared at him for a moment. Then she went to the kitchen to make coffee.

On the radio, the sportscaster shouted and shouted, as if nothing in the wide world mattered except that football game.

I asked the woman if I could use her telephone. I called Bin and told her that we were on the ground and safe, in Herndon. Then I called the Associted Press and the United Press. I wanted to be sure that no false stories would be broadcast about us, but I was unsuccessful. In his Sunday evening broadcast, Drew Pearson announced that we had crashed.

When we were rested, we walked back down the road to get our suitcases. A dark figure emerged from the falling snow and trudged toward us. He wore rubber boots and a fireman's helmet.

"You seen an air pilot around here?" he shouted. "Folks are swearing some damn fool airplane flew right past their windows and underneath the water tower! I been hunting for the pilot ever since!"

I led him to the Navion, sitting by itself in the meadow. I said that it had no locks, and that any kid could climb into it and start it up.

"Don't worry about that," he said. "Melvin here is a good darky; he'll watch over it."

We walked over to the shack. Melvin came out with his four kids clutching onto the back of his coat and peering at us around his waist.

"Now Melvin," said the fire chief, "you do like I tell you and don't let no damn fools near that plane."

"Yessir!" said Melvin. He nodded and touched his cap.

There was one drug store in Herndon. We waited there until Bin arrived in my station wagon and picked us up. We started off for Washington. It was still daylight, but the cars that crept along the road all had their headlights on—the falling snow was so thick.


I flew all over the nation in the Navion. My travels served to remind me that it was one thing to preach liberalism in the North and another to practice it in the South.

I was elected as the national chairman of the American Veterans Committee in 1949, with a black professor of law at the University of Chicago as my running mate. I set out on a national tour in the Navion in 1950, with our national organizer and our public relations man.

We flew South in stages until we landed at Tallahassee. There, the principles that we as Northerners had professed so easily were put to the test.

There was an all-white university, Florida State, in Tallahassee, and an all-black college, Florida A. and M. Students were not permitted to cross the street from one campus to the other in 1950; black and white students were not permitted to meet.

I spoke at a convocation in the black college. The faculty were assembled in their robes on the stage of the auditorium. I shook the president's hand after he introduced me. I heard a low, incredulous murmur in the crowd of two thousand students who faced us.

I spoke about the necessity of practicing what we preached in America. I said that the American Veterans Committee was determined to do its part in changing a society whose veterans had to pass through two doors, one marked White and the other marked Black. I said that I and my staff men would stay on when the convocation was over to meet with any veterans who were willing to meet with us.

A score of black students waited for us when the crowd trooped out of the auditorium. We scheduled a meeting for that afternoon, and 150 black veterans turned up.

Bill Pawling, our regional organizer, was a white Southerner. He told the veterans that while we had no Tallahassee chapter, we did have a number of individual members at Florida State. He said that if the A. and M. veterans would join up *as individuals,* we could go on from there.

The black veterans shook their heads. No, their leader said; they had listened to my speech; they assumed that I meant what I had said. They wanted one interracial chapter in Tallahassee or nothing at all.

Bill nodded. He said, "All those who are prepared to join together in one Tallahassee chapter please stand."

Every one of the black veterans stood up. They went on to elect their own organizing committee.

Bill appeared to be elated. Inwardly, he was sick at heart. He feared that he would not be able to find a single white veteran in Tallahassee who would be able to afford the risk of joining an interracial chapter. If he was right, we would leave the black veterans of Tallahassee disillusioned and embittered.

We walked across the street to the Florida State campus. Bill hunted down an old-time liberal who was a member of the faculty.

The man had been a *New Republic* subscriber for fifteen years. He believed in everything that we stood for. He listened to our story; he shook his head.

"If you go ahead and set up an interracial chapter," he said, "the authorities in both institutions will be forced to expel every student and every faculty member who joins it. You will ruin us."

"What can we do?" I asked him.

He said, "Get out of town!"

We hunted down our twenty white members. Some were Southerners; some were Northerners who had come to Tallahassee because it was cheaper to get a degree in Florida than in the North.

One married veteran said that he had been corresponding with a black veteran. They had not dared to meet. I asked him if he would meet with the Black Organizing Committee. He knew what the penalties were, but he and three other whites chose to take the risk.

We thanked them and flew away, over the pine wastes of Alabama. We held two meetings in Texas that vigilantes tried to break up. We pushed our way against the gales that blew through the San Gorgonio Pass and came to the Pacific. We turned north along the coast of California, past wild cliffs and tawny hills. We circled Mount Shasta and crossed the Wilamette Valley, all pink and white since the cherry, the pear, and the apple trees were all in bloom. We flew up the Columbia River and over the summits of snow-covered peaks to Idaho. We climbed to fifteen thousand feet—as high as we or the Navion could go—to cross the Teton Mountains and the Wind River Range. We came down in Cheyenne, long after nightfall. We flew on to Minneapolis.

In Minneapolis, I was handed a special delivery letter by our welcoming committee. It was from Bill Pawling.

Our Tallahassee chapter had been formed, Bill said. It had held its first meeting in the second story of a building in the town. Policemen with pistols drawn had broken into the meeting room. They had arrested our members and taken them to jail. There, they were told that they would be expelled from the two colleges unless they disbanded their chapter. They were standing fast.

We set out on the last leg of our journey on May 25, 1950. We were homesick by then and very tired. We had flown ten thousand miles, and I had made thirty speeches, all in the course of twenty-six days.

It was a full day's flight from Minneapolis to Washington. We started early and made a hurried stop for fuel at a small field outside Chicago. I told the lad who stood at the gas pump to fill both tanks of the Navion while we grabbed a cup of coffee.

The bill for the gas seemed a little low to me, but I had no time to make sure that the tanks were full.

We flew on across Indiana and into Ohio. My two companions snored as they slept. I tuned my automatic direction finder to the C.B.S. station in Zanesville, the town where I planned to land once again for fuel. The station was broadcasting a discussion about European federation, my favorite cause.

I glanced at the gas gauge as I listened to the discussion. It was edging toward Empty. I let the Navion rise with the air currents, just in case. . . .

Zanesville appeared at the far end of a troubled landscape. We had been flying for two and a half hours by then. If the tanks had been filled, we had gas for thirty minutes more.

The panelists were talking about cartels when the engine died. The propellor went on turning over in the wind; it made a soft, whistling sound. The speakers went on talking; my companions woke up and looked around.

I established a gentle glide; we headed for the airport. I could see, as we lost altitude, that it was on a plateau above the city, and that it was fronted by some formidable cliffs.

I heard sepulchral voices from my air force days: *Never stretch a glide.* I looked around for a pasture that would serve for a forced landing; I saw only steep gullies and razor-backed ridges, planted with corn.

I stretched the glide. The Navion came in fast with wheels and flaps up. We crossed the cliffs with thirty feet to spare; I dumped the wheels with the emergency switch. We sank a little lower than we should have done at eighty miles an hour; then the Navion raised herself as the wheels touched down and the struts straightened out.

We crossed two runways where air liners were waiting to take off. We rolled onto the concrete apron of the airport and came to a halt fifty feet from a gas pump. We pushed the Navion the last fifty feet. A mechanic strolled over to us and asked how many gallons of gas we wanted.

We flew on to Washington, where another letter was waiting for us from Tallahassee.

Our chapter chairman had suffered a nervous breakdown as the result of the strain to which I had subjected him. The chapter members had refused to disband, under the threat of expulsion from the two colleges, but they had suspended their activities.

That was in 1950, when the National Association for the Advancement of Colored People was an underground organization in the South, and Martin Luther King was unknown.

# TWO SOCIALISTS

AT dawn on June 25, 1950, the armies of North Korea crossed the Thirty-Eighth Parallel—the boundary line established by the Allies at the time of the Japanese surrender—and invaded South Korea.

The Soviet Union had absented itself from the United Nations meetings. The UN was free to act, and it called upon its member states to "furnish such assistance to the Republic of Korea as may be necessary to repel the armed attack and to restore international peace and security in the area." The United States and several smaller nations responded promptly and sent armed forces to join in the defense of South Korea.

The issue seemed perfectly clear to me. *The New Republic* gave its full support to our war effort.

I learned, when I flew to England, that my view was not shared by the intellectuals to whom I had once turned for guidance. For some of them, America, far from being a principal supporter of the world organization that they called "Uno," was the main threat to world peace.

I telephoned my old friend Kingsley Martin, the editor of the *New Statesman,* when I arrived in London. He invited me to lunch at his club on Pall Mall.

He had, as it turned out, also invited his associate G. D. H. Cole to lunch that day.

I was the first to arrive at the club. Cole was led to the room where I was waiting. We had never met, but, apparently, he knew who I was. He came toward me; before I could open my mouth, he said,

"I am on the side of the North Koreans!"

I said, "Why?"

"Because I'd rather have Russian bases than American bases in Korea!"

"Do you think that is the issue?"

"Why else do you think there's a war?"

Kingsley arrived at that moment. He had a habit of adjusting his opinions to the person that he was with, and he was plainly embarrassed at finding himself with both Cole and me. He saw that we were arguing about Korea and hastened to change the subject.

"All of England," he said, "can now be divided into two segments: those who shudder when the American planes fly overhead and those who don't."

"Which segment do you belong to?" I asked.

Kingsley turned to me with his Suffering Christ smile, as if to say, *"You should know better than to try and pin me down."*

At luncheon, Cole insisted on dragging the conversation back to the Korean War. "You took the wrong line on Korea," he told Kingsley. "You should have insisted that the war is a civil war. Then there would have been no grounds under the charter for Uno to become involved in it."

Kingsley clicked his tongue in self-depreciation. "Why didn't I think of that!" he cried.

"My real hope," said Cole, a little later, "is that in the next war, England will play the role that France played in the last war. She will start the war but she will not finish it."

"Quite!" cried Kingsley.

"Which side would you be on?" I asked Cole.

"The Russian side, of course!"

"Why?"

"Because I'd rather live in a socialist world than a capitalist world."

"And you think that Russia is a socialist country?"

"Of course!"

Kingsley smiled again. "You realize," he said to Cole, "that in the event that the Russians conquered Britain, we two would be the first to be arrested."

It gave them a delicious *frisson* to contemplate being manhandled by some burly Red Army soldier. It was a bit like two bejeweled old dowagers insisting that, come the revolution, they would be the first to be dragged to the guillotine.

# GOODBYE, GUY

MASSACHUSETTS Avenue descends in gentle curves from Cathedral Heights to Rock Creek. It passes over the creek and runs on into the center of Washington.

The British embassy stands half-way down the hill. An access road cuts into the avenue above the embassy and separates it from the Naval Observatory.

I parked my car on the access road, one morning in March 1951. I went into the embassy to talk to an economist about an editorial that I was writing for *The New Republic*. At noon, I headed back downtown.

A man was standing with his back toward me, on the corner of the access road and the avenue. He was waving vainly at the taxis as they rushed past down the hill. I halted at the corner and he turned toward me. He was Guy Burgess.

He climbed in beside me. "Can you drop me downtown?" he asked. "I've lost my car, or rather, it's been taken from me. I'm having a hell of a time getting around."

He had bought a second-hand Lincoln he said. He had driven it to Charlottesville, or some such place, to give a lecture. He had been arrested three times for speeding; each time, he had claimed diplomatic immunity. The governor of Virginia had protested; the ambassador had impounded his car.

"I don't suppose you would lend me your car," he said.

"No," I said. "I wouldn't."

He smiled and shrugged his shoulders.

"What are you doing in Washington?" I asked him.

"I've been here since October," he said. "I'm working on Far Eastern affairs."

Since October. In October 1950, South Korean and American troops had crossed the Thirty-Eighth Parallel and had advanced to the Yalu River. There, they had been ambushed by massive Chinese forces. Four hundred thousand Chinese soldiers had routed the troops commanded by General Douglas MacArthur. Heavy fighting had followed, in which many Americans had been killed.

October. If Guy was in Washington in October, I thought, he would have known of our plans to advance into North Korea. He would have sent that information to Moscow if at all possible. The Kremlin, in turn, would have handed it to Peking. If I was right, Guy could have caused the deaths of many American soldiers.

That thought left me numb.

"If you were here since October," I said, "you must have known about our plans."

"Everyone knew about them!"

"Including the Chinese?"

"Of course! They did their best to warn you not to get too close to the Yalu River. We passed the warning along to you; so did the Indians. No one here would listen. MacArthur said that the Chinese were bluffing. Acheson and the C.I.A. agreed with him.

"Acheson sees himself as another Metternich," he added. "He thinks he can prop up every rotten dictator in the world with American power. Well, he can't! I tell you that as a friend of the United States. If you try it, you'll fail!"

I no longer felt numb. Instead, anger rose within me.

"You told me in 1949 that you were going to leave the Foreign Office. You gave me your word."

"Did I say that? Perhaps I did.

"I believed at the time that I was about to leave the Foreign Office," he added. "I actually did go on an extended tour. I did almost leave when I returned, but they insisted on finding another job for me. Then they posted me here."

"You broke your word to me," I said.

"Yes. Well," he said, "this is where I'm getting off if you will pull over."

I pulled into the pavement. "Look," I said. "We're at war now. If you aren't out of the government within a month from now, I swear to you, I'll turn you in."

Guy looked back, smiling, as he climbed out of the car.

"Don't worry," he said. "I'm about to sail for England and as soon as I return, I'm going to resign.

"Goodbye, if I don't see you again," he said.

"Goodbye, Guy."

That was in March. On Friday, June 8, the *Washington Post* carried a banner headline on its front page: TWO BRITISH DIPLOMATS "DISAPPEAR" IN EUROPE, FLIGHT TO RUSSIA FEARED.

The story, filed by the United Press in London, continued: "A Foreign Office announcement said Donald Duart Maclean, 38, Head of the American Department, and Guy Francis de Moncy Burgess, 40, a Specialist in Far Eastern affairs, have been missing from their posts since May 25 and have been suspended for being absent without leave."

The story added that, after reading the announcement, the chief of the information branch of the Foreign Office answered questions put to him by reporters:

Q: Is there anything to indicate they went to Russia?
A: I have no information on that.
Q: It has been suggested that a third person was involved. Can you say anything about that?
A: I have no knowledge of any third person.
Q: I simply don't understand this. The whole matter doesn't make any sense.
A: You're telling me!

Saturday's *Post* carried a message from Maclean to his wife and one from Guy to his mother, which read: "Terribly sorry for my silence. Am embarking on a long Mediterranean holiday. Do forgive."

On Sunday, the *Post* reported that the hunt had shifted from France to Italy. Fifteen thousand policemen were engaged, it said, in the biggest manhunt "since the collaring of the Nazi war criminals in 1946."

On Monday, the *Post* reported that the manhunt had extended to Florence, Rome, Prague, and Istanbul. The *Post* went on to say that an anonymous informant had told the *Daily Express* that the two diplomats were heading for Moscow.

I had never heard of Maclean, but, knowing Guy, I guessed that the anonymous informant was right, and that Guy had lied once again in telling his mother that he was off for a Mediterranean holiday.

I was ready at that moment to tell the authorities all I knew. With that in mind, I went to see the British official whom I knew best in Washington.

"I have some information about Guy Burgess that I want to give to the British government," I said.

My friend smiled at me and said, "You too?

"My dear fellow," he added, "you will have to take your place at the end of the line. And I should warn you, the line runs all the way around the block."

It was almost as if the British government did not want to hear what I and others had to say. It was all too embarrassing.

Should I take my place at the end of the long line? Many people, I gathered, were giving information about Guy to the authorities. It would lead them inevitably to Anthony. He would, I was certain, refuse to admit his role. And until he chose to tell all that he knew, what would be gained by my testimony? Anthony, I believed, had long since given up the world of espionage for his true profession of art history. If his past role was known to the authorities, that would suffice.

I should have gone to the end of the line and waited there; I know that. Instead, I told myself that Guy was gone forever, and that Anthony had been rendered harmless. With mixed feelings of relief and uneasiness, I went back to my own work.

# BREAKING APART

MY sister's family broke up in the years that followed the war. A few years later, the family created by my father and mother was broken apart for a second time.

The immediate cause of the break was the management of my mother's fortune.

She gave up her American citizenship in 1936. She placed her American properties, including Westbury and *The New Republic*, in trust. She made her five children life tenants of the trust and, initially, named the Royal Trust Company of Canada as her trustee.

The assets of the trust were no more than its debts when it was created. Thanks to the expansion of the American economy and the skill of Milton Rose, the equity grew substantially over the next fifteen years.

My mother chose in 1951 to make Milton Rose and me her trustees. Her action deeply offended my brother, Whitney. He felt that, as the eldest son, he was entitled to control the family fortune. He believed that he was the only family member who had sound business sense. He resented the use of family funds to support the *United Nations World*. He regarded *The New Republic* as a waste of money.

At Whitney's suggestion, a family conference was held at Darting-ton in April 1951. It began in a spirit of reconciliation. Two days later, our family was broken apart.

Whitney left for London before the rest of us were awake. A note from him indicated that he would deal with us through his solicitor.

My mother followed him to London and waited for him at his house. It seemed impossible that, in one meeting, she could break through his defenses. But he was so overwrought that his deepest feelings burst from him.

"I lay awake and cried all last night," he told her. "I wished that you had never borne me."

He was determined, he said, to break away from the family trust. He would hold Milt and me personally responsible for the losses incurred on the estate in Old Westbury and on *The New Republic* unless we relinquished his family's share of the trust.

Whitney's interests were segregated. The rifts that were opened in 1951 did not extend to his wife and children, and they healed over before our mother died. I mention them here only because they brought about a change in my own life, by forcing the sale of our home in Old Westbury and of *The New Republic*.

Milt and I put our home up for sale when we returned to America. From then on, we were there on borrowed time. Our days there were like scenes from *The Cherry Orchard*: in each moment of stillness, we could hear the sounds of the axes chopping down the cherry trees.

My mother came over to Old Westbury in October 1951. We walked the estate together. It was a misty day; the autumn air was chill, and the mist narrowed the world around us. The trunks of the trees were dark; the dead leaves that clung to their branches were amber, ochre, and scarlet.

She had placed her favorite trees around the house: Liquidambar and phellos oak on the lawn; weeping cherries at the entrance to the Chinese garden that she and my father had designed when they re-turned from Peking. We walked through the garden, around to the playhouse, and back through the arched lane of lilacs. We knew that before the summer was over, the bulldozers would be at work.

My mother spent a week in the basement at Westbury, setting aside a few of her papers and burning the rest. Bin and I went back in December to sort out our own papers and pack up our trunks.

By then, the water had been turned off in our house. The pipes dripped in the darkness of the basement; the matting was beginning to rot on the floor of the porch. The house was deserted, save for George Bennett, my father's old *aide-de-camp*, who lived on there in a room in the attic. For him, the boundaries between life and death had dimmed, as they dimmed for the watchkeeper in Henry James's story *The Altar of the Dead.* George would have had nothing to live for, once the house was sold. He killed himself.

The estate was sold to a local developer. We managed to find homes for our tenants, and jobs for the gardeners. We brought in an auctioneer, and on April 1, 1952, a crowd assembled on our front lawn to bid for our belongings. The butchers, the bakers, the grocerymen were all there from Westbury with their wives. They wanted to own the items that bore my mother's monogram: pillowcases, sheets, and bath towels were bid up to five times their value; so were the glasses, the knives and forks, the picnic baskets that my mother and father had shared before the First World War.

A real estate agent bought the canopied bed in which Edith Randolph Whitney had died. A hardware merchant bought the highboy that had stood in my mother's bedroom. His wife wrote to me a week later to say that, in a drawer of the highboy, she had found a yellowed envelope containing a lock of Whitney's hair. I could have it back for ten dollars, she said.

I waited until the auction was over; then I bought the leftovers— the sets of Conrad, Tolstoy, and James that my mother had treasured; the portrait of President Monroe that my father had purchased from Monroe's granddaughter; the sofas that we had romped on as children.

One month later as I was eating breakfast in our house in Virginia, an immense van pulled up outside our door. Two teamsters climbed down from its cabin and lugged our purchases in.

I offered them each a cup of coffee. They joined me at the table. As they sipped the coffee, one of them looked across at me.

"Don't remember me, do you," he said.

"I'm afraid not."

"I used to be a groom in your Uncle Harry's stables, back in Old Westbury. You used to watch us as we worked.

"Dressed us all up in his racing colors, your Uncle Harry did," the teamster went on. "Big buttons on our jackets with his initials on them; as if we belonged to him."

"I remember," I said. Biddy had come upon the last of those buttons in an old steamer trunk at Westbury. She had made them up as cuff-links for her friends.

"Hard work it was then," said the teamster. "Low pay. Now it's high pay for taking it easy.

"You know where I'd like to be now?" he said. "Back with your Uncle Harry."

One year later, I acted as chairman of an A.V.C. banquet in New York. The crowd wandered out when the speeches were over, but one lad waited at the end of the dais to speak to me.

"You remember me?" he said.

"Of course," I lied.

"From those A.V.C. picnics at Old Westbury. I was with the North Shore Chapter."

"I remember."

"Some of the best days we ever had were at those picnics. Five hundred vets and their wives, laying around on your lawns. They couldn't believe there could be a place as beautiful as yours."

"Thank you."

"You sure you're going to speak to me after what I'm going to tell ya?"

"Of course I am."

"I wouldn't tell ya, only my wife said I had to."

"Go on."

"Okay! My dad was the one who bought your place. Joe Gariano. He pushed a vegetable cart when he was young."

"That's fine."

"You aren't mad with me?"

"Why would I be mad?"

"Okay. This here's my wife," he added. "We had great times playing with our baby on Sundays in your Chinese garden."

"I'm glad."

"Now it's being broken up into half-acre lots. Look, Mister Straight, don't ever come out there no more!"

I did not intend to go back. Yet, week after week, I had a recurring dream. I was staying in the house that was no longer ours. The windows were cracked; the carpets were threadbare. The staff was unpaid. I was there on sufferance; the new owners might, at any moment, arrive to dispossess me. I knew that I had to leave but I could not; I loved the place too much.

The dream haunted my sleep for twenty years. Then, as the deputy chairman of the National Endowment for the Arts, I went to a conference that was held a few miles from Old Westbury. We had an hour each day for luncheon, and while everyone else was eating, I borrowed a car and drove back to my old home.

Most of the trees were still standing; the gravelled roads were in place. A dozen split-level bungalows surrounded the main house. Ernest Thompson Seton might have compared it to a moose, held at bay by a pack of wolves.

A disabled moose. Half of the house, I could see, had been torn down, demolishing the kitchen, the pantry, the laundry, my father's study, where I had seen my mother weeping.

I stood by the front porch, and a Lincoln Continental pulled in beside me. A woman climbed out of the car. Her hair was in curlers; she explained that she had driven her daughter to ballet school.

I introduced myself, and she led me inside. A bar had been made out of the closet where we had stored our coats and skates. It was flanked by two powder rooms: *His* and *Hers.*

The new owner apologized as she led me through the house. I insisted that it was a good experience for me, and I meant it. I never had the dream again.

*The New Republic* was the second casualty of the break within my family.

It had become once again a respected journal of opinion. It had a strong staff, a distinguished group of contributors, a devoted reader-ship, and a clear position on the critical issues of the day. A wise man, Francis Biddle, shocked Walter Lippmann by telling him that it was a better magazine than it had been in Lippmann's day.

The readers and the contributors of *The New Republic* did not know that it had only a few months to live.

Milt telephoned me in December 1951. *The New Republic,* he said, was in worse financial shape than we had supposed. Our legal advisers wanted us to close it down at once; he felt that at best, we might keep it going until the spring.

We went over the records together. Then we went to see Dan Mebane, who had taken over as publisher once again after Wallace's departure.

Dan had come to the magazine as a young apprentice. Now his hair was white. We told him that we were planning to sell it to anyone who would undertake to keep it going.

"No," Dan said, "better not."

He swept his arm across the bookcase that stood behind his desk. There, in stately rows, were sixty volumes of *The New Republic,* bound in black leather.

"They are a storehouse of all that was fine in American thought in our lifetimes," he said. "It would be better to close down *The New Republic* in a dignified manner than to see it dishonor its own tradition."

I could not argue with Dan. I worked on a draft on our final editorial when I returned to Washington. I told Helen Fuller that she would have to find another job. I read through the articles that we were planning to publish in the next issue. They were worthy articles, but they had little to do with my mood. I pulled them out and published instead the essay that Richard Tawney had published in the London *Athenaeum* in December 1917. It was entitled *The Sword of the Spirit.* Its words seemed to bear both upon the war that the United Nations was fighting in Korea and on the conflict that had divided our family: ". . . The destruction, by the effort to achieve victory, of the moral principles which alone can justify a war, is the commonest lesson of history. It is the defeat which men prepare for themselves as the danger of defeat by the enemy becomes more remote. . . ."

Helen, when she had recovered from the shock of my warning, said that she and the other members of the staff would work without pay while we searched for some new supporters. James Newman came out to my house in Virginia to plead with me. "I've disagreed with you on many issues," he said, "but it would be a national tragedy if *The New Republic* were to go down."

It seemed to me then that I had given in too easily. I called Milt and said that, if necessary, I would pay for the magazine out of my own savings while I hunted for a friend who could keep it going.

Did I have any cause for bitterness? Among the Christmas cards on our mantlepiece was one from my young friends Marge and John. Twice I had carried Marge to a taxi when the pain induced by her pregnancy became unbearable. She carried her baby to term and it was born with cancer. At Christmas in 1950 her doctor had asked for permission to allow the baby to die.

My own children seemed very precious to me. I helped to nurse them when all four came down with bronchitis in mid-December.

Susie was three. She insisted on a bedtime story.

"What shall our story be about?" I asked her.

"The bobwhites," Susie said.

It had been a harsh winter. A heavy snowfall had been followed by freezing rain. From under the sagging branches of the boxwood, a flock of bobwhites had ventured every morning to eat the grain that we scattered for them on the snow.

One afternoon, two hunters stalked our bobwhites. They drove them out into our front field while I was at work and shot two before the flock whirred back to the shelter of our woods.

I made up a story about the two dead bobwhites and the twelve live ones. In some obscure way, it was about the long life and the imminent death of the journal that my parents had nurtured, and which, left to my care, was about to die.

Susie listened to the story, enthralled. At its end, she asked, "Are the dead ones alive?"

# IN THE DAYS OF McCARTHY

BOB La Follette, the Senior Senator from Wisconsin, was a liberal Republican and a good friend of mine. He was up for re-election in 1948.

Robert Hannigan, Truman's political manager, offered La Follette a choice. If he would give up his party and run as a Democrat, Truman and the trade unions would back him. If he refused, they would help to defeat him in the Republican party primary.

La Follette refused to give up his party. Hannigan and the unions boycotted his campaign. They helped to bring onto the national stage the man who defeated La Follette and who went on to become a United States Senator—Joseph McCarthy.

McCarthy made a speech at a veterans rally sponsored by the A.V.C. He made no impression on us. He went on to champion a group of Nazi prisoners of war. That gained him nothing. Then, at the urging of a priest at Georgetown University, he turned his attention to Communist infiltration of the State Department. At Wheeling, West Virginia, he said, on February 9, 1950: "I have here in my hand a list of 205—a list of names that were made known to the Secretary of State as being members of the Communist Party and who nevertheless are still working and shaping policy in the State Department."

That assertion, which McCarthy himself disowned, ushered in one of the most dishonorable decades in the history of American politics.

The newspapers and the networks became instruments of McCarthy's, relaying his charges without concern for the truth. Conservatives who should have defended our institutions and traditions became the accomplices of an adventurer without principle or restraint. Republicans who had been the guardians of political virtue egged McCarthy on.

McCarthy played a leading role for the Republicans in the elections of 1952. From then on, he became an encumbrance rather than an asset to his party; but he did not understand that.

> *You taught me language; and my profit on't*
> *Is, I know how to curse.*

McCarthy had been taught how to savage the government of the United States while the Republicans were out of power. He continued to savage it after Eisenhower moved into the White House.

"He's a son-of-a-bitch, but he's our son-of-a-bitch." So said Charles Wilson, Eisenhower's secretary of defense. McCarthy ceased to be their son-of-a-bitch when he attacked and disrupted their Department of the Army.

Belatedly and reluctantly, the army undertook to defend itself. The televised confrontation between McCarthy and the army followed.

The stage was a Senate subcommittee. I remember well the opening day of its hearings in the Senate caucus room. McCarthy himself had difficulty in working his way to the subcommittee table that day. I was seated by the table, and, as he passed behind me, he paused and gave the base of my neck a playful squeeze.

I wrote a book about the hearings entitled *Trial by Television*. I made hundreds of speeches attacking McCarthy in Wisconsin and in a score of other states. People used to come up to me after I had spoken to thank me for being brave enough to attack McCarthy. That always embarrassed me, for I never felt intimidated by him.

One characteristic of McCarthyism was the indiscriminate nature of the onslaughts that it provoked against individuals in America. Thus, I was never seriously threatened during the McCarthy years, but my sister, Biddy, was blacklisted, and Gustavo Duran, who was married to my wife's sister, was persecuted by McCarthy until he was almost destroyed.

Biddy became an actress of national renown when she returned to the theater. She was chosen by Jed Harris to play a leading role in Arthur Miller's study of persecution, *The Crucible*.

Arthur Kennedy played the martyred John Proctor in the play that opened on Broadway in January 1953. Biddy played his wife, Elisabeth. E. G. Marshall, well known for his many roles on television, was the Reverend John Hale.

The play was well into its run when one evening Marshall took Biddy aside.

"Have you been getting any roles in television?" he asked her.

Biddy shook her head.

"I had three performances lined up before we opened," Marshall told her. "They've all been canceled."

Biddy remembered then that she had been asked to appear in two television plays and both had been canceled, for no reason.

Others in the cast, they discovered, had been cut out of television shows after *The Crucible* had opened. A follower of McCarthy who owned a grocery chain in upstate New York had informed Kraft and other sponsors of television dramas that he would boycott their products if the actors and actresses who had been blacklisted appeared on their programs.

Marshall, like my sister and others in the cast, had never been active in politics. Their sole error, in the eyes of the McCarthyites, was that they had appeared in Arthur Miller's play.

Some months later, Biddy received a telephone call from a priest who was a faculty member in a Catholic university.

"I understand that you are on the blacklist," he said.

Biddy acknowledged that she had been unable to obtain any new roles in television.

"Are you prepared," said the priest, "to sign a sworn statement affirming that you are not now and never have been a member of the Communist party or of any other organization designated by the attorney general as subversive?"

"I suppose so," Biddy said.

"Are you further prepared to affirm in writing your unswerving loyalty to the Constitution of the United States?"

"Of course."

"Very good," said the priest. "In that case, for a fee of five hundred dollars, I can have you removed from the blacklist."

───⌒∞⌒───

In a free society, men and women learn to respect the rights of others. For that reason, political leaders look on those with whom they disagree as opponents, not as enemies.

McCarthy stood outside the traditions of a free society. He had to characterize his victims as enemies in order to justify his efforts to destroy them. So when his followers William F. Buckley and L. Brent Bozell wrote a book in praise of him, they entitled it *McCarthy and His Enemies.*

One of McCarthy's victims, whom Buckley and Bozell identified as his enemy, was Gustavo Duran.

Gustavo was born in Barcelona in 1906. He went to the university and the Conservatory of Music in Madrid. He lived in Paris from 1928 to 1934, working as a pianist and earning his living by dubbing films for Paramount Pictures.

He was not involved in political activities of any kind in Paris. He joined the armed bands of the Spanish Republic when it was attacked by Franco; he became the military commander of an army brigade. He was portrayed as a hero by two masters of twentieth-century fiction: Ernest Hemingway and André Malraux.

For Hemingway, Gustavo was both subject and collaborator. The dialogues of the Spaniards—Pablo and Pilar and the Gypsy—in *For Whom the Bell Tolls* are in part Gustavo's work.

In turn, if there is a continuous thread in Malraux's novel, *Man's Hope,* it is the growth in wartime of the young Spaniard, Mañuel. He too is a film editor by profession and a pianist by avocation. He is drawn from Gustavo Duran.

Mañuel is first seen as a volunteer, manning a telephone center at the outbreak of the fighting. He calls one station after another: "sawing the air with a ruler as if he were beating time."

Mañuel is appointed a company commander in the renowned Fifth Regiment. A professional soldier, Colonel Ximenes, is assigned to help him. Ximenes tells him: "Courage is a thing that has to be *organized* . . . you've got to keep it in condition, like a rifle."

The full meaning of those words becomes clear when a group of volunteers in Mañuel's company are sentenced to be executed as deserters.

Malraux describes one deserter "rubbing his cheeks frantically against Mañuel's muddy top-boots." He says of Mañuel: "Never had he realized so keenly the necessity of choosing between victory and compassion. Stooping, he tried to push aside the man who was clinging to his leg. The man clung desperately, his head still bowed, as if in the whole world nothing but that leg could save his life. . . ."

The deserters are executed. The next morning, as Mañuel's company marches past him, a captain cries "Eyes-Left!"

"All heads turned smartly toward Mañuel," Malraux tells us. He adds: "It was the first time the command had been given in the regiment; it was perhaps the first time it had been given on the entire Madrid front."

Mañuel understands: "It had been necessary to kill—not enemies but men of his own—volunteers. And he had done it because he was responsible to each of the men who were now passing before him."

He says to Ximenes: "To command is to serve, nothing more and nothing less. . . . But . . . every step I've taken towards becoming a better officer has estranged me more and more from my fellow men."

"And what did you expect," asks Ximenes; "That you could sentence men to death without a qualm?" "The real struggle," he adds, "begins when you have to contend against a part of your own self . . . it's only from such inner conflicts that a real man emerges."

Mañuel and his brigade join the International Brigades and defeat the Italians at Guadalajara. He pauses in a church in the captured city and plays a Palestrina *Kyrie* on its organ. It stirs up his longing for his past life and, finding a gramophone, he listens to a recording of the Beethoven Sonata *Les Adieux*. It becomes, for him, the voice of Man's hope.

These scenes were taken from Gustavo's life in wartime. The novel ended with the playing of the sonata; his life went on.

He was holding the coastal city of Valencia when the fighting ended in Spain. The city was surrounded and taken by Franco's soldiers. Gustavo was to be executed on the day after its capture.

He spent the night wandering through the city in the hope of finding someone who might help him to escape. He went to the American consulate and pleaded with the consul, a Foreign Service officer.

The consul refused to help him. "You picked the wrong side," he said.

Gustavo held out his hand to the consul. He wandered on through the city. He found no one who could help him, and, at dawn, he returned to the consulate.

The consul stood in his doorway. "I could have saved your life," he said, "and I refused to. Yet, you held out your hand to me; why?"

"Why not?" Gustavo said.

The consul handed him the address of a British diplomat. The diplomat drove him through Franco's lines to a launch in the harbor.

The launch took him to a British destroyer that was waiting offshore. "I saw the trousers of a British sailor ruffle in the breeze as the destroyer got under way," he said later. "I knew then that I was going to live."

He landed penniless in London. By chance, he met my old friend Michael Young. Michael took him to Dartington, where Bin's sister, Bonte, was living. My mother acted as a matchmaker, and they were married in Totnes.

They wanted to live in America. To come here, Gustavo needed a visa. His chances of getting one were none too good, but I went nonetheless to call on the head of the visa division, Mrs. Ruth Shipley.

Mrs. Shipley was an ardent conservative, but she was kind to me. "I knew your father well," she told me. "He was the greatest consul the United States ever had."

I lost no time in handing her Gustavo's papers. She studied them carefully.

"I see that he fought in Spain," she remarked. "Which side was he on?"

"The right side, Mrs. Shipley," I said.

She stared at me for a moment. Then she signed the papers and let Gustavo in.

The Durans came to live at old Westbury. Their three children were the same ages as ours, and our families were inseparable. We shared a house on Martha's Vineyard each summer. At Christmas, our charades were transformed from entertainment to high drama when Gustavo appeared as Urban the Seventh, with a bath robe wrapped around his torso and a brass bucket on his head.

His taste was impeccable, his knowledge formidable, his talent overwhelming.

Once, for example, when we went to a party on Martha's Vineyard, Gustavo noticed a score propped up on a piano.

"What's this?" he asked the son of our host.

"*The Rhapsody in Blue,* scored for piano alone," wailed the boy. "It's impossible to play."

"Nonsense!" said Gustavo. He played the score off on sight while the boy looked on, stunned.

On another evening that summer, we went to an illustrated lecture on "The Generation of '98," given by a fellow-exile of Gustavo's who had become a professor of Spanish literature at Wellesley.

The lights were turned down. The first slide appeared on the screen. It showed a whitewashed house.

"Ah yes," said Gustavo. "The birthplace of the poet, Antonio Machado, in Seville."

He gave a summary of the way in which Machado employed images in order to evoke memories and dreams. Then, "Next slide!" he said.

He went on to give an hour's lecture on the generation of '98, accompanied by forty-nine slides, all of which he identified without hesitation. The professor of Spanish literature worked the projector and, at the end, stood up to receive her share of the applause.

"Some day there would be peace," Malraux wrote in the final scene of *Man's Hope.* "And he, Mañuel, would become another man, someone whom he could not visualise as yet."

That certainly was Gustavo's intention. He had no sympathy for simplistic ideologies and little interest in politics. He wanted to create a new life for himself, but his past was forcibly recalled by men who were willing to destroy him in order to advance their own ends.

Gustavo was naturalized as an American citizen in December 1942. He worked with Nelson Rockefeller on projects related to the arts. Then, in the belief that his skill and his experience were needed in more important tasks, Ernest Hemingway persuaded him to go to work for the American ambassador to Cuba, Spruille Braden.

In 1945, Braden was made ambassador to Argentina. In the absence of any indigenous opposition, he became the principal antagonist of the Argentine dictator, Juan Peron.

The United States government published a *Blue Book* in 1946, outlining Peron's wartime collaboration with the Nazis. Peron struck back by accusing Gustavo of being an agent of the Soviet Secret Police.

The charge was supported by Franco. It was taken up in America by Representative J. Parnell Thomas, soon to be chairman of the House Committee on Un-American Activities. It was echoed within the government by Edwin Pauley, an oil man who had backed Truman and had been rewarded with a high position in the Department of State.

Gustavo was subjected to a full loyalty investigation by the department. He stayed on until he was cleared; then he went to work for the United Nations.

There, he was pursued by Senator Joseph McCarthy.

On August 30, 1951, McCarthy made a speech to the Annual Convention of the Veterans of Foreign Wars. Standing on a raised platform, he unveiled a seven-foot photograph of Gustavo, wearing a uniform that McCarthy claimed was that of the S.I.M., an organ of "the Russian Secret Police."

The uniform was that of an officer in the Spanish Army. As an officer, Gustavo had indeed been assigned by the Spanish government to work in the S.I.M. He had insisted, after a few weeks, on returning to his brigade.

The New York *Daily News* noted that McCarthy was lying. *Time*, in its issue of October 22, 1951, chose Gustavo's case to document its charge that McCarthy was an unprincipled demagogue. McCarthy's response was characteristic: his agents stole *Time*'s dossier on Gustavo. McCarthy threatened to release the file unless Henry Luce, the publisher of *Time*, apologized to him. Luce refused to apologize, so McCarthy fed excerpts from the dossier to Fulton Lewis and to his other allies. They redoubled their attacks on Gustavo, branding him disloyal.

In their book, *McCarthy and His Enemies*, Buckley and Bozell devote an entire chapter to Gustavo. It reads today as if the authors were engaged in pinning dead butterflies to their pages rather than describing their fellow citizens.

Did it matter that when Gustavo's daughters went to school, they were accosted by other children who cried: "There go the daughters of the traitor, Gustavo Duran?"

From 1945 until 1955, Gustavo was forced to defend himself against charges of disloyalty to the country that he had chosen as his home. Trygve Lie, the secretary general of the United Nations, refused to defend him. His passport was taken from him although it was essential to his work.

The unending, insidious campaign against him was harder for Gustavo to bear than the enemy fire he had endured in Spain. When I flew to Wilton in September 1951 to pick up my children, I found him sitting in the sunlight like a patient after an operation; his eyes closed, his mouth agape; his skin dead-white in hue.

I sat down beside him. I said that many others had lived through McCarthy's accusations. I said that the good in America far outweighed the evil.

"It's no use, Michael," he said. "It's like an allergy. The first time it strikes, I'm hardly affected; the second time, the effect is violent. If it strikes again, I don't know what will happen to me."

He sat in silence as we ate our luncheon. Bonte begged him to answer when he was spoken to. "Bonte!" he cried out in anguish, "I am ill, I am ill!"

Three weeks later, I flew to Old Westbury, where the Durans were living. I had made an appointment to see Mrs. Shipley about Gustavo's passport, and I needed to know as much as she did about his past.

Bonte met me at the door of their cottage in the cobbled courtyard. She looked pale and haggard.

"You should know," she said, "that Gustavo is a changed person. He used to be lighthearted. Now he's silent and arbitrary. Even his own staff at the United Nations is turning against him.

"Two days ago, his assistant, Donald McGranahan, brought him the issue of *Time* that defended him. Donald thought it would please Gustavo, but, when he saw the photograph of McCarthy in it, he flung it in Donald's face.

"I called Donald to tell him that Gustavo is really ill. It's true. Last night he lay on our carpet and cried. 'I'm not a strong man,' he kept saying; 'I'm not strong.' "

Inside the cottage, I could hear Gustavo playing one of the Goldberg Variations on his piano. The music stopped in the middle of a bar and he came to the door.

We talked until he was weary. I walked down to the main house to spend the night. I was alone there, and the house was deserted. I found it hard to sleep.

Early the next morning, I stopped by Gustavo's cottage to drive him to New York.

"No more talk," he said, as he climbed into the car. "If the choice is to go on talking about my case or to go to jail, then I prefer to go to jail."

Two days later, I went to the State Department to see Mrs. Shipley. She looked at me warily from behind her desk.

"Who do you wish to bring in this time?" she asked.

Evidently, I had gained quite a reputation for sponsoring the visa applications of former Communists, including Stephen Spender and Gustav Regler.

"I've come to talk to you about my brother-in-law, Gustavo Duran," I said.

"There's very little that I can say."

"Mrs. Shipley, why is the department denying him his passport?"

"You know the law."

"If the department is acting in obedience to the McCarran Act, then it must have reason to believe that Gustavo is a member of the Communist party or that he is disloyal."

"We have to obey the spirit as well as the letter of the law."

"In either event," I said, "I'd like to offer my testimony for what it's worth, based upon my experience in opposing the Communist party in the American Veterans Committee."

"I didn't know that you were active in the A.V.C."

"I'm the national chairman," I said, flying toward every break in the clouds.

"The secretary of state may withhold passports when it is in the national interest to do so."

"That is a matter for you and the secretary to determine, isn't it?"

"It is."

"Well?"

"We have to consider the individual, the purpose of the trip, and the sensitivity of the area to be visited."

"The individual is a practicing Catholic; the trip was ordered by the secretary general of the United Nations; the areas to be visited are

Chile and Equador. It seems to me that your decision is easy."

"The area is a sensitive one. It is close to Argentina."

So that's it, I thought. We have to thank Juan Peron for Gustavo's miseries.

"You realize," Mrs. Shipley said, "that your brother-in-law may travel without a passport."

"Mrs. Shipley, he came here as an exile. He loves this country. He needs to know if it accepts him as a citizen or not. His health depends upon it."

"It would be easier if he didn't travel for a year."

"His job requires him to travel."

"You realize that if his passport is withheld, nothing is said by the department, while if he travels on an American passport the public may protest."

"Some part of the public is going to protest if his passport continues to be withheld."

"It is all very difficult."

The decision on Gustavo's passport would be made, she said, by officials "anxious to protect the secretary of state." I thanked her for that information. With her permission, I repeated my story to Acheson's assistant, Marshall Shulman. He understood, and he was kind.

Gustavo was given back his passport; the skies cleared. Looking back, it is hard to believe that the Loyalty Board of the Department of State required Gustavo to answer charges such as these:

> That in April, 1951, you attended a meeting to celebrate the 20th Anniversary of the Spanish Republic.
>
> That, on at least one occasion, you said you were sorry you had become an American citizen.

—◦◦◦—

For Biddy, the age of McCarthy was characterized by intimidation; for Gustavo, it meant persecution. In contrast, I was never threatened, save in the clumsy and inept efforts of two congressional committees to turn me into an informer by testifying falsely about my liberal friends.

I was angered by the injustice of those days. I was infected by the tensions that they engendered. I sensed that they would seem unbelievable in time; for that reason, I kept a notebook in which I recorded my experiences.

The pages that follow in this chapter are taken from my notebook. They are footnotes to an age, but for me they retain some value because of the time at which they were written.

October 15, 1951

Our old friend, Virginia Durr, called up to invite us to dinner. Her guests of honor, she added, were to be the ambassador of the People's Republic of Poland and his wife.

We drove to the Durrs' house on Seminary Road. We moved into their living room. A number of aging New Dealers and their wives had arrived before us.

Virginia beckoned to us to come and be introduced to her guests of honor. "Your Excellency and Madame Winiewicz," she said, "may I present the editor of *The New Republic* and Mrs. Michael Straight."

The ambassador bowed. He was tall, handsome, well groomed, and as cold as ice.

He had been a leading Socialist intellectual in Poland, so Mordecai Ezekiel whispered to me. He had supported the Communist government when it suppressed his friends.

Madame Winiewicz was also tall, but her gray hair was a bit disheveled. There were dark hollows under her cheek bones, and her eye sockets were dark and deep. Throughout the evening, we remembered later, she kept staring at Bin.

Food was never a high priority at the Durrs'. We hurried through dinner, then Virginia seated us all in a circle.

"Before we all get to conversing again," she said, "I'd like His Excellency to repeat what he was saying to me at the table."

The ambassador cleared his throat. He delivered a few pleasantries about our gracious host and our charming hostess. In venturing a few comments to her, he added, he had not supposed that they were worthy of repetition to such a distinguished gathering. It was not his province, he said, to be critical of the nation to which he was so fortunate as to be assigned by the Polish Peoples Republic. Nonetheless . . .

"I said to our hostess," he continued, "that my wife and I were watching your television last evening. There, on the news, was a film, of the arrest of eleven leaders of your Communist party. They were pushed into a police wagon and taken off to prison. *In tsains!*

"I told our hostess that my wife and I were distressed," said the ambassador. "We were deeply distressed!"

He was right about the news program. Eleven ranking leaders of the Communist party had been arrested the night before and taken off to prison—in handcuffs, not chains—under the provisions of the Smith Act.

In many editorials in *The New Republic,* I had attacked the Congress for passing the Smith Act, the Supreme Court for upholding it, and the Department of Justice for enforcing it. I was under no compulsion to defend the actions of the Truman administration in arresting the Communist leaders, but I would be damned if I would let a Soviet puppet instruct me in political morality. I had been living under a good deal of tension and in the long wait to be fed, had emptied four glasses of Virginia's sweet sherry.

Everyone nodded as the ambassador voiced his deep distress. No one spoke. From a distance, I heard my own voice:

"What was it that distressed you?"

"To see them taken off to prison!" the ambassador cried.

"Did it distress you when the Polish Socialists were taken away to prison by your government—and shot?"

There was a long moment of silence. I could see Virginia glaring at me while Cliff, her mild-mannered husband, sucked on the stub of his cigarette and stared at the floor.

"Criminals!" cried the ambassador. "A few criminals may have been detained. A few anti-Socialist elements. A few may have been disciplined —at the insistence of the people."

"Only a few?"

The ambassador was taken aback. "Who are you Americans to criticize?" he cried. "You have never been invaded! You have never been bombed! You have never lived under the Nazis! Who are you to interfere?"

Everyone around the circle nodded. Everyone hoped that I would say no more; but there was too much pent-up anger in me to be kept down.

"You were the one who criticized!" I said. "You are the ones who interfere! You attack Mrs. Roosevelt and everyone else in this country who believes in peace! You undermine Walter Reuther and everyone else who works to strengthen our democracy! You talk about peace and cooperation, and all the time you keep on——"

"We? . . . We have done nothing!" the ambassador cried.

"You know what I mean! The Communist leaders that you're so distressed about; you know what they're doing! You'd better make up your minds whether you want world peace or world revolution, because you can't have them both!"

It was brutal. It might have grown worse, but it was brought to a sudden end.

We were seated as we shouted at each other. Suddenly, there rose above us the gaunt figure of Madame Winiewicz.

She glared at all of us. Then, "I do you all a favor!" she shouted. "I do my husband and all of you a great favor! I shoot you all!"

She raised her bony arms in front of her, with her long forefingers joined together. "*Ach! . . . ach! . . . ach! . . . ach! . . .*" Pivoting slowly, she mowed us all down in a burst of imaginary machine-gun fire.

We sat in silence, unable to move or to speak. Slowly, she lowered her arms to her sides. She stood there, swaying.

The ambassador looked at his watch. He stood up. Once again, he was calm and cold.

"Well," he said. "I see it is getting late. We must not keep our driver waiting any longer. We must be going."

"Come!" He gripped his wife's elbow and led her to Virginia. "A most enjoyable evening!" He bowed to all of us and steered his wife to the door.

We all stood up. There was nothing more to say. Virginia reappeared at the doorway. Everyone filed past her.

"Most enjoyable. . . ." "So nice!" "You must come and see us, now that we're settled in. . . ."

Virginia called up the next morning. The ambassador apparently had telephoned, not to apologize but to explain. His wife, he explained, had been upset by a strange coincidence. One of the guests, Mrs. Straight, had borne a most remarkable resemblance to their daughter.

"How interesting," said Virginia.

Yes, said the ambassador, it was very interesting. His wife, he repeated had been upset by the resemblance. Their daughter had been killed in Warsaw at the end of the war.

-----

November 29, 1951

A man came into *The New Republic* office today. He insisted on talking to me, alone.

A gaunt, pock-marked Negro; he sat down beside my desk and asked for a cigarette.

He had been living in Europe with his child, so he said. The State Department had been giving him pin money to spy on Negro Communists. Oh sure, the Communists trusted him. He had been a member of the party in California.

Unable to make it on his State Department allowance, so he said, he had written to McCarthy, offering to spy for him. McCarthy hired him, he said, to frame John Carter Vincent, an old China hand who was the United States envoy in Switzerland.

The State Department was a bit miffed, so he said, when they learned that he was taking money from McCarthy. They told him to make up his mind just who he was spying for.

"I picked McCarthy," he said; "he had more dough."

He then forged some papers, so he said, linking Vincent to the local Communists. The Swiss government caught him and he ended up in jail.

He was brought back to America, he said, to face a Senate subcommittee. McCarthy's staff got to him first. Life is easy in Venezuela they told him, especially if you start off with $5,000 in a local bank.

"I turned down their offer," he told me. "I hired a photographer, and he took a picture of me with McCarthy's staff man.

"I showed him a positive," he went on. "I kept the negative in my hotel room. They stole it from me.

"Things have changed," he complained, "since I was here last."

"How did you expect to be treated," I asked him, "after what you did?"

"Things have changed," he said.

"Well, what can I do for you?" I asked him.

"I don't know," he said. "Keep in touch, I guess."

-----

March 20, 1952

We employed a press clipping service for *The New Republic*. The bundle that arrived in March included a copy of a broadsheet named HEADLINES, edited and published by a man named Joseph Kamp.

Kamp, I remembered, was an associate of Gerald L. K. Smith.

Smith's journal, *The Cross and the Flag,* had been attempting to prove that Dwight D. Eisenhower was the presidental candidate of the Jews. In a similar spirit, the entire issue of HEADLINES was devoted to vilifying Eisenhower. On one side of its center-spread was a photograph of Eisenhower greeting a Soviet marshal on the Elbe. On the other side was a long quotation from my editorial in praise of Eisenhower, under the headline "EVEN RED MIKE LIKES IKE."

The story struck me as hilarious. But as Milt Rose pointed out, we were facing a court accounting in which I might be accused of leading *The New Republic* too far to the Left.

With the accounting in mind, a letter went off to Mr. Kamp under the letterhead of Milt's law firm. It informed him that the term "Red" had been held to be libelous *per se* in a New York court. It summarized my own record in opposing the Communist party in *The New Republic* and the A.V.C. It stated that unless Mr. Kamp published a full retraction in HEADLINES, we would take him to court.

To my amazement, Kamp replied by return mail. He was glad to be given the facts, he said, and would be happy to publish a correction in his next issue.

The following issue of HEADLINES did, indeed, contain a correction. He was delighted, said the editor and publisher, to point out to his readers the record of my opposition to the Communist party. His reason, he added, was that it was well established that the most dangerous Reds were the anti-Communist Reds.

Milt climbed up one side of his office wall and down the other. I could not stop laughing. It was, I thought, the only funny thing that had happened to us in quite a while.

━━◦◦◦◦◦━━

December 23, 1952

In October 1952, a bulky package arrived by registered mail in the office of our family fund, the William C. Whitney Foundation. It proved to be a twenty-four-page questionnaire, prepared by the Select Committee of the House of Representatives created to investigate tax-exempt foundations and comparable organizations.

We were instructed to respond in full to all of the questions and to return the questionnaire in short order to the Select Committee.

Most of the questions were tiresome rather than threatening. A few were pointed:

Question Number Nine: Have you made investigations of individuals who are connected with the foundations and did any of your investigations reveal anyone who had been connected in any way with subversive organizations or organizations that had been cited?

Question D-14: Has your organization made any grant, gift, loan, contribution or expenditure, directly or indirectly, to any individual, individuals, group, organization or institution . . . which has been criticized or cited by the Un-American Activities Committee of the House of Representatives or the Subcommittee on Internal Security of the Judiciary Committee of the United States Senate?

I had not, in fact, belonged to any of the organizations that the Select Committee identified. In contrast, Max Lerner, who was one of our directors, had belonged to many left-wing groups during the Depression. I talked to Max, and with his endorsement, we filed our answer to Question Number Nine: "One of the directors, prior to his election as a director, had permitted his name to be listed as a sponsor of several organizations which were later cited. However, at the time of his selection, he had severed all connections with such organizations."

Our foundation had been established by my mother in 1926. All but a handful of the grants that came within the Select Committee's definition had been made before Biddy or Max or Milt or I had joined the board. In answer to Question D 14, we said: "The Foundation made no grants or contributions directly or indirectly to any organization or institution subsequent to citation. Grants were made on several occasions to organizations and institutions which were later cited . . . such organizations and institutions at the time . . . enjoyed tax-exempt status by a ruling of the Treasury Department."

Needless to say, Milt and I, as Secretary and President of the foundation, were summoned to appear before the Select Committee. So, the morning of December 5, 1952, found us waiting in an ante-chamber on Capitol Hill. Seated beside us, waiting to be called in his turn, was Marshall Field, a well-known philanthropist from Chicago.

At 9:30 A.M., Milt and I were ushered into the private office of Harold Keele, counsel to the committee. He motioned to us to sit, facing him. Then he looked up, frowning, as if he were a headmaster about to chastise two wayward boys.

His purpose, said Mr. Keele, was to bring about corrective action rather than to punish those who were guilty of past errors. With this in mind, he added, he had arranged this private session with us. If we would cooperate in private, in advancing the goals of the committee, he would, in turn, see to it that we would be spared a public humiliation.

We thanked him. We sat there. Mr. Keele turned over the pages of our written statement until he came to our *Answer to Question Number Nine.* He shook his head.

Our answer saddened him, Mr. Keele said. Sadly, he asked if we would enlighten him on the identity of our misguided board member who had joined so many subversive organizations.

I said that the board member in question was the well-known columnist Max Lerner, and that the summary of his past political affiliations had been submitted to the Select Committee at Mr. Lerner's request.

I went on to describe how Max had been reviled by the Communist party and its allies during the years in which he had served on our board.

Mr. Keele cut me short. Our foundation, he said, had supported the Southern Conference for Human Welfare and a number of other organizations to which the chairman of the Select Committee had taken strong exception.

I said that I understood the Chairman's feelings—and I did. He had been a sworn enemy of progress in his native state of Georgia.

"I suggest to you," said Mr. Keele, "that it was Max Lerner who advocated making these objectionable grants. If you will concede that much," he added, "and if you will assure me that corrective action will be taken in regard to your board member, then I think that I can say on behalf of the committee that no public examination of your grants will be called for."

I said that we were sorry, but we could not agree that Mr. Lerner was responsible for the offending grants; we could not concede that they were improper since they were made to organizations certified as educational or philanthropic by the Treasury Department, and we would not invite Mr. Lerner to resign from our board.

Sadly, Mr. Keele shook his head.

At 10:35, the Select Committee was called to order, the Honorable Aime J. Forand presiding. That, in itself, was a disappointment to Ed Harris of the St. Louis *Post Dispatch*. The chairman of the committee had been Representative Eugene Cox of Georgia. He had promised Ed and other members of the press that he would give me a good working-over. But that was before the Thanksgiving recess. Representative Cox, who was known as "Goober," had gone home for Thanksgiving. He had stuffed one too many mouthfuls of turkey into himself and had died of a stroke.

We took our seats at a table facing the committee. A teletypist sat beside us, tapping our sentences out in shorthand onto a tape that laid itself in neat folds into a little black coffin.

The questions moved along at a brisk pace until we arrived at the exchange recorded on pages 910 and 911 of the official transcript:

MR. FORAND: What was the original purpose of the Foundation according to your instrument of organization?

MR. ROSE: It was broadly stated that general educational and eleemosynary purposes organized under the New York Membership Corporation Law [sic].

Mr. Forand's question is perfectly lucid; Milt's reply is gibberish—because of that one word, *eleemosynary.*

I was watching the long, pale fingers of the stenotypist, tapping out Milt's explanation of our purposes. He came to the word *eleemosynary,* and his fingers froze in mid-air.

It was as if the stenotypist had died, and *rigor mortis* had instantly set in.

The stenotypist called for a halt in the proceedings. He fished a pencil out of his pocket. He started to write the word out on the margin of his tape; he stopped once again.

He asked the chairman to spell the word; the chairman turned to the committee counsel; the counsel motioned to Milt. Milt spelled out the word. It was saved for posterity, but the sentence in which it was embedded was garbled forever. It served Milt right.

The hearings started up again. Mr. Keele brought us to our misguided

board member. I spoke out in defense of Max. Mr. Keele told the committee that we had supported Frontier Films and the Institute for Pacific
Relations. Representative Forand failed to cry out in anguish as Cox
would have done.

Mr. Keele moved on.

MR. KEELE: Mr. Straight, have you changed your views with reference
to whether the Communist Party in this country constitutes a clear and
present danger from what they were in 1950, shall we say?

Evidently he had dug up the testimony I had given as chairman of the
A.V.C.

MR. STRAIGHT: I testified on the McCarran Act sir. I said that . . . my
own experience led me to believe that the McCarran Act would not
help people like myself to set back the Communist Party in the factories
and the organizations where the front lines existed. I still hold the view
that legislation is not the final answer and may, in fact, be a hindrance.
. . . I regard the Communist Party as a source of espionage and of
subversion.

MR. KEELE: You are quoted here as saying: "We don't believe that the
Communist Party today is a clear and a present danger."

MR. STRAIGHT: Yes. I was using that phrase in relation to Justice
Holmes' famous dictum as to whether a danger, clear and present,
existed, compelling this country to take action in the legal suppression
of this group.

MR. KEELE: I take it from what you have said that . . . you would say
that the Communist Party is a clear and present danger today, is that
right?

MR. STRAIGHT: I certainly would; yes.

MR. KEELE: I have no further questions, Mr. Chairman.

"Whereupon," the transcript notes, "at 12:05 a recess was taken until
2:00 P.M. this day."

We walked out of the Committee Room. We bore no bruises, but I was
ashamed of myself for giving in on the "clear and present danger" point.

Mr. Keele led Marshall Field into his office and shut his door. Marshall
showed some irresolution, so in the public session that followed, Keele
flayed him unmercifully.

Our trial, I assumed, was over. I was mistaken. Three weeks later, as
I read the *Washington Post* at breakfast, I saw my name on the front page.

The Select Committee, the *Post* reported, had taken sworn testimony
from a "former leader" of the Communist party who affirmed that he
knew me well.

"When did you know him?" Mr. Keele asked the witness.

"Back in the thirties," the witness answered. He added that my name
"was a household word in the councils of the party's Central Committee."

"Is he to the best of your knowledge a member of the Communist
party?" Keele asked the witness.

"I doubt very much whether he's actually a card-carrying party member," the witness replied, "because I doubt that he's the type that would bind himself by card-carrying discipline. But I might be wrong."

The witness was identified by the *Post* as a paid informer for the Bureau of Immigration.

I called the chief of the bureau and asked how it felt to have a perjurer on his payroll. Then I drove up to Capitol Hill. I waved a copy of the *Post* in front of Mr. Keele. I pointed out to him that I was a boy of seven, living in England, at the time when his witness knew me well.

Mr. Keele was discomfited. He said that his witness was a reliable man. He agreed to check the matter further with his chief informant, the one-time editor of the *Daily Worker*, Louis Budenz.

"Well?" I said, when I went back to see Mr. Keele, a few days later. "What did Mr. Budenz have to say?"

"He said that *The New Republic* had called him a worm."

"Was that all he said?"

"He gave you a clean bill of health," said Mr. Keele unhappily.

"Well," I said, "that's something."

"Did you call him a worm?" asked Mr. Keele.

"I don't know, but I'll find out."

It was not a term that we normally used, but I had hired my old boss, Harold Ickes, as a columnist. I discovered that he had indeed called Budenz "a worm" in one of his columns.

I was lucky. Budenz could so easily have called me a good comrade in return.

--~∞~--

In what his associates described as an effort "to take over McCarthyism from McCarthy," Herbert Brownell, the attorney general of the United States, denounced Harry Truman as a near-traitor and accused him of knowingly promoting a Soviet spy, Harry Dexter White.

I was infuriated by Brownell's debasement of his office. I ranted on about him at our dinner table until I was interrupted.

"Daddy," said David, aged eleven, "is Jimmy Brownell Herbert Brownell's son?"

It hadn't occurred to me that the attorney general had a son, and that the son was a member of David's class in the Sidwell Friend's School. I tried to evade the question, but Bin answered it.

"Yes, he is, Dave."

"I'll fix him!"

"No you won't!" I said. "You won't even mention it to him. He's not to blame."

"I will mention it to him!"

"Look Dave, I happen to think that Jimmy's father did a terrible thing today. It may spread new hatreds across this country, but we're not going to add to them by spreading hatreds of our own. We're not going to hold Jimmy responsible for the acts of his father."

David looked up at me, baffled.

"Do you understand?"

"I think so."

---

November 2, 1953

"You've got a headache?" said Dinah, not quite three. "You take a thermometer and you put it in your behindness. You take it out and look at it, and if you've got a pertemperature, you eat an aspirin."

"Thank you, Dinah," I said. But an aspirin was no remedy.

I telephoned my friend Roger Kennedy in the Department of Justice. "How could the attorney general make that statement about Truman?" I asked.

Roger was silent for a moment. Then, "If you think that the great domestic issue is subversion," he said, "then you must concede the right of the incoming administration to re-state the record."

"Even though the issue itself has been settled?"

"Has it been settled?"

"You know that it's been settled, Roger."

"I hope that it's been settled. I'll call Steve," Roger added, "then I'll call you back."

He called back half an hour later.

"What did Steve say?" I asked.

"He said: 'If you believe in the objectives of the Eisenhower administration, then you must accept whatever political measures are necessary to keep it in power.'"

---

November 16, 1953

I went to dinner at the home of Duncan Phillips, the founder of the Phillips Gallery and a liberal of the old school. Francis Biddle and Marquis Childs, the columnist, were there.

"I cannot believe that the American people will let Brownell get away with these disgraceful attacks," said Duncan.

"I'm afraid that they will," I said.

"Don't they understand that it's McCarthyism in executive clothing?"

"Yes, and they still suspect that McCarthy was right."

"Who began this round?" Duncan asked."

"Hoover," said Mark. "J. Edgar himself. McCarthy was his mouthpiece. Brownell is his captive. He's getting even with Roosevelt, at last."

"Brownell may be Hoover's captive, as you say," said Francis, who had been Roosevelt's attorney general. "Every attorney general is to some degree his captive.

"I remember," he went on, "that when I took over the Department of Justice, Hoover began at once to feed out stories and rumors to cut me down.

"I realized that he was bitter about being left out of my inner council, so I created a new advisory group, largely to give him a place to sound off.

"He was very useful; often sound. He was also cruel, vindictive, and reactionary. I told him that he should make a liberal name for himself. I sent the F.B.I. to the South on civil liberties cases. Hoover hated every minute of that assignment, and he did a superb job.

"He came to like me," Biddle continued. "We used to sit together for hours while I listened to his gossip. He was the greatest gossip in Washington; he knew every trivial, damaging detail that there was to know. He filled me up with salacious stories about Mrs. Roosevelt and Joe Lash; how she wrote to Joe every day; how the letters were intercepted and reported back by Joe's commanding officer in the Pacific, and how furious Roosevelt was when he found out about it. He sent the officer to the front at once! Oh, Hoover had hundreds of stories about Mrs. Roosevelt, but his consuming interest was immorality among boys and young men."

I described the refusal of Lou Nichols, Hoover's public relations man, to talk to me about the implications of the Brownell charges. "Not that we have anything against you," Nichols had added. "We're just not talking."

"A curious statement," I said.

Mark laughed. "Last November," he said, "when the election was safely behind us, I wrote a column proposing that a nonpartisan commission be created to investigate the whole question of infiltration of the government. I added that it should be given access to F.B.I. files. And that was all I said.

"Within a few days, a flood of attacks broke out against me. Walter Winchell threw out a number of foul rumors about me. Morris Ernst called me dirty names. Half a dozen columnists went after me, for no apparent reason. Fulton Lewis devoted three broadcasts to denouncing me. He said that I had become the chief spokesman for a Communist-inspired plot to overthrow the government of the United States.

"Lewis made it pretty clear that his source was the F.B.I. So I called up Lou Nichols. I said, 'Lou, what's going on?' He laughed. 'We've been waiting for you to call,' he said; 'you'd better come over for lunch.'

"So I went. 'Now, look here Lou,' I said, 'You know perfectly well that I'm not part of any Communist plot.'

" 'Oh, sure,' he said.

" 'Then why did you put out that story about me?' I asked.

" 'Our friends needed some copy,' Lou told me.

"I said, 'Now come on Lou, that's not good enough.'

" 'No, it isn't,' he said.

" 'I'll tell you why we put the story out,' he added. 'We put it out because we don't like this commission of yours and we're going to kill it.'

" 'Oh Lou!' I said; 'you're not serious!'

" 'We're very serious,' he said. 'If this commission is created, the Commies will get onto it. Then they'll be into our files.'

" 'Why, that's absurd!' I said.

" 'No, it's not;' he said, 'and anyway, it's what we think.'

"He said, pretty broadly, that if I knew what was good for me, I'd lay off the idea for good. The treatment I'd been given, he said, was just a warning; just a reminder, for my own good."

"Hoover is a dangerous man," I mumbled.

"Of course he's dangerous!" Francis said.

---

November 20, 1953

The Senate Caucus Room was jammed as tightly as a subway car in the rush hour. I fought my way around a pillar to see what was going on. A photographer promptly clambered up onto my shoulders.

The doors of the Caucus Room were forced open. A wedge of policemen pushed their way in. In the center of the wedge was J. Edgar Hoover. His face was bloated and veinous; the veins were scarlet and purple.

At the sight of Hoover the crowd in the room stood up and cheered. He took his seat in a witness chair, and Herbert Brownell sat down beside him.

The gavel pounded; the cameras began to whirr. Brownell read aloud a letter from Hoover. It amounted to proof, he said, that Truman had promoted Harry Dexter White when he knew him to be a Soviet spy.

The letter said, ". . . the evidence indicates. . . ."

Robert Morris and Julius Sourwine, the staff attorneys, helped Brownell to flesh out his charges. The Republican senators backed him up. Butler, a Democrat, made Brownell admit that White had been transferred from the Treasury but not promoted. McClellan worked Brownell into a corner and, his voice dry with disdain, dismissed him.

Brownell gathered up his papers and departed. Hoover, when he was asked to testify, managed to shift the argument to a denunciation of the ban on wire tapping.

I rode back downtown with Scotty Reston and Bill Lawrence of the *New York Times.* I followed Reston to his office.

"I supported Stevenson, not Eisenhower," I said. "I've been wondering why I feel betrayed."

Reston turned furiously on me. "Why should you wonder!" he cried. "This is the dirtiest trick you've ever seen, and ever will see!"

---

February 5, 1954

Once again, the Congress was investigating foundations. This time, Milt and I were summoned to the New York offices of an attorney named Rene Wormser, who was counsel to a House subcommittee.

"Mr. Rose and Mr. Straight, to see Mr. Wormser," we said.

The receptionist spoke into an ivory-colored telephone. Down the carpeted corridor came an expansive man, dressed in a white shirt, a black, woven tie, and black suspenders.

Big Brother! I said to myself.

Mr. Wormser was very genial. So was his partner, Mr. Koch. They worked as a team.

"Have you heard our definition of 'subversive'?" asked Mr. Wormser.

"No," we said, "tell us."

"Something that undermines a foundation!" cried Mr. Koch. We gasped with laughter.

"Now," said Mr. Wormser, putting on a solemn air. "Let us get things straight. We are counsels to a congressional committee that is investigating foundations. You gentlemen represent a foundation; one that has made a number of mistakes. The committee is anxious to find out why you made those mistakes, and you can be of great help to us by being cooperative."

"Are you saying that your principal interest is investigating past mistakes?"

"No, no! Mr. Koch and I are more concerned with larger issues. But, you understand, the committee has some politicians on it, and this is an election year."

"We understand," Milt said.

"Now!" said Mr. Wormser, leaning forward, "just how did you come to make those mistakes? Who brought forward these unpleasant projects? What staff member analyzed them? Which board members voted for them, or against them? Were one or two individuals responsible for the great majority of grants that the committee may conclude were unwise? We would be very glad to have that information."

"We gave to no organization," said Milt, "that did not have a Treasury Department ruling of tax-exemption."

"That is no standard," Mr. Wormser said.

"Do you mean," Milt asked, "that foundations such as ours are supposed to have larger resources for investigation and appraisal than the Government of the United States?"

Mr. Wormser shifted his ground.

"Would you agree," he said, "that you have made mistakes?"

"Hundreds," said Milt.

"Of the subversive variety?"

"One or two."

"Very interesting!"

"However," I said, "we may disagree as to what we mean by mistakes. For example, I don't believe that the grant that we made to the Institute of Pacific Relations was a mistake."

Mr. Koch coughed loudly.

"You had better not mention the I.P.R. here," said Mr. Wormser. "Mr. Koch is very sensitive on the matter of the I.P.R."

I asked Mr. Wormser how he would define 'mistakes.'

"I will tell you," said Mr. Wormser. "I will do even better by giving you an example of a 'mistake' made by a very large foundation. We have uncovered a case in which a very large foundation financed a study of cybernetics, and the study, when it was published, contained criticisms of capitalism. Now would you say that was right?"

"Every year," I said, "we receive an application from the League for Industrial Democracy that openly criticizes capitalism and has a Treasury Department ruling. Are you saying that we are not entitled to support the league?"

"I will tell you my theory," said Mr. Wormser. "The money you are spending under today's very high tax rates belongs to the people of the United States in the sense that they would otherwise collect it in taxes. I question very much whether the people have not the right to ask whether their money should be spent on behalf of ideas that the majority strongly disapprove of."

I choked on the obvious rejoinder: that in repudiating the prerogatives of private property, Mr. Wormser had staked out a position well to the left of the groups that the Whitney Foundation had 'mistakenly' supported.

My final sketch, in these notes on the McCarthy era, revolves around the prickly personality of Owen Lattimore.

The collapse of the Chiang Kai-shek regime in 1949 coincided with McCarthy's rise in American politics. In the squalor that characterized our politics, China became a divisive issue within the United States.

Searching questions were in order relating to China; they were not asked. Instead, scapegoats were sought and identified by McCarthy and his allies. Chief among them were the Institute for Pacific Relations and its one-time officer, Owen Lattimore.

From the privileged sanctuary of the Senate, McCarthy claimed that the I.P.R. had delivered China to the Communists, and that Lattimore was "the top Russian espionage agent in the United States."

Brien McMahon, a Democratic Senator and a Catholic, was deeply shaken. "I thought that at last he'd stumbled on some real information," McMahon told me. "I checked all the sources. I satisfied myself that, once again, Joe had no proof to back his charges up. He just wanted to see his name on the front pages."

Lattimore demanded a Senate hearing to respond to McCarthy. In sworn testimony, he stated: "I have never consciously or deliberately advocated or participated in promoting the cause of communism anywhere."

I barely knew Lattimore. I did not particularly like him. But I printed his testimony in full in *The New Republic*. A few weeks later, the Senate committee that heard his testimony cleared him of the charges McCarthy had brought against him.

Those charges should have been laid to rest. Instead, they were picked up and pressed by McCarthy's ally Senator Pat McCarran. He kept Lattimore for twelve days in a witness chair, in the belief that in his exhaustion, he might commit some blunder.

McCarran took testimony about Lattimore that was subsequently proved to be false. He denied to Lattimore the right to cross-question his accusers, to respond to their charges, to present his own defense in an orderly manner, and to learn what had been said about him in executive sessions of the committee.

That was in February 1952. In August, McCarran succeeded in placing his protégé, Roy Cohn, in the Justice Department.

Lattimore had said: "I am not and never have been a Communist, a Soviet agent, sympathizer, or any kind of promoter of communism or of Communist interests." Cohn prepared an indictment of Lattimore, charging him with lying.

The indictment went before Judge Luther Youngdahl. He dismissed it, saying that it was "so nebulous and indefinite" that a jury would have to engage in speculation in order to arrive at a verdict.

Youngdahl held, in effect, that a perjury charge had been turned into an ideological charge by the indictment. His opinion was upheld by a Court of Appeals. He was attacked, quite improperly, by the Justice Department, in a statement that it termed an "Affidavit of Bias and Prejudice." He responded by calling the affidavit "scandalous."

A young Republican lawyer who admired Youngdahl happened to be working at the time for a broadcast network. He was assigned to do a report on the Lattimore case. He came to share Youngdahl's opinion—that the conduct of the government was scandalous.

The network had no interest in pursuing a story that would incur the wrath of the McCarran Committee and the Justice Department if it were told. So the Republican lawyer called me. We agreed that he would write a lengthy story on the case for *The New Republic,* and we agreed that he would sign it with a pseudonym. The name that he chose for himself was Brian Gilbert, an Anglicized version of Sir Walter Scott's character Brian de Bois Guilbert.

The December 27 issue of *The New Republic* in 1954 carried as its lead article "New Light on the Lattimore Case," by Brian Gilbert. A footnote added, "Brian Gilbert is the pen name of a well-known Washington commentator on political affairs."

The opening lines of the article were written in Brian's urbane style: "Toward the end, they say, Pat McCarran lost his enthusiasm for Roy Cohn, but, by then, the damage had been done."

The article went on to make three grave charges against the Government of the United States:

> The Subcommittee of the Senate Judiciary Committee had overstepped the boundaries of legitimate Congressional investigation in its interrogation of Owen Lattimore.
>
> Senator McCarran in his capacity as Chairman of the Senate Judiciary Committee had brought improper pressure to bear upon the Executive Branch by making Senate confirmation of James McGranery as Attorney General conditional upon the prosecution of Lattimore.
>
> The Department of Justice had acted improperly in submitting to McCarran's pressure, and in prosecuting Lattimore.

Brian did not defend or criticize Lattimore, noting only that his truculence did not help him. He pointed out that the government lawyers believed that Lattimore had lied in making his general denial. He added that no facts had been presented to support their belief. They had claimed simply that Lattimore had influenced others. Brian concluded, "No law makes mere influence a crime."

A week or so after the article was published, a telephone call came in for me at *The New Republic.*

"Mr. Straight?"

"Yes."

"This is Jay Sourwine."

"Yes, Mr. Sourwine."

"You know who I am?"

"Yes, indeed."

"Good! I'm sure we'll get along very well."

"I hope so."

"Mr. Straight, I am, as you know, counsel to a Senate committee. The members of my committee have read with great interest the article that you published entitled 'New Light on the Lattimore Case.'"

"I remember it."

"Mr. Straight, they were particularly interested in the assertion made in the course of the article that the committee had encouraged perjury."

"I see."

"They regard that as a very serious charge, Mr. Straight, a very grave charge. They are most anxious to determine what facts were in the possession of Mr. Gilbert that led him to make such a grave and serious charge."

"I understand."

"Mr. Straight, I realize that you are merely the editor of *The New Republic* and not the author of the article in question."

"I take full responsibility for it, Mr. Sourwine."

"Yes. Nonetheless, Mr. Straight, it is Mr. Gilbert in whom the committee members are interested. They are anxious to meet with him, Mr. Straight, in order to consider his charges. Would you please be kind enough to give me his telephone number so that we may arrange a meeting."

That made me pause.

"Mr. Sourwine," I said, "I can't do that at the moment. But I'll tell you what I will do. I will call Mr. Gilbert and I will tell him of your request."

At that, Sourwine paused.

"I assume that I will be hearing from you shortly." he said.

"Very shortly, Mr. Sourwine."

I grabbed another telephone and called Brian.

"Holy Cow!" he cried. "I can't go up there! They'll murder me, and the network will bury me!"

"You'd prefer not to talk to Mr. Sourwine?"

"You bet I'd prefer not—if I can help it!"

I called the number that Sourwine had given me. I explained to him that I had spoken to Mr. Gilbert and that, for reasons I had to accept, Mr. Gilbert had decided that he could not meet with the committee.

There was a long pause.

"Mr. Straight, do you realize what you are saying to me?"

"I think so."

"I can hardly think so. I am speaking to you, Mr. Straight, as an official of the United States Congress. I am relaying instructions to you given to me by members of that body. Contempt of Congress, Mr. Straight, is a very serious act; a *very* serious act indeed, in the opinion of the members of my committee."

"I'm sure it is, Mr. Sourwine."

"Mr. Straight, I urge you with the utmost seriousness to reconsider your position. I urge you further to press upon Mr. Gilbert the gravity of this situation and to do all that you can to induce him to reconsider his position. Mr. Straight, will you do that?"

"Certainly, Mr. Sourwine."

"I will be awaiting your further call, Mr. Straight."

I telephoned Brian. "Look," I said. "I have no objection whatever to being cited for contempt. I have a predilection for martyrdom, and I have a lot of reading to catch up on if I do go to jail. However, it's possible that, one way or another, they'll catch up with you; and that will make it worse for you, when they do."

"I'll think it over," Brian said.

He called back in an hour, chuckling in his irrepressible way. "I've got an idea," he said, "and I'm going to try it out."

"Come on, Brian, what is it?"

"Call me Hiram Spaulding," Brian said.

An hour later, the telephone rang again. Rusty, who ran our office, covered the mouthpiece of her telephone with her hand. She whispered, "It's that awful man again."

"Yes, Mr. Sourwine."

"Mr. Straight? . . . I have good news to share with you. I've just had a long and a most profitable talk on the telephone with Mr. Gilbert's attorney, a Mr. Hiram Spaulding, not of this city. He understood perfectly why the senators were so disturbed, and he came up with what I regard as a most constructive proposal. He said that he and his client——"

"He *and* his client?"

"Pardon me. He said that he would advise his client to meet in private with members of the committee. He was most persuasive, and I believe he will prevail upon Mr. Gilbert to see it his way."

"I'm sure he will," I said.

Two days later, Brian Gilbert paid a call upon the members of the committee, without his attorney. They had expected to see an unkempt radical; instead, they faced a well-groomed young Republican. Some intensive grilling followed, but the committee concluded that the net cast out by Sourwine had caught an unappealing fish.

Once again, the story should have ended there but did not. An envelope arrived at *The New Republic* office late in January. It bore the imprint of the American Committee for Cultural Freedom and contained a Letter to the Editor from its executive director, Sol Stein.

The letter, which we published, began by noting that the committee was not concerned with Lattimore's *legal* guilt or innocence. It went on to state, "It is difficult to see how anyone can seriously question the legitimacy of the statement that Lattimore was 'a conscious and articulate instrument of the Soviet conspiracy.' "

It ended by praising the McCarran Committee investigation as "certainly worth the cost to the American taxpayer."

Brian replied to Stein's letter. He wrote in part,

> My article was about the impropriety of the indictment of Owen Lattimore. Mr. Stein begins by saying that his remarks do not concern this matter. He then presents what he chooses to characterise as a "critique" of my article. . . .
>
> Mr. Stein asks incredulously if I wish to infer that the McCarran Committee suborned perjury. I refer Mr. Stein to Mr. Harvey Matusow.
>
> . . . I neither defended nor criticized Mr. Lattimore in my article. As one who would protest the lynching of any man, innocent or guilty, I concerned myself with the dangerous precedents and procedures established in this case. But, Mr. Stein, speaking in the name of "freedom" would have me kept silent, because, by protesting the procedures, I "may seem to have the effect of absolving [Lattimore] from the charge of Communist sympathies."
>
> If Mr. Stein wrote in his own name, we could dismiss his arrogance without more ado. But, he writes in the name of "Cultural Freedom" and apparently speaks for a Committee formed to advance "Cultural Freedom." The Committee's officers include Norman Thomas, George Counts, Arthur Schlesinger, Jr., David Riesman, Richard Rovere, Elliot Cohen, Peter Viereck, Hans Kohn and others. And so, I for one want to be told: did they approve of Mr. Stein's statement, issued in their name? And, do they endorse it now?

I mailed Brian's comment out to the officers of the committee. I waited for their replies to come in. They were important to me. I had taken my punishment for aligning myself with Henry Wallace. I had set out to identify myself with the liberal intellectuals of America. If they were to fail on this issue, then, I felt, my disillusionment would be hard to overcome.

Slowly the replies to our query came to my desk.

The first letter was from Richard Rovere, the political correspondent of *The New Yorker.* He wrote that the executive committee was within its rights in releasing the letter—as if that were the issue.

The second letter was from the historian Herbert Muller. He said, "It is humiliating that a nation confronted by life and death issues should be distracted by an hysterical search for scapegoats. Even if guilty, Mr. Lattimore has done far less harm to the democratic cause than Senators McCarran, Jenner, McCarthy and their fellow-travellers."

Arthur Schlesinger, Jr., wrote: "1. I disapprove of the prosecution of Mr. Lattimore. 2. I find it hard not to believe that Mr. Lattimore was for many years a sympathiser with Communist and Soviet practises. 3. I saw the Stein letter in advance of publication and I thought that the A.C.C.F. ought to find better things to do than harry Lattimore."

David Riesman wrote to say that he had resigned from the executive committee of the A.C.C.F. because of the Stein letter. He added, "To put the whole weight of the A.C.C.F. behind the pursuit of an already beleaguered man, living in limbo and not permitted to teach classes, was an act of inhumanity."

'An act of inhumanity. . . .' That act was fully supported by Norman Thomas, who had dedicated his life to the advancement of humanity. It was given government sanction, since the Committee for Cultural Freedom was supported largely by public funds, turned over in secret by the C.I.A.

The committee's action was for me a measure of the spiritual corruption that characterized the McCarthy years. The letters of Riesman, of Muller, and of Schlesinger suggested that we were on our way back to health.

Our journey took less time than I had supposed it would. Four months after Brian's article appeared in *The New Republic,* the Department of Justice abandoned its prosecution of Lattimore, taking pains to pin the responsibility for the prosecution upon the previous administration. We had helped, Brian believed, to raise the costs to unprofitable levels for the prosecution; for the defense, they were already unconscionably high.

Here, I should add a footnote to my story:

We heard nothing from Lattimore in the course of our dispute. In May 1955, I drove a British friend, Anthony Crosland, to Baltimore to visit his wife's relatives. Among the men and women who had gathered in their sitting room, I recognized the owlish face of Owen Lattimore. I walked across the room to greet him. He cut me dead.

# STRIGANOV

"THERE'S a man here I want you to meet," said Adam Watson, a Soviet specialist at the British embassy. "His name is Striganov. He's the political counselor at the Soviet embassy. He's the brightest, the best, the most *reasonable* of all of their men."

We walked across the lawn at the home of the British cultural attaché to the bar where Striganov was waiting for a drink. It was May 1954.

I had not talked to any Russians since 1942, when I said goodbye to Michael Green. I had no desire to meet them. Yet it was part of my work as an editor to talk to them, and I still believed that communication at a personal level was essential if we were to avoid war.

Striganov had the lean look of a professor. He was very intelligent; very correct. We agreed to meet again, and from then on we met for lunch once a month. We followed a strict protocol, treating each other in turn. He would take me to lunch at the Mayflower Grill; I would take him to the University Club. Both places were within a block of the Soviet embassy.

We spoke frankly at our luncheons. I found that reassuring. Still, there were conventions that I did not fully understand. One day, for example, I said that I was bringing along an assistant editor of *The New Republic* to luncheon. Striganov said nothing, but he arrived with one of his assistants. The poor man had obviously been roped in at the last moment. He had not even had time to catch my name.

"What is our host's name?" I heard him whisper to my assistant editor.

"Straight, as in straight line," my friend said.

"Ah!" said the Russian. A little later, he turned to me.

"Mister Straight Line, a moment ago you were saying. . . ."

At times, Striganov would telephone and ask if we could have lunch that day or the next day. On those occasions, a pattern emerged in our conversations. Striganov, I came to realize, had received a telegram from Moscow, querying him about some domestic development in American politics. It was up to him to send a prompt reply.

It was easy to spot the query; Striganov would bring it out between the main course and the dessert. I would wait for it, picking away at my salad. When it came, I would answer, thinking to myself: *First your answer must be the truth as you see it; secondly, it must make sense to Striganov's bosses in Moscow; thirdly, it should seem to be a sound answer to the C.I.A., which will surely intercept Striganov's cable on its way East.*

Thus on one occasion, when our main course had been cleared away, Striganov began:

"Vice President Nixon has made a speech in Miami."

"To the Annual Convention of the American Legion."

"Yes. It is a harsh speech in our opinion; a warlike speech."

"Well?"

"I am interested in your opinion. What does the speech portend to you?"

"Mr. Striganov, you have been to the ballet?"

"Of course."

"You know that ballet dancers follow certain conventions, so rigid that all of their movements in any work may be written out in a score."

"Of course."

"Well, if you are a politician in America, you must also follow certain very rigid conventions. If you are making a speech to farmers, you must advocate higher price supports. If you are speaking to Jews, you must pledge yourself to defend the new state of Israel. Otherwise, you will not be elected."

"And?"

"If you are speaking to the Annual Convention of the American Legion, then convention requires that you demand that our defenses be strengthened; that our stance be stiffened; that our opposition to Godless communism be made the cornerstone of our foreign policy. That is what the Legionnaires expect to be told, and that is what any aspiring politician must tell them."

"Including Vice President Nixon."

"Of course."

"It is not to be taken as a departure from the established policies of President Eisenhower?"

"If there was to be a new policy, it would not be announced by the vice president. And it would not be presented to the American Legion."

"I see."

The dessert arrived. Striganov attacked it with enthusiasm. The answer I had given him was, I was convinced, the right answer. And it was the one that he hoped to hear.

At times, talking to Striganov was like shifting one's attack from one side of the board to the other in a game of chess.

One morning, for example, the *New York Times* carried a story about a student riot in a provincial university in the Soviet Union. The students, the *Times* reported, had rebelled against the compulsory courses that were being given on Marxism-Leninism.

I mentioned the story to Striganov when we had lunch that day.

"A fabrication of your capitalist press," he said.

"Maybe," I said. "But let me suggest an alternative interpretation to you.

"In times of crisis, it may be necessary for the ruling powers in any state to give great emphasis to matters of doctrine and ideology. But if the goals of society are accepted, and the state is secure, then doctrine and ideology become less important. Students will want to get on with their studies in order to advance in their professions. And they may resent it if they have to take time off from their chemistry and their engineering to listen to lectures about Marxism. So, it could be argued that if there were student riots against those courses, that would be a sign of strength and of stability, not of weakness in the Soviet state."

"I see what you mean," said Striganov. A little later he added, "It appears that there may have been some minor disturbance at a university."

On another occasion, when Striganov and Gil Harrison and I were having dinner, Gil mentioned that at a few critical moments, the course of his life had been determined by what he could only describe as chance.

Striganov nodded. He had studied to be an engineer, he said. A matter of chance had led him to give up engineering for diplomacy.

"It's interesting that you should say that," said Gil. "You are of course a Marxist, and I'd always supposed that Marx's theory of determinism left no place for chance in shaping our lives."

"Marx was speaking of societies; I am an individual," Striganov said. "Even in the Soviet Union," he added, "there are individuals."

One day, in the summer of 1955, Striganov telephoned to see if I was free for lunch. We met in the Mayflower, since it was his turn to pay. When the waiter was taking away the leftovers of our main course, Striganov turned to me.

"A delegation of Soviet writers is to visit the United States. In October. They will come to Washington. Their leader will be the secretary of the Union of Soviet Writers, Mr. Boris Polevoy."

"Maybe we can all have lunch."

"They have said that they would like to visit an American writer. In his home."

"We'd be happy to invite them all for dinner."

That apparently was what Striganov wanted to hear. It was the last that I heard of the Soviet writers for two months. Then, in October, the *Washington Post* announced that the delegation had arrived in Washington, and that the Soviet ambassador had held a reception at the embassy in their honor.

That day, at noon, Striganov telephoned.

"The delegation that I spoke to you about has arrived in Washington," he said. "They would like to accept your kind invitation to dinner."

"When?"

"Tomorrow night."

Striganov began to give me the names of all of the delegation. As I wrote them down, I thought of a few complications.

"How will you all come out to our house?"

"I will drive them, in my car."

"You may not be able to find the way."

"I will have no trouble. I drove out to your house this morning," he added, "just to make sure."

"You did?"

"I followed a map to a Green Spring Road. You have a red brick house with pine trees all around it."

"That's the one."

I telephoned Bin and Anya, our Polish nurse, to warn them. Next, I rounded up the friends that I could count on: Gil and Nancy Harri-

son, Bev and Louise Bowie, Ed Harris of the *Post-Despatch,* Ted Dud-
ley of the C.I.O. Then I went out and bought a dozen bottles of
whiskey, vodka, and gin.

The Russians arrived half an hour early. The whiskey, the vodka,
and the gin were set out on a side table, and we started in.

Polevoy was loud-mouthed. He laughed a good deal and drank a
great deal. The others seemed nondescript, save for a sallow and
suspicious man who was said to be their translator.

I stayed beside Polevoy. He asked to be shown around our house.
I led him up the steep and narrow stairs to our second floor, where
David and Mike lived. The rest of the delegation followed us, and we
all crowded into David's tiny room.

David, aged thirteen, was sitting on his bed, surrounded by an
immense array of plastic tanks, bombers, fighters, destroyers, aircraft
carriers, and battleships.

Polevoy was delighted. He shouted something in Russian and let
out a resounding guffaw.

Striganov translated. "Mr. Polevoy congratulates your son. He is
a big munitions maker!"

We headed back downstairs. Mike joined us and, at my request,
brought to Polevoy a bound volume of the newspaper that the
Straight and Duran children had put out for two summers on the
Vineyard—the *Green Spring Menemsha Gazette.* As luck would have it,
Polevoy opened up the volume at Part Three of Mike's serial *The
Spies.*

Mike's illustration showed a large airplane heading for Moscow
with the secret blueprints of *The Flying Waffle,* hotly pursued by seven
American jet fighters. "Very good!" cried Polevoy. He demanded to
know what the story was about.

Mike looked up at me.

"You're on your own," I said.

He explained with great tact that the blueprints had been stolen by
agents of an unknown power.

Polevoy seemed truly impressed by the *Gazette.* He waved a five-
dollar bill in Mike's face as his subscription. Mike was reluctant to take
it. We agreed at last to a cultural exchange: our magazine for one of
theirs. Polevoy made some heavy-handed joke about the response of
John Foster Dulles to this bold initiative. Then he drew Striganov
aside. He whispered to Striganov, and Striganov in turn whispered to
me.

"Mr. Polevoy wants to be sure," he said, "that if he puts you on
his mailing list, that will not get you into trouble."

I laughed, but I was touched by his concern.

A few weeks later, Striganov telephoned to say that he would soon be returning to Moscow to head the United States department of the Soviet Foreign Ministry. I suggested that before he left, he and his family might like to come out for a Sunday lunch. He agreed. So, once again, the black Soviet limousine drew up outside our door—this time with Striganov, his wife, and their daughter, Natasha.

Mrs. Striganov was blonde and docile. She could barely speak a word of English. She and Anya managed to talk back and forth, one in Russian, the other in Polish. They talked about children, cooking, and schools.

Striganov also talked about schools, as we sat under a walnut tree. Evidently, when he went out of his compound to visit an American family, it was necessary for him to record that he had spent an hour indoctrinating them on some positive aspect of Soviet society. So, I was given a rather long-winded account of the rise in literacy, in school attendance, and in graduate degrees in the Soviet Union.

It was a lovely spring day. The lilacs were in bloom; a mockingbird was singing in the walnut tree. I sat in silence until Striganov had completed his set piece. Then I said, "May I ask you a question?"

"Of course!"

"If, as you say, the Soviet people are becoming better educated, better read, more sophisticated, will that make it harder for the Soviet government to . . . ah. . . ."

"To lead them around by the nose?"

"Well, yes."

"Yes, it will make it harder," Striganov said.

Susie was eight years old. Natasha was about her age. They sat on a sofa together. Soon they were communicating in the one language they shared:

"Mickey Mouse?"

"Howdy Doody?"

"Hopalong Cassidy?"

Natasha pronounced each name very carefully; she knew them all.

They laughed together; then Susie led Natasha up to her bedroom. When they came down again, Susie was carrying a bundle of plastic horses, and Natasha was clutching Susie's Queen Doll.

The Queen Doll had been Susie's principal Christmas present. She was two feet in height; she wore a long, white satin dress. She had joints for her elbows, her fingers, and her knees. She had what appeared to be human hair. She had long eyelashes, and if she was tilted back, her eyelids closed. If you pinched her in the right place, she made a faint squeak.

Natasha rocked the Queen Doll to sleep in her arms. She woke her up and fed her. She combed her hair and talked to her. She took off her shoes and put them on again. She placed the Queen Doll at her

side when we sat down to eat lunch. She took the Queen Doll along
when Susie led her down to the pond to see the ducks and the Canada
Geese.

At three o'clock, Striganov stood up and said that they had to be
going. He looked down at Natasha, and Natasha's grip tightened on
the Queen Doll. We glanced a bit anxiously at Susie, but she had
nothing to fear.

"We must be going, Natasha," Striganov said once again. "You
must give up the Queen Doll."

Natasha clutched the Queen Doll against her small chest. She
looked up at her father. Her eyes were bright with tears.

Striganov spoke quietly but very firmly in Russian. Natasha stood
up and handed the Queen Doll back to Susie. Then she ran out of the
house.

Striganov seemed to feel that some explanation of her conduct was
called for. "It is necessary for Natasha to get good grades," he said.
"She works very hard. As you can see, she has no time for dolls."

That was the last that we saw of the Striganovs. I believed then, as
I do today, that he knew nothing of my own past. The friendship that
we shared was open and honest. It could not, I felt, lead to harm; it
did in fact lead to one unexpected result.

In May 1956, I received a letter from Walter Lacqueur in London.
"I suppose you know," he wrote, "that the latest issue of *Oktyobr* has
a long article about you and your family by Boris Polevoy."

I borrowed a copy of *Oktyobr* from the State Department. I had it
translated, and I published it in *The New Republic*. It was necessary, of
course, to note a few errors in the article, and one or two assertions
that were misleading. But heavy-handed as it was, it was nonetheless
revealing. It portrayed an American family whom the readers of *Oktyobr* must have envied. They were opposed to the party in power, yet
they were well off. They thought for themselves and spoke for themselves. And in describing our cultural exchange plan, Polevoy turned
the story on himself. It was he who had voiced the fear that I might
be punished for subscribing to a Soviet publication; I had laughed.

Did it matter at all? I could not argue that our encounters would
change the course of events in any way, yet I felt reassured as I read
over Polevoy's lines. It seemed to me that the infinitesimal echoes of
my laughter might be heard by other anxious people in his vast and
alien land.

# ESPECIALLY WHEN I LAUGH

IN the months that followed the break between my mother and Whitney in 1951, I searched for wealthy liberals who might take over *The New Republic*. I flew to Dallas to see Stanley Marcus and to Los Angeles to talk to Gifford Phillips. I spent hours with Marshall Field in Chicago and with Averell Harriman in New York. They all had their own reasons for saying no, and the quest seemed hopeless. Then, at the last moment, two friends of mine said yes.

Nancy Blaine, the granddaughter of Mrs. Anita McCormick Blaine of Chicago, was a dedicated liberal, like my mother, and one who looked on the fortune that she would inherit from her grandmother as a public trust.

Gil Harrison had given no thought to journalism as a career. But he had been the editor of the *Daily Bruin,* the student newspaper at the University of California at Los Angeles. And in 1951, he had reached a decisive moment in his own life.

Gil had gone on to found the World Veterans Federation after leaving the American Veterans Committee in my hands. We went as delegates from the A.V.C. to the conference of the federation that was held in Rome in the summer of 1951. We were joined there by Nancy. Gil and I spent three days arguing with nationalists and neutralists. Then the three of us drove out to the Villa d'Este. We wandered for hours in the darkness, through that enchanted world of water, falling through light.

We met again in New York, late in 1952. By then, Gil and Nancy were married. I spoke of my desperate and fruitless efforts to find a new owner for *The New Republic*. Gil agreed to become its publisher and to take full responsibility for it when Nancy came into her inheritance from Mrs. Blaine's estate.

Mrs. Blaine died in February 1954. A year went by before her estate was settled. We borrowed, we begged, we emptied our own pockets during those months; we managed to keep *The New Republic* afloat.

I continued to be the editor of *The New Republic,* until 1956, but the essay that I wrote for our Fortieth Anniversary issue in 1954 was really my farewell—to *The New Republic* and to the world of politics.

I went to see Felix Frankfurter to seek his guidance on my essay. We spoke about my parents and about Herbert Croly. He spoke of his own years with the magazine. Then I made a casual reference to the unconditional nature of America's commitment to freedom of speech.

Unwittingly, I touched on an inflamed nerve.

In the thirties, a New Deal Congress enacted progressive legislation; the Supreme Court struck it down as unconstitutional. Frankfurter criticized the Court for its lack of judicial restraint; so he became a hero of the liberals.

In the fifties, many restrictions were imposed upon freedom of expression by Congress and by local authorities. Frankfurter refused in the name of judicial restraint to strike down those restrictions. In contrast, William O. Douglas and Hugo Black reaffirmed the power and the duty of the Supreme Court to protect our constitutional liberties. To his chagrin, Frankfurter saw Douglas and Black rise to heroic stature while he sank into disrepute.

Frankfurter had welcomed me into the world in 1916. When I took my stand with his enemies, he turned on me in a fury. He pounded the top of his desk until his *pince-nez* fell off his nose. He shouted at me for ten minutes, barely pausing for breath.

I sat in silence, filled with a cold disdain. Frankfurter wound down at last; he sat there, his small frame heaving. He glanced down at his desk and spied a small container. He pushed it across his desk toward me.

"Have a cough drop," he said.

Another long-time associate of *The New Republic*, Richard Crossman M.P., was in the United States when I was preparing my essay. He spent five days holed up in the Waldorf Astoria. Then he flew back to London and wrote an article for the *New Statesman*, equating our Loyalty program with the Nuremberg Laws of the Nazis and declaring that liberalism in America was dead.

I called my essay "The Ghost at the Banquet." I quoted Crossman's verdict that we who had gathered for a Fortieth Anniversary celebration were dead. I maintained that, on the contrary, we had overcome the worst excesses of McCarthyism.

"Late in 1954," I said, "the patient seems to be rising, even while Mr. Crossman draws the winding sheet over an empty bed."

The essay was a long one; it ended,

I don't believe in Mr. Crossman's vision. I don't recognize the land he describes. The loyal Americans I know are not fearful of infection. Those who suffered agonies from the Loyalty checks are all doing useful and constructive work. The young men who have come to me from the F.B.I. have never asked me to denounce a friend as a "secret carrier" of Communism for what he said twenty years ago. And, if I knew of any "secret carriers" in sensitive positions today, I wouldn't suppose that keeping that knowledge to myself was an act of affirmation of my liberal faith. I'm short of breath from shouting about the excesses of the Loyalty Program, but, I know of no citizen branded traitor today because, yesterday, he practiced

Americanism. As one of "the opinion formers who supported the New Deal, Republican Spain and the Russian Alliance," I rub the neck that Mr. Crossman weeps for; I feel no scar.

All conviction of course, is intuitive in the end. My own intuition, like Mr. Crossman's, was pessimistic until now. The experiences which brought me into politics were the sight of the Hunger Marchers trudging toward London, and the loss of close friends in Spain. All of us are bound by such early training, and the death of the Spanish Republic led me to expect the worst.

Mr. Crossman and his friends have gone a little further down that road until they need disaster like a drug to keep them on the march. So do those who blame society as a means of concealing the bitter truth—that the cause of their unhappiness lies within themselves.

I don't trust these people any more; I don't feel that they are my own. I have no compulsion to quarrel with a society that has permitted me to work for what I believe in. On most of the occasions on which I differed with the majority of Americans, I can see now that the majority was right, and I was wrong.

On the broad front of progress, the regulars are advancing in America. The scouts are out in front, where they should be. Of course they stumble into pitfalls, lose their ways, retrace their steps, and pause for rest.

Those who cry out in alarm that all is lost because a few days pass without good news remind me of the story told by Adlai Stevenson after the 1952 campaign.

A scout was found by troopers in our early days, with three Indian arrows in his back. They revived him with whiskey and, when he could whisper, they said: "It must hurt awfully."

"It sure does," he said, "especially when I laugh."


I might have hung on in public life after I left *The New Republic*. A few of my friends nudged me in that direction. I would have been tempted to listen to them when I was thirty; at forty, my political ambition had drained away.

I was not a political leader who had found a temporary base in journalism. I was a writer who had been sucked into political action during years of crisis.

Those years were over. My interest in politics had receded until, at ebb tide, the mud flats were dry.

I had made many errors; I had done what I could. I wanted to turn from the present to the future; I wanted to create something of lasting value.

I needed to recapitulate my own experience in order to come to terms with it. To do that, I had to cast off the shreds of journalism that clung to me. I had to place myself in another time and in a different setting. I had to find the right metaphor.

The Indian wars offered that metaphor to me. Their setting on the Western plains was majestic and largely unaltered. Their origins lay in the collision of contrasting civilizations—the collision that had shaped the lives of my generation. The inward conflicts that they engendered—between conscience and duty—were the conflicts that concerned me.

The charred ruins of a frontier fort reached out to me during the months I spent in Wyoming in 1956. The colonel who built the fort stepped forward as my central character. As a humanist, he had tried to prevent a confrontation with the Indians who surrounded him. As a commander, he had been unable to control his own men. The outcome was the Fetterman Massacre, the second battle in recorded history in which there were no survivors.

I worked blindly on the story until I stumbled onto Aristotle's *Poetics.* At that moment, all of the characters were cast, and each detail fell into place.

That novel led to a second work about the massacre of a band of Indian prisoners by a fanatical clergyman-turned-soldier. It began as a study of fanaticism; it became a hymn of praise to the essential goodness of most Americans.

It is as the author of these works that I would choose to be remembered. The writing of them is not a part of this story. The works speak for themselves, if they speak at all.

"The writer," as Joseph Conrad said, "seeks recognition of the work, not of the man. Once the last page is written, the man does not count."

# DINAH

THIS book is a political memoir rather than an autobiography. It dwells on my childhood in an effort to explain my responses to the circumstances that I faced later on. It does not deal in any depth with life within my own home.

The pages that follow center on my daughter Dinah. They concern a chapter in her life that made all other matters seem remote and unimportant to me. They take their place here for that reason, and because she made the summer of 1956, when she was five years old, the most memorable of all summers for me.

Rather than attempting to recreate those days, after so many years

have passed. I am turning here to the letters I wrote to my mother at
the time.

-----◈-----

June 3

Weynoke, Virginia
    ... In two weeks, we all head West. I and the boys will fly off first in
the Navion; it should be an exciting journey. Niagara Falls the first night;
then Cleveland, to see a baseball game. A tour of the River Rouge plant
in Detroit; a night in Iowa; then on to my old base, Rapid City. We'll drive
from Rapid to Deadwood, where Wild Bill Hickock and his enemies
linger on; then we'll fly to Sheridan, Wyoming. Bin and the girls will meet
us there, and we'll spend seven weeks on a nearby ranch. . . .
    I've been reading Charlie Siringo's autobiography to the boys in prepa-
ration for our trip. Next, we'll read *The Conspiracy of Pontiac*. . . .

-----◈-----

June 24

Saddlestring, Wyoming
    ... We're settled in this heavenly place, and, for the first time, I have
an idle morning. Dinah rushed back to her cabin as we were saddling up.
I'm staying with her, happy for this chance to write to you.
    Our first outing, yesterday was a bit rough for a five-year-old. Black
clouds rumbled over the mountains on the Western horizon as we walked
to the corral. We set out nonetheless on our first ride, with a lad of
fourteen as our guide.
    We rode in single file up a narrow canyon, Mike on a white gelding;
David on a Roan. Susie rode a small horse named Fatso; Dinah was on
Whitesox, his pal. Neither one rode on a lead rein.
    The lad, who had no experience, led us up an almost vertical bank and
over a rock ledge. The girls clung onto their saddle horns, and showed
no fear. Then, in an upland meadow, we were struck by a sudden hail-
storm. The mountains were shrouded behind dark streamers; the wind
was cold; the hailstones stung our faces and hands. Dinah's mouth began
at last to quiver. We led her horse down a steep hill and into a Cottonwood grove. We huddled there while our guide set off in search of a way
home.
    We waited, soaking and shivering, until the lad came back. Then,
following him in single file, we led our horses down a ledge and across
a ford.
    The storm blew over. The sun glistened in the swift water. A lazuli
bunting sang in a cottonwood tree. We dried out quickly in the summer
wind, and our spirits revived. Dean Thomas, the foreman of the ranch,
rode out in search of us. He found us and led us back, and, since Dinah
had picked him out to be her future husband, she had to act like a
grown-up.
    This morning, in her resolute way, she announced in the corral that she
was not going riding. Dean, the foreman and future husband, will change

that by tomorrow. Meanwhile, she is looking at books that she cannot yet read, and I'm able to write to you. . . .

———∞———

July 8

Saddlestring

. . . It's seven thirty in the evening. Shadows lean across the plains, cast by the mountains that tower to the west of us. Bin, Susie and Dinah are off on an evening ride; Mike is listening to a baseball game on his radio. David is trying to catch a large trout that he spotted in the stream that rushes past beneath our window.

We ride every morning. Dinah enjoys it now, and sits solidly on White-sox. Susie whacks away on Fatso's flanks in a vain effort to make him trot.

The wild flowers are fading now, but for two weeks they were celestial: the valleys golden; the hillside meadows blue with lupins, beardtongues and bluebells. Wild roses were massed among them, and Indian paint-brush. And the most delicate white flowers: star-of-Bethlehem and white geranium; mariposa lily; and the little ones: Anemone and saxifrage and the small-flowered everlasting.

The wranglers make a point of knowing about nothing save horses. "What's this?" I ask . . . "What's that?" "Well," says Barney, the Old Timer who has taken the lad's place as our guide, "that's a regular old pitch pine . . . that's nothing but an ornery old red leaf. . . ."

We are in the center of a great historic battlefield—the Fetterman Massacre took place on the road between Buffalo and Sheridan; the Wagon Box Fight was on the ranch next to ours. Buffalo, the nearest town, was the setting of a famous battle between settlers and the hired gunmen of the cattle owners known as the Johnson County War.

Hank Horton, who owns this ranch, has collected many old books about these memorable events. I read them to the boys each evening. They listen, but I'm the one who is stirred and shaken by the ghosts who live on around us.

David is oppressed by the nearness of everyone. Dinah in contrast is on her own for the first time, and she loves it. At five, she is perfectly self-contained. She never undertakes more than she can handle; she never resents doing less than the others. She fell into the swimming pool yesterday, and sank to the bottom. She came up sputtering and a Southern lady who was sitting at the pool side bent over.

"Can you swim dear?" she asked.

"No, as a matter of fact, I can't," Dinah said as she sank down again.

The Southern lady fished her out, and is still telling everyone who will listen about Dinah's presence of mind. . . .

———∞———

July 18

Saddlestring

. . . The boys and I rode up into a wilderness area last week. Four hours upward, along narrow trails; through forests of ponderosa pine, until the pine gave way to Engelmann Spruce, standing tall in the upland meadows.

We camped out in a log cabin. Pack rats and whiskey jays made off with everything that wasn't tied down. Chipmunks ran over us as we lay in our bedrolls, looking for crumbs to eat, and a small, ice-cold stream danced in the sunlight by the cabin door.

We rode in under Cloud Peak, until we came to three absolutely clear lakes. We could see great rainbow trout moving in and out of the whitened limbs of dead trees, thirty feet down.

David mastered his fear of riding and pushed his horse down some fearsome trails, waving his cowboy hat in the air. Mike caught a number of trout and threw them back. We climbed until, at midsummer, we came to a region where, beneath the spruce trees, the ground was covered in snow.

A sudden snowstorm overtook us on our way back to the cabin. Our light shirts and bluejeans were no protection against the driving snow and sleet. We hunched over, eyes closed, letting our horses find the way. By the time that we arrived back at the cabin, I was so numb that I could barely turn the lock in the cabin door. We started a fire, once we were in the cabin; soon we were warm and dry.

Dinah rides with no fear now. Susie looks as settled as any ranch hand in her saddle. She and the boys and I are flying to Glacier Park next weekend. It should be an exciting time for all of us. . . .

---

July 28

Denver

. . . I asked Milt to telephone you today about Dinah since it seemed impossible to call you from here and I didn't want to wire.

We've been through a pretty rough time, but her chances now seem to be quite bright.

Two months or so ago, she complained of stiffness in her back after a fall. Syd Ross, our pediatrician, checked her in Washington. She'd been checked before by two specialists. Nothing at all showed up.

At H. F. Bar, she announced once or twice that she wasn't going to ride because her back hurt. Each time she showed up smiling at the corral and rode with zest. She loved her horse, Whitesox. Only once, when I led her over an unavoidable gulley and Whitesox made a sudden leap, snapping her neck, did she complain. I told her not to be silly, in my impatience to catch up with the others.

Bin noticed that she was raising herself from her bed by rolling over and pushing herself up by her hands. Then, she began to run a low temperature.

We took her to Sheridan for a check. Her patch test for T. B. showed up *positive*. So Bin took her down to Denver.

Dinah was given all the relevant tests in Denver. She never complained, and, once again, nothing at all showed up. The X rays were faultless; the top orthopedist who came in as a consultant with three other specialists gave her a clean bill of health. They all said that she could go back to H. F. Bar.

That was two days ago. Bin felt Dinah's neck the next morning as they were getting ready to drive to the airport. For the first time, Dinah complained of tenderness. So, Bin took her back to the hospital. A new set of X ray plates were made of the base of her neck. They showed an advanced deterioration of one whole side of her vertebrae, right on the spinal column.

The conclusion of all of the specialists was that the growth was malignant and that she had not long to live.

We had been planning a trip to Glacier Park. We delayed it when Bin and Dinah flew to Denver. Then, the good news came that Dinah was all right, so we started off.

We had a few troubles on the way. The engine kept on cutting out but I was able to keep it going. So we arrived at Cut Bank, a tiny air strip, four hundred miles North of H. F. Bar and eight hundred miles from Denver.

We drove on from Cut Bank to the Park. We settled in at a Lodge; the boys arguing over the beds, and Susie setting out her clothes in her quiet, methodical way. We hiked ten miles the next day, through that spectacular country. The following morning, as we were setting off on a four-hour ride, the emergency call came through.

We set off in our rented car for Cut Bank. A police escort, sent out by the ranch, picked us up and swept us on, much faster than I cared to drive.

I left the Navion at Cut Bank, with instructions to replace the fuel pump. I chartered a flight back. We landed at Sheridan; I left the kids there. I flew on and arrived at midnight at the hospital.

Poor Bin was utterly exhausted. Dinah, in contrast, was cheerful and wide awake.

She was in traction, with a pad that she called her crumb-catcher, fastened around her chin and weighted down behind her bed. We had a long talk about the tricks she had played on the doctors and the secrets she had learned before she sank into sleep.

She awoke at seven this morning. We read Thornton Burgess for an hour. She was given a hypodermic at eight-thirty; it didn't have much effect.

She went off, smiling, to the operating room. The doctors were wonderful; they allowed Bin to stay with her until the anesthetist put her under.

We waited for two hours outside the operating room. Dinah's back was opened up; sections of the tumor were removed and analyzed. Then, at last, half a dozen doctors in white gowns came out to talk to us.

Their faces were grave, but their report was hopeful. The slides indicated a giant-cell tumor, which they felt was benign and could be treated by radiation.

We collapsed, holding onto each other.

The surgeon, Charles Fried, who had lost a kidney through cancer, went back into the operating room. He cut into Dinah until her spinal cord came into view. He shelled out the tumor.

After three hours, an oxygen tent appeared with Dinah inside it. She

was in shock of course; her skin was pale blue. But now, at two-thirty, she
is smiling, as best she can. After being violently sick, she is asking for her
beloved apple juice.

Now that the operation is over, the physicians can be explicit. Craig
Johnson, the pediatrician who first saw Dinah in Denver, has just been
with us. He told us that the chances were one in ten that the tumor was
benign. In all, there have been just twelve cases like Dinah's in the history
of the Denver Children's Hospital; not one was in a child of Dinah's age.
It is so rare that the plates which they took will be used in classes from
now on, to aid in diagnosis.

Well . . . it was close. In fact, an Episcopal minister came in this morning
to say a prayer which sounded very much like a last rite. He came back
this afternoon, a trifle embarrassed. Grateful as we were, we were ready
even for him.

We're far from secure, of course. Dinah will have radiation here. It may
not be pleasant, and there's no assurance that the tumor will not grow
again. But, she's alive, and there's no present prospect of increasing pain.

Anya arrives tonight. Bin's mother will fly out on Saturday to be with
the kids at H. F. Bar. We'll find a place to stay in Denver while the
radiation treatments continue. After a month, Dinah should be able to fly
home.

It seems too good to be true—that she's still with us. Bin saved her life,
I'm sure, by insisting on that final check.

--<∞>--

August 3

Denver. . .

Dinah keeps us going all day long with demands for stories and games.
She's doing very well. She's been in pain, of course—she had to be given
thirty-one shots. She never cried or whimpered. She objected only to
being uncovered by strangers and having a tube thrust inside her. That
was a mortifying experience for a five-year-old.

Now all that is over. She came out of the oxygen tent after three days.
The intravenous feeding ended on that same, great day. Her lungs filled
out again. The color came back into her face. She ran a fever for a week,
but no complications set in.

Soon, she was as lighthearted as she ever was. She made up jokes about
all of the doctors. The resident, Dr. Butterfield, became Doctor Buttercup
and then Doctor Butter-and-Bread-and-Honey. Her eyes brightened when
Craig Johnson appeared. She made me bend down close to her lips; she
whispered, "Doctor Johnson picks his nose!"

The Episcopal minister, an incongruous little Englishman, appeared,
doing his duty rounds. He chucked Dinah under her chin and made
animal noises in a vain effort to get her to talk to him. He gave up in time;
at that moment, she pointed to a poster of a naked baby on her bedroom
wall. She said, "I bet you wouldn't dare show your tummy button like
that!"

Yesterday, her brace arrived. It consists of a corset, covering all of her stomach; a steel rib running up her back to the base of her skull and a steel cage, padded with rubber, fitted around her chin. We dreaded its arrival, since she will have to wear it for months to come. But Dinah clasped it to herself at once, saying that it was beautiful. She calls it her girdle and bra. She wants us to buy it so that she can wear it always.

She put it on for the first time today. She emerged grinning from her hospital room to set out on a tour of her floor in her wheel chair.

The tumor has been established as a giant-cell tumor of the least aggressive kind. Specialists in Denver, in Washington and in New York, all agree that radiation is called for now. So Dinah starts her radiation on Monday: two hundred roentgens a day, for ten days.

We will stay on in Denver through August. Luckily, after a long and a futile search for a home, the Travelers Aid Society found us a furnished house with its own garden in the nicest part of the city. It's a Spanish-style bungalow, cool and spacious. Dinah can move around in it instead of being cooped up in a hotel room, and buying groceries and cooking will fill out our days.

August 9

Denver

Your cards, covered with pictures of horses, all arrived. Dinah cherishes them.

She has a large collection of drawings by her bedside. Dean Thomas, who draws in his spare time, sent her a drawing of Whitesox. He has a crestfallen expression, and the thought that he is missing her is the only thought that brings Dinah to the verge of tears.

We're settled in our Spanish bungalow. It's on an avenue shaded by Elms. It's warm during the days, and cool at nights. Once a week or so, clouds darken into thunderstorms above us. The rest of the time it's still.

Dinah marches about on her matchstick legs, indignantly thrusting aside any hand that reaches out to help her. She wears her brace for two hours at a stretch now, and she's able to walk around the house.

Shrubs and flowers are planted around our bungalow. There is an old player-piano in our living room. We sit before it pumping away while it pounds out *Yessir, That's My Baby* and *Tea for Two*.

Most of the day is spent in play-acting. We are summoned to Dinah's bedside. She re-enacts her days in the hospital over and over, with humor rather than resentment. Her dolls go to the hospital; they are operated on; they wake up and go home. Their emotions are normal, but they have odd names. Dinah usually plays the part of a little girl whose name is Silver; her best friend is called Hairy. I am assigned the part of a downtrodden little waif named Frogbelly. The script, as in all serious drama, adheres to its own, internal logic. Poor Frogbelly always ends up badly.

We drive to the hospital every morning for the radiation. We drive back through the park. We explore new paths each day; today we came upon the Denver Zoo. Dinah insisted on walking through the zoo; we found bird houses, monkey houses, and an enclosure with an elephant that trudged around in circles, pushing a log.

It's a good life. Dinah doesn't mind the radiation. She loves the hospital staff. She kept on telling everyone how handsome Dr. Buttercup was, and, when she left the hospital, the nurses gave a party for her with all kinds of presents. There were Japanese paper balls for example—the kind you unwind and unwind until nothing is left but a button or else a scrap of paper with a motto printed on it. Dinah unwound one ball until it ended in a button. *Peddle Your Fish Elsewhere* it said. She pinned it on her chest and lay in wait for Craig Johnson, the little pediatrician who is always talking about the trout that he catches in the mountain streams. Dr. Johnson appeared, and Dinah asked him very politely if he had caught any more trout. Yes indeed said Dr. Johnson, and he would bring them to the hospital to show them to her. She pointed to her button; he leaned over and read it, and we all laughed until we cried. . . .

⚬

August 18

Denver

. . . We're happy here, and reassured. There had been some concern about the amount of radiation that Dinah should be given—there's so little information to go on. Now, the first series of treatments is completed, with no ill effects. In fact, Dinah, who weighed thirty-seven pounds, has put on three more.

She walks a good deal now, holding onto one of our hands, for our sakes, as she explains, not for hers. She leads us through the past weeks in innumerable dramas. Poor Frogbelly! By now, she's endured at least one hundred enemas!

Each day, we go to the zoo. We end up in front of Dinah's particular friend, a crow, who, when he is provoked for long enough squawks: "Oh, shut up!" This afternoon, we took Dinah to her first movie: *M. Hulot's Holiday.* Dinah marched up and down the aisles of the movie house in her brace, tapping strangers on their shoulders and crying, "Isn't it funny!"

We feared that the operation would isolate her from her own age group. Not at all. She marched across to the neighboring garden where four children were playing. She stood beside them in silence for a moment; they stared at her. She pointed at her brace, and she told them about it in the most matter-of-fact way. Then they all played together. They come over to our house now in the afternoons. All five of them sit at our dining-room table playing *Little Stinker.* Dinah sits bolt upright in her brace. It gives her a spinsterish air. . . .

⚬

September 1

Weynoke

. . . We're home again. Dinah, Susie, and Susie's friend, Carol, are lying on the lawn, playing with Mister Hooley, a dachshund puppy that she demanded and was, of course, given. She named him for M. Hulot.

We had a final conference in Denver with Charles Fried, the surgeon. He pressed Dinah's scar inadvertently and apologized.

"Thanks for scratching me where I itched," Dinah said. He'd never smiled, but he smiled at that.

Bin asked him what Dinah could do, and what she should not do. He mentioned the obvious hazards—high diving and so on.

"Ask him about riding!" Dinah whispered to Bin.

"What about riding?" Bin asked.

"Horses?" said Doctor Fried.

Dinah looked up at him. "Did you ever try to ride a steer?" she said. She laughed until her thin frame shook, and he had to laugh with her.

Now we are home, a thousand miles from Denver. Nonetheless, the dramas go on. Dinah dictates the scripts, as always, and assigns the parts.

She invariably plays the nurse. "Now, honey," she says to the one who plays the little girl, "this won't hurt much."

I am usually the little girl. I have to squirm, whimper, yell, and cry as I am subjected to the endless succession of "pertemperatures," blood tests, shots, and medicines.

The "pertemperature," of course, is given in the "rector." Dinah, the nurse, examines it with great solemnity. She has mastered every detail of hospital life, and everything must be exactly as it was in Denver.

Each morning, she puts on her cowboy boots and bluejeans, her cowboy shirt that fits over her brace, and her cowboy hat. Despite the pain and the uncertainty of those days, she clings to her memory of the West.

At night, her fears rise to the surface. She insists that Bin stay at her bedside. She lies awake, and talks in the darkness. Two nights ago, she wanted to talk about Stalin. Last night, more out of curiosity than dread, she talked about death.

Weynoke                                               November 27

. . . Dinah cranes her neck so much now that the brace seems superfluous. The Neurosurgeon who watches over her says that soon we can replace it with a collar.

Meanwhile, the summer seems to be receding in her consciousness. Mister Hooley commands the center of her stage now, not that he cares.

Dinah insisted on entering him in a local dog show. He disgraced us by sitting on his haunches and scratching himself in front of the judge.

Dinah is not one to accept defeat. The dog show is now re-enacted in our living room. Dinah is the judge; the contestants are Mister Hooley and our mongrel, Parsley; the results are predictable.

Dinah stands, hands on hips, in front of the fireplace. "Lead in your dogs, please!" she commands.

Bin and Mike drag Mister Hooley and Parsley into the room.

"Now . . . may I see them led around!"

The two entries are dragged around the carpet.

"Okay! . . . May I have the prizes!"

I bring in a large bone and a little bone.

Dinah holds out the large bone. "First Prize goes to Mister Hooley!"

Mister Hooley lies down on the carpet, licking his prize. Parsley gets the second prize and gnaws on it. Bin tries to leave since she has a lot of work to do, but Dinah cries out.

"Wait . . . wait! What I really want is for the people to be the dogs and the dogs to be the people!"

That takes some imagination. I don't mind being a dachshund, but Mister Hooley balks at leading me around.

# JAMES

WE spent the summer of 1958 on Martha's Vineyard. James Cornford, John's son, joined us there.

He was tall and dark, like his father. He had more charm, more humor than John; he was not resolute or tense. Twenty-one years had passed since I had last seen John, but when James smiled sidelong, John was there, beside me. They swung a golf club in the same way.

For Dinah, aged seven, it was love at first sight. She marched into our bedroom one morning and delivered a well-rehearsed speech.

"I know you don't think he's very handsome, but I'm in love with him and he's nearly in love with me, so is it all right, and will you give your consent?"

"Consent to what?"

"To our marriage, of course!"

"You and James?"

"Naturally!"

We consented, provided that they would wait until Dinah was eighteen. James would be thirty-four by then, and that was not too old in her opinion. So she agreed.

"How do you know that he's nearly in love with you?" I asked.

"He calls me 'Beautiful.' "

She ran off, immensely pleased, to tell Anya that her parents had consented. As far as she was concerned, the wedding was as good as arranged.

She led James up the hill above our house each evening. She sat with him there in the best *Wuthering Heights* tradition. She smiled bravely and waved goodbye, as a fiancee should, when James departed, heading for California in a borrowed *Volkswagen*.

# A FUNERAL IN
# MISSISSIPPI

I RETURNED to my first vocation—writing—after 1956. I remained a liberal, committed to the advance of minorities and of poor people in America. It was a stance that became increasingly parochial as those constituencies gained self-assurance. That was made suddenly and painfully clear to me in 1963.

The American Veterans Committee gave its annual award to the chairman of our Jackson, Mississippi, Chapter in 1963. His name was Medgar Evers, and he was the leader of the young and the militant blacks throughout his state.

Evers wrote to us to say how much the award meant to him. He posted his letter in Jackson. Four hours later, he was assassinated by a white Mississippian who believed in white supremacy.

The Jackson chapter asked me to be a pallbearer for Evers. I and two other A.V.C. members flew to Jackson. It was June, and the city was steaming. We were assigned three bunks in a dormitory in an all-black college. I was taken to a mass meeting in a church where I was supposed to speak.

Fifteen hundred blacks had crowded into every pew in the church, and every aisle. They were chanting, clapping, crying. I stood in a crowded aisle, wondering what I would say if I were called up to the stage.

I sensed that the mood of the audience was unlike any mood that I had known. That was made plain when a knot of black veterans formed around me. "Don't worry," one of them said to me. "They don't all hate you because you're white."

The speakers were mostly older ministers. They were trying to keep their congregations under control. They kept on repeating that they hated the murder of their brother Medgar, not the murderer. They also said that no threats, no bans, no white politicians or policemen would deter them from doing what they had to do.

The first assertion was met with silence; the second with stamping and cheers.

A light-skinned black, dressed in overalls, took the microphone. He was David Davis, a leader of the Student Non-Violent Coordinating Committee. The committee no doubt had stood in past years for nonviolence. Now, Davis's voice, his words, his gestures, all conveyed an ungovernable anger that was, in itself, an incitement to violence; or so it seemed to me.

Sentence by sentence, Davis raised the pitch of his anger. The veterans around me pressed closer to me, and I glanced around to mark the Exit signs.

"You want to see the enemy, your enemy?" Davis shouted at the climax of his speech. "You want to meet him, face to face? Well, you can! He's here, right here in this church!"

Hundreds of Blacks in the crowd looked around. A good many stared at me. Enough is enough I thought to myself, and I and my bodyguard began to edge toward the nearest Exit.

"I'll show you your enemy!" Davis raised his right arm and pointed at the crowd of mesmerized blacks. "You are your own enemy!" he screamed. "Your enemy is you!"

He was striking at the passivity that had immobilized the black community; it was passive no longer. I knew that as I left the church, surrounded by my protectors. Evers had expressed the rising temper of the blacks and he had been murdered. His death marked a point of no return.

Tensions were rising day by day in Jackson. The city newspapers that had referred to blacks as monkeys were frantic; the students had been forbidden to take part in any demonstrations. White policemen were patrolling every street on their motorcycles, revving up their engines to hide their own fears.

A funeral march through the city had been called for by the Jackson Chapter of the National Association for the Advancement of Colored People. The mayor, foreseeing bloodshed, had banned the march. The N.A.A.C.P. in turn swore, on the day that I arrived in Jackson, that they would disregard the ban. That was what the speakers in the church had meant when they had said that they would not be deterred from doing what they had to do.

It seemed certain that the day would end in violence. But Evers, in addition to being the local leader of the N.A.A.C.P., was a member of the Masons. The Masonic lodges of the Jackson blacks proved to be sources of stability as the day wore on.

I and my friends walked with our chapter to the Masonic Hall. On every street corner, white policemen in helmets were standing, their pistols in their holsters. Beside each policeman, a black Mason stood, in his purple hat.

Five thousand people crowded into the hall. Black leaders had flown in from all over America. Newspapermen were there from all over the world. Fifteen cameras were pointed to the microphone that stood on the stage, ready to bring the voices of the speakers to millions of men and women.

It was a tremendous moment, and it was lost. The N.A.A.C.P. was in charge of the service. Its primary emotion appeared to be jurisdictional jealousy.

No white was permitted to speak—that did not matter. Ralph Bunche was there in the audience; so was Martin Luther King. Neither one was allowed to mount the stage. "Why didn't you speak?" I asked them. "We weren't asked to," they replied. "For God's sake!" I protested. They looked at me with sad smiles.

Bunche was a black who had succeeded in a white society. King was a rival leader. Like the whites who were present, they were not welcome. Yet there was a role for me. A French television crew standing beside me were utterly bewildered; they could not provide a running commentary on the scene. So, for two hours, I and another A.V.C. member became commentators for the French networks.

No one knew when the meeting began if the march that was to follow would be sanctioned. We knew only that we would march, ending up, if need be, in jail.

The banks of television cameras spoke more eloquently than the orators of the N.A.A.C.P. to the mayor of Jackson. Halfway through the meeting, a message arrived from the mayor. Since the march would be orderly, the Mayor decreed, since it would take place on a Saturday when business would not be inconvenienced and traffic would be light, and since the police would be present to keep it in hand, we could proceed, along a route of the mayor's selection and at a time of his choosing.

We marched in silence through the streets of Jackson: the corpse in its bier, borne by black officials of the N.A.A.C.P.; the Masons in their purple hats; the rest of us following along. Crowds of expressionless blacks and hostile whites stared at us as we passed; photographers darted around, and mounted policemen on their motorcycles roared up and down our ragged column.

We arrived at last at our destination: a funeral parlor for blacks. We left Evers there and headed for the airport. A few minutes later, the first bricks sailed through the air.

Martin Luther King was on our plane, flying north. "I'll make a humanist out of him," said Algernon Black, the Leader of the Ethical

Culture Society. He asked King to join us, and for the rest of the flight we sat together.

"Did God know that Medgar Evers would be assassinated?" Black asked King.

"I must believe that."

"In that case, did He sanction the assassination?"

King smiled. "There are questions," he said, "which it is not given to us to answer."

King stood his ground; Black danced around him, jabbing and weaving. King was the traditionalist in that sparring match; Black was the rationalist; Black was still condescending; King was no longer deferential.

I listened, but my mind was drifting. I had seen one age erode as a student Communist; now, as a liberal, I sensed once again that the best days of the movement to which I belonged were over.

# THE END OF SILENCE

ON March 26, 1981, the *Daily Telegraph* of London published a lengthy despatch from Washington under the headline: AMERICAN KEPT BLUNT'S SECRET FOR TWENTY-SIX YEARS.

That is a long time to keep a secret. Why did I wait so long?

In wartime, we and the Russians were bound together by a common objective. Lord Louis Mountbatten employed a high-ranking Communist, J. D. Bernal, as his scientific adviser; Winston Churchill held that Communists might be employed save in the intelligence services.

We felt deeply indebted to the Russians in those years for bearing the main burden of the fighting against our common enemy. Then, in 1946 and 1948, Stalin crushed the independent governments of Poland and of Czechoslovakia.

Was it not plain by then that the Soviet state had forfeited its claim upon the allegiance of free men?

It was plain to me. On three occasions between 1949 and 1951, I drove my car to the British embassy with the intention of walking in and asking to see an intelligence officer. On a fourth occasion, I took up with my cousin, a high official of our Central Intelligence Agency, my fears about the infiltration of the British intelligence services. I wanted to tell my story. I needed one beckoning word or gesture to lead me on. Without it, I lacked the resolution to carry my impulse through.

It was not only a matter of sharing my knowledge with a few officials. My story would result in a trial in England; it would be leaked to a congressional committee in America; I was certain of that. Within a few months, I would be facing Anthony Blunt in an English courtroom, or else I would find myself in a witness chair facing Senator McCarthy.

These were not easy prospects to face. They seemed to threaten the well-being of a national journal, and of two other families in addition to my own.

In the recesses of my own conscience, the balance shifted from a sense of dread to one of obligation as the spirit of McCarthyism receded. I still needed some external force to trigger into action my sense of what was right.

That external force was brought to bear upon me in a most improbable way, in the summer of 1963.

It was in that year that the United States Government accepted a limited but continuing responsibility for the advancement of the arts in America.

-◦◦-

The belief that the arts formed a part of the pursuit of happiness was well established in our Age of Enlightenment. It had been set aside during the era of Andrew Jackson, when democracy was broadened from the political to the social realm of our society. From then on, the utilitarian values that Charles Dickens excoriated in *Hard Times* prevailed in America as they did in England. The arts were denigrated as the pastime of the privileged. The Benthamite criterion of *the greatest good for the greatest number* denied all sanction for public patronage of the arts.

It was Keynes who identified Bentham's rule as "the worm which has been gnawing at the insides of modern civilization" and who, in England, first proposed the creation of a national arts council. After twenty years, we followed England's lead.

Franklin Roosevelt, to be sure, put our artists to work along with our butchers and our bakers. The arts programs that he created were brilliantly successful, but they were short lived. Their primary purpose, of providing jobs, was undermined when unemployment declined. Their secondary purpose, of using artists as propagandists, collapsed with the collapse of the New Deal.

The identification of the arts with the New Deal left a legacy of hostility among Republicans and conservative Democrats. Nonetheless, four underlying elements in our society argued for public patronage of the arts:

A sympathetic technology that made the arts available to all Americans;

An increasing appetite for the arts;

An increasing ambition among artists to broaden their audiences; and

An expanding economy, which seemed to sanction an expansive attitude within our government.

In addition, programs established in support of the arts in Britain and in New York State were seen to be successful.

President Truman called upon the Fine Arts Commission, a small agency with limited functions, to prepare recommendations on a national program for the advancement of the arts in America. President Eisenhower sent the commission's report with his endorsement to Congress. There, it was interred in the House Rules Committee.

President Kennedy was young and impatient. He sent the report of the commission once more to Congress in 1962. When Congress failed to respond, he acted on his own. He appointed August Heckscher as his consultant on the arts. He directed his staff to find a vigorous successor to David Findlay, the wise but aged chairman of the Fine Arts Commission. He set in motion the steps that would lead in time to the creation of an Advisory Council on the Arts.

It was then that I was brought onto the scene.

I had finished my two novels in 1962. Good causes were hard to find. The American Civil Liberties Union was well established; trade unionists and blacks no longer felt the need to lean on white liberals; I had done my bit for planned parenthood and women's rights, the preservation of our national parks and the control of handguns; the protection of whales, dolphins, and baby seals.

My mother-in-law, a wonderful woman, was convinced that I needed some job to keep me occupied. She enlisted the help of her close friend Senator Paul Douglas. Unknown to me, he set out to secure my appointment to the one area of government that he knew would appeal to me—the arts.

Douglas went to the White House three times on my behalf. Thanks to his efforts, I was called in to meet with Hecksher and with President Kennedy's special assistant, Arthur Schlesinger, Jr. To my amazement, they asked me how I would like to be the chairman of the Fine Arts Commission.

That was in May, 1963; it happened to be an awkward time for me. I had started on a third novel, and for the moment, I was preoccupied with my youngest daughter, Dorothy. She had dictated and illustrated a book that, in due course, would establish her in the *Guiness Book of World Records* as the youngest published author. She had also broken her arm—so badly that for a time it seemed that it would have to be amputated.

For those reasons and others, I said that I had no interest in becoming chairman of the commission.

In June 1963, Bill Walton was named chairman of the Fine Arts Commission. He had been the head of the Washington office of *The New Republic,* and he was a good friend of mine. He brought new vitality to the commission—a federal agency responsible for monuments and historic districts. At the same time, he worked with Schlesinger in organizing a more ambitious and inclusive agency to advance the arts in America.

President Kennedy created the agency—the Advisory Council on the Arts—by an Executive Order in June 1963. It was to consist of a chairman, the heads of several federal agencies, and thirty private citizens. In making known his action, the president added, "I shall shortly announce the names of those private citizens whom I am asking to serve."

Once again I was called to the White House. Arthur Schlesinger handed me the list of private citizens whom the president had selected. My name was on the list, followed by the discreet notation *Collector* and, in red pencil, the presidential check.

Membership on the council required little time and no administrative responsibility. It was in perfect accord with my background, my developing interests, and my desire to renew some acquaintance with the world that lay beyond my door.

I was happy with the appointment, but from day to day, the situation was changing.

The appointment of the council was to be followed by the creation of the administrative arm of the new agency, the National Endowment for the Arts. The endowment would be small at first but in time it would grow. It would be shaped by its chairman, an individual who would also be chairman of the council.

Who then was to be the chairman? "We've given a great deal of thought to that question," said Bill Walton, on the third occasion on which I was called back to the White House. "We've decided that the chairman should be you."

I was stunned by the suggestion. I had never pictured myself in that role.

"We're convinced that you are the best man for the job," Bill said. "You're a novelist in your own right and a damned good one. You're respected by the arts organizations. You have many friends in Congress. Above all, you and the president will get along well together.

You come from the same backgrounds; you share the same interests; you're bound to like each other."

"What does he think?"

"I've talked to him about you," Bill said. "He's all for it.

"Think it over," Bill said at the end of our meeting. "Give me a ring tomorrow."

All of my thoughts were on the chairmanship that evening. I stood in awe of it, as I had stood in awe of the presidency of the Cambridge Union as a lad of nineteen.

It was not an easy assignment. There were no precedents to follow in 1963; there was no conventional wisdom to serve as a guide. The chairman would have to decide what arts should be funded by the federal government and in what ways. He would have to deal with the trustees of the Metropolitan Opera and with black militants; with egomaniacal conductors and with unintelligible poets. He would have to gain the confidence of Congress and the press. He would have to recruit and manage a large staff.

I had met the challenge of the Cambridge Union in 1935. Could I handle the chairman's job? I had turned my back on the troubled world of politics when I left *The New Republic.* In my small study, surrounded by stacks of books and piles of papers, I had come to feel secure, as an animal feels secure in its burrow. I was envious of the success of others, but was I ready to be drawn out of my burrow, to face the predators who stalked the halls of Congress and the offices of the press?

"I have the solution," I said to Bill Walton when I telephoned him the next morning. "You become the chairman of the council; I'll take your job on the commission."

Bill laughed. "Oh no you won't!" he said.

That evening, I went over every aspect of the job with Bill. We agreed that I could handle it as well as anyone else whom we could name.

"How long have we got to think about it?" I asked.

"A few days at most," Bill said. "The president is ready to go, but we'll have to clear you with the leaders in Congress. Then there's the F.B.I. check. That takes time, and there's no time left if we're going to get Congress to approve you this year."

The F.B.I. check . . . I hadn't thought about that. It would mean going over all of the old charges that the House Un-American Activities Committee had made against Louis. It would mean raking over all the lies that McCarthy had told about Gustavo.

And my own past?

Without any warning, a disposal regurgitates its half-digested meal of garbage, slop, and dirty water into the kitchen sink. In the same way, unwelcome images that I had long ago disposed of came flooding to the surface through the sinkhole of my memory.

*Don't worry,* I told myself, back in my snug little burrow in Virginia. *An F.B.I. check would turn up nothing on you.*

Unless a Soviet defector had mentioned my name.

And if he did? I gave them nothing save for reports of my own opinions.

*An F.B.I. check would turn up nothing,* I kept telling myself. Much later, as I lay in the darkness, I thought, *That's not the point.*

If I become the chairman of the arts endowment and of the council, I thought to myself, I would be opening myself up to blackmail. . . . No, I decided, that's being melodramatic. But my name would be constantly in the newspapers. At any moment, some former member of the Cambridge Communist movement could say: *"Why . . . I knew him!"*

The story would be carried in the newspapers. I could not deny it. If I admitted that it was true, then I would be in an indefensible position. I would have accepted a White House appointment under false pretenses. I would have betrayed the trust that the president and Arthur and Bill and many others would have placed in me.

All right, I decided; I'll tell a part of my story: the part that will cause me and everyone else the least pain—I'll tell Arthur and the F.B.I. that I was a Communist back in Cambridge. I'll admit that much.

And no more?

I knew, even as I thought about it, that it was no use.

*You knew, back in 1947,* I told myself, *that you would have to tell your story one day. You pretended to yourself that all that you lacked was the opportunity. That was how you clung to the remnants of your self-respect through all those years.*

*Well,* I said to myself, *now the opportunity is here, right here in front of you. It's been handed to you at last by Arthur and Bill.*

*You have no choice now,* I told myself; *you have to take the opportunity.*

*And if I do? Maybe,* I told myself, *the F.B.I. will keep my secret. Maybe the president will understand that those days in Cambridge were part of another age. He was a student in England, after all; he will understand.*

*There's a chance,* I told myself, *a bare chance that I could tell my story and still be the chairman.*

A part of that notion held fast through the hours of darkness; the rest of it crumbled. I slept for an hour or two; when I awoke, I knew what I had to do.

I telephoned Bill Walton and told him that I could not accept the chairmanship. I said, "There's too much explaining to do."

"Explaining?"

"About Louis; about Gustavo; about all of my family ghosts."

"Ah! Every family has its ghosts!"

"Not like mine. Then there's my own past as a radical."

"Oh hell! We've all been radicals; the president knows that!"

"I'm from another age. It's hard to explain one age to another."

"He understands that, I tell you; he——"

"Bill, I just can't do it."

———◦∞◦———

Arthur Schlesinger had a handsome office in the East Wing of the White House. I went to see him there. I told him the whole of my story; he listened in silence. His secretary came in after twenty minutes to tell him that some distinguished intellectual from Latin America was waiting to see him. "He'll just have to wait," Arthur said.

I asked Arthur to withdraw my name as the prospective chairman of the Arts Council. He said that he would. I said that I wanted to tell my story to the F.B.I. He called the attorney general, Robert Kennedy.

The next day, I went to the F.B.I. entrance of the Department of Justice. It had always seemed like hostile territory to me. The interior of the building was colorless and antiseptic. My steps resounded as I walked along its marble corridors in search of the man whose name Robert Kennedy had given to me.

His name was Cartha de Loach; he had no idea of who I was or why I had come to see him. I blurted out a sentence or two; he called in a stenographer and told her to take down my words.

The three of us sat down at a table. They waited.

I said, "Where shall I begin?"

De Loach thought for a moment. He still did not know why I was there.

"Well," he said at last, "why don't you say that you have come here on your own volition. That's always good for a start."

I started off at a fast rate; the stenographer could not keep up with me. She looked up, pleading with me. We started again.

*"My name is Michael Straight. I reside at Weynoke, Virginia. I have come on my own volition to the Federal Bureau of Investigation and the statement which I am about to make is volunteered by me without any pressure or intimidation of any kind."*

I looked at de Loach; he nodded. "That's good," he said.

*"I lived as a small boy in Old Westbury, Long Island. I and my brother and sister moved to England when I was ten. I went to school there, and on to the London School of Economics and then to Cambridge University. It was at Cambridge that I was approached by members of the Communist . . .*

"Hold it right there!" cried de Loach. "You've come to the wrong place!"

He went into his inner office and closed the door. Ten minutes later, he came back with a sheet of paper torn off a telephone pad in his hand.

"You're to go to this building," he said, giving me an address on Connecticut Avenue. "You're to tell the guard at the entrance to take you to William Sullivan. He's the deputy director of the F.B.I. He's waiting for you."

Sullivan was seated at a large desk in a large office. He stood up when I stepped into the room. He was a small man.

He came toward me with his hand outstretched. "Thank you for coming in," he said.

I thought, *Those are the kindest words that were ever spoken to me.*

We talked for a few moments about inconsequential things. Then Sullivan turned to me.

"There's a young agent on my staff who knows you," he said. "When I heard that you were coming over, it occurred to me that you might want to give your statement to him."

He pressed a button on his desk. A young man stepped into the room. He was very neat; very clean.

He, too, came up and shook my hand. "You don't remember me," he said.

His blue eyes and the shape of his lips stirred up some dim memory within me but I could not get a grip on it. I shook my head.

"I'm Jimmy," he said; "Jimmy Lee."

From Old Westbury; the small boy, my own age, to whom Miss Gardner gave my castoff clothes—the second son of my mother's head gardener, Harry Lee.

If there was any pride left in me, it was stripped away at that moment. Sullivan had acted out of kindness; my humiliation was complete.

I sat down at a long table with Jimmy Lee and a stenographer. I started off again,

*"My name is Michael Straight. I reside in Weynoke, Virginia. I have come on my own volition to the Federal Bureau of Investigation; the statement which I am about to make. . . ."*

It took an hour or more to complete my statement. Jimmy Lee listened, nodding sympathetically from time to time. He asked me about my mother when I had finished. I asked him about his parents, and his brother, Harry. I never saw him again.

I was too weary to read when the day was over, and too unnerved to rest. A great burden had been lifted from my shoulders, but, as it is with many such burdens, it would be some time before I was aware that it was gone.

I went to a movie at the MacArthur Theatre. I thrust my dollars under the slot in the glass face of the kiosk. Close beside me, a voice murmured, "Good evening, Mr. Straight."

The F.B.I. stenographer was sitting inside the kiosk, issuing tickets for the evening show. I did not tell her that she had taken a week off my life.

I spent a good many hours with Sullivan in the days that followed. He asked me a number of searching questions about the appeal of communism for the intellectuals of Europe. He told me wonderful stories about his early days with the F.B.I. He had, for example, been on the F.B.I. team that hunted down the notorious killer, John Dillinger. Weighed down with guns, as they were, the team paused for rest in a café. The senior agents called for black coffee; Sullivan asked for a lemonade. The leader of the team breathed heavily until the waitress had departed. Then he turned on Sullivan. "For as long as you're with Mr. Hoover's F.B.I.," he said, "don't ever again disgrace him by asking for a lemonade!"

I found it hard to believe that Sullivan could be close to Hoover. In fact, he became Hoover's principal antagonist within the bureau. He returned from lunch one day to find the door to his office padlocked. He retired to his home in New Hampshire. He was walking in his woods when he was shot and killed by a deer hunter.

I spent the best part of June in the Old Post Office on Constitution Avenue, working with F.B.I. agents. They worked in pairs, and they made a habit of asking sudden, unexpected questions. That pattern of interrogation, I decided, had been perfected in order to catch the people whom they were questioning off guard. In my case, they learned that I had nothing to hide, so in time we settled into a less calculated exchange. Yet I could see that from time to time they reverted to the techniques that they had been taught. They made their own checks between our sessions, and they seemed reassured whenever they came up with some corroborative detail. "I was living with two friends in Georgetown," I would say, and one of them would murmur, "At 2811 Dumbarton Avenue." He had been leafing through old telephone directories and was reassured by his discovery. It was something solid in the midst of so much that was incomprehensible, a rock to stand on in the marshes of the past.

In one of our sessions, the agents came in with a sheaf of papers. "Take a look at these," one of them said, "and tell us if you see Michael Green."

On each sheet of paper there were rows of faces. Some looked like reproductions of passport photos; others were blurred as if they had been taken with telephoto lenses from second-story windows or from within parked cars.

Heavy-set faces; scowling faces; Slavic faces. . . . I scanned them row by row. On the fourth page, his black hair stiff, his mouth no longer smiling, his close-set eyes staring at me, was Michael Green.

It was almost as startling as if I had run into him on a street corner. "That's him!" I cried.

The two agents nodded. One of them excused himself and left the room.

I did not ask what Green's real name was or who he was. We did talk about his wife. I had mentioned her midwestern accent and her auburn hair. The agent told me that she had come from Kansas. He did not know how she had met Green or when, or what her maiden name had been.

What had become of them? The F.B.I. men were not sure. Green, they said, had been recalled to Moscow; no more had been heard of him.

I spent the rest of June in the offices of the F.B.I. The agents, for the most part, were impersonal and interchangeable; their haircuts were fresh; their shoes were shined; they wore drip-dry shirts; they seldom smiled.

We spent forty or fifty hours in interviews, shook hands, and forgot each other. But many loose threads were left lying around, and so, for four years, the bureau continued to call me. My relations with it came in time to center in one man—an old-timer whom I knew as Agent Taylor. He wanted his weekends free so that he could play his round of golf; he was laying his plans for his retirement. We trusted each other completely and became good friends.

In 1969, the White House asked me to go as a judge to the Moscow Film Festival. I went to see Taylor.

"What do I do," I asked him, "if I'm approached by a Russian intelligence agent?"

"Don't worry," he said. "They'll never approach you again."

"And if they do?"

"They won't," said Taylor. And he was right.

—⟨∞⟩—

You bear a burden for many years; you say to yourself, *Once I rid myself of this burden, everything will be different. I'll stand upright; I'll sleep well; I'll be considerate of other people because I'll respect myself; I'll be happy.*

It does not work out that way; it did not for me. Our bodies and our spirits become adjusted to the burdens that we bear, and when they are lifted from us, we do not spring back into the ideal shapes that we picture for ourselves in our fantasies.

I spent the summer of 1963 on the Vineyard, and the autumn in Greece. It was a good life, but it was not freed from anxiety. The anxiety that I had learned to live with remained within me; like the web woven by a spider, it attached itself to other things.

I returned to my home in Virginia. I had nothing to keep me occupied; nothing to look forward to. I thought to myself: *I am a writer.* I gathered the notes that I had stuffed away in my desk. I went back down the mine where the writer works alone and in the darkness. I went back to my novel. I thought *What I'm writing may not be remembered, but here, at least, I'm in the company of great men.* I could pause over my typewriter and hear the faint echoes of other men deep in the mine; Conrad, muttering to himself as he labored over his sentences; Chekhov, coughing; Yeats, scratching one line of a poem and trying out another.

In November, a dry autumn ended in steady rain in Virginia. Our pond rose until it brimmed over; it became very dark, save for the rich reflections of the trees that bordered it; maple and dogwood; red oak and persimmon. The Canada geese rode on the dark water, restless and alert as the days grew chill. Each evening, they turned to face westward until, at some unseen signal, they heaved themselves into the sky, uttering their bitter cries.

Dorothy, aged five, gained a sense of the fragility of life after her arm was broken. "Daddy," she said, one evening, "what would you do if you could lasso the morning?"

"If I could *what?*"

"If you could lasso the morning; what would you do?"

"I'm not sure, any longer. What would you do?"

"I'd play with my horses. I'd never stop."

She joined me in my study whenever some illness kept her from school. She played with her plastic horses on the carpet while I wrote at my desk. We were in the study together on the morning of November 22 when Lorraine, our laundress, burst into the room. She was sobbing uncontrollably; it took Dorothy and me a minute to learn what had happened.

I was dry-eyed as we listened to the radio reports from Dallas. Dorothy began, very slowly, to cry.

"I wish it were all a dream," she kept on saying. Then she said, "Poor Caroline!"

An hour later she said, "Why couldn't it have been someone else!"

"Who for example?"

"Well . . . Rockefeller or Khrushchev."

There, the year ended for me.

# BLOWING THE GAFF

THE exchange of information between British and American intelligence services was inhibited by distrust and suspicion at the time when
Guy Burgess and Donald Maclean fled to Moscow. It was perhaps for
that reason that seven months passed before the information that I
gave to the F.B.I. reached England.

In July 1963, Sullivan asked me if I would repeat my story to the
British intelligence services. I told him that I would be glad to, and
that I would fly to London to see them if that seemed best. I heard
no more until Sullivan called me in January 1964.

"A friend of mine is flying in from London," he said. "If you're
willing to talk to him, we'll meet at the Mayflower Hotel."

Sullivan met me in the lobby and took me to see Arthur Martin, a
British intelligence officer from M.I.5. We talked for twenty minutes,
then Sullivan left us.

In contrast to the F.B.I. agents, Martin was sophisticated and urbane. We were able to move at once to the core of my story.

I went over the entire story with Martin. I repeated my own conviction that it was Guy Burgess, who had drawn Anthony Blunt into his
network and had directed him in Cambridge. Plots such as the one to
send me back to J. P. Morgan and Company were, I said, expressive
of Guy: clever, imaginative, somewhat playful, utterly devoid of family feelings.

Martin asked if I could name anyone else who had been recruited
by Burgess and Blunt. I mentioned my dead friend who had balked
when he was approached by Anthony. I said that I had no hard
evidence, but that I believed that Leo Long had been brought into the
network.

Martin said nothing, but when I mentioned Leo, he let out a deep
sigh.

"You may not believe this," he said, when our first interview was
completed, "but this is the first hard evidence that we've been able
to obtain on Burgess and Blunt."

"You mean that none of the people who came forward in 1952 had
any hard information to offer?"

"Hearsay and rumor, the odd remark made by Burgess to some pal
of his when he was drunk. Nothing more.

"This will be most useful to us," Martin added, "but I'm afraid that
Blunt will continue to deny everything, even when we tell him that
we've talked to you.

"If I am right," he continued, "then we must consider our next

318

steps. Would you be prepared to confront him? We would be present, of course."

"I'm prepared to do whatever you want me to do," I said. "If you tell him that you've talked to me, and he denies it all, then we'll confront him in private. If he still refuses to talk, then I'll say that I'll tell my story in an open court."

"We'll keep that in mind," said Martin. "We'll be in touch with you."

---

I worked on my novel. I had little hope that it would be published. In contrast, *How the World Began,* which Dorothy, aged four, dictated and illustrated with magic markers, was a great success. And rightly —in its flights of fancy it made my work seem earthbound.

Dorothy's leg was broken soon after her arm had healed. I was furious with the boy who had caused the accident; she remained lighthearted. She developed a fever one morning when she was six; her mother discovered the telltale lumps behind her ears and told her that she had German measles. "Well," Dorothy said, "thank goodness I'm not pregnant!"

In September 1964, I flew to London to be with my mother. Arthur Martin met me at her flat in Upper Brook Street. We walked down South Audley Street to a house used by the intelligence services. He opened a cupboard and took out a bottle of Scotch—a nice contrast to the inhibitions that his employers had laid upon Michael Green. He offered me a whiskey and water with no ice in it. I explained that I was a wino. He kept the drink for himself, and, in that sparsely furnished house, we sat down in the only available chairs.

Anthony, said Arthur, had given up and confessed. He had, in the course of many interrogations, named his Russian and his British colleagues; he had described the material that he had turned over to the Soviet government; he had provided the intelligence services with a great deal of information. There were some gaps, however, between his story and mine, and, in the belief that we could jog each other's memories, the intelligence services had decided that it would be a good idea for us to meet.

Martin asked if the meeting would be too painful for me. I said once again that I would do whatever he wanted me to do.

"Right!" he said. "We'll meet him at his flat tomorrow."

He gave me the address, 20 Portman Square, and the time of our meeting. Then, "There is one request that he made," Martin said. "It is that you get there fifteen minutes early. He wants to have a few words with you alone."

"And you want me to do that?"

"Why not?" Martin said.

I set my watch very carefully the next morning. I allowed myself plenty of time. It was a short walk from Upper Brook Street to Portman Square. I arrived there six minutes early. I walked around the block, peering into several shop windows. *This is the sort of scene that belongs in a movie,* I thought to myself, *only it's been filmed too many times.*

I went to the front door of Anthony's building at the appointed time. I pressed the button under *Blunt.* The door opened; I walked up the stairs. Anthony was standing at the entrance to his flat. He looked pale and skeletal, as he always had; he did not appear to be broken in spirit. I had assumed that he would be bitterly hostile; I was surprised by his thin-lipped smile and the grip of his hand.

We walked into his spacious living room. I glanced at the paintings on the walls. I was in no hurry to talk but was aware of his sense of urgency.

"I asked if I might see you alone for a few moments," he said. "I just wanted to tell you: Thank God you did what you did!

"I was sure that it would all become known, sooner or later," he added. "I couldn't muster up the strength to go to the authorities myself. When they said that you had told them your story, it lifted a heavy burden from my shoulders. I was immensely relieved."

"I'm glad that you told me that," I said. "I'd assumed that you would be bitter."

"I am curious about one thing," he said. "Why did you act when you did?"

"Because of the arts," I said. "Because our government finally decided to support the arts.

"Kennedy was going to make me the head of his new arts agency," I added. "That forced me to face up to it at last.

"The real question that has to be answered," I said, "is, Why didn't I act long ago?"

"I see. We always wondered how long it would be before you turned us in."

With that, we came to a new equilibrium in our relationship. It was not a matter of forgiveness; theologians insist that it is not given to us to forgive. Yet, men and women must strive to surmount the injuries that they inflict upon one another day after day.

In the larger context of war, Wilfred Owen wrote of "the reciprocity of tears."

The power to heal lies in the present, not in the past. For Anthony and for me, it lay in the arts. He was a preeminent authority on the paintings of Nicholas Poussin. I had bought a landscape by Gaspard Dughet, the chef's son, who had become the brother-in-law of Poussin and his greatest pupil. It was a dark, romantic painting with shepherds and a stream in the foreground and, in the distance, a mountain with a ruined castle standing in silhouette against the evening sky.

I had read that Cézanne spent days in copying the paintings of Poussin. I saw in my landscape all that Cézanne had portrayed in his many studies of the *Mont Ste Victoire*. I asked Anthony if he agreed. We were talking about Dughet and Cézanne when the doorbell rang and Arthur Martin came in.

We talked for an hour or so. I remember very little of what was said. The question of immunity from prosecution was never mentioned, but, for some reason that I cannot recall, the matter of confidentiality did arise. I had never asked that my own story be kept held in secret by the American or British governments. Arthur Martin did mention the possibility that, at some point, the story might come out. I said I was prepared for that; Anthony was not. "If the story should be published," he said, "that would be absolutely devastating for me."

⎯⦅∽⦆⎯

I met Anthony once again, in the house on South Audley Street. The British authorities had come upon a minor discrepancy in my testimony, and Anthony, who had spent many days with them by then, was able to assist us in clearing it up. We walked together along South Audley Street when our meeting was over. He said that the authorities had come to trust both of us; that was important to him, as it was to me.

An intelligence officer was with us at our second and last meeting —not Arthur Martin, for Martin had been taken off the case. He had been fired by Sir Roger Hollis, the Head of M.I.5, according to Chapman Pincher; the reason, Pincher adds, in his book *Their Trade Is Treachery* is that Martin was probing too close to the core of Soviet influence within the British intelligence services. It was this action, taken by Hollis, Pincher maintains, that led to Hollis himself falling under suspicion. Of this, I know nothing.

For more than ten years, after 1964, I continued to meet at rare intervals with British intelligence officers. They came in pairs to the hotels at which I stayed in London. I usually stayed at the Connaught, and my bedroom was often not much larger than my bed. The three of us would find some place to perch; a member of the British team would reach into his pocket and fish out a tape recorder.

"Would you mind frightfully if I turned this thing on?"

"No, not at all."

"It's so convenient."

We reviewed in the most minute detail my days with Anthony and with Michael Green. We moved on to the Communist cells in Cambridge. The British government, after years of inactivity, was attempting to identify all of its citizens who held positions of public trust and who were, or had been, members of the Communist party. With that in mind, the intelligence officers and I pored over many pages of photographs and long lists of names, dividing them into nonmembers; student activists, like myself; hard-core members of the party; and "moles." The "moles" we divided in turn into those who were heading for nonsensitive professions and those who would in time gain access to sensitive material.

For every "mole" whom I felt that I had to identify, I was able, I believe, to help clear a score of men and women who had joined the student movement as I did but would not have embarked upon careers directed toward subversion and based upon deceit.

The last action that I undertook for the British intelligence services was in the seventies. It was to clear my old friend Brian Simon of any role beyond the open and avowed one that he still carried on as a member of the Central Committee of the Communist party of Great Britain.

With that, my role as an informer came to an end.

It is a role that is despised in every country and in every context. It runs counter to a determination that we all share—not to inflict pain upon others.

In his autobiography *Witness,* Whittaker Chambers describes the anguish he suffered when he became an informer against the Soviet agents who had been his accomplices and friends. He found his justification in the conviction that he was acting as an instrument of The Almighty in a titanic struggle between communism and Christianity.

I did not picture myself in any such grandiose role. I believed simply that the acceptance of individual responsibility is the price we must all pay for living in a free society.

Chambers had some deepseated need to believe that he and the Almighty were battling against the odds. I felt no such need. I was convinced, as were the British intelligence officers with whom I worked, that, sooner or later, my one-time comrades would wish to sever themselves from any shred of allegiance to the Soviet Union. Even party stalwarts like Brian could not blind themselves for long to the oppressive nature of the Soviet regime. And, as Justice Holmes said, "Time wears away many fighting faiths."

I asked few questions of the men who questioned me; I didn't know what use they would make of the information I gave them; I could not tell where it would lead. I never asked that my own role be kept a secret; I was not bound by any pledge of secrecy. I guessed that, sooner or later, the story would appear in the newspapers. I was sure that it would not be made public by me.

A good many books and articles were written about Guy Burgess and Donald Maclean in the years that followed their flight to Moscow. They provided little in the way of information and rarely mentioned Anthony Blunt. None of them mentioned Leo Long.

Then, in the late seventies, limited access to the files of government agencies in Washington was authorized under our Freedom of Information Act. The English author Andrew Boyle obtained some of the files on Burgess and Maclean. He was aided, so he wrote, by retired officials of the Central Intelligence Agency and by a former senior executive of the British Secret Service. Boyle was prevented by the British libel laws from naming Anthony Blunt as a member of Soviet network, but in his book *The Fourth Man,* he came so close to naming Anthony that the whispers reverberated through the offices of the British press and the halls of Parliament.

That forced the Prime Minister, Mrs. Margaret Thatcher, to act.

Under the heading *Written Answers to Questions,* the transcripts of the House of Commons for Thursday, November 15, 1979, record the following exchange:

*Mr. Leadbitter* asked the Prime Minister if she will make a statement on recent evidence concerning the actions of an individual whose name has been supplied to her in relation to the security of the United Kingdom. *The Prime Minister:* The name which the Hon. Member for Hartlepool [Mr. Leadbitter] has given me is that of Sir Anthony Blunt.

In April, 1964, Sir Anthony Blunt admitted to security authorities that he had been recruited as a talent spotter for Russian intelligence before the war, when he was a don at Cambridge, and had passed information regularly to the Russians while he was a member of the Secret Service between 1940 and 1945. He made this admission after being given an undertaking that he would not be prosecuted if he confessed.

He first came under suspicion in the course of inquiries which followed the defection of Burgess and Maclean in 1953. . . . The Security Service remained suspicious of him and began an intensive and prolonged investigation of his activities. During the course of the investigation, he was interviewed on 11 occasions. He persisted in his denial and no evidence against him was obtained.

Early in 1964, new information was received which directly implicated Blunt. It did not however provide a basis on which charges could be brought.

In the debate that followed, on November 21, 1979, Mrs. Thatcher repeated her statement about the "new information" that had reached the prime minister's office 'early in 1964.' She added that she was not at liberty to reveal the source of the 'new information,' and for days, the British press engaged in a futile guessing game. The source was, of course, myself.

Several leaders of the House of Commons, including a former

Prime Minister, James Callaghan, declared that the truth about Anthony Blunt would never be told. In contrast, the Attorney General, Sir Michael Havers, described in vivid terms the scene on April 23, 1964, when Anthony was informed by British intelligence officers that I had told them my story.

*The Attorney General:* . . . He was told of the new information. . . . He maintained his denial. He was offered immunity from prosecution. He sat in silence for a while. He got up, looked out of the window, poured himself a drink and, after a few minutes, confessed.

In the weeks that followed the prime minister's statement, Anthony was stripped of his knighthood and driven into hiding. Newspaper headlines affirmed that more traitors would be named, and one "fifth man" was cited: a scientist whom I had never heard of named Dr. Wilfred Mann. A sense of outrage spread in the patient and tolerant people of Britain. It seemed to me that it was generated by two feelings: a deeply felt resentment that Anthony, by accepting an appointment as the keeper of the Queen's paintings, had brought the Royal family within the circle of his subversion and a deeply felt suspicion that in granting Anthony immunity from prosecution, the ruling class of Britain was, once again, using its special privilege and influence to protect itself.

These feelings seemed to settle in the winter months. Then, in late March, the issue was brought to the boiling point a second time by the publication of the excerpts from Chapman Pincher's book.

I was awoken by a telephone call from London, on the day that Angus Macpherson's story appeared in the *Daily Mail.* In the week that followed, my telephone rang night and day.

My mind was made up on the day that I first talked to Angus Macpherson. I would not take advice from an attorney, since that would imply that I had something to conceal. I would talk to any reporter who called me and would answer, candidly and truthfully, any question that was put to me.

I held to that decision through fifty-nine interviews. For six months, it seemed to me that my decision had been the right one.

There were a few unwelcome moments. A Washington radio station, to cite one example, called me to ask if I would consent to a telephone interview. I consented. I sat waiting by the telephone and listening to the station. "And now," said the interviewer, "we go to Maryland to talk to the spy who came in from the cold."

It was the flippancy of the comment as much as the injustice of it that upset me. But the great majority of the men and women who interviewed me were serious and fair. Many of them were baffled by my story; none of them was unkind.

It was in October 1981 that my decision to answer every question came back to haunt me.

My telephone woke me up at daybreak on that morning. The call was from London.

"Mr. Straight? . . . Simon Freeman here . . . from the *Sunday Times.*

"A new book has just been published over here," said Freeman. "It's by Nigel West. You talked to him, I suppose."

"Six months ago."

"Right. He says that you named two other possible Soviet agents to M.I.5. Is that true?"

"I named one."

"Very well. West goes on to say that Blunt confirmed to M.I.5 the involvement of one of the two men you had identified. He says that a confrontation was arranged with the man at Brown's Hotel, and that it lasted five hours."

"I know nothing about that."

"What about the man himself then? West says that he admitted to having been a Soviet agent."

"What else does he say?"

"I'll read it to you. He says that the man assured M.I.5 that he had long since abandoned Marxism. He had held a sensitive post in military intelligence during the war but had long since ceased to have access to secrets."

"Would you read that again?"

'. . . had *long* since abandoned. . . . had *long* since ceased. . . .' Plainly the law of libel was guiding West's hand. He was publishing Leo's name without actually naming him. But, once again, the rumors would spread until Mr. Leadbitter would hand another slip of paper with the words *Leo Long* on it to the prime minister and would ask for her comment.

I knew then that Leo's days of anonymity were over, but I said nothing. I did not want to be the one to give his name to the press.

Freeman broke the silence. "Mr. Straight," he said, "do you know who Nigel West is referring to?"

"I think so."

"Would you tell me his name?"

"I would if I thought it would serve some vital purpose. I can't see that it does."

It was Freeman's turn to pause.

"Mr. Straight," he said after a moment, "let me speak not as a reporter but as an Englishman. These names are going to come out, sooner or later. The timing is more important than you know. A Commission of Inquiry is meeting now. If the names come out after it has cleared the security services—and it will clear them—then the

British people will be understandably bitter and disillusioned in their
government. I put it to you that by giving me the man's name now,
you will be doing him and this country a service."

It was a strong argument. I said, "Why don't you see if you can talk
to a man named Leo Long."

Two days later, Freeman called me again. He sounded unnerved.

"I've just come from seeing Leo Long," he said. "He's given me
the whole story."

"Was it hard for him?"

"He said more than once that he was going to commit suicide. His
wife is gravely ill, and that makes it worse for him."

"But you're going to run the story."

"On Sunday morning."

I thought, *What have I done?*

On November 1, 1981, the *Sunday Times* published its story. As an
official in military intelligence, Leo stated, he had turned over "top
level stuff" to Anthony throughout the war. He had, apparently,
continued to serve as second-in-command of intelligence operations
in the Allied Control Commission in Germany until 1952; yet, the
*Sunday Times* said, "he remained undiscovered until 1964."

"Discovery came," the *Sunday Times* continued, "when an American, Michael Straight, who had himself spied for the Russians, made
a statement to the F.B.I." I had, the story said, named Blunt, Long,
and a scientist named Alastair Watson—a comment that was untrue,
since I had never named Alastair Watson in that capacity.

The story continued: "Long was telephoned by Blunt and told:
'Michael has blown the gaff on us.' Long says: 'Blunt told me he was
terribly sorry. I went around to his flat to talk about it. Blunt told me
that the best thing to do was to come clean. He arranged for me to
meet the security people. . . .' "

Leo voiced his deep remorse to Freeman and to the host of reporters with whom he met on the day that the article by Freeman and his
team mate Barrie Penrose appeared. The London *Times* led its story
with the comment that "The Soviet Union could not have had a better
placed 'mole' inside British intelligence at the moment of its greatest
peril . . ."

"Mr. Long's confession," said the London *Times*, "is bound to
rekindle the parliamentary disquiet. . . ." The debate in Parliament
followed, in fact, in a week's time.

The House of Commons Report for November 9, 1981, includes
the following transcript:

## MR. LEO LONG

*Mr. Canavan* asked the Prime Minister whether she intends taking any steps in view of recent information about the espionage activities of Mr. Leo Long.

**The Prime Minister:** Early in 1964, Leonard Henry Long was named to the Security Service by Mr. Michael Whitney Straight, the United States citizen who identified Mr. Anthony Blunt, as someone else whom Mr. Blunt might have attempted to recruit as an agent for the Russian Intelligence Service. When Mr. Blunt made his confession in April 1964, he admitted to having recruited Mr. Long before the war and controlled him during it.

Mr. Long was then seen by the Security Service. He asked for immunity from prosecution; this was refused, but he was told that he was not likely to be prosecuted if he co-operated in the Security Service's inquiries. He then made a detailed confession.

The *Sunday Times* as I have noted, identified me as the American "who had himself spied for the Russians." From that misstatement of fact, all other newspapers took their cues. The London *Times* described me as "an American who had spied for the Russians." So did the *Daily Telegraph* and every other newspaper that I was able to obtain. Reuters and the United Press International sent the same description of me to all their overseas subscribers; so, across the United States and throughout the world, I was identified as a one-time Soviet spy. The *Guardian* went further than that in reporting Anthony Blunt's statement that Leo and I were his only two recruits. "ALL TRAITORS HAVE BEEN NAMED CLAIMS BLUNT" was the *Guardian's* headline. Having put words that he had not used in Anthony's mouth, the *Guardian* went on to state quite falsely that I had admitted spying.

It was necessary at that moment to take some action to protect my children, if not myself. In a letter to the London *Times,* I said that its characterization of me was simply not true. "I did give my own appraisals of the political situation to a gentleman who called himself Michael Green," I wrote, but "I did not seek, nor was I given access to, any sensitive information. I did not provide any such information to Mr. Green or to anyone else."

My comment caused a number of letters to be written to me from England, one from a leading barrister. If what you say is true, he wrote, then I strongly advise you to file a series of libel suits against the British newspapers. You can collect very large sums in damages at very little expense. Your failure to do so will lead my friends and I to conclude that you have not told all the truth.

I found it hard to explain the reasons for my failure to defend myself. I was influenced by my own solicitors, who advised me that the costs of legal action would be substantial. I wanted to concentrate upon the writing of this book. I had, also, a deeper, less acceptable reason. I felt that I had inflicted a great deal of pain upon Anthony and Leo and Leo's wife when their names were spread across the front pages of the British newspapers. I was more than willing to bear some part of the punishment.

# THE FUTURE WILL BE MERCIFUL

THE House of Commons, in considering the prime minister's statement about Anthony Blunt, centered its attention on the questions of accountability and immunity. It was generally agreed that the British government acted wisely when it offered Anthony immunity in 1964.

But immunity from what? Was the government's commitment limited to an assurance that there would be no prosecution in a British court of law; or did it imply that there would also be no prosecution in the British press?

The question was raised in the debate of November 12, 1979, by the attorney general of Great Britain, Sir Michael Havers.

*The Attorney General:* . . . Generally, apart from the question of whether it would be right for the Crown to take the initiative in naming a man as a spy when there was no evidence on which to prosecute him, it seems to me that anonymity should usually be inherent in the granting of immunity.

Many people no doubt concluded, upon reflection, that the attorney general's statement was both compassionate and wise. Others plainly disagreed.

It is not for me to sit in judgment upon those who told what they remembered, to Andrew Boyle, to Chapman Pincher, and to Nigel West. They felt, I am sure, that only when the story of the Soviet network in England was fully told, would the British people be prepared to take the steps that were necessary for their security. Beyond that, I sense in their action some of the sadness and resolution that is voiced in Abraham Lincoln's Second Inaugural Address: " . . . if God wills that . . . every drop of blood drawn by the lash shall be paid with another drop drawn with the sword, it must be said 'the judgments of the Lord are true and righteous altogether.' "

Do the judgments of the Lord require that those who have acted against their country not be allowed to go in anonymity to their graves? It is not for me to say. Thanks to the magnanimity of Richard Nixon, I had enjoyed eight richly rewarding years as deputy chairman of the National Endowment for the Arts before the day came in 1981 when I returned to my home to find Angus Macpherson and his photographer waiting for me. From that day to this, my family and my friends have been supportive of me, and no one has set out to punish me.

We punish ourselves, but punishment is not enough. We seek to protect our own families; we struggle to write our own epitaphs. For those reasons, when Angus Macpherson handed me the story about myself, I knew that I would have to write this book.

"Speech after long silence; it is right. . . ." So Yeats begins his poem. It ends

> *Bodily decrepitude is wisdom; young*
> *We loved each other and were ignorant.*

Yes; but I feel none of Yeats's rage at growing old.

The last chapter of *Under Western Eyes* serves better for me as an ending to this book.

The central character of Conrad's novel, you will recall, is Kirylo Sidorovitch Razumov, the student of St. Petersburg who betrays his fellow student Victor Haldin to the secret police. Haldin had assassinated the tsarist minister of state.

Haldin is hung. Razumov is sent to Geneva to spy upon a group of Russian exiles. There, he meets Natalia Haldin, sister of the man whom he has betrayed.

Natalia treats Razumov with reverence, believing him to be the trusted comrade of her dead brother. Razumov is undone by her love. He stands before her in the climactic scene of the novel. He says, "Do you, Natalia Victorovna, believe in the duty of revenge?"

She answers, "Listen Kirylo Sidorovitch, I believe that the future will be merciful to us all. Revolutionist and reactionary, victim and executioner, betrayer and betrayed, they shall be pitied together when the light breaks on our black sky at last. Pitied and forgotten; for without that there can be no union, and no love.

# NOTES

### AFTER LONG SILENCE (pages 11–13)

The paragraphs handed to the author on March 24, 1981, were published in the *Daily Mail* on March 24 and in the London *Times* on March 25. They were included in the first edition of Chapman Pincher's book *Their Trade Is Treachery:* Sidgwick and Jackson, London.

In the revised edition of his book, published by Bantam Books in 1982, Mr. Pincher substantially altered the paragraphs quoted here.

### MY FATHER (pages 13–17)

Willard Straight's letters, diaries, and other papers are in the archives of Cornell University. They are quoted at length in *Willard Straight,* by Herbert Croly, the Macmillan Company, New York, 1924, and in *Whitney Father, Whitney Heiress,* by W. A. Swanberg, Charles Scribner's Sons, New York, 1980.

### MY MOTHER (pages 17–24)

Dorothy Elmhirst's American papers are in the Cornell archives; her American years are described in *Whitney Father, Whitney Heiress.* Her English papers are in the Dartington Hall archives; her life in England is set forth by Michael Young in *The Elmhirsts of Dartington,* Rutledge and Kegan Paul, London, 1982.

The passage from James Naylor is taken from *My Special Anthology,* by Dorothy Elmhirst, published after her death by Dartington Hall Press, Totnes, Devonshire.

### MY BROTHER, MY SISTER, AND I (pages 24–29)

Ernest Thompson's comment is taken from his introduction to *Lives of the Hunted,* Charles Scribner's Sons, New York, 1901.

### LEONARD ELMHIRST (pages 29–32)

Leonard Elmhirst describes his early life, his days at Cornell, his meeting with Dorothy Straight, and their work on the student union in *The Straight and Its Origin,* Willard Straight Hall, Ithaca, New York.

The correspondence of Leonard and Dorothy Elmhirst is in the Dartington archives and is quoted at length in *The Elmhirsts of Dartington.*

### DARTINGTON HALL (pages 32–34)

Leonard Elmhirst's description of Dartington is published in *The Elmhirsts of Dartington.*

The history of Dartington Hall is splendidly set forth in Anthony Emery's *Dartington Hall,* Oxford University Press, 1970. The early days of the experiment are described by Victor Bonham Carter and W. B. Curry in *Dartington Hall,* Phoenix House, London, 1958, and Exmoor Press, Somerset, 1970.

### A PROGRESSIVE EDUCATION          (pages 37–42)

W. B. Curry, headmaster of the school from 1931 to 1937, describes his approach in *Dartington Hall,* Phoenix Press and Exmoor Press.

*Le Tombeau sous L'Arc de Triomphe,* translated by Cecil Lewis, was published by the Century Company of New York and London in 1928 under the title *The Unknown Warrior.*

### LONDON: THE PULL OF THE LEFT          (pages 46–57)

Ford Maddox Ford's comment, made when he was sixty-three, is quoted in *The Life and Work of Ford Maddox Ford,* by Frank MacShane, Routledge and Kegal Paul, London, 1965.

*The London School of Economics,* by Sir William Beveridge, Robson Books Ltd., London, 1977.

### JAMES AND JOHN          (pages 57–62)

James Klugman's family background and his schooling are recounted by Anthony Boyle in *The Climate of Treason,* Hutchinson, London, 1979.

John Cornford's letter to Margot Heinemann is quoted in *Journey to the Frontier,* a fine double portrait of John Cornford and Julian Bell, by Peter Stansky and William Abrams, W. W. Norton, New York, 1970.

### CAMBRIDGE: MY COMMITMENTS          (pages 77–83)

John Cornford's poems are quoted in *Journey to the Frontier.* W.W. Norton, New York, 1970.

### ON THE EVE          (pages 83–86)

This chapter is a revised version of an article published in *The Cambridge Review,* autumn 1936.

### THE APOSTLES          (pages 92–96)

Keynes's essay is published in *Two Memoirs,* Rupert Hart-Davis, London, and Augustus M. Kelley, New York.

### BREAKING THE TIES          (pages 106–110)

Julian Bell's letter to his mother is quoted in *Journey to a Frontier.*

### "MICHAEL GREEN"          (pages 128–130)

The author, acting under the Freedom of Information Act, asked the F.B.I. to advise him as to the name, identity, and fate of "Michael Green." His request was not granted.

### THE NEW REPUBLIC          (pages 158–162)

Justice Holmes's comment is taken from *Holmes-Laski Letters, 1916–1935,* edited by Mark DeWolfe Howe, Harvard University Press, 1953.

### PUSHING AMERICA TOWARD WAR (pages 162–165)

Henry L. Stimson's comment about Roosevelt, and Roosevelt's remark to Henry Morgenthau are quoted on pages 91–2 of James McGregor Burns's book *Roosevelt, the Soldier of Freedom,* Harcourt Brace Jovanovich, New York, 1970.

## THE BEST OF DAYS  *(pages 167–170)*
*Make This the Last War* was published by Harcourt Brace and Company, New York, and by George Allen and Unwin, London.

## THE WILD BLUE YONDER  *(pages 173–194)*
I have called the disgraced cadet Ernest W. Thompson because I cannot obtain his name.

## HENRY  *(pages 203–224)*
This chapter is a revised and expanded version of a brief memoir published in *The New Republic* following Wallace's death in November 1965.

## DIES IRAE  *(pages 227–240)*
Eric Hoffer's book, *The True Believer,* was published by Harper, New York, 1951.

Elizabeth Bentley's comment is taken from her book *Out of Bondage,* Rupert Hart-Davis, London, 1952, and is quoted in David Caute's *The Great Fear,* Simon and Schuster, New York, 1978.

A. Rossi's book, *A Communist Party in Action,* was published by Yale University Press and by Oxford, 1951.

Abraham Lincoln's comment is quoted in Carl Sandburg's *Abraham Lincoln, War Years,* vol. II, p. 168; Harcourt Brace, New York,

## IN THE DAYS OF McCARTHY  *(pages 257–284)*
My book on the Army/McCarthy Hearings, illustrated by Robert Osborn, was published by The Beacon Press, Boston, in 1954. It was re-published with some shorter works by Devon Press, Berkeley, Calif., under the title *Trial by Television and Other Encounters.*

The passages from *Man's Hope* are taken from the 1979 edition published by Grove Press Inc., New York.

## ESPECIALLY WHEN I LAUGH  *(pages 291–294)*
The 40th Anniversary Issue of *The New Republic* is dated November 22, 1954.

My two novels were: *Carrington,* published by Alfred A. Knopf, Inc. New York, 1960; Jonathan Cape, London; and Dell Publishing Co., New York; and *A Very Small Remnant,* published by Alfred A. Knopf, 1963; Jonathan Cape; The University of New Mexico Press, and Dell.

Joseph Conrad's comment, quoted at the end of the chapter, was made in a letter to Arthur Symons and is contained in Symon's *Notes on Joseph Conrad,* Myers and Co. London. n.d.

## DINAH  *(pages 294–303)*
Dinah's recovery proved to be complete. She is now an elementary school teacher.

JAMES                              *(pages 303–304)*

James Cornford is now director of the Nuffield Foundation.


THE END OF SILENCE          *(pages 307–317)*

Dorothy's book *How the World Began* was dictated and illustrated by her when she was four. It was published by Pantheon Books in 1964. She is still listed in the *Guinness Book of World Records* as the world's youngest published author.


BLOWING THE GAFF          *(pages 318–328)*

The landscape by Dughet is now in the Cornell Art Museum.

# APPENDIX A

Photograph of the Cambridge Union Society taken in 1937 (see page 185). (back): Hon. R. C. Maugham[1], R. M. Patel, N. Singleton, J. H. Watson, F. Thistlethwaite[2], E. Welbourne, L. A. Humphrey, A. H. Gordon, A. P. Astbury, L. Long[3], I. Henderson, G. H. Jackson, J. Dollar, F. K. P. Vinter, C. N. Parkinson, D. W. Ewer, W. H. Dutton. (middle): M. H. Dobb[4], R. A. De La Sota, A. S. Eban[5], C. J. H. Churchill, R. E. Swartwout, J. N. Emery, S. M. Kumaramangalam[6], L. K. Jha, P. B. Hague, Hon. P. Butler, G. W. Guthrie-Jones, P. G. B. Keuneman[7], D. G. Bosanquet, Sirak Herony, J. Boon, A. J. Alexander, H. G. Atherton, Stanley S. Brown. (front): P. R. Noakes, G. B. Croasdell, C. Fletcher-Cooke[8], M. W. Straight, H. M. the Emperor of Ethiopia, R. V. Gibson, H. E. Blaten Gueta Herony, F. Singleton, P. J. Noel-Baker[9], H. L. Elvin, J. M. Simonds.

1. nephew of Somerset Maugham
2. later Vice-Chancellor of East Anglia University
3. confessed in 1964 to being a Soviet spy
4. later the marxist Emeritus Reader in Economics at Cambridge University
5. later deputy Prime Minister and then Foreign Minister of Israel
6. became a prominent Communist in India
7. later general secretary of the Communist Party of Sri Lanka
8. later a Conservative Member of Parliament
9. Lord Noel-Baker later founded the World Disarmament Campaign

# INDEX

# INDEX

339